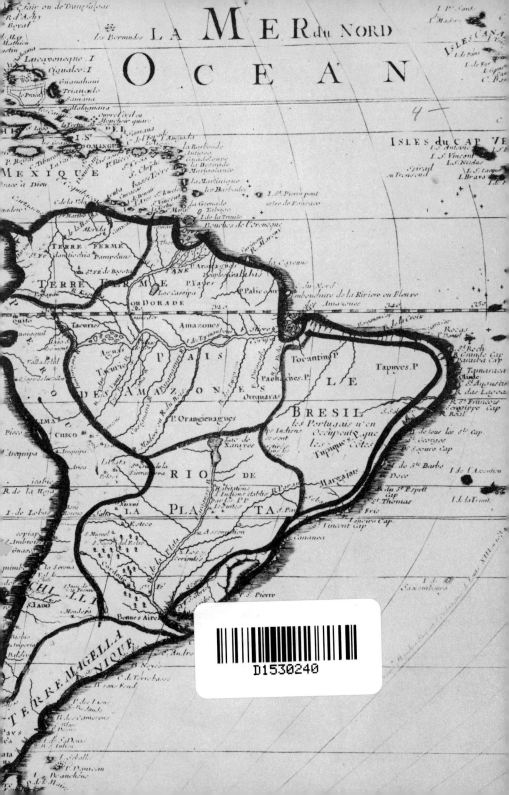

The

SOUTHERN

AMERICAS

A New Chronicle

ABEL PLENN

Creative Age Press · New York

48- 6040

FOR DORIS AND TOPI
AND THE RISING GENERATIONS
OF ALL THE AMERICAS

VVVVVVVVV

FOREWORD

An increasing awareness of the need to help bring about a more fundamental understanding of the people and problems of the southern Americas among the men, the women, and the youth of this country, has motivated the writing of this book. The work was begun with the clear realization—emanating from periodic travels in different parts of Latin America and the Iberian Peninsula, and studies concerning those areas, which have been carried out in the course of the past twenty years—that its fulfillment would be one of the most difficult which a writer, or for that matter, even a formal historian, might undertake.

The chief difficulty has been the problem of comprehending and interpreting—by means of an accurate presentation that might, at the same time, appeal to the popular American taste—the growing complexity of social and cultural attitudes arising out of the Latin American people's long struggle for freedom and self-expression.

But that struggle is still in the making. And it is through this very fact that the complexity of Latin American traditions and aims has, in many respects, become part of a larger pattern of historical development in which at least the aims are approaching closer and closer to our own more or less independently established directions as a people.

More recently, newer challenges resulting from the Second World War and its ideological implications have, inevitably, helped to change the nature of our search for a greater insight into the backgrounds of Latin American society. From a matter of academic interest, humane endeavor, or profitable enterprise, the broadening quest for a fuller and more profound rapport between the Americans of the United States and the Americans of the rest of the hemisphere has, slowly but irrevocably, become part of a vital national need.

In the following pages I have attempted to portray the historical development of the southern Americas, from the earliest times to the present day, as an unbroken march, a constantly changing panorama of dramatic events involving personalities from every cultural group and recounted by actual participants or immediate observers. While I have sought to show the rise of the other American countries in major historical terms as a single and all-encompassing social phenomenon, within the unavoidable limitations imposed by the scope of the subject I have also tried to indicate special peculiarities proper to certain countries and, even more, to certain areas—such as the Negro influences in the Caribbean and the Indian strains in Mexico, Guatemala, and the Andean countries.

In substance this book is an authentic document, constructed from personal accounts, private and public letters, diaries and speeches, and similar primary and contemporaneous sources. Many of the chroniclers and narrators represented in the book were active participants and, not infrequently, leaders in the events related.

Through my own commentary, sometimes brief, at times necessarily lengthy, I have sought to link the chapters and sub-chapters into which the book is divided. The chief purpose of the commentary, which appears in oblique type in the printed version of this book, has been to furnish the reader with essential background and continuity—always with an eye on the larger narrative, however, and on the importance of bringing its most significant aspects into relief.

In other words, while the selecting and ordering of basic source material used as the body of the book has been conditioned throughout by the desire to achieve a work of real documentary value (the excerpts chosen are virtually unedited, except for the application of modern forms of spelling and punctuation), my primary concern both as author and editor has been to tell a story: the story of the heroic resistance and the intrepid struggle against vast human and natural obstacles which have gradually transformed the southern Americas from a conglomerate of widely disparate, ancient Indian cultures into an integral part of the intricate and changing new world of today.

In this ambitious undertaking—the outlines of which I began to envision fifteen years ago, when I was studying and travelling in Mexico—I have been aided and encouraged in many ways by people, both living and dead, too numerous to mention here. I am especially indebted, however, to my wife, Doris Troutman Plenn, whose devotion and whose painstaking criticisms as well as suggestions have so greatly contributed to the development and completion of this project.

I am also most grateful to the Library of Congress for its helpful courtesy in extending the use of its study-room, Hispanic Division, and other facilities to me over a long period, and to the publishers and others mentioned below for their generous and kind cooperation in allowing me to reprint copyrighted material used in the body of this book. The sources from which this material and all other quoted passages have been selected are cited in part in the text, and in full in the "Bibliographical References" included in the Appendix.

Finally, to the publishers of this book—in particular to Eileen J. Garrett, editor-in-chief, to Harold Vursell, editor, and to Harry Feltenstein, who prepared the manuscript for publication—I can do no less than express my deepest appreciation for the warm understanding and discerning care with which this work has been treated from its initial reading to its present form.

Grateful acknowledgment for the use of copyrighted material is due to the following:

The American Geographical Society for permission to quote from *The Discovery of the Amazon*, translated by Bertram T. Lee, edited by H. C. Heaton; copyright, 1934.

D. Appleton-Century, Inc. for permission to quote from *Insurgent Mexico* by John Reed; copyright, 1914.

Columbia University Press for permission to quote from *Costa Rican Life* by John and Mavis Biesanz; copyright, 1944.

Fisk University Press for permission to quote from *A History of Ancient Mexico* by Fray Bernardino de Sahagún, translated by Mrs. Fannie Bandelier; copyright, 1932.

The Inter-American for permission to quote from "Editor's Eye-Witness" by Scott Seegers, "Scourge of the Andes" by Lilo Linke, and "Open Letter to North Americans" by Alejandro Vallejo; all copyrights, 1946.

Robert M. McBride & Company for permission to quote from *The True History of the Conquest of Mexico* by Captain Bernal Díaz del Castillo, translated by Maurice Keatinge; copyright, 1927.

The New Masses for permission to quote from "Letter from Alcala de

Henares" by Pablo de la Torriente Brau; copyright, 1937; and from "I Met the Monster" by Jesus Menéndez; copyright, 1946.

The New York Times and Milton Bracker for permission to quote from "The Glass Bookshop" by Milton Bracker; copyright, 1946.

Charles Scribner's Sons for permission to quote from Theodore Roosevelt: An Autobiography; copyright, 1925.

G. Butler Sherwell for permission to quote from Antonio José de Sucre by Guillermo A. Sherwell; copyright, 1924.

Tomorrow Magazine for permission to quote from "Impressions of a Roving Peruvian" by Manuel Seoane; copyright, 1943.

The Vanguard Press for permission to quote from The Banana Empire by Charles David Kepner, Jr. and Jay Henry Soothill; copyright, 1935.

The Washington Post for permission to quote from "An Awful Lot of Inflation in Brazil" by Emily Towe; copyright, 1946.

A. P.

New York City
December 1947

CONTENTS

Book Two · ROOT: THE COLONY

Book Three · STEM: THE INDEPENDENCE

THE SOUTHERN AMERICAS

· A New Chronicle ·

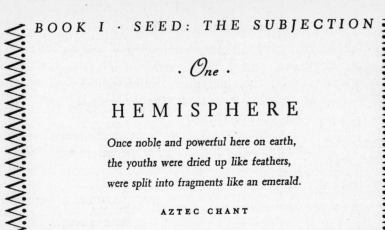

· One ·

HEMISPHERE

Once noble and powerful here on earth,
the youths were dried up like feathers,
were split into fragments like an emerald.

AZTEC CHANT

THE LAND

How long had she slumbered?

What centuries, millennia, aeons had rolled by?

The clouds moved ponderously above her, and above them, above the mist and through the pink and rough-edged mist of her half-waking, she saw her mountains rise.

From where she lay, she saw them rise above her world: out of the steaming forests where the fat and curling rivers nursed against the thousand-breasted mother of them all, the Amazonian offspring of that great inland sea no longer remembered; out of the salt of both her present oceans, her Caribbean sea that holds the hurricane's eye, her gulfs and all her little bays; out of the sand of her shores and the sand of her deserts; out of the grit and clay, the wounding dust and rock-strewn gorges, out of the mud of all her tablelands.

Out of all these—the grain of sand, the speck of dirt, the smallest pebble in the creek—her cordilleras rose to the sun. They were her jewels. They were her necklace of splendor with many names.

The names were dead or the names were changed, but the sierras were there, gleaming in the sun, towering from the heights of the Earth planet in their identity of old. And even the names—even the sound of the dead and the changed and changing names of the sierras and their multiple valleys, even the sound and the sight and the perfume of the

3

names of the surrounding rivers and plains, and of all that the land encompassed—were not forgotten in the fire and light of her sun, or in the
water and ice flying in the whistling winds that blew around her where
she lay. For she was the land itself, as she was the many lands and the
many names that belonged to them.

She was less than the hemisphere of the west of which she herself
formed a large part, and yet she was more. For she was a whole world,
infinite in her changing vastness and in the endless horizons of the common destiny before her.

She was the southern Americas, half-waking where she lay:

Her long hair of grass and thicket buckled and braided over the 32nd
parallel. Left arm stretching to the sea of the Caribs, thumb dipping to
the Mexican gulf. Other arm extended, from her shoulder in the west,
down the Sierra Madre, past her delicate Isthmus waist, to the Andes
where thighs of silver and gold lift to the world's own ceiling—and her
warm, verdant belly, the Amazon! The bulge of Brazil? Her left knee—
the leg drawn back, away from Antarctica (but the toes of her feet
blanket-warmed in the dazzling snow of Fuegia, Land of Fire).

And so, back through the ages in snow that would be called fire,
and on freezing heights in tropic latitudes, paradoxical and permanent,
the southern lands of half a sphere half-awoke to many sounds.

One of the sounds was a chant and a myth of the Maya folk. They inhabited the peninsula of Yucatan and, through their brother tribes, the
Quichés, all the surrounding soil that curved like a narrowing snake
south toward the hemisphere's waist.

Their myth was chanted and it told of the first beginnings of their
world far beyond the ten thousand years or more of their own origins.
Their first beginnings were also those of all the other aboriginal folk of
the hemisphere, from Labrador down to Fuegia, from the Antilles across
to the Galápagos. So that, although the symbolism and the language of
their myth was Maya, the story it told was about the world that was inhabited by all of them—about how it rose out of the distant night:

It was in the period Katun II Ahau when the Bee God came forth
to blindfold the face of the God-of-the-Thirteen-Heavens. . . . Then
the God-of-the-Thirteen-Heavens was seized by the god Nine-Lords-of-

THE LAND 5

the-Night. Then it was that fire descended, then the rope descended, then rocks and trees descended. Then came the beating of things with wood and stone. Then the God-of-the-Thirteen-Heavens was seized, his head was wounded, his face was buffeted, he was spit upon, and he was thrown on his back as well. Then he was despoiled of his insignia.

The Book of Chilam Balam of Chumayel

. . . There would be a sudden rush of water when the theft of the insignia of the God-of-the-Thirteen-Heavens occurred. Then the sky would fall, it would fall down upon the earth, when the four gods, the four *Bacabs* of the cardinal points, were set up, who brought about the destruction of the world.

Then, after the destruction of the world was completed, they placed a tree to set up in its order the yellow cock oriole.

Then the white tree of abundance was set up. A pillar of the sky was set up, a sign of the destruction of the world; that was the white tree of abundance in the north.

Then the black tree of abundance was set up in the west for the black-breasted *mut* bird to sit upon.

Then the yellow tree of abundance was set up in the south as a symbol of the destruction of the world, for the yellow-breasted bird to sit upon, for the yellow cock oriole to sit upon, the yellow timid *mut*.

Then the green tree of abundance was set up in the center of the world as a record of the destruction of the world.

The number-sign of another *katun* period was set up and fixed in its place by the messengers of their lord. The red *Piltec* was set at the east of the world to conduct people to his lord.

The white *Piltec* was set at the north of the world to conduct people to his lord.

The God-of-the-Tenth-Heaven was set up at the west to bring things to his lord.

The yellow *Piltec* was set at the south to bring things to his lord.

But it was over the whole world that He-Who-Fertilizes-the-Maize-Seven-Times was set up. He came from the seventh stratum of the earth when he came to fecundate Itzam, the Earth-Crocodile, when he came with the vitality of the angle between earth and heaven.

They moved among the four lights, among the four layers of the stars. The world was not lighted; there was neither day nor night nor moon. Then they perceived that the world was being created.

Then creation dawned upon the world. . . . Then a new world dawned for them.

MEN OF MAIZE

They came from the west, they said, from lands forgotten and gone. And from the east, from a lost continent, they said they came. There were those who must have known how the early ones trekked down from icy Bering, having crossed all Mongol Asia. And others that must have heard of the other old ones pushing to the west, out of Iceland, Greenland ice and wasteland, thence south, and then still farther south— always south, migrants moving toward the meridian's hearth.

They were the earth-men, color of its clay, tanned in its fire, reddened in the smoke of burning ochre. And their hair was like the night. And their eyes like rubbed obsidian. They were bony in the cheeks and high in the chest, with faces square and massive as a slab of living rock (and the face and body hairless, smooth as a cocoon).

And where they came from could be anywhere. But what they came from—what the air, what the water, what the earth, what the root from the earth and the herb from the root and the plant from the herb, what the food from the plant, what the food that was life, what they came from—was inside themselves as it was outside everywhere. Out of the tiny plant, tzenzontli, out of the Mexican land, grew the mighty sustainer of men. Maize it was called, and it moved with the men: southward, ever southward, through the lands of the Mayas, south to the lands of their brother Quichés:

And here begins the time when it was decided to make man, and to search for the thing that might serve as man's flesh. And the creators and shapers, Tepeu and Gucumatz—thus were they known—said: "The time for the dawn is now here, in which everything—everything—must be at last perfected, and our sustenance must be made. . . ." They met, and they came in large numbers. And they

The Popol Vuh—Sacred Book of the Quichés

went to consult in the darkness of the night; and searching, they took counsel, they consulted, and they grew sorrowful here. And thus did their knowledge spring into being, into clarity, and they found what they were looking for—the thing that might serve as man's flesh. And it was almost time for the sun, the moon and the stars to dawn over the shapers.

From Paxil and from Cayal . . . came the yellow and white ears of corn. And these are the names of the animals that brought the food: the wildcat, the wolf, the chocoy, and the crow—these four animals revealed to them the yellow and white ears of corn. . . . And from this was made the flesh of man who was already formed, and this was man's blood. And this was placed there by the creators: the ears of corn.

And thus they rejoiced at having found a beautiful land, full of sweet things, of many yellow and white ears of corn. . . . Then, grinding the yellow and white corn, the goddess Xcumane made nine drinks, and eating and drinking began, and then man's flesh and fat were created. . . . It was done by the shapers who . . . then had a talk about creating our first fathers and mothers. . . . And their flesh was only yellow and white corn; nothing but food was the arms and legs of men, our first fathers.

Four was the number of the created ones—and only food was their flesh. . . .

They were only shapes and creatures, they had no fathers or mothers. We only call them men—who were not born of women . . . but were shaped and created by the creators called Tepeu and Gucumatz. And when they were made into men . . . they were men who spoke and talked, saw and heard, moved and sensed. They were good, beautiful men, and their appearance was that of men, and they could breathe.

And looking, their gaze came to see everything, and they knew all that there was in the world—and when they looked, they turned to look again, and their gaze moved over all that there is in the sky and all there is on earth.

And there was nothing that could block their gaze from all that there is. It was not necessary for our first fathers to walk or run in order to see all that there is in the sky—they could stand in one place and see it all.

Great was their knowledge. And their features excelled those of the trees, the stones, the lake, the sea, the mountain, and the plain. And they were precious men.

MIGRATION

They were precious men. They were men of peace who could also prove themselves great warriors.

Over the whole hemisphere there were such men and such tribes. But there were also the fiercer warrior tribes. These stalked and captured and killed and ate the men of peace who lived by hunting beasts and birds and by tilling the soil with the rude planting-stick and even with their bare brown hands.

In the Caribbean there were the gentle Arawaks—patient growers of cotton, agile spinners of thread, clever weavers of patterned cloth. They lived in the islands that sit on volcanoes in the sea of hurricanes. And they feared that bottomless sea. They feared its deeps. They feared its tempests and quakes.

But more than all these, man was their darkest fear:

Man, the maker of many canoes that flew up from the mainland coast —up from the southern continent and over the sea, up from island to island, the warriors' canoes like sharp-beaked birds bringing man, the hunter, on sea and land, man with the spear and the arrow and club. And man's name was a thing of dread. Man's name was Carib.

The eater of men and the eater of his own children born of his captive women. The mutilator of the captive boys, whom he dealt with as women until they were men ripe for the cannibal repast. This was the Carib of the brutal ways who was also the clever maker of swift canoes and deadly arrows pointed with fish-spines or tortoise shell or the strangling poison called curare.

Across the islands of the Caribs' sea, and up and down the two great continents of the west. Up and down its coasts, circling its endless mountains, defiling along its river banks and through its canyons and caverns—over the whole hemisphere, in fact—roamed the restless aborigines, the red folk of the land, the peaceful ones and the warriors, too.

From hollowed tree-trunk to sheltered cave, campfire to hearth, the red folk moved on. Where were the roots and the berries, the shellfish, the birds and the game? Where was the food, where was the quiet without the sudden arrow in the heart? They hunted out of hunger, but slowly and surely their search was for soil.

Where was the soil with sun and water to give them maize? Where could the corn grow and men take root? Their search was for soil, and the trail was marked by their bones and the broken bits of gods they made and destroyed.

Gods of bark and feather and shell. Men died, tribes died, and their gods died with them. Only the tangled trail ahead. And hunger. And a little hope in the fresh-made god.

The search went on for centuries. And in the long night of migration, broken by periods of settlement and growth, powerful cultures arose and flourished and in time decayed and were conquered or were overrun and supplanted by new and vigorous groups. This was the cycle that repeated itself hundreds of times over the whole hemisphere. One of the last great migrations took place in Mexico in the early part of the twelfth century A.D.

Out of their Place-of-the-Seven-Caves, somewhere in the north and center of Mexico, out of the Place-of-the-Herons, went the seven Aztec tribes. Across the central valley they went, back and forth, for ten times twenty years. Across Anahuac, where earlier folk, the Toltecs, had once raised temples of stone. Across the valley moved the "little Mexicans," and their little god with the long name moved with them.

At this place the wife of one of the leaders was delivered of a child, on which account the site is called Mixiuhtlan, which means place-of-birth. In this manner and in this water their idol brought them nearer and nearer to the place where he had decided they should build their great city, which was very near that location. It so happened that those there began to look around to see if there was any place in that part of the lagoon fitted to found and people a city, because on the dry land there

The Codex Ramírez—Mexico in the 14th Century A.D.

would be no way of establishing themselves, as it was all inhabited by their enemies. Running about and wandering from one place to another among the reeds and grasses, they found a spring where they saw many beautiful things which they greatly admired, all of which their priests had previously prophesied, telling them that this would be the city designated by their idol.

The first thing they found at that spring was a white and very beautiful savin, from the foot of which flowed a brook. Soon they saw that all the willows which were around what they thought was the spring were entirely white and without a single green leaf, and that all the canes and reeds were white.

While they were standing and looking at these with great attention, there began to come out of the water absolutely white and beautiful frogs, and the water that issued from two rocks was so clear and limpid that they were very well satisfied. The priests, remembering what their god had told them, began to weep with joy and gladness, and gave full vent to their feelings of pleasure, saying:

"Now we have found the place which we were promised. Now we have seen the place of comfort and rest for the weary Mexican nation. We have nothing else to ask. Be consoled, sons and brothers, for what our god has promised us we have now found. However, be quiet and do not say anything, but let us return to the place where we were staying, where we will await what our god, Huitzilopochtli, commands us."

So they returned to the place they had left, and on the following night, Huitzilopochtli appeared in a dream to one of his ministers and said, "Now you are satisfied that I have not told you anything that did not turn out to be truthful and you have seen the thing that I promised you would find in the place where I was going to take you. However, wait, for there is even more for you to see. You will remember how I commanded you to kill Copil, the son of the sorceress who claimed to be my sister, and how I ordered you to tear out his heart and throw it away in the canes and reeds of this lagoon—which you did? Know now that the heart fell upon a rock and from it there sprang a nopal, a cactus plant, and this was so large and beautiful that an eagle built his home in it, and there on the treetop he maintained himself, eating the best and finest birds to be found there. And there he spreads out his large and beautiful wings and receives the warmth of the sun and the freshness of the morning. Go there in the morning and you will find the beautiful eagle on the nopal, and around it you will see a great quantity of green, red, yellow, and white feathers of the elegant birds on which the eagle sustains himself. To this place, where you will find the nopal with the eagle above it, I have given the name Tenochtitlan."

. . . On the morning of the following day the priest had all the people, old and young, men, women, and children, gathered together, and standing before them he began to tell them about the revelation he had received, dwelling on the great manifestations of regard and the many acts of kindness they had received day after day from their god. After a long harangue, he concluded, saying:

"The site of this nopal will be the place of our happiness, peace, and rest. Here we will increase in numbers and add prestige to the name of the Mexican people. From this home of ours, shall be known the force of our valorous arms and courage, our undaunted hearts by means of which we shall conquer all the nations. . . . And we shall become the rulers of gold and silver, of jewels and precious stones, of rich feathers and shawls. . . . From this place we are to start to become rulers over all these people, their fields, their sons and daughters. Here shall they be compelled to serve and pay tribute to us, and in this place there shall arise a famous city, the queen and ruler over all the other communities, where kings and lords shall be received in court, where all shall congregate, and a city to which all shall look up as to a supreme court. For that reason, my children, let us walk between these canebrakes, between these reeds and grasses that grow in the thicket of this lagoon, and let us seek for this site of the nopal, which undoubtedly is to be found here, since our god has said so, for up to the present all he has told us has come true."

After the priest made this speech, all the people knelt and rendered thanks to their god. Then, separating into different groups, they entered the thicket of the lagoon and looked in every place until they came to a brook which they had noticed the previous day, but which had then contained water that was clear and limpid.

Now the water that flowed from there was quite reddish, almost like blood, and the brook seemed to flow into two arroyos, in the second of which the water was so blue and thick that it inspired them with fear. Although they felt that there was something mysterious about it, nevertheless they went on, looking for the sign of the nopal and the eagle.

Proceeding in this way they finally came to the sign of the nopal on top of which was perched the eagle with wings spread out to the rays of the sun, absorbing its heat and holding in its claws a gorgeous bird that had very precious and gleaming feathers. When they beheld this they knelt down and did reverence as to a divine object.

The eagle saw them and he also knelt, lowering his head in the direction in which he saw them. When they noticed that the eagle was kneeling before them, having now seen what they had so earnestly desired, they all began to weep and utter shouts of joy and happiness.

TWO FESTIVALS

In 1325 the Aztec city was founded. The city rose with the corn. And the little god grew. Huitzilopochtli! Huitzilopochtli! Left-Handed Hummingbird—war-god who sat on the left of the moon-god, war-god wearing the hummingbird dress—feathers the symbol, with flowers, with jade, of life at its best, of all that was precious (and hummingbird feathers most precious of all).

Huitzilopochtli! They made him their war-god, sprung full-blown—
with cotton shield and sword of obsidian—out of the bundle of feathers,
out of his mother's womb. He grew from stick to clay to stone to marching temple to pyramid: his home on the summit, close to the sun, close
to the gods of the moon and the stars, close to the gods he had come to
conquer. And men who led, and men who followed, touched their brows
to the earth before him. Once, twice, thrice to the earth before him.
Blue was his color. And his sign was the flint-knife. And War was his
word.

War was their will. War was the way to win their world. They had
wandered and wept. Now War was the way.

War and the captured ways of the conquered (the victor was wise).
The Flowery War to capture the other gods and their power and the
power that beat like a drum in the heart of man and his blood (the
flower-liquid, the jade-studded water, the feathered stream, the liquor of
life). They took the others' gods for themselves. And the captive heart
and nectar-blood went to the war-god.

The liquor of life was their gift to the god who would give them rain,
give them maize, give life to their land, and multiply their men, make
them good warriors, make them all warriors (even the women, out of
whose womb their world would grow). Warriors and stars in the west:
these were the women that fought and fell in the battle to bear the folk
of the future. War was the way, as it was for the stars that fought to
win the sky each night.

War and the wisdom of all the vanquished. They took their knowledge from the plateau dwellers, the heirs of earlier master-builders that
came and went before them. They took their knowing of season and
soil, of skill to shake power and plenty from the monster earth (stuffed
with corn and circled with snakes) from the heirs of the Toltecs, the
Olmecs, the masters before the Maya. And what they took from the
nomad tribes—the Chichimecs and the nameless ones—was little enough,
and more than enough. Enough of their ways of hardy hunters in the
mountain maze to win that world for the Mexican men. Power was
born, and its name was Aztec.

Born the painters of skin and stone, the artists in gold and feather,
cotton and clay. Born the leaders in law, the distributors of land, the
wise men of the temple on the pyramid top, the masters of music and

dance. Born the poets and the poet-kings (Nezahualcóyotl of the verse like chocolate, like the fragrance of toasting maize, like the beverage brewed from his favorite flower). Born the pyramid-planners and temple-builders. Born the warrior-captains—knights of the Eagle, knights of the Jaguar. And born the statesmen. Born the great confederacy of the three great city-states. Born that union to last until some comet crossed their sky.

Great was its growth, mighty its men, multiple its gods. And everywhere were the vanquished, learning now the ways of the victor (some learned with love, but others swore vegeance). To the west and the north and the east moved the Aztec army, through the virgin forests and over the mountains. And behind them came their men of magic and medicine, their merchants, their seers and their statesmen. Clad in the rainbow, like a plumed serpent the column moved. Then to the south, always south. Southward they marched, and their war-god marched beside them—carved in stone by the skilled of the land, carved in rigid stone but alive as the men on whose shoulders he rode. Southward down to the Zapotecs, down to the Chiapanecs, down to the crumbling Mayas and Quichés. Their banners were bright. But tribute was their toll.

Tribute and slaves for the blood-sacrifice. The gods multiplied. The pyramids rose.

The pyramids rose with the city—Tenochtítlan, heart of the empire!—that rose with the corn, that rose with the precious liquor, the blood of precious men lost in the Flowery War. Above the pyramids rose power. And then above the power, privilege.

Even at home in the city of power, there were the privileged and there were the poor.

Four or five days before the festival of Hueytecuilhuitl, the king and all the people prepared a festivity for the poor—not only of the town proper but of the entire province—in order to feed them. They prepared a certain beverage, which they called chiampinolli, in great quantities. The beverage, mixed with chian-flour, was then placed in a canoe. Everybody drank that beverage in bowls. . . . Each one of those present drank one or two such bowls . . . children, men and women, no one being left out. If they couldn't finish it all, they saved what was left

By Fray Bernardino de Sahagún, a Faithful Chronicler

over. Many brought separate bowls or pots to put the leavings in, and in case they had no container of any kind they simply poured it into their laps.

No one went to drink twice, but everybody got as much as he could or cared to drink. If he came back for more, they slapped him with a green cornstalk.

After all had partaken of the *chiampinolli* they sat down and rested. They gathered in small groups and talked with one another, and there was much merry-making. It was then that they would drink the left-overs or give them to their small children.

At dinnertime, which was the noon hour, they would again sit in their proper order: the children, boys and girls with their fathers and mothers. Once everybody was seated, those who were to distribute the food fastened their blankets to the waist, as the etiquette of that service demanded, and likewise tied their hair with reed-mace in the shape of a garland or wreath to prevent it from falling over their eyes.

Then they began to serve. This they did by taking up large quantities of *tamales* to distribute them to all their guests from beginning to end of the long rows. They gave each one as many as he could hold in one hand, and there were many varieties of *tamales*. . . . All those who served took special care of the children, boys or girls, and some of the officials and hosts gave extra large quantities to their friends or relatives. No one took twice, for if anybody dared to do so, he received a whipping with a twisted twig of reed-mace and, furthermore, he lost all he had taken the first time and whatever had been given to him.

It happened that those who were at the very end of the line did not get anything; therefore, everybody tried to reach the most advantageous place possible in order to receive his allotted portion. Those who were left without any cried and were irritated, saying, "In vain have we come here, since they don't give us anything." And they went from group to group that were eating to see whether they might obtain something. They did not even desist when slapped or ill-treated, but kept on tarrying among the others and making comments.

This feast which the rich lord made for the poor lasted eight days, because this same time each year there is a great lack of all food staple, and famine is widespread: many died of hunger during this period.

As soon as this festivity was over, the festival of the month began, and when the sun had left the court of the temples, the singing and dancing started. In the court there were a great many braziers, almost two yards tall, and so large in circumference that two men could barely span them. They stood in a row, and at nightfall they lighted fires in them, and by that light the people danced and sang.

The dancing was started by the singers, who came forth from the houses of their order, singing and dancing in couples, and between each two of them was a woman. The people who danced this were all specially chosen men, such as captains and other valiant men well versed in matters of warfare. . . .

The women were very richly dressed in blouses and skirts elaborately embroidered in different manners and of very costly material. . . . These women danced with hair flowing. . . .

The men also were very elaborately dressed; they wore a blanket of cotton very thin, like a net. Those among them noted for their bravery and who were entitled to wear a ring in the lower lip wore these mantles or blankets embroidered with small white shells. . . . All men wore earrings made of some common material, but those who were at the head wore copper earrings with gold pieces hanging from them, and the lip-rings were of the same material and style. . . .

The common people adorned themselves with yellow beads which, although they were also made of marine shells, were of little value.

Men who had made captives in some war wore a tuft of plumes on their heads in order to distinguish them, for this demonstrated that they had captured enemies. Captains wore plumes on their back, which showed their valor. . . .

The king at times was present at this dance. At other times he did not come out. Just as he chose.

The dancers either danced holding hands or else with their arms about their partner's waist, all of them keeping good time in lifting their feet, taking a step forward or backward, and in making the turns. They danced . . . till night, stopping at nine. As soon as the one who beat the drum and the *teponaztli*, or hollow-log drum, stopped, they all stopped and started to go home.

The chieftains among them were accompanied home with torches carried before them. The women dancers assembled after the dance, and those who were in charge of them took them to the houses where they were wont to gather. They were not allowed to disband or go with any man except the chieftains. If one of these women were called by some in order to give her something to eat, they were obliged to call also one of the matrons who were in charge of them. In such cases they gave them food and blankets to take home with them; the food that was left after they had eaten, they also were allowed to carry home with them.

If any one of the principal soldiers desired to take one of these girls home with him, he spoke secretly to the matron in charge to bring her to him. . . . The matron would take the girl to his house or wherever else he might order to have her taken, but she would bring her at night and take her back also in the dark.

WHATEVER ITS NAME

Southward moved the warriors, and the other tribes fled before them. In jungle and in forest, canyon and cavern, the weaker sought refuge—only to find the victor was there, welcoming war, hand on his sword, with the wizard of the flint-knife standing behind him poised for the sacrifice (hearts for the war-god). The victor was there, waiting for tribute. What shall it be?

"Let it be toil, whatever its name."

Cocoa and crocodiles, feathers and fish, shields of quilted cotton, pieces of jade and bags full of turquoise, soft hammocks of thread, blouses embroidered with strands from the sun (and women to wear them).

The tribute was toil whatever its name: sweet-smelling resin to burn in the temples, stone masks for the gods, silver and gold wrought in their image.

The tribute was toil:

The new king, in order to obtain prisoners for the sacrificial ceremony and for the feasts, after making great preparations set out for a very populous and great province called Tehuantepec—where some Mexican merchants and majordomos, going there to collect tributes for the great king of Mexico, had been maltreated, and in some instances killed. In addition to these misdemeanors, these people had rebelled against the royal crown. So the king went in person to restore the province, taking with him a large number of soldiers from all over his kingdom and carrying along with him large quantities of provisions. Great feasts were celebrated and great banquets with the richest of foods given to them by all the cities and towns through which they passed.

Again, The Codex Ramírez: The Heavy Tribute

Finally he arrived at the place where the Mexicans were to attack the enemy. They were prepared for them, although greatly astonished at seeing the Mexican king himself at the head of the army and so large a number of soldiers come so quickly to a country so far removed from their own.

Although the number of troops of that province was very great—not reckoning the neighboring tribes that had come to their help—the king was not in the least dismayed; but arming himself in his accustomed fashion, with sword and shield in his hand, he placed himself at the head of his army and gave battle valorously. Thus fighting there fell upon him and his men an innumerable mob of people, shouting and shrieking, and the air became thick with arrows, throwing-sticks, javelins, and other missiles.

He feigned flight and was followed by this multitude until he came to a place where many of his soldiers lay concealed, hidden and covered by straw. These allowed the people of Tehuantepec to pass them in pursuit of the king, and then, suddenly bursting out from under the grass and forming into the shape of a half-moon, they fell upon the rear. Then the king turned and returned to the fray with his men on another part of the field and fell upon the center of the enemy, inflicting very great slaughter.

They took a sufficient number of prisoners for the coronation sacrifices.

Then he immediately turned with great fury upon the city and the temple, all of which he devastated and destroyed. Not content with this, he took vengeance upon the neighboring provinces that had been incited to war by the enemy and that had aided them. Thus he inflicted great punishment upon all the provinces he had conquered, and he did not cease until he reached Huatusco, a port of the southern oceans—for up to that point did his kingdom extend.

He returned home with great triumph, the whole world filled with admiration for him. Great feasts were held and banquets given all along the road. He entered his court in the midst of universal applause. All the priests and the young men of the temple, the colleges and the children's schools went out to meet him and performed the customary ceremonies. . . .

Having arrived at the temple, he made his adoration and obeisance before his god, Huitzilopochtli, thanking him for his victory and offering him many spoils of great value and rarity which he had brought with him: extremely large seashells with which he was to make new musical instruments for his temple, and trumpets, and flutes, and other such objects.

Then they proceeded immediately to the coronation celebrations. And these were so marvellous that people from all parts of the world came to witness them—even their enemies. These also came to see the tributes piled up in the royal plaza . . . in far greater numbers than were ever known.

LESSON IN STRATEGY

Moving southward, nearing the Isthmus waist, the Aztecs stopped. If they had gone a little farther, they would have reached the narrow waters and their voices would have been heard by those other men of maize who called themselves the children of the sun.

Silently they came to life, those Andean tribes of the sun, out of their own place-of-the-caves. And steep and labyrinthine was their climb.

Up the existent wall of a continent they went, scaling the continent that would be known as South America, scaling it northward and back, to south and to east, from the Pacific up from the parching plain by the sea, up from the new heights, burrowing through boulders with stone and with flint. With fiber bridge tying the mountains, tying the sky, pulling their way up to the summits. Scaling the continent, up to their temple-roof, their home, their city, up their conqueror's sky, up to their city of silver and stone.

Their city of herdsmen of the sheep of the land (virgin vicuña, like water, like air, like mist of the mountain). City of craftsmen who studied the sun and knew the secret it told of time and the cycles. Time for the spectrum, time to scatter it in cloth and in clay. Time for the old ones, the old ones and mummies, time to warm them with music and wine.

City of builders of bridges and dams, of makers of highways. City of masters. City they called the world's navel. City of Cuzco—eye of the Andes:

Where power moved in a golden litter and men spoke his name in a hush and a whisper.

Inca!

They arranged that the Inca Ccapac Yupanqui should again command the army, as he had shown so much prudence and valor in former cam-

paigns, as well as all the other qualifications of a great captain. He was
to take with him the prince who was heir to the empire, and his nephew,
named Inca Yupanqui. He was a lad of sixteen years, and had been initiated as a knight with all the ceremonies . . .
The Inca Garcilasso de la Vega: in that very year. His father desired that he
From the Royal Commentaries
should acquire experience in the art of war,
which was so highly esteemed by the Incas. They assembled fifty thousand soldiers. The Incas, uncle and nephew, setting out with the first
third of the force, marched as far as the province called Chucurpu. . . .

Thence they sent the usual summons to a province called Pincu; and
the inhabitants, both seeing that it was useless to resist the power of the
Incas, and knowing how good they were to all their vassals, replied that
they rejoiced to become a part of the empire of the Incas, and to receive
their laws. Having received this answer, the Incas entered the province,
and sent thence a similar summons to the other neighboring districts,
the chief among which are Huaras, Piscopampa, and Cunchucu.

These, instead of following the example of Pincu, rose in arms, assembled together, and setting aside their local animosities, resolved to combine in defending themselves against a common enemy. Their reply was
that they would rather all die than receive new laws and customs, and
worship new gods; that they did not want them, and did very well with
their ancient customs, which had been those of their ancestors, and well
known in ages gone by; and that the Inca ought to be satisfied with what
he had already tyrannically seized, having, with the excuse of religion,
usurped the lordships of so many curacas, or chiefs.

Having sent this reply, and seeing that they could not resist the power
of the Inca in the open country, they agreed to retire to their fastnesses,
carry off the supplies, break up the roads, and defend the difficult passes:
all which they prepared to execute with great speed and diligence.

The General Ccapac Yupanqui was not the least put out when he received the defiant and insolent reply of the enemy, for his magnanimity
enabled him to receive, with the same composure, both good and evil
words, as well as good or ill success. But he did not neglect to prepare
his army, and, having received intelligence that the enemy had retired
into their fastnesses, he divided his force into four parts of ten thousand
men each, each division advancing to the fastness which was nearest,
with orders not to engage the enemy, but to blockade their positions and
reduce them by hunger.

The general himself, with his nephew, remained to give assistance
wherever it might be called for. And to provide against any chance of the

supplies of provisions running short, owing to everything having been carried off by the enemy, the general sent to ask his brother the Inca to order the surrounding districts to collect and forward to his camp double the usual quantity.

Having taken these precautions, the Inca Ccapac Yupanqui awaited the result of the war, which broke out fiercely, with much loss of life on both sides because the enemy defended the roads with great obstinacy. And, when they saw that the Inca did not assault their strongholds, they sallied out from them and fought with desperation, throwing themselves on the arms of their opponents, and the natives of each of the three provinces vying with each other as to which should show the most resolute valor, and so excel the other two.

The Incas merely stood on the defensive, waiting until hunger and the other sufferings caused by war should oblige them to yield. And when women and children were found in the fields or in the abandoned villages, they were fed and treated with kindness, and then sent to their fathers and husbands to show them that the Incas did not come to oppress them but to improve their condition.

This was also done as an act of military strategy, so that the enemy might have more mouths to maintain, more to guard and take care of, and be more hampered than they would have been without women and children. It was also thought that the hunger and suffering of their children would afflict them more than their own hardships, and that the weeping of the women would cause the men to lose heart, and surrender more readily.

The enemy did not fail to recognize the kindness with which their women and children had been treated, but their obstinacy was such that they would not give way to any grateful feeling, being rather hardened than otherwise by these benefits.

Thus both sides persisted in the war for five or six months, until the besieged began to feel hunger, and to see their people becoming feebler than the children and more delicate than the women. These evils increased more and more until, with common consent of captains and soldiers, each fortress appointed ambassadors to go, in all humility, to the Incas, ask pardon for the past, and offer obedience and homage for the future.

The Incas received them with their accustomed clemency, and, with the kindest words they could think of, admonished the conquered people to return to their homes and, by continuing good vassals, merit the favor of the Inca, so that the past might be forgiven, and never more remembered.

The ambassadors returned to those who had sent them, very well satisfied at the good result of their mission, and, as soon as the reply of the Incas was known, there was great rejoicing. In obedience to the mandate, they returned to their villages, where their necessities were re- lieved—and the double supplies which the Inca Ccapac Yupanqui had applied for at the beginning of the war proved to be much needed. For the vanquished people had a year of scarcity, having lost all their crops through the war.

LOVE BUILDS A DAM

They gave them law-givers and men to spread justice over the land. Men to teach the Inca faith and men to lead the rites. Men to count the revenues and keep the accounts on the many-colored quipu knots. Men to divide the land and the herds—allotting a share for the Inca, and for his sister-wife, and for the offspring by the other women; allotting a share for the temples that honored the sun, and the vestal virgins that honored the temple.

And they gave the vanquished hope. There was beauty with their benevolence, there was science with their subtle skill. There was achieve- ment. And there followed the story and poem to remember it by.

There was the chain of aqueducts built across the giant range carry- ing the water down to the desert land, down to the dying land to bring it new life in the miracle of a channeled spring, to bring it rebirth in the bath of its magical flow from the dams: it came down from the heights of the Andes. It flowed.

And there was the legend tying the dream to the deed, as they tied the skies to the mountains, the mountains to springs, to dams, to ducts, to the life-giving act, to the vision.

. . . There was a very beautiful girl belonging to the *Ayllu Copara*, the Copara lineage, who, seeing one day that the maize crop was drying up for want of water, began to weep at the small supply that came from one of the smaller dams she had opened. The god, Pariacaca, happened to be passing by, and seeing her, he was captivated by her charms. He

*Narratives of the Rites and
Laws of the Incas*

went to the dam, and taking off his *yacolla*, or cloak, he used it to stop up the drain that the girl had made. He then went down to where she was trying to irrigate the fields, and she, if she was afflicted before, was much more so now when she found that there was no water flowing at all.

Pariacaca asked her, in very loving and tender words, why she was weeping, and she, without knowing who he was, thus answered: "My father, I weep because this crop of maize will be lost and is drying up for lack of water."

He replied that she might console herself and take no further thought, for that she had gained what he had lost, namely, his love; and that he would make the dam yield more than enough water to irrigate her crop. The girl, Choque-suso, told him first to produce the water in abundance, and that afterwards she promised willingly to yield to his wishes.

Then he went up to the dam, and, on his opening up the channel, such a quantity of water flowed out that it sufficed to irrigate the thirsty fields and to satisfy the damsel. But when Pariacaca asked her to comply with her promise, she said that there was plenty of time to think about that.

He was eager and ardent in his love, and he promised her many things, among others to conduct a channel from the river which would suffice to irrigate all the farms. She accepted this promise, saying that she must first see the water flowing, and that afterwards she would let him do what he liked.

He then examined the country, to see whence he could draw the water; and he observed that . . . a very small rill came from the ravine of Cocachalla, the waters of which did not flow beyond a dam which had been thrown across it. By opening this dam and leading the water onwards, it appeared to Pariacaca, it would reach the farms of the *Ayllu Copara*. . . .

So he ordered all the birds in those hills and trees to assemble—together with all the snakes, lizards, bears, lions, and other animals—and to remove the obstruction. This they did; and he then caused them to widen the channel and to make new channels until the water reached the farms.

There was a discussion as to who should make the line for the channel, and there were many pretenders to this duty who wished to show their skill as well as to gain the favor of their employer. But the fox, by his cunning, managed to get the post of engineer. . . . Then a partridge came flying and making a noise like *pich-pich*, and the unconscious fox let the water flow off down the hill.

So the other laborers were enraged, and they ordered the snake to take the fox's place and to proceed with what he had begun. But he did not perform the work as well as the fox. And the people to this day deplore that the fox should have been superseded, saying that the channel would have been higher up and better if this had not taken place. And because the course of the channel is broken . . . they say that is the place where the fox let the water flow off, and which has never since been repaired.

After the water had been brought to irrigate the farms in the way that is still working, Pariacaca besought the damsel to keep her promise. She consented with a good grace, but proposed that they should go to the summit of some rocks called Yanacaca.

This they did. And there Pariacaca obtained his desires, and she was well repaid for her love when she knew who he was.

She would never let him go anywhere alone, but always desired to accompany him. He took her to the head-works of the irrigating channel which he had constructed for her love. There she felt a strong wish to remain, and he again consented, so she was converted into a stone, while Pariacaca went up the mountains.

PEOPLE WITHOUT A CHIEF

The Andes: tied, stamped with the seal of the Incas moving downward, south, to the Amazon, and east, cracking the rim, to the emerald of forest and jungle.

And the lands to the north: seized in the beak of the Aztec lords advancing in feathers and flame, the free land fading.

The free land the nameless margin narrowing closer to border of Aztec and Inca. Narrowing, shrinking, the lands with the nomad hunters, the city-less sowers of manioc and maize, the folk still free of toll of tribute, crouched in the long and lengthening shadow of Aztec and Inca over their world.

The tread of some was soft and fearful. But others stamped defiance and hate.

There were eaters of berries, of the wild thistle, of the nut of the

palm and the heart of the maguey. There were eaters of game uncooked
and eaters of smoked flesh of the pig and the deer and the furred creatures of forest and plain. Eaters of fish. And eaters of men. And some
wore nothing on bodies of sun and fire, and slept scanning the mirror of
the moon overhead for their image. But others might draw the envy of
Inca or Aztec for their dress and their jewels and maybe even their towns
and their ways: emerald-wearing folk like the Chibcha, whose lands lay
between the giant twain and who worshipped their lakes and their glittering chieftain dipped in dust of gold.

The Otomí, the men of the Yaqui, the Tarahumar. And a hundred
others that roamed the edge of the empire of the north, pummeling its
borders, defying its desire to subdue them, taunting the men of Tlaxcala and the others who paid the tribute of toil.

And at the opposite end of the hemisphere, far to the south in the
Andes—still unconquered by Inca might—were the Araucanians, the
warriors of the west. These were Quirandís in the pampas. And in
the Amazon: the Caribs' cousins, eaters of men—the cruel Tupinambá.
The Guaraní, the Guato, and the Guaycurú—the tribes of the Paraguay, the folk on the Paraná. And along the Iapaneme there were people
of mirth, people without a chief.

These people are agriculturists, sowing maize and other roots, hunting
and fishing a great deal, both fish and game being abundant. Men and
women wear the skins of wild animals, except a few, who only cover
their privities. They tattoo their faces in points and lines, and pierce the
lips and ears. Their canoes are only large enough to contain two or three
persons at a time. They are exceedingly light,
The Commentaries of Alvar
Núñez Cabeza de Vaca   and the skill with which they manage them is
admirable. When going up or down the river,
the motions of these canoes are so swift that they appear to be flying. . . .

They fight in their canoes on the river as well as on land; nevertheless,
they traffic with one another, bartering bows and arrows for canoes,
which are supplied to them by the Guaxarapos and Payaguás, besides
other things. So they become, by turns, friends and enemies with one
another.

When the waters are low, the people from the interior come and live
on the banks of the river with their wives and children, and pass their

time in fishing, for the fish are abundant and very fat at this season.

They lead pleasant lives, dancing and singing day and night, like persons who are relieved from all anxiety about food. But when the water begins to rise, which is in January, they retire inland, because at that season the floods begin, and the waters rise six fathoms above the banks of the river.

At such time the country is under water for over one hundred leagues inland, spreading over everything like a sea, so that even tall palms and other trees are covered, and vessels may pass over their summits. This usually happens every year, when the sun crosses one tropic and approaches the other. . . . At such times the natives keep very large canoes in readiness for this emergency; and in the middle of these canoes they throw two or three loads of mud, and make a hearth.

The Indian then enters with his wife, children, and household goods, and floats on the rising tide wherever they like. He lights a fire on the hearth to cook his food and for warmth, and thus he voyages for four months of the year, or as long as the floods last.

While the waters are rising, he lands at certain spots not yet inundated, and kills deer, tapirs, and other wild animals which have escaped the flood. As these retire into their channels, he returns the same way, hunting and fishing, and not leaving his canoe till the banks whereon he is wont to dwell are uncovered.

It is a sight to see the enormous quantity of fish left on the dry land after the waters have subsided. This happens in the month of March or April, when all that country smells awfully bad, owing to the poisonous mud which covers it. At this period all the natives . . . were very ill . . . and, as it is then summer in these parts, it is barely endurable. In the month of April the sick begin to recover.

All these Indians spin the thread, of which they make their nets, of a kind of teasel. These teasels are pounded and thrown into muddy pools; after leaving them there fifteen days, they take them out and scrape them with mussel-shells; the fiber is then clean and white as snow.

This tribe, unlike others, has no chief; they are all fishers and woodsmen, inhabiting the borders of the country.

THE PLUMED SERPENT

There were men with chiefs and men without them. Nomad tribes who worshipped the helping moon in the hunt. People who sang to the sun as it sprinkled its seed of flame on their fields. And folk of the towns and cities sheltered in the shade of towering temples and pyramids, that slept with a nude and knowing eye on the stars.

They charted the courses of the stars. They built their stony calendars of science and symbol. Into the cold of the constellations they breathed their own fire of fancy, peopling the familiar sky with gods sired from the intimate stars.

The sun was the spring of life to some. To others the moon of silver was the sister-and-wife to the lord of light. There were many that danced to the water and wind that swept down from the skies. And there were the leaders of old they made into gods. There was Quetzalcóatl.

The Plumed Serpent, they called him in the lands north of the Isthmus. He was the seer with the beard of gold and the skin that was white. He was the Morning Star.

And long before the Aztec or the Inca conquerors appeared, he and the ones like him in the other lands of the hemisphere were all the glory that shone in the sky and over that whole aboriginal world.

Quetzalcóatl, Plumed Serpent, was revered and considered a god, and in ancient times they worshipped him in Tulla. He had a very high temple with many steps, which were so narrow that there was not room enough for one foot. His statue was always stretched out and covered with blankets; the face was very homely, the head long, and he wore a very long beard. His subjects were all workmen

Fray Bernardino de Sahagún: Concerning The Plumed Serpent

in the mechanic arts and skillful in cutting the green stones called chalchihuites; also in the art of smelting silver and making other objects. All these arts had their origin and commencement with Quetzalcóatl, who had houses made with those precious green stones called chalchihuites and others made of silver, still others made of red and white shells, others all made of boards, and again others of turquoises, and some all made of rich plumes. . . . Furthermore they say he was very wealthy, that he had whatever he needed for eating and drinking, that the corn was exceedingly abundant, and the squash or gourds were very large, a fathom in circumference; the ears of corn were so big that they had to be carried in the arms, and also the reeds of the wild amaranth were very tall and thick, and that they climbed them like trees. They sowed and gathered cotton of all colors as, for instance, red, bright red, yellow, purple, whitish, green, blue, dark brown, gray, orange and tawny; these colors of the cotton were natural, as thus the cotton grew.

They say, moreover, that in the said town of Tulla they reared many and different kinds of birds of rich plumage in many colors . . . as well as song birds who sang very sweet and softly.

Quetzalcóatl also owned all the wealth of the world in gold, silver, and the green stones called chalchihuites, and other precious things; he had a great abundance of cocoa-trees of different colors, which are called xochicacatlao.

The said subjects of Quetzalcóatl were also very wealthy, and did not lack anything at all. They never suffered famine nor lack of corn; they never ate even the small ears of corn, but rather heated their baths with them, using them instead of firewood.

They also say that the said Quetzalcóatl did penance by pricking his limbs and drawing blood, with which he stained the maguey points; that he bathed at midnight in a spring. . . .

The time came when the good fortune of Quetzalcóatl and the Toltecs came to an end, because there appeared against them three necromancers, by the names of Huitzilopochtli, Titlacahuan, and Tlacahuepan, who played many tricks in Tulla.

Titlacahuan was the one to invent the first fraud, because he turned himself into an old man with very gray hair, and in this disguise he went to the house of Quetzalcóatl, saying to his pages: "I want to see and speak to the king."

They replied: "Clear out, go away, old man, you cannot see him because he is ill, and you would annoy him and leave him sorrowful." The old man thereupon said: "I must see him!"

The pages replied: "Wait," and they went to tell Quetzalcóatl how an old man had come to speak to him, saying, "Sir, we have thrown him out to make him go away, but he refuses, saying that he is going to see you by force." Quetzalcóatl said, "Let him come in here and appear before me, because I have awaited him for many days."

Thus they went to call the old man, and he entered where Quetzalcóatl was and said to him: "My son, how are you? Here I have a medicine which you must drink." Quetzalcóatl answered, saying, "Well and good that you came, old fellow; it is for many days that I have been expecting you!"

The old man asked Quetzalcóatl, "How are you in body and health?" To this Quetzalcóatl replied: "I am very ill; my whole body aches; I cannot move my hands and feet."

The old man said to the king: "Sir, you see here the medicine I brought you; it is very good and wholesome, and whosoever drinks it becomes intoxicated; if you should wish to drink it, you will become intoxicated, but you are to get well, and it will soften your heart; it is going to remind you of the sufferings and anguish of death or of your life."

. . . Quetzalcóatl drank again and became drunk, and he commenced to cry very sadly and had a turn of heart which softened so that he wanted to leave. . . .

A great many more tricks were thus played on the Toltecs, because their good luck had left them, and Quetzalcóatl, feeling great sorrow for them, agreed to leave Tulla and go to Tlapallan. Therefore he ordered that all the houses of silver and shells which he had caused to be built be burned, and he had all his other very precious things buried in the mountains or clefts; he changed the cocoa-trees into others called mezquite, and he, moreover, commanded all kinds of birds of rich plumage, such as the quetzaltolotl and the tlauchquechol, to go farther on. . . .

Quetzalcóatl prepared to take the road leaving Tulla, which he did. He arrived at a place called Quauchtitlan, where there grew a large tree, big and tall. He went close to it and asked his pages for a mirror, and they gave it to him; looking at his face he said, "I am old now," and he thereupon called the place Huehuequauhtitlan, the Place of the Old Eagle. . . .

Looking back towards Tulla, he commenced to cry very bitterly, and the tears he shed hollowed and perforated the rock on which he thus sat, resting and weeping. . . .

Continuing on his way, he came to another place called Coahpa, where the necromancers met him in order to prevent him from going any farther, saying to Quetzalcóatl, "Where are you going? Why did you leave your town? To whom did you commend it? Who is going to do penance?"

Quetzalcóatl, responding to the conjurors, told them: "In no way can you prevent my departure, for I have to leave forcibly."

The said necromancers again asked Quetzalcóatl, saying, "Where are you going?" and he replied, "I am going as far as Tlapallan."

"What for are you going there?" asked the necromancers, whereupon he replied, "They came to call me and the Sun is also calling me."

To this they answered, "Well and good; go then, but you are to leave here all the mechanical arts, such as the smelting of silver, stone- and wood-carving, painting, making feather-work, and other trades." The necromancers took everything away from Quetzalcóatl and he commenced to throw all the valuable jewels he had taken with him into a spring. . . .

Quetzalcóatl continued on his way, and as he got farther on between the two mountain ranges . . . all the pages who accompanied him, and who were dwarfs and hunchbacks, died from the cold. He mourned deeply the death of his pages and, crying very bitterly, singing his song of sorrow and sighing, he saw the other mountain range. . . .

It is moreover said that Quetzalcóatl created and built houses under ground which are called *mientlancalco*, and he also ordered a large stone to be so erected that it can be moved with the little finger. They say that even if there were many men who meant to move the stone, it wouldn't move, even though there be a great many.

There are other noteworthy things Quetzalcóatl did in many towns, and he gave names to all the mountain ranges, forests, and sites.

When he reached the seashore, he ordained a raft to be made of snakes of the kind which is called *coatlapechtli*. He entered it and sat down as in a canoe. And thus he left, navigating on the sea. . . .

He left by the sea. And by the sea he promised to return. For he was The Plumed Serpent, The Precious Twin: the star of the east that shot his arrows of light, and the planet of peace that rose in the west. He was the Morning and the Evening Star.

Great and fearful, fraught with omen, was the scope of the story of the star that was prophet, that was priest, that was lord of learning and lore, that was symbol of all the glory that was ended. And the symbol survived, and even the hope of the promised return. It shone in the sagas of lost leaders, of the departed seer of seers, that were spoken and sung up and down and across the lands of the living red folk.

Among the Aztecs, where temples honoring the departed teacher and demi-god bore his symbol of the plumed serpent, he was known as Quetzalcóatl.

To the south, in the lands of the Mayas, there were mammoth stones carved, and sacred folding-scrolls painted with precision and fancy, and buildings hewn, with labyrinthine glyphs and picture-writing on them— in homage to the lost leader they also knew as The Plumed Serpent. But they called him Kukulcán.

Farther south, where the Quiché kings had ruled, colossi of stone ringed with the sign of the feathered serpent recalled the teacher of many skills, the god who had gone but was well remembered still as Gucumatz. Green were the feathers of Gucumatz, and he was The Serpent of Learning.

From north to south they sang of the long-gone seer of seers with the many names, and they sang of the cities he built and the folk of fame and achievement he fathered. Of glorious Tulla and Teotihuacán—the City of Gods with the mighty pyramids consecrated to sun and moon— on the Mexican plateau. Of the early Mayas and Quichés to the south, and the debris and dust that lay on the land where their leaders of old had lived: of Chakanputún, of Mayápan, of Palenque, and Copán.

And farther still to the south, south among the Andes, they spoke and they sang of the wise men of the times before the Inca, of the people of the Great Chimú, of the learned folk of Tiahuanaco—the city that vanished forever.

Northward and to the south, towards the west and to the east, sowing the salt of grief and yearning up and down the whole land, the red folk chanted their woe, remembering their departed seers, their cities lost and buried, their great brothers gone. They remembered the promised return of the gods from the sky and the sea—but where was the hope, and where the food and the nourishment, in the word of a god? And sadness made the song. Sorrow and longing, and chants of scarceness and toil swept with the winds over the living and over the whole body of the whole land, filling the land with dark echoes:

Where is Tulla, what of Mayápan! And Copán! And Tiahuanaco! How did they die, how did their glory and greatness go? How did they go before Aztec or Inca ever loomed upon the land? When did they vanish; by what hand was their power slain and their cities buried under the dust under the wind?

And who can tell for whom is the dust that comes with the veering winds? Whose is the storm that sweeps the winds in from the shores to which the gods promised to return, that sweeps in from the sea?

They looked to the sea that was the east, unknown and infinite, with fear and yet with hope. They looked with awe that was not without longing. The red folk looked to the east.

VOYAGERS

> . . . who unto the West
> Have through a hundred thousand perils run . . .
> Be willing never to renounce the quest
> Of the unpeopled world behind the sun.

DANTE

EAST VIA WEST

Out of the east they would come, they were told, the new bearers of new life—out of the east from the sea.

And maybe they knew even more than they were told by their sooth-sayers, searching the signs in the skies and the seas, and the pattern of entrails of birds. Maybe the birds that were living came to them out of the skies they were searching, and the waves came from the seas, carrying the signs that were truly signs and not omens or dreams: bits of alien wood, perhaps, that spoke to them of other soil beyond their sea.

Or maybe they listened to one of their runners, one in the long and almost endless lines of men moving in relays across their land, listened as he told of some lone voyager dead on some lonely shore, some voyager cast out of the sea: a being white—unlike a man!—and clad in cloth from another world. Yes, maybe they saw and smelled and sensed the signs multiplying along the shores and out of the sea, that lands of other beings lay to the east.

But no one told them of that other East beyond the east. No one sounded the warning: there are unknown lands to the east that look to other lands to an East that is golden with spices and cities without number! And men of different nations and faiths are fighting to take the trade of the golden East from each other.

Men of Venice and Cadiz, Lisbon and London, Aleppo and along the

31

Red Sea out to the Indian Ocean, out to the islands of spice and gold, across to Cathay and the mighty lands of the Khan! They are charting new routes (the old routes are closed in the fighting) that lead to the goal of the Indies of spice!

Charting the sky and the winds, and studying the earth with more than the naked eye! With quadrant and compass made with the skill of their body and brain. Studying the earth and finding it spherical. Studying the earth and finding at length that the way to the east—like some demon's device!—may lie to the west:

1474 it was when a sane man of Florence—Paolo the Physician, he was called—went on record as favoring the west to get to the East.

I have already spoken with you respecting a shorter way to the places of spices than that which you take by Guinea, by means of maritime navigation. The most serene King now seeks from me some statement, or rather a demonstration to the eye, by which the slightly learned may take in and understand that way. I know this can be shown from the spherical shape of the earth, yet, to make the *Letter of Paolo Toscanelli to* comprehension of it easier, and to facilitate *Fernan Martins (June, 1474)* the work, I have determined to show that way by means of a sailing chart.

I, therefore, send to his Majesty a chart made by my own hands, on which are delineated your coasts and islands, whence you must begin to make your journey always westward, and the places at which you should arrive, and how far from the pole or the equinoctial line you ought to keep, and through how much space or over how many miles you should arrive at those most fertile places full of all sorts of spices and jewels.

You must not be surprised if I call the parts where the spices are "west," when they usually call them "east," because to those always sailing west, those parts are found by navigation on the under side of the earth. But if by land and by the upper side, they will always be found to the east.

The straight lines shown lengthways on the map indicate the distance from east to west, and those that are drawn across show the spaces from south to north. I have also noted on the map several places at which you may arrive for the better information of navigators, if they should reach a place different from what was expected, by reason of the wind or any other cause; and also that they may show some acquaintance with the country to the natives, which ought to be sufficiently agreeable to them.

It is asserted that none but merchants live on the islands. For there the number of navigators with merchandise is so great that in all the rest of the world there are not so many as in one most noble port called Zaitun. For they affirm that a hundred ships laden with pepper discharge their cargoes in that port in a single year, besides other ships bringing other spices.

That country is very populous and very rich, with a multitude of provinces and kingdoms, and with cities without number, under one prince who is called Great Khan, which name signifies *Rex Regum* in Latin, whose seat and residence is generally in the province, Cathay.

PRELIMINARY AT PALOS

Paolo's letter was sent to Fernan Martins, Canon at Lisbon. And a copy went to another friend living in Lisbon, a man of the Genoese nation, interested in travelling, especially on water, in a ship with sails, and himself at the helm.

Looking to the west from his ship of the moment, looking out of the market ways of the Mediterranean, wandering even into the ocean sea, and looking out from as far as Madeira and the Azores, he seemed almost to see the East.

He remembered the others who said it lay out there. He recalled the words of a cardinal, and the words he had read of a university chancellor in Paris. And there were the reports of strange carved sticks found at Ferro. And the calculations along with the talk by the pilots, the skilled sailors of ships, the navigators like himself. There were the learned men he conversed with—in Portugal where he married a navigator's daughter and inherited the old man's instruments and charts, in England by proxy of Bartholomew his brother, and in Spain among some wise ones in the monasteries, and even a cardinal or two.

He went from one to the other, finding agreement with what he proposed, meeting a nod of approval, encountering friends to free him from the reaching hands of bigots who feared his belief in the lands in the East lying westward, who feared the change his contemplated act might bring. Their cry was the cry of heresy, as it had been with others before him. But he found friends to succor him, though he wanted more than protection and moral comfort. From his own land, to Portugal, to Spain, to England by his brother's proxy, and to Spain once more he moved, seeking the ships with the sails and the men to man them.

Like a man of notoriety, he became known by various names. Among the Genoese, the Venetians, his friends in Florence, he was Cristóforo Colombo. In London they referred to him as Christopher, the brother of Bartholomew, who came to plead his cause. And in Granada, in the south, where the Catholic kings were running the last Moors out of the Spain they had held for eight hundred years, the man was called Cristóbal Colón.

Among the tents in the shadow of the heights of the Alhambra, there was the sailor again, hat in hand, his feet on the dry, burning soil, seeking his ships with sail, pleading, petitioning, begging for the ships and the crew and the needed provisions, promising their majesties more wealth and more power than the vanquished Moor had won. It was there to the west, he told them, across the water—where Cipango, which was later known as Nippon, where Cathay, where India, and the isles of spice and gold lay. Jewels and gold and golden cinnamon and glittering saffron. And a treasure of trade with the countries of the Great Khan that waited, west from the Azores. Treasure for their majesties, wealth and finery for Ferdinand and Isabella—and power forever over the people brought together beneath the banner of Aragon and Castile.

And, at last, Castile was cunning, there was craftiness in Aragon.

Granted, they said, granted, when Christopher alias Cristóforo alias Cristóbal was turning his feet toward France. Granted—but let the people pay for it! Let the rabble run the risk. Let the people of Palos pay:

Don Ferdinand and Doña Isabella, by the grace of God, King and Queen of Castile, Leon, Aragon, Sicily, Granada, Toledo, Valencia, Galacia, Majorca, Seville, Sardinia, Corsica, Murcia, Jahen, Algarve, Algesira, Gibraltar, and the Canary Islands, Count and Countess of Barcelona, Lords of Biscay and Molina, Dukes of Athens

From Ferdinand and Isabella—
"Outfit two caravels"

and Neopatria, Counts of Rousillon and Cerdan, Marquises of Orestan and Goziano, to you, Diego Rodríguez Prieto, and to all other persons inhabitants of the town of Palos. Greeting:

You are well aware that in consequence of some offense which we received at your hands, you were condemned by our council to render us the service of two caravels armed at your own expense for the space of twelve months whenever and wherever it should be our pleasure to demand the same, this service to be rendered under certain penalties as stated more at length in the sentence given against you.

And, inasmuch as we have ordered Christopher Columbus to proceed with a fleet of three caravels, as our captain, to certain parts of the ocean, upon a matter connected with our service, and we desire that the two caravels, the service of which you owe us as above said, should be placed at his disposal—we hereby order that within ten days from the sight of this letter, without delay or waiting for any further directions, you have in complete readiness the said two armed caravels for the service of the above said Christopher Columbus in the enterprise upon which we have dispatched him, and that they be placed at his command from that time forth; and for the crews of the said two caravels we order him to pay you forthwith four months' wages at the same rate with which the crew of the other caravel is paid, being the common allowance for ships of war.

The vessels thus placed under his direction shall follow the route ordered by him on our part, and obey him in all other orders, provided that neither you nor the said Christopher Columbus, nor any other person belonging to the said caravels, shall proceed to the mines nor to the countries in that neighborhood occupied by the King of Portugal, our brother, as it is our desire to adhere to the agreement existing between us and the said King of Portugal upon that head.

And having received a certificate from the said captain that he had received the said two caravels from you, and is satisfied with the same, we shall consider you as having discharged the obligation imposed upon you by our council as above said, and we hereby declare you henceforth free from the same. But in the event of the non-fulfillment of or procrastination of the above order, we shall forthwith command the execution of the penalties contained in the aforesaid sentence, upon each one of you and your goods.

The above requisition is to be complied with throughout, under pain of our displeasure and a penalty of ten thousand *maravedis*. . . .

ALIVE AS THE DAY

It was cheaper to outfit the caravels, the people of Palos concluded. To the little port of Palos, then, went the man some called Columbus: a man weary of waiting, but more than willing to wait in that seaport in the south. More than willing to wait as the two caravels of Palos and a third ship leased by himself were made ready for the voyage.

Quite willing, he was, even to see the springtime slowly travel into summer that year of 1492, as he looked over the job being done. Or to watch the other vessels, with their sails or without, swaying in the sultry harbor. Or gaze upon the ships being loaded with the sad, unwilling exiles, see them hoist their sails for Africa and slip out—no sound but the weeping—taking the Jews from Ferdinand's and Isabella's kingdom. Or look out at the horizon and with a vigilant eye bring the appearing ships into the haven, see them coming slowly to the near shore:

And listen to the tales they bring, examine the cargo—delighting in the new kinds of wood for ships and furniture and buildings that were beginning to change the architectural face of Iberia and the continent. Sampling the sweet sugar while hearing the news brought from the ports they had touched on the Guinea coast, from Finisterre and the lands of Europe to the north, or from Ferro in the Canaries lying more west than south.

Willing and eager in fact to hear the reports of ships of the other nations slowly learning the secrets of the great ocean sea and the lands that it held. Stories of ships of the Genoese and men of Florence and Venice, of the restless sea-rovers from Holland and from France, of the Scandinavians and their lanes to Iceland. Of the British moving out of Bristol, northwestward to Greenland and maybe farther west still. And above all, and in particular, of the westward-lying waters washing the islands of the rival Portuguese:

Of Fayal in the Azores, of the islands of the Madeiras, and the cluster called Cape Verde. And of the isle of Porto Santo—where Christopher's own father-in-law had sailed in the service of that prince of men and navigators, Don Henrique of Portugal:

Prince Henry, the pure, who chose for his motto the will to do good.

Conqueror in Africa, colonizer, patron known to the nations of that known world. Henry, the true prince, dead these two and thirty years, but alive as the day still, alive as the sun that he and his scholars and seamen of every land and every faith watched come up and set and rise again over his lookout at Sagres, where Europe met the sea. Alive and exemplary still was the figure of Henry, the prince of discoverers.

He was there at Palos, appropriately, in the little port busily engaged in big preparations. He was there in the calculations and the sailing instruments, in the charts handed down by himself and his navigators to heirs by marriage and calling. He was there in the mind of Christopher, and he was among his company of men in the tales of all who had heard of him and even some who had known him:

This noble Prince was of a good height and stout frame, big and strong of limb, the hair of his head somewhat erect, with a color naturally fair, but which by constant toil and exposure had become dark. His expression at first sight inspired fear in those who did not know him; and when wroth—though such times were rare—his countenance was harsh.

A Portrait of Prince Henry, by Eannes de Azurara

Strength of heart and keenness of mind were in him to a very excellent degree, and beyond comparison he was ambitious of achieving great and lofty deeds. Neither luxury nor avarice ever found a home within his breast—for as to the former, he was so temperate that all his life was passed in purest chastity, and as a virgin the earth received him at his death again to herself.

And what can I say of his greatness, except that it was pre-eminent among all the princes of the earth? He was indeed the uncrowned prince, whose court was full of more numerous and more noble vassals of his own rearing than any other.

His palace was a school of hospitality for all the good and high-born of the realm, and still more for strangers. And the fame of it caused there to be a great increase in his expenses: for commonly there were to be found in his presence men from various nations so different from our own that it was a marvel to well-nigh all our people, and none of that great multitude could go away without some guerdon from the Prince.

All his days were passed in the greatest toil, for of a surety among all the nations of mankind there was no one man who was a sterner master to himself. It would be hard to tell how many nights he passed in the which his eyes knew no sleep. And his body was so transformed by the use of abstinence that it seemed as if Don Henrique had made its nature to be different from that of other men. Such was the length of his toil and so rigorous was it that . . . the people of our kingdom had a proverb that the great labors of this our Prince "conquered the heights of the mountains"—that is to say, the matters that seemed impossible to other men, by his continual energy were made to appear light and easy.

The Infant, Don Henrique, was a man of great wisdom and authority, very discreet and of good memory, but in some matters a little tardy— whether it were from the influence of phlegm in his nature or from the choice of his will, directed to some certain end not known of men. His bearing was calm and dignified, his speech and address gentle.

He was constant in adversity, humble in prosperity. Of a surety no sovereign ever had a vassal of such station, or even of one far lower than his, who held him in greater obedience and reverence than he showed to the kings who in his days reigned in Portugal, and especially to the King Affonso, his nephew. . . . Never was hatred known in him, nor ill-will towards any, however great the wrong he might have done him. And so great was his benignity in this matter that wiseacres reproached him as wanting in distributive justice, though in all other matters he held the rightful mean. . . .

The Infant drank wine only for a very small part of his life, and that in his youth, but afterwards he abstained entirely from it. He always showed great devotion to the public affairs of these kingdoms, toiling greatly for their good advancement, and much he delighted in the trial of new essays for the profit of all, though with great expense of his own substance. And so he keenly enjoyed the labor of arms, and especially against the enemies of the holy faith, while he desired peace with all Christians. Thus he was loved by all alike, for he made himself useful to all and hindered no one.

His answers were always gentle, and therewith he showed great honor to the standing of every one who came to him, without any lessening of his own estate. A base or unchaste word was never heard to issue from his mouth.

He was very obedient to all the commands of Holy Church, and heard all its offices with great devotion. Aye, and caused the same to be celebrated in his chapel with no less splendor and ceremony than they could have had in the college of any Cathedral Church. And so he held all sacred things in great reverence and treated the ministers of the same with honor, and bestowed on them favors and largess.

Well-nigh one half of the year he spent in fasting, and the hands of the poor never went away empty from his presence. . . .

I would fain end . . . with an account of that noble town which our Prince caused them to build on Cape St. Vincent, at the place where both seas meet: to wit, the great Ocean sea and the Mediterranean sea. But of the perfections of that town it is not possible to speak here at large, because when this . . . was written there were only the walls standing, though of great strength, with a few houses. Yet work was going on in it continually.

According to the common belief, the Infant purposed to make of it an especial mart town for merchants. And this was to the end that all ships that passed from the East to the West should be able to take their bearings and to get provisions and pilots . . . for here ships can get shelter against every wind—except one that we in this kingdom call the cross-wind.

A SAILOR NAMED RODRIGO

There were winds that cried to the sailor to take shelter. And winds that pleaded for sails to the west.

August was the month, the day the third, the year 1492, when three ships heeded the call of the wind blowing off Palos, off Spain. Three were the ships that sailed that day with the wind crying to Christopher, and Christopher crying the order from his small flagship, the Santa María, to the men on his vessel, to his captains and men on the smaller Niña and Pinta, slowly moving, their sails waving a stately farewell, out of the haven, away from Palos and Spain.

By written authority from their Catholic majesties, and by written directions from the doctor-astronomer-geographer, Paolo Toscanelli, whose letter and whose map he carried; by the blinding vision of the East he sought in accordance with the times; by his full fresh title, still unused—Christopher, now the Admiral, hearing the cry of the wind, and grateful for it, gave the order:

Westward.

Toward the west and south, to the Canaries and beyond, westward into nothing.

August disappeared, dissolving in sky, in sea, in nothing. The voyage lengthened, moving into fear as the sailors saw the steadfast needles of the compass change, and change again—with none, not even the Admiral, knowing the real reason why. The Admiral, meanwhile, hid the truth from them of the distance they sailed each day and night, hid the terrible truth from them by keeping one log that was accurate and another to show to them.

Maybe they suspected—but even if they did not, they saw the days and the nights melt like a cursed calm into the sameness of sea and sky. They noted the change of the needles again, the compass turning to chaos before their eyes. And they watched the wind blow harder to the nothing in the west—wondering through tears turning to ice how they would ever return!

The three ships had never seemed frail before: they had reached the Canaries, why not beyond? But now their frames of wood, their masts and decks, their tossing sides, shook to the sickening sound of the murmurs swelling louder among the men against the Admiral. In the three narrow wakes of the ships, September was left behind. In the vanishing wakes of the three ships still sailing into the unknown, October began, and the men pleaded with the Admiral to point the ships around before it was too late. Turn back, they begged, it is Autumn already, October is here!

The first five days sped by like the wind, taking them farther each night from fresh food, fragrant with clean oil pressed from the plump green olive, from the smell of cool wine pressed from the purple and the olive grape, from joy pressed from the olive-tinted bodies of the swaybacked wenches with olive-irised eyes. Taking them farther from the olive soil of Spain, the land that was poor, the land that was held by the noble few and worked by the many like them, the land that took a lot and gave little—but the land they knew. Even a small square of soil to stand on, hungry amid the sweat and interminable toil, was better than braving this threatening sea without end. And they yearned to go back.

The Admiral shook his head. Yet he must have known, as well, perhaps, as the rest whose plea he denied, that the strain and the uncertainty and fear would never carry them through that month if the course continued westward. And the course continued westward into nothing.

Over the three ships, then, rose the shadow of longing become discontent, the changeless prison of water and sky changing their discontent to anger to fright to terror, nearing the point of more than probability when a crew of maddened men, confronting the figure they had begun to fear and to hate as that of a fanatic who had become an oppressor, would inevitably commit mutiny. And then, the fateful week:

Saturday, 6th of October: The Admiral continued his west course, and during day and night they made good forty leagues—thirty-three being counted. This night Martín Alonso said that it would be well to steer south of west, and it appeared to the Admiral that Martín Alonso did not say this with respect to the island of Cipango. He saw that if an error was made, the land would not be reached so quickly, and that consequently it would be better to go at once to the continent and afterwards to the islands.

Journal of the First Voyage, 1492, of Christopher Columbus

Sunday, 7th of October: The west course was continued; for two hours they went at the rate of twelve miles an hour, and afterwards eight miles an hour. They made good twenty-three leagues, counting eighteen for the people.

This day, at sunrise, the caravel, Niña, which went ahead, being the best sailer, and pushed forward as much as possible to sight the land first, so as to enjoy the reward which the Sovereigns had promised to whoever should see it first, hoisted a flag at the masthead and fired a gun, as a signal that she had sighted land, for such was the Admiral's order. He had also ordered that, at sunrise and sunset, all the ships should join him; because those two times are most proper for seeing the greatest distance, the haze clearing away.

No land was seen during the afternoon, as reported by the caravel Niña, and they passed a great number of birds flying from N. to SW.

This gave rise to the belief that the birds were either going to sleep on land, or were flying from the winter which might be supposed to be near in the land whence they were coming. The Admiral was aware that most of the islands held by the Portuguese were discovered by the flight of birds. For this reason, he resolved to give up the west course, and to shape a course WSW. for the two following days.

He began the new course one hour before sunset. They made good, during the night, about five leagues, and twenty-three in the day; altogether twenty-eight leagues.

Monday, 8th of October: The course was WSW. . . . The sea was like
the river at Seville. . . . The weed seemed to be very fresh. There were
many landbirds, and they took one that was flying to the SW. Terns,
ducks, and a booby were also seen.

Tuesday, 9th of October: The course was SW., and they made five
leagues. The wind then changed, and the Admiral steered W. by N.
four leagues. Altogether, in day and night, they made eleven leagues by
day and twenty and one half leagues by night. . . . Throughout the night,
birds were heard passing.

Wednesday, 10th of October: The course was WSW., and they went
at the rate of ten miles an hour, occasionally twelve miles, and sometimes seven. During the day and night they made fifty-nine leagues,
counted as no more than forty-four.

Here the people could endure no longer. They complained of the
length of the voyage. But the Admiral cheered them up in the best way
he could, giving them good hopes of the advantages they might gain
from it. He added that, however much they might complain, he had to
go to the Indies, and that he would go on until he found them, with
the help of our Lord.

Thursday, 11th of October: The course was WSW., and there was more
sea than there had been during the whole of the voyage.

They saw sandpipers, and a green reed near the ship. Those of the
caravel, *Pinta,* saw a cane and a pole, and they took up another small
pole which appeared to have been worked with iron; also another bit of
cane, a land-plant, and a small board.

The crew of the caravel, *Niña,* also saw signs of land, and a small
branch covered with berries. Everyone breathed afresh and rejoiced at
these signs.

The run until sunset was twenty-six leagues.

After sunset the Admiral returned to his original west course, and
they went along at the rate of twelve miles an hour. Up to two hours
after midnight they had gone ninety miles, equal to twenty-two and
one-half leagues. As the caravel, *Pinta,* was a better sailer and went
ahead of the Admiral, she found the land and made the signals ordered
by the Admiral.

The land was first seen by a sailor named Rodrigo de Triana.

(But the Admiral, at ten in the previous night, being on the castle of
the poop, saw a light, though it was so uncertain that he could not
affirm it was land. He called Pero Gutiérrez, a gentleman of the King's
bedchamber, and said that there seemed to be a light and that he

should look at it. He did so and saw it. The Admiral said the same to Rodrigo Sánchez of Segovia, whom the King and Queen had sent with the fleet as inspector, but he could see nothing, because he was not in a place whence anything could be seen. After the Admiral had spoken, he saw the light once or twice, and it was like a wax candle rising and falling. It seemed to few to be an indication of land. . . . When they said the Salve, which all the sailors were accustomed to sing in their way, the Admiral asked and admonished the men to keep a good lookout on the forecastle, and to watch well for land; and to him who should first cry out that he saw land, he would give a silk doublet, besides the other rewards promised by the Sovereigns, which were 10,000 maravedis to him who should first see it.)

At two hours after midnight, the land was sighted at a distance of two leagues. They shortened sail and lay by under the mainsail without the bonnets. The vessels were hove to, waiting for daylight. . . .

The Admiral and his crews waited for daylight to see how their ships might fit into the shape of the land. They waited in their ships on the warm new water sparkling like jewels of the East, the vessels riding at anchor, the sails shortened, waiting to see what the land was like when daylight came, awake and watchful, with the unknown land before them.

Awake, recalling the ocean sea behind and no longer unknown. They had but to send the word back, and the sea would grow heavy with ships, the empty waves would swell with caravels, their sails full in the welcoming wind!

And how soon the word would be given, how soon the world would know, they little suspected. How soon the sea behind them would fill with the world's ships without number, multiple sails flying in a multitude of winds.

All the winds were crying westward, to clash with the shout of the sea and the surf, to clash with the cries of the birds over the barren reefs, to carry the lost echo of cries from shipwrecked men cast on the ocean sea, cast on the rocks, scattered and dark upon the sea slowly filling with light.

Now Columbus' men waited for daylight, waited not knowing that the land was waiting, too. The dark shape of the land waiting where she lay:

Her wild night hair falling over the valleys of the California Indians, her small feet faintly stirring before the snowy Fuegian dawn, the green of her Amazon belly beginning to glow again. The long night lifting, waking first the tips of her Caribbean-island fingers pointing east, coloring them first with the gold and phosphorescence of the bays of the Bahamas:

Her fingers of Carib fire stretching toward the light in the east, the light rising higher, higher, hurrying now to come down slowly over the whole awakening body of the land, waiting westward where she lay.

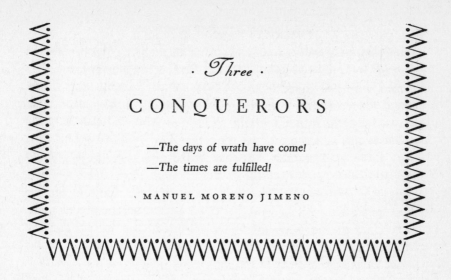

· *Three* ·

CONQUERORS

—*The days of wrath have come!*
—*The times are fulfilled!*

· MANUEL MORENO JIMENO

PRELUDE ON COZUMEL

Even before the Admiral and his sailors saw the land, there were the people standing naked on the shore. There were the people crying welcome, the men and even some women falling down and kissing the ground, lifting their eyes to the gracious skies that had sent them the long-awaited gods returning.

Before the land could be seen clearly, there were the red folk already with the shining black hair: some in canoes, others swimming, racing through the water to the ships' boats. There were the people with bodies of fire painted in every color, moving swiftly to the boats where the Admiral and his captains stood startled and staring in awe, and then no longer startled, but staring with an eye for booty and trade and power over body and soul of subjects claimed for Catholic majesty by the flag of Ferdinand and the ensign of Isabella planted on the new-found soil. Staring now not without covetousness at the naked red folk with the straight limbs and the small and beautiful eyes, at the bits of gold gleaming in their noses, at the welcoming hands bringing them green parrots fluttering, solid skeins of cotton thread of many colors, and a multitude of precious things the Admiral found were worth recalling, but too tedious to recount.

Bringing the gifts as they sped through the water, giving them for nothing or for anything at all. And what they got was mostly broken pieces of crockery and hawks' bells and beads of worthless glass.

These were the innocent Arawaks whom the neighboring Caribs hunted. These were the folk who hated war, caring nothing about wearing arms or even clothes, knowing so little of arms that they took the Spanish swords by the blade that made the blood appear, knowing little in that respect, but impressed at once by the steel and iron brought by the white-skinned gods from the east.

The gods in the armed boat smiled now on the naked folk and the bright land, green with many trees, that gave such pleasure to look upon.

These are the outer islands of the East that lead to Cipango and Cathay, the Admiral wrote. From the landfall in the Bahamas to the land of Cuba that he thought was Japan, and then thought was Cathay, he continued to the island that would be called Hispaniola. He continued in subsequent voyages to Puerto Rico and Jamaica and other islands in the Caribbean Sea, touching Trinidad and perhaps the mainland of the southern continent, calling all the lands discovered—The Indies of the West.

The name remained long after Spain and the old world knew better, knew this was not the sought-for East, but part of a hemisphere that lay between Castile and Cathay, knew that the people they called Indians were not the subjects of the Khan or even of the East, knew most keenly and most consciously that the marvels of gold and spice reported found by the Admiral lay waiting in a world that was new, a world that lay west.

Then over the ships rose the sails, and over the ocean-sea's horizon rose the fleets of ships. From every cranny of Europe, men avid for the promise of treasure and goods, for land and power, men eager for the certainty of adventure even without the gamble for glory, made their way to the ports, to the ships, to the new world waiting in the west: from Holland and from France, Britain and Bavaria, from the city-states of Italy, from Flanders, from Sweden, from Norway and Poland, from the kingdom of Denmark they came. But to the lands of the south in the new-found western world, first and foremost went the men from Portugal and Spain—the two Catholic countries upon whom the writing, shaping hand of Pope Alexander VI had bestowed the new-found hemisphere.

And one of the first, from one of the poorest corners of Spain, was Hernán Cortés, coasting up by way of Cozumel, off Yucatan, toward the untouched Mexican mainland. Cortés with his small fleet and his little band of men of little or no schooling, soon to write a lasting story with sword and shot and, in a few instances involving honest and simple soldiers of fortune like their fellow who answered the roll-call to the shouted name of "Díaz," christened "Bernal," in words as lasting as the remembered deed:

Cortés now sent for me and a Biscayan named Martín Ramos, in order to question us as to our opinions of the meaning of the word "Castillán," so frequently repeated by the Indians of Cotoche, when we came with Captain Hernández de Córdova; adding that he was convinced that it must allude to some Spaniards in that country: for which reason,

Captain Bernal Díaz on the Conquest of Mexico

he questioned the native chiefs upon the subject. They all answered in the affirmative, and certain Indian merchants then in Cozumel assured us that they had spoken to them a few days before.

Cortés was anxious to obtain their release, and being informed that compensation would be expected, he amply provided his messengers for the purpose. By these persons he sent letters to them, and he ordered for this service two light vessels, with twenty crossbow-men and musketeers under the command of Diego de Ordas. One ship was to remain at the point of Cotoche for eight days, while the messengers went and returned, and the second was to bring the report to Cortés how the business proceeded.

The places where the Spaniards were said to reside were distant from the point of Cotoche only about four leagues. The letter which Cortés sent was as follows: "Gentlemen and brothers, here in Cozumel I have been informed that you are detained prisoners by a cacique. I request as a favor that you will forthwith join me. I send a ship and soldiers, with whatever is necessary for your ransom; they have orders to wait eight days. But come with all dispatch to me, from whom you shall receive every assistance and protection. I am here with eleven ships and five hundred soldiers, with which I will, with the assistance of God, proceed to Tabasco, Pontonchan, etc., etc."

The merchants of Cozumel, to whom this business was intrusted, being embarked, the ships crossed the gulf, and the letters were in two days received by a Spaniard named Jerónimo de Aguilar, together with the beads sent for his ransom. He immediately waited upon his master, who accepted them with satisfaction, and gave him his liberty. Aguilar then went to his companion, Alonso Guerrero, and having made known his business, Guerrero replied to him as follows:

"Brother Aguilar, I am married; I have three sons, and am a cacique and captain in the wars; go you in God's name; my face is marked, and my ears bored; what would those Spaniards think of me if I went among them? Behold these three beautiful boys; I beseech you give me for them some of these green beads, and say that my brother sent them as a present to me from our country."

The man's wife who was present now became greatly enraged and said in her language, "See this slave how he comes to seduce my husband!"

Aguilar persevered in advising the other not to lose his precious soul for the sake of an Indian, or at any rate if he could not part from his wife and children, to bring them with him; but he could not be induced to quit his home. When Aguilar saw that it was impossible to move him, he came with the Indian messengers to the part of the coast where the ships had been stationed.

But they had already sailed, for the eight days to which De Ordas considered himself limited, and one more, were expired. And De Ordas, despairing of the return of his messengers, had gone back to Cozumel. So that Aguilar was forced to return with great sorrow to his Indian master.

Cortés was exceedingly displeased at De Ordas for returning without the Spaniards or even those whom he sent in quest of them. . . .

In the beginning of the month of March, we set sail. . . . We had sailed but a few hours when a signal gun and cry of alarm informed us that the vessel of Juan de Escalante, which contained the bread for the fleet, was in danger, having sprung a leak. This forced us to put back to the place from whence we had sailed. . . .

The Indian messengers and Aguilar, hearing of our return, joyfully hired a boat and crossed the gulf to join us. Intelligence of the arrival of a large canoe was given to Cortés by some soldiers who had gone out to hunt wild swine. Whereupon he ordered Andrés de Tapia and two others to go and see who and what these Indians were, who came to us thus without apprehension.

Aguilar was not in his appearance to be distinguished from a native, and he had hardly the pronunciation of his own language; his only words at first were "Dios," "Santa María," and "Sevilla." His color was as dark as a native, and he was marked like them. He had a few rags about his shoulders and waist, an oar in his hand, and the remnant of an old book of prayers tied in a bundle on his shoulder.

When he came into the presence of Cortés, he, like the rest of his companions, squatted down upon his hams, and everyone was looking for the Spaniard. At length, to the enquiry of Cortés, he replied, "Here he is," and then coming forward, he was immediately supplied with proper clothing.

THE UNPREDICTABLE WAYS

There were the portents in the air at last. In the entrails of birds opened by the wizards with the matted locks, the sign of a cross and the shape of a curious sword appeared. The Mexicans' chief of chiefs, the wizard-warrior, Moctezuma, had fitful dreams that left the sleeper's cheek discolored. And then, the fiery comet crossed the Aztec sky.

And finally, more final than the Aztecs knew, there were the ships coming in from the sea, up from the coast; and from the ships white-skinned beings with beards, stepping out on the eastern shore where The Plumed Serpent had left the land.

Although it was reported widely that the new arrivals were the gods returning to bring back the glory of yore, as the approaching echo of their footsteps on the land grew louder, Moctezuma's spirits waned. The power of the gods, he knew, was wondrous: awesome were their omens and their prophecies—but unpredictable the whims of their demanding ways! He sent the visiting lords from the sky a treasure of gifts far surpassing those that the other captains had received from the chiefs now subdued in Cuba, Hispaniola, Puerto Rico, and other islands in the Carib sea and even the rich land of the narrow Panama isthmus, washed by the two vast ocean seas.

But the gods were not content: they did not turn back as Moctezuma hoped and did not dare to hope. They did not stop. Nor did they promise to come no farther than the place where they set foot and which they called "The True Cross"—"Vera Cruz"—or the points just beyond. In fact they promised nothing, moving irresistibly up the steady ascent toward the heart of the Aztec empire where the emperor's heart was growing more melancholy. And the sound of their feet marching toward Tenochtitlan rang in Moctezuma's ears like the lightning that spoke from the fiery mouths of the fearsome metal monsters they dragged in their midst, like the thunderous neighing that came from the two-headed thing of terror—the beast that was one with its rider, like the fire roaring from the ships left burning behind them, blocking the way back.

The gifts grew larger, the offerings came faster by the relay of gasping messengers from the man of Aztec power: like a man bewitched, now turning mute and immobile with the breath of doom blowing cold at his heart: the sound of the feet tramping up from the coast, from the plain, the din of beasts and metal and metal monsters approaching, the stubborn feet moving west and upward, pounding to the high plateau holding the heart of his empire. Stop them now, his chieftains urged, stop them now before it is too late! Gods or no gods, they mean us no good! Stop them now. . . .

But it was too late by the time the band of white-skinned ones with the beards and the fearful beasts of iron and flesh reached the land of the deadly enemies of the Aztec Confederacy, reached the land of Tlaxcala. Too late by the time Cortés could talk to Tlaxcala after the fight: the red bodies scattered, the limbs severed by steel, and the breasts torn open by lead as the flint knife of sacrifice had never been able to do in the Flowery War of the Aztecs. Havoc was the aim of this new kind of warfare brought by the gods from the east—havoc and instant death, with no time for the capture, no time for the rite, no time for the sacrifice and the gift of the warm, beating heart. There was only fire and steel and death and the furious feet of the two-headed beast, encased in iron and pointing the lance that slew where it struck.

Too late: the fighting was over and Tlaxcala was more than willing to listen. It was too late by the time Tlaxcala could understand through the tongues and the lips of the two that stood by the side of Cortés. More than the cannon and horses, more than the iron armor, more than the death in an instant borne on the points of their steel swords and lances by Cortés and his few hundred men, more than the trampling horses thundering over the hordes defending their homes, was the worth of those two who stood at the side of the captain: Aguilar, the man he found on Cozumel, and Malinche, the Mexican woman he had won for his bed and his brain.

Malinche heard her native speech, her tongue uttering the meaning in the Maya she had learned in the south. Aguilar heard her words in the Maya he had learned, but his lips formed the words in the speech that was native to him and to the man they called their captain: Cortés. Listening, then, in more than wonderment, Tlaxcala watched the words and the speech from Cortés that came from the lips of Aguilar and the tongue of the woman known as Malinche.

And Tlaxcala became the faithful ally of invasion, furnishing the numerous army while the Spaniards brought the arms of fire, the iron armor and the swords and lances of steel, the terror of the horses, the courage of their captain and his guile, which spoke through the tongues of the two that moved beside him.

The red blood of the red folk began to flow upward, up the plateau, up to the four great causeways that led to the doomed city. The blood flowed up, into the heart of the city that was the heart of empire, out of the heart of the captive Moctezuma, slain by the stones of his wrathful subjects driving the startled invader out of the city in the night that was briefly the night of sorrow for Cortés and his conquerors.

The blood flowed down that night when scores of the conquerors were slain by the arrows shot from the darting canoes on the great lake, and others sank to the bottom of the lake with their bellies gorged with food and drink and their clothes turned to lead from the silver and gold loot they were laden with.

But the respite for the red folk was brief. Cortés came back with his soldiers and Indian allies fresh and replenished, his brigantines new. The long, cruel siege of the city began. And the blood flowed up in rivulets turning to streams around the feet of the conquering captain and all his men. The blood flowed up in streams turning to a crimson tide, turning the waters of the Aztecs' lake of lakes red, as the siege went on. In the storm of resistance that rose with the red man's realization that the white men of guile and massacre were only men, the siege went on:

As soon as it was day, I caused our whole force to be in readiness, and the heavy guns to be brought out. And the day before, I had ordered Pedro de Alvarado to wait for me in the square of the market place, and not to attack the enemy until I arrived. Being all assembled, and the brigantines drawn up ready for action on the right of the houses situated

Dispatches of Hernán Cortés to the Emperor Charles V

on the water, where the enemy were stationed, I directed that when they heard the discharge of a musket, the land force should enter the small part of the city that remained to be taken and drive the enemy towards the water where the brigantines lay. And I enjoined much upon them to look for Cuauhtémoc (their "cacique" or chief, and nephew of the late Moctezuma) and endeavor to take him alive, as in that case the war would cease.

I then ascended a terrace and, before the combat began, addressed some of the nobles whom I knew, asking them for what reason their lord refused to come to me, when they were reduced to such extremities, adding that there was no good cause why they should all perish, and that they should go and call him and have no fears.

Two of the principal nobles then went to call their lord. After a short time there returned with them one of the most considerable of all these personages, named Cihuacoatzin, a captain and governor over them all, by whose counsels the whole affairs of the war were conducted; and I received him with great kindness, that he might feel perfectly secure and free from apprehensions. At last he said that the cacique would by no means come into my presence, preferring rather to die; and that his determination grieved him much, but that I must do whatever I desired.

And when I saw that this was his settled purpose, I told the noble messenger to return to his friends and prepare for the renewal of the war, which I was resolved to continue until their destruction was complete. So he departed.

More than five hours had been spent in these conferences, during which time many of the inhabitants were crowded together upon piles of the dead—some were on the water, and others were seen swimming about, or drowning in the part of the lake where the canoes were lying, which was of considerable extent. Indeed, so excessive were the sufferings of the people, that no one could imagine how they were able to sustain them. And an immense multitude of men, women and children were compelled to seek refuge with us—many of whom in their eagerness to reach us threw themselves into the water and were drowned amongst the mass of dead bodies.

It appeared that the number of persons who had perished, either from drinking salt water, from famine or pestilence, amounted altogether to more than fifty thousand souls. In order to conceal their necessitous condition from our knowledge, the bodies of the dead were not thrown into the water, lest the brigantines should come in contact with them; nor were they taken away from the places where they had died, lest we should see them about the city. But in those streets where they had perished, we found heaps of dead bodies so frequent that a person passing could not avoid stepping on them.

And when the people of the city flocked towards us, I caused Spaniards to be stationed through all the streets to prevent our Indian allies from destroying the wretched persons who came out in such multitudes. I also charged the captains of our allies to forbid, by all means in their power, the slaughter of these fugitives. Yet all my precautions were insufficient to prevent it—and that day more than fifteen thousand lost their lives.

At the same time the better classes and the warriors of the city were pent up within narrow limits, confined to a few terraces and houses, or sought refuge on the water—but no concealment prevented our seeing their miserable condition and weakness with sufficient clearness. As the evening approached, and no signs of their surrender appeared, I ordered the two pieces of ordnance to be levelled towards the enemy to try their effect in causing them to yield.

But they suffered greater injury when full license was given to the allies to attack them than from the cannon—although the latter did them some mischief. As this was of little avail, I ordered the musketry to be fired, when a certain angular space where they were crowded together was gained and some of the people thrown into the water. Those that remained there yielded themselves prisoners without a struggle.

In the meantime, the brigantines suddenly entered that part of the lake and broke through the midst of the fleet of canoes, the warriors who were in them not daring to make any resistance. It pleased God that the captain of a brigantine, named García de Holguín, came up behind a canoe in which there seemed to be persons of distinction—and when the archers who were stationed in the bow of the brigantine took aim at those in the canoe, they made a signal that the cacique was there, that the men might not discharge their arrows. Instantly our people leaped into the canoe, and seized in it Cuauhtémoc, and the lord of Tacuba, together with other distinguished persons that accompanied the cacique.

Immediately after this occurrence, García de Holguín, the captain, delivered to me on a terrace adjoining the lake, where I was standing, the cacique of the city . . . who, as I bade him sit down, without showing any asperity of manner came up to me and said in his own tongue that he had done all that was incumbent on him in defence of himself and his people, until he was reduced to his present condition—that now I might do with him as I pleased. He then laid his hand on a poniard that I wore, telling me to strike him to the heart.

I spoke encouragingly to him, and bade him have no fears.

Thus the cacique being taken a prisoner, the war ceased at this point, which it pleased God our Lord to bring to a conclusion on Tuesday, Saint Hippolytus' day, the thirteenth of August, 1521.

THE CHANCE OF A LIFETIME

The war for the Mexican capital ceased, but the war between the conquering whites and the folk of the land was only starting. Over the Aztecs' slain city of cities, over its pyramids and temples, the man with the beard and the mailed fist raised the cross and the banner of Spain. Hernán Cortés, now the Conqueror, the Gran Capitán who had helped to win Cuba, rode out of the city of death, over the ruined causeways, and down to the south, down to the lands they called Guatemala and Honduras, planting the cross as he went, planting the cross and hanging the captive chief, Cuauhtémoc—after bidding him "have no fears." Over the slain Cuauhtémoc and all the chiefs massacred by Alvarado and the other companions of Cortés for refusing to divulge by entreaty or by torture where the supposed Aztec treasure lay, over the Aztec fields and along the canals, Cortés and his conquistadors planted the cross and raised the conquering banner of Spain.

Southward, other white-skinned gods, soon to be recognized as men, were marching still farther, carrying the cross and the banner of power of Isabella's and Ferdinand's successor: Charles I. Moving through conquest and marriage from Austria, from Germany, to Spain, to Naples, to the Lowlands and the ports of the North Sea, the spanning power of Charles I of Spain, who was also Charles V of Germany, was also rushing now over the new lands in the west, rushing southward to the waist of the Isthmus where the Aztecs once had stopped and where the banner of Spanish power was already being raised by others than Cortés, by men led by a man named Balboa.

One had been a swineherd back in Spain, a cousin of the same Cortés who set the pattern for the overthrow of the pagan empire in the west.

He passed from swineherd, to adventurer, to man of tireless enterprise, to the titled rank of Marquis: Don Francisco Pizarro.

He was a man with ambition and with many relatives, a man whose feverish eye was fixed on the fabulous lands of the Incas from the seat of their empire he had finally reached. He came to see, he said—

But there was little of the disinterested spectator about him. Particularly when the chance of a lifetime of lifetimes presented itself in the form of a pending visit from the lord of Peru and the Andes, a visit from Atahualpa the Inca himself:

After dawn, the Marquis Don Francisco Pizarro arranged his troops, dividing the cavalry into two portions—of which he gave the command of one to Hernando Pizarro, his brother, and the command of the other to Hernando de Soto. In like manner he divided the infantry, he himself taking one part and giving the other to his brother, Juan Pizarro.

Pedro Pizarro: The Conquest of the Kingdoms of Peru

At the same time, he ordered Pedro de Candia with two or three infantrymen to go with trumpets to a small fort which is in the plaza of Caxamarca and to station themselves there with a small piece of ordnance which he carried in the field. And that when all the Indians—and the Inca, Atahualpa, with them—had entered the plaza, the Spaniards would make Candia and his men a signal, after which the firing should begin and the trumpets should sound. And at the sound of the trumpets, the cavalry should dash out of the large *galpón*, or shed, where they were in readiness, and wherein many more of them might have been hidden than there were in their troop.

The *galpón* had many doors, all those on the plaza being large, so that they might easily allow those who were within to dash out mounted. At the same time, Don Francisco Pizarro and his brother, Juan Pizarro, were in another part of the same *galpón* so as to come out after the cavalry. Thus it was that all were in this *galpón*, without one of them being lacking.

Nor did they go out into the plaza, because the Indians did not see what sort of troops they were and because it would put fear into their hearts when they all came out together. All decked their horses' trappings with bells in order to fill the Indians with fear.

When all was thus with the Spaniards, the news was carried to Atahualpa by some Indians who were spying about that all the Spaniards were waiting in readiness in a *galpón*, full of fear, and that none of them dared to appear on the plaza. And in very deed the Indians told the truth, for I have heard that many of the Spaniards made water without knowing it, out of sheer terror.

On learning this, Atahualpa bade them give him food to eat, and he ordered that all his men should do likewise. These people had the custom of dining in the morning, and it was the same with all the natives of this kingdom. The lords, having dined, were wont to spend the day drinking until the evening, when they supped very lightly. . . . Then, having dined, finishing about the hour of high mass, Atahualpa began to draw up his men and to approach nearer to Caxamarca.

When his squadrons were formed in such wise that they covered the fields, and when he himself had mounted into a litter, he began to march. Before him went two thousand Indians who swept the road by which he travelled, and these were followed by the warriors—half of whom were marching in the fields on one side of him and half on the other side, and neither half entered upon the road itself at all. In like manner, he bore with him the Lord of Chincha riding upon a litter, which seemed to his men a wonderful honor—for no Indian, no matter how great a lord he might be, ever appeared before the Inca save with a burden upon his back and with naked feet.

Then, too, so great was the amount of furniture of gold and silver which they bore, that it was a marvel to observe how the sun glinted upon it. Likewise, there marched before Atahualpa many Indians singing and dancing. This lord required for his going over the half league, between the baths where he was and Caxamarca, the time between the hour of high mass . . . and three hours before nightfall.

Then the Indian troops having arrived at the entrance of the plaza, the squadrons began to enter it to the accompaniment of great songs. And thus entering, they occupied every part of the plaza.

The Marquis Don Francisco Pizarro, observing how Atahualpa had now drawn near to the plaza, sent Padre Fray Vicente de Valverde, first bishop of Cuzco, Hernando de Aldana, a good soldier, and Don Martinillo, the interpreter, with orders to go and speak to Atahualpa and require it of him in the name of God and of the King that he subject himself to the law of our Lord Jesus Christ and to the service of His Majesty—and to say that the Marquis would regard him as a brother and would not consent that any injury be done to him nor any damage be done to his land.

When the Padre had arrived at the litter in which Atahualpa travelled, he spoke to him and told him the things he had come to say. And he preached unto him the matters pertaining to our holy faith, they being declared by the interpreter. The Padre carried in his hands a breviary from which he read the matters which he preached. Atahualpa asked him for it, and the Padre closing it, handed it to him.

When Atahualpa had it in his hands, he did not know how to open it, and he threw it upon the ground. The Padre called upon Aldana to draw near to Atahualpa and give him the sword. And Aldana drew it and brandished it—but did not wish to plunge it into the Inca.

When this occurred, Atahualpa told them to get them thence, as they were mere scurvy rogues, for he was going to have all of them put to death. Hearing this, the Padre returned and related all to the Marquis. And Atahualpa entered the plaza with all his pomp and the Lord of Chincha in his train.

When they had entered the plaza and had seen that no Spaniard made his appearance, he asked his captains where were these Christians who failed to appear. And they said to him: "Lord, they are in hiding for very fear."

The Marquis Don Francisco Pizarro, seeing the two litters, did not know which was that of Atahualpa, so he ordered Juan Pizarro, his brother, to attack one with the infantry, and he would attack the other. This being ordered, he made the signal to Candia—who began to fire, and at the same time caused the trumpets to sound. And the cavalry came out in troop formation, and the Marquis with the infantry. . . .

And it all happened in such wise that, with the noise of the firing, and the blowing of the trumpets and the bells on the horses, the Indians were thrown into confusion and were cut to pieces. The Spaniards attacked them and began to slay them, and so great was the fear which the Indians had, and so great was their anxiety to flee, that, not being able to pass through the gateway, they threw down a portion of the wall around the plaza. . . .

The Marquis attacked the litter of Atahualpa, and his brother that of the Lord of Chincha—whom they killed there in his litter. And the same fate would have been Atahualpa's had not the Marquis been there, because they were unable to pull him out of the litter, and although they slew the Indians who bore it, others at once took their places and held it aloft. And in this manner they spent a great time in overcoming and killing Indians. . . . Out of weariness a Spaniard made as if to give Atahualpa a blow with a knife in order to kill him—and the Marquis

Don Francisco Pizarro prevented it, and by his prevention the Marquis received a wound in the hand from the Spaniard who wished to slay Atahualpa.

Because of this, the Marquis gave loud cries, saying: "Let no one wound the Indian on pain of death!"

Hearing these words, seven or eight Spaniards were spurred on, and they rushed upon the litter from one side, and with great efforts they turned it over on its side. And thus was Atahualpa made a prisoner.

"WE WENT ON KILLING"

They took him in Cajamarca, one of the many cities that bowed to the Inca with feet bared and a burden placed on the back. It was in Cajamarca that he was dragged from his litter, dragging his empire with him.

He promised them a roomful of gold and a roomful of silver if they would spare his life. And the offer of wealth became his doom and that of the land he wanted to spare. They gave their promise and they took the treasure: dividing it among themselves after sending the king in Spain his royal share. They melted down the treasure of gold and silver beauty carved in the warm figures and symbols of sun and moon and bird and beast and god and man, melted it down to ingots cold as the wind in the Andes. And the rest they gambled among themselves.

They took the Inca treasure and they spared the Inca's life for the little while it took to pit the royal captive against his own captive: Huascar, his half-brother and challenger of his throne. And when Huascar was dead, they took the life of Atahualpa, dragged from the overthrown litter, whose life they promised to spare. But they gave him the privilege of escaping death at the burning stake providing he embraced the faith of the cross and the book he had thrown to the ground in bewilderment. He accepted the offer and this time they kept their word: they let him meet his death by the twist of the string, they permitted him to go to his death by strangling. In Cajamarca where he fell.

In his last bewildered gasp the last of the great empires of the red folk died. The fighting went on, but the empire was dead. The fighting went on: over the immense provinces ruled from Cuzco, the eye of the Andes, over the cities and towns won by the folk now leaderless, but proud in the knowledge of conquering achievement. The fighting went on over the dams and the bridges and roads built by the people of builders: lost and leaderless now, facing the fire that filled their aqueducts in the Andes with their own blood running down from the skies, down the canals and the ducts, spilling over the dams, down to the desert, down to the shore—painting the sand of the desert and shore red with blood in the final gasp of the Inca.

And power belonged to Pizarro, with all his brothers and cousins. Power over the Inca kingdoms and power over the hotheaded rivals from Spain bent on conquest in these kingdoms. Power over the die-hard Almagro and the grasping Alvarado, who was bribed to go back to the northern lands, back to Cortés who had his own factions to fight. Power for Pizarro in the name of Spain and the person of Don Francisco and all the other Pizarros, power over all factions and power over the numberless followers of the strangled and slain Inca chiefs. Power over the treasure of towns and fields, over mines of silver and gold, over the vast herds of grazing sheep of the land.

Power moving in all directions out of Peru, mostly east and south, mostly by land, but also by sea. Power moving in the name of Pizarro and his brethren and cousins, relaying power with care and calculation to their friends and their fellows:

Handing it at length to a man who was stout of body and restless in mind, firm in his obstinacy and obstinate in his firmness and his cruel ways. A man commissioned to execute the next to impossible task of winning the western strip of the Andes stretching down to Magellan's Strait, the strip that would some day be referred to as Chile. The power was handed to this man on condition that he lead his hundred and fifty men and their thousand Indian allies southward to settle the land of the Araucanians who were skilled in their own ways of war and who were still unconquered by Inca or by Almagro and the other Spaniards that had tried the thing before him.

Pedro de Valdivia was the name he bore, and he took the road down the burning coast, preferring, if need be, to perish from heat and from thirst rather than freeze in the mountain ways as others had done before him. Southward down the coast he went.

Striking at last a vale he liked near the sea, Valdivia founded a town, calling it Santiago; then he moved on. He moved inland to cross new *rivers, giving them new names, claiming and settling the soil for Spain whatever the cost in toil and blood.*

So as not to risk the horses, I went up the river to look for a better crossing; after we had gone two leagues, a great number of Indians showed themselves on our road; Captain Alderete attacked them with twenty mounted men, and they threw themselves into the river, and he with his men after them. When I saw this, I sent another thirty mounted

A Letter from Pedro de Val- divia to Charles V

men to support them, for over twenty thousand Indians had showed themselves on the other side. They crossed, and a very good soldier got drowned because he had a treacherous horse.

They killed a great number of Indians and came back in the evening with over one thousand sheep, whereat all the men were very glad, for after all, if the soldier does not die of hunger, he finds his merit in dying in the fight.

I went on two or three leagues farther up the river and camped there. For the third time, a lot more Indians came up to stop my crossing. There, although the water came above the horses' saddles, it was gravelly. I fell on them with fifty horsemen, and gave them a right good lesson. Very many were laid out on those plains, and we went on killing for a league and more. I came back in the evening.

Next day I again crossed the river with fifty mounted men, leaving the main body on this other side. And I rode two days toward the sea, above the neighborhood of Arauco, where I came upon so thick a population as to frighten one, and I at once turned round, as I did not dare to stay longer away from my camp, in case it should suffer injury while I was away.

I rested eight days there, riding about hither and thither always, and taking cattle to feed us wherever we should camp; and so struck camp. I again crossed the Nivequeten river and went towards the coast down the Biubiu. I camped half a league from it in a valley near some freshwater lakes, that I might look for the best district from there. I stayed there two days looking at places, giving all heed to keeping a good watch: half of us watched half the night, and half the other half of the night. . . .

I went to look at where, in past years, I had resolved to make a settlement, which is one and a half leagues this side of the great river which I have called Biubiu, in a harbor and inlet than which there is none better in the Indies, and a big river falling into the sea round a headland, with the best fishing in the world, with many sardines, bream, tunny-fish, cod, lampreys, soles, and a thousand other kinds of fish; and on the other side another small stream that runs the whole year with very soft and clear water.

I moved camp hither on the 23rd of February to get supplies from the galley and a small vessel which the Captain Juan Bautista de Pastene (my lieutenant-general by sea) was bringing me. He was coming along the coast, and I had ordered him to look for me in the neighborhood of this river.

Next day I set to work in the morning to make a fence where we could come out to fight when we should choose and not when the Indians should egg us on. It was of very thick trees set against one another and fastened together like a wattle-fence, and a very wide and deep ditch around us. It was to give, too, some rest to the *conquistadores* in the matter of keeping the watches. For up till then, the keeping watch had been a most wearisome thing owing to the men being always armed and every night, there being no one to look after sick and wounded. And we made it with our hands within eight days, so good a one and strong that it could be defended against the finest and most warlike nation in the world.

When it had been made, we all went inside of it, and I allotted quarters and lodging to each one; and we took up a convenient position for this on March 3 of this year, 1550.

Nine days later, the 12th of this month, I having had news three days earlier that the whole land was gathered together and that countless Indians were coming down upon us—we had not been able to go and seek them out owing to our work on the stronghold and we had been expecting those bulls every day—and so, at vespertide, there appeared within sight of our fort, on some ridges, over forty thousand Indians, with as many more behind who could not show themselves.

They came on with the utmost boldness, in four divisions of the most splendid and fine Indians that have ever been seen in these parts, and with the best equipment of sheep's and llamas' skins and undressed seal skins of many colors (which looked very handsome) and great plumes on headpieces of those skins like the great hats of priests—such, that there is no battle-axe, however sharp, which can hurt those that wear them—with many arrows and spears twenty and twenty-five *palmos* long, clubs, and staves. They do not use stones for fighting.

Seeing how the Indians were coming to attack us from four sides, and

that the squadrons could not give help to one another—as they meant
to besiege us and fight with us for the fort—I ordered Captain Gerónimo
Alderete to go out at one gate with fifty mounted men and break
through a squadron that was coming against this same gate and was a
musket-shot away from it. And no sooner had the mounted men come
up than the Indians gave way and turned; and the other three squadrons,
seeing them broken, did the same. The pursuit went on till nightfall.

NO SILVER BUT THIS

The pursuit for power over the footloose hunting tribes of the southern
Andes went on till nightfall, and then went on till the sun rose again,
and on until dusk, and another night unending.

Led by other men of conquest, the chase spread across the mighty
peaks and beyond, to Patagonia, south to the Strait and beyond, to the
north, up and down the precipitous, hostile banks of snaky rivers coiling
through the continent. Hunting the wild hunters, the conquerors moved
across the highest Andean heights to the pampas rolling from the eastern
shore. They moved almost to the estuary of the Rio de la Plata, the
River of Silver, the full-skirted curvesome Plate.

But here earlier conquerors made their landfall, landing here and
looking rapt at the easy swell of the pampas, breathing deep the clean
air blowing cool off the wide white river—the rib of water joined to the
spine of the south Atlantic sea. Among the new ones landing here were
men who spoke the speech of their Spanish commanders with the
accents of folk out of Flanders and Germany. They were men who
served the banking firms of Augsburg and Antwerp, the firms favored
by the Emperor Charles V.

There were men like the fearless failure, Pedro de Mendoza. Men
like some of the men under him: men like his ill-fated brother, Diego,
men like Martínez de Irala, cutting his way up the Paraguay, settling
that land, making the first foundations last. And men that spoke the
speech of Castile in strange accents, men like a certain fighting Bavar-
ian. Ulrich Schmidt was his name, he insisted. But his fellow-con-
querors from Castile found it easier to call him Schmidel.

Schmidt or Schmidel, he came with the others in search of the treasure
of silver the Indians of the Paraguay were said to own and be willing to

trade. They came prepared, with a cargo to barter for Paraguay silver. But there was only the argentine sheen on the water. No silver but this: the argentine magic of the great estuary where the silver rib of river was joined to the spine of the Atlantic of the south.

Schmidt or Schmidel, he stayed to take part in the killing and conquering, in the hunger and horror. He stayed to become a part forever of that initial expedition, lavish in ships and money and men, and the struggle to settle the Plate. He became a part of the desperate struggle as well as the patient chronicling thereof:

So, by the grace of God, we arrived at Rio de la Plata, Anno 1535, and found there an Indian place inhabited by about two thousand people, named Charúas, who have nothing to eat but fish and meat. These, on our arrival, did leave the place and fled away with their wives and children, so that we could not find them. This Indian people go quite naked, the women having only their privities covered, from the navel to the knees, with a small piece of cotton cloth. Now the captain, Pedro de Mendoza, commanded to bring the people into the ships again, and to convey them to the other side of the Paraná. . . .

Voyage of Ulrich Schmidt to the Paraguay and La Plata

There we built a new town and called it Buenos Aires—that is, in German, Guter Wind.

We also brought from Hispania on board the fourteen ships seventy-two horses and mares.

Here also we found a place inhabited by Indian folk, named Quirandís, numbering about three thousand people, including wives and children, and they were clothed in the same way as the Charúas, from the navel to the knees. They brought us fish and meat to eat. These Quirandís have no houses, but wander about, as do the Gypsies with us at home, and in summer they oftentimes travel upwards of thirty miles on dry land without finding a single drop of water to drink.

And when they meet with deer or other wild beasts (when they have killed them), they drink their blood. Also if they find a root called cardos, they eat it to slake their thirst. This—namely, that they drink blood—only happens because they cannot have any water, and that they might peradventure die of thirst.

These Quirandís brought us daily their provision of fish and meat to our camp, and did so for a fortnight, and they did only fail once to come to us. So our captain, Pedro de Mendoza, sent to them, the Quirandís, a judge, named Juan Pabón, with two foot-soldiers, for they were at a distance of four miles from our camp.

When they came near to them, they were all three beaten black and blue, and were then sent back again to our camp. Pedro de Mendoza, our captain, hearing of this from the judge's report (who for this cause raised a tumult about it in our camp) sent Diego de Mendoza, his own brother, against them with three hundred foot-soldiers and thirty well-armed mounted men—of whom I also was one—straightway charging us to kill or take prisoners all these Indian Quirandís and to take possession of their settlement.

But when we came near them, there were now some four thousand men, for they had assembled all their friends. And when we were about to attack them, they defended themselves in such a way that we had that very day our hands full. They also killed our commander, Diego de Mendoza, and six noblemen. Of our foot-soldiers and mounted men, over twenty were slain, and on their side about one thousand. Thus did they defend themselves valiantly against us, so that indeed we felt it.

The said Quirandís use for their defense hand-bows and darts which are made in the shape of half-pikes, and the head of them is made out of flint-stone, like a flash; they have also bullets made out of stone with a long piece of string attached to them, of the size of our leaden bullets at home in Germany.

They throw such bullets round the feet of a horse or a deer, causing it to fall. It is also with these bullets that they killed our commander and the noblemen, as I have seen it done myself. But the foot-soldiers were killed by the aforementioned darts.

Thus God Almighty graciously gave us the victory, and allowed us to take possession of their place; but we did not take prisoner any of the Indians. And their wives and children also fled away from the place before we attacked them. At this place of theirs we found nothing but furrier-work made from marten or so-called otter; also much fish, fish meal, and fish fat. There we remained three days and then returned to our camp, leaving on the spot one hundred of our men, in order that they might fish with the Indians' nets for the providing of our folk, because there was there very good fishing.

Every one received only six half-ounces of wheaten flour a day, and one fish every third day. The fishing lasted for two months, and if one would eat a fish over and above one's allowance, one had to go four miles for it.

And when we returned again to our camp, our folk were divided into those who were to be soldiers, and the others workers, so as to have all of them employed. And a town was built there, and an earthen wall, half a pike high, around it, and inside of it a strong house for our chief captain. The town wall was three foot broad, but that which was built today fell to pieces the day after, for the people had nothing to eat and were starved with hunger . . . and it became so bad that the horses could not go. . . .

It happened that three Spaniards stole a horse and ate it secretly, but when it was known, they were imprisoned and interrogated under the torture. Whereupon, as soon as they admitted their guilt, they were sentenced to death by the gallows, and all three were hanged.

Immediately afterwards, at night, three other Spaniards came to the gallows to the three hanging men, and hacked off their thighs and pieces of their flesh, and took them home to still their hunger. A Spaniard also ate his brother, who died in the city of Buenos Aires.

Now our chief captain, Pedro de Mendoza, saw that he could not any longer keep his men there, so he ordered and took counsel with his head men that four little ships (called brigantines) should be made ready, which must be rowed, and three more yet smaller ones. . . .

And when these seven little vessels were ready and equipped, our chief captain ordered all the people to assemble, and sent Jorge Lujan with three hundred and fifty armed men up the river Paraná in order to find out the Indians and so obtain victual and provisions. But as soon as the Indians were aware of us, they wrought us the most abominable piece of knavery, by burning and destroying all their victual and provisions and their villages, and then all took to flight. In consequence whereof we had nothing to eat but three ounces of bread. One half of our people died during this voyage through hunger. Therefore we had to return again to the said place, where was our chief captain.

Pedro de Mendoza desired to have a relation from Jorge Lujan, our commander, as to the circumstances of our voyage, why so few of them had returned, since they had only been absent for five months. To whom our commander answered thus: the people died for hunger, since the Indians burnt all the provisions, and then took to flight, as has been related before.

After all this, we remained still another month together in the town of Buenos Aires, until the ships were prepared.

At this time the Indians came in great power and force, as many as twenty-three thousand men, against us and our town, Buenos Aires.

There were four nations of them, namely, Quirandís, Charúas, Chechuas and Timbús. They all meant to go about to destroy us all. . . .

And when they first came to our town, Buenos Aires, and attacked us, some of them tried to storm the place, others shot fiery arrows at our houses, which, being covered with straw (only the house of our chief captain, covered with tiles, excepted), were set on fire. And so the whole town was burnt down.

Their arrows are made out of cane, and carry fire on their points. They have also a kind of wood, out of which they also make arrows, which, being lighted and shot off, do not extinguish, but also set fire to all houses made out of straw.

Moreover, they burnt down four great ships which were half a mile distant from us on the river. The people who were there, and who had no guns, hearing such great tumult of the Indians, fled out of these four ships into three others which were not far from these, and did contain cannon.

But seeing the four ships burning that were lighted by the Indians, the Christians set themselves on defense and fired at the Indians, who becoming aware of this, and hearing the firing, soon departed from thence and left the Christians alone. All this happened on St. John's Day, Anno 1535.

All this having happened, our people had to return into the ships again, and Pedro de Mendoza, our chief captain, gave the command to Juan de Ayolas, and put him in his place to be our commander and rule us. But when Ayolas mustered the people, he found no more than five hundred and sixty men who were yet alive, out of two thousand five hundred, the others being dead and having been starved for hunger. God Almighty be gracious and merciful to them and to us. Amen.

PIONEER FOR PORTUGAL

Higher up the coast there were other men speaking the conquering tongues of Spain, of France, of Portugal, with accents freshly brought from Flanders or from Germany where the Fuggers and the Welzers were busy financing the voyages. There were men like a certain gunner from Wolfhagen, born to the German tongue. Staden was his name and the name of his fathers from Hesse. But his friends and his fellows knew him as Hans.

Hans was his name to his Portuguese fellows concerned with settling the coast that lay north of the Plate, northward up the coast, slanting east, rounding the bulge, then westward slanting to the mouth of the river of rivers still unknown. To the coast of their world in the west named for the treasure of brazil-wood it held, went the first conquerors in the new-found lands from the kingdom of good Prince Henry, the discoverer of discoverers.

Up and down the coast held by the Caribs' kin—the dreaded Tupinambás—the Portuguese had sailed before and since Cabral made an admitted landing there in the year 1500. Springing to shore, at length setting their feet firm on the cannibal coast, came the first folk from Portugal since the shipwrecked "man of lightning," Caramurú, landed there to become a native chief. To the northern coast of the lands in the west opened to Portugal by the marking hand of the Pope and the treaty that followed, came the pioneers that set their sails from Lisbon.

And among them came Hans Staden of Wolfhagen, who sailed and fought in the service of Portugal, sailing then for the glory of Spain, meeting shipwreck, and landing near the first Portuguese colony at Santos.

Hans Staden, born to adventure, busy again at his gunner's trade for the little kingdom now become the great empire with lands in the East, with lands and people in Africa, with lands and people and treasure untold in the wilderness known as the land of the precious dyewood called brazil.

Hans Staden in the wilderness. Hans the pioneer:

As I was going through the forest, I heard loud yells on either side of me, such as savages are accustomed to utter, and immediately a company of savages came running towards me, surrounding me on every side and shooting at me with their bows and arrows. Then I cried out: "Now may God preserve my soul." Scarcely had I uttered the words when they threw me to the ground and shot and stabbed at me. God be praised they only wounded me in the leg, but they tore my clothes from my body, one the jerkin, another the hat, a third the shirt, and so forth.

The History of the Captivity of Hans Staden of Hesse

Then they commenced to quarrel over me. One said he was the first to overtake me, another protested that it was he that caught me, while the rest smote me with their bows. At last two of them seized me and lifted me up, naked as I was, and taking me by the arms, some running in front and some behind, they carried me along with them through the forest at a great pace towards the sea where they had their canoes.

As we approached the sea I saw the canoes about a stone's throw away, which they had dragged out of the water and hidden behind the shrubs, and with the canoes were great multitudes of savages, all decked out with feathers according to their custom. When they saw me, they rushed towards me, biting their arms and threatening me, and making gestures as if they would eat me.

Then a king approached me, carrying the club with which they kill their captives, who spoke saying that having captured me from the Perot, that is to say the Portuguese, they would now take vengeance on me for the death of their friends, and so carrying me to the canoes, they beat me with their fists. Then they made haste to launch their canoes, for they feared that an alarm might be raised at Brikioka, as indeed was the case.

Before launching the canoes, they bound my hands together, but since they were not all from the same place and no one wanted to go home empty-handed, they began to dispute with my two captors, saying that they had all been just as near to me when I was taken, and each one demanding a piece of me and clamoring to have me killed on the spot.

Then I stood and prayed, expecting every moment to be struck down. But at last the king, who desired to keep me, gave orders to carry me back alive so that their women might see me and make merry with me. For they intended to kill me *kawewi pepicke*, that is, to prepare a drink and gather together for a feast at which they would eat me. At these words they desisted, but they bound four ropes round my neck, and I was forced to climb into a canoe, while they made fast the ends of the ropes to the boats and then pushed off and commenced the homeward journey.

There is another island close by the one where I was captured, in which water-birds nest which are called guará, and they have red feathers. The savages asked me whether their enemies, the Tupinikin, had been there that year to take the birds during the nesting season. I told them that the Tupinikin had been there, but they proposed to visit the island to see for themselves if this was so, for they value the feathers of these birds exceedingly, since all their adornment depends upon them. . . .

The savages made for this island, hoping to take the birds, but when they were a distance of some two gun-shots from the place where they had left their canoes, they looked back and saw behind them a number of Tupinikin savages with certain of the Portuguese who had set out to recapture me. For a slave who was with me had escaped when I was taken and had raised an alarm.

They cried out to my captors that unless they were cowards they would turn and fight. My captors turned about, and those on the land assailed us with blow-pipes and arrows while we replied. My captors then unbound my hands, leaving the cord still fastened to my neck, and as the king had a gun and a little powder which a Frenchman had given him in exchange for some Brazilian wood, I was forced to shoot with it towards the land.

After both parties had skirmished for a time, my captors, fearing that those on shore might be reinforced with canoes and might give chase, made off with three casualties and passed about a gun-shot distance from the fort at Brikioka where I had been stationed, and as we passed, I had to stand up in the canoe so that my companions might see me. They fired two large guns from the fort, but the shot fell short.

In the meantime some canoes had set out from Brikioka in pursuit, hoping to overtake us, but my captors rowed too fast, and when my friends saw that they could do nothing, they returned to Brikioka.

MAN AND RIVER

Wandering through the wilderness filled with death, fearing the death that lurked in the ceaseless rain and the hunger waiting in the sudden, barren wastes, in the lethal vine, in the poisonous reptile or bug. Fearing the danger from these or the prowling beasts no more than the threat from men who were eaters of men. Wandering through the wilderness filled with killers and eaters of men, and sometimes fleeing from their jaws and, at long last, finding succor among friends—as Hans, the pioneer, was finally favored to do. Sometimes finding safety and shelter. But more often meeting pain and hunger, and death with both. This was their part.

There was the job of conquering the new continent of people. And there was the job of plumbing the wilderness, the dark labyrinth of forest and mountain and jungle and river that lay wrapped like a strangling growth around the great beating heart of the whole continent. Plumbing the wilderness was the slower task, and even slower in coming was the bare recognition of the deed. There were even times when the name of the man who plumbed the worst of the wilderness choking the continent was all but forgotten forever.

From their conquered lands in the Andes near the equator, the Spaniards saw where a river began. And one of them found the men to follow him, and with equal faith and fervor to follow the unknown course. Fifty-eight men they were in all, and even the record of that first voyage down the world's river of rivers might have been lost with the all-but-forgotten name of the leader. The record of that particular side trip of four thousand miles down the ever-branching water that flowed through the land of long-haired warriors believed to be women—the land of the ancient amazons, they thought—might have been lost but for Fray Gaspar de Carvajal, who happened to go along, a priest with an eye for detail and a mind and a heart to revive it and make it flow in the telling.

And so the said Captain Orellana picked out fifty-seven men, with whom he embarked in the aforesaid boat and in certain canoes which they had taken away from the Indians, and he began to proceed down his river with the idea of promptly turning back if food was found. All of which turned out just the reverse of what we all expected, because we did not find food for a distance of two hundred *A Friar's Report of the First* leagues, nor were we finding any for ourselves, *Trip Down the Amazon* from which cause we suffered very great privation. . . . And so we kept going on, beseeching Our Lord to see fit to guide us on that journey in such a way that we might return to our companions.

On the second day after we had set out and separated from our companions, we were almost wrecked in the middle of the river because the boat struck a log and it stove in one of its planks; so that if we had not been close to land, we should have ended our journey there. But matters were soon remedied, thanks to the energy of the men in hauling the boat out of water and fastening a piece of plank on it, and we promptly started off on our way with very great haste.

And, as the river flowed fast, we proceeded on at the rate of from twenty to twenty-five leagues a day, for now the river was high and its power increased owing to the effect of many other rivers which emptied into it on the right from a southerly direction. We journeyed on for three days without finding any inhabited country at all.

Seeing that we had come far away from where our companions had stopped and that we had used up what little food we had brought along, too little for so uncertain a journey as the one that we were pursuing, the Captain and the companions conferred about the difficulty, and the question of turning back, and the lack of food—for, as we had expected to return quickly, we had not laid in a supply of food. But, confident that we could not be far off from some settlement, we decided to go ahead, and this at the cost of no little hardship for all.

And, as neither on the next day nor on the following one was any food found nor any sign of a settlement, in accordance with the view of the Captain I said Mass, as it is said at sea, commending to Our Lord our persons and our lives, beseeching Him, as an unworthy man, to deliver us from such manifest hardship and destruction—for that is what it was coming to look like to us now, since, although we did wish to go back up the river, that was not possible on account of the heavy current. . . . To attempt to go by land was out of the question. So that we were in great danger of death because of the great hunger we endured.

And so, after taking counsel as to what should be done, talking over our affliction and hardships, it was decided that we should choose of two evils the one which to the Captain and to all should appear to be the lesser, which was to go forward and follow the river—either to die or to see what there was along it, trusting in Our Lord that He would see fit to preserve our lives until we should see our way out.

And in the meantime, lacking other victuals, we reached a state of privation so great that we were eating nothing but leather, belts, and soles of shoes, cooked with certain herbs, with the result that so great was our weakness that we could not remain standing. . . . Some on all fours and others with staffs went into the woods to search for a few roots to eat, and some there were who ate certain herbs with which they were not familiar—and they were at the point of death, because they were like mad men and did not possess sense.

But, as Our Lord was pleased that we should continue on our journey, no one died.

Because of this suffering as stated, a number of the companions were quite disheartened, to whom the Captain spoke words of cheer. And he told them to exert themselves and have confidence in Our Lord, for since He had cast us upon that river, He would see fit to bring us out to a haven of safety. In such a way did he cheer up the companions that they accepted that hardship.

On New Year's Day of the year 1542, it seemed to certain of our companions that they had heard Indian drums, and some said they did and others said no. But they became somewhat happier over this and pushed on with much greater diligence than was customary with them. And, as neither on that day nor on the next was any inhabited country actually seen, it became evident that it was imagination, as in reality it was. And, in consequence of this, both the sick and the well were becoming so greatly downhearted that they thought that they could no longer escape with their lives.

However, the Captain sustained them with the words which he spoke to them. And, as Our Lord is the father of mercy and of all consolation, who restores and helps him who calls on Him in the time of greatest need, they took heart. And so it was that, it being Monday evening, which by count was the eighth of the month of January, while eating certain forest roots, they heard drums very plainly very far from where we were. And the Captain was the one who heard them first and announced it to the other companions.

And they all listened, and they being convinced of the fact, such was the happiness which they all felt that they cast out of their memories all the past suffering, because we were now in an inhabited country and no longer could die of hunger.

ROLL CALL

The ships of the conquerors kept coming. They came from Spain and they came from Portugal. And then the Spanish ships began to come from the nearer points already conquered: from Cuba and from Hispaniola, which was also known as Española, and as Haiti, and even as Santo Domingo.

There were newcomers coasting up and down the shores of the conquered lands who had been there before. And there were others who were destined to die without having set foot on the new-won land that was still not won in many places—not won from the folk and not won from the sea or the storm.

Some perished with the land before their eyes. Others lived to tell the story, shedding the tears without shame as they looked back with sorrow.

Men like Alvar Núñez Cabeza de Vaca, a conqueror in both great continents of the west, who tramped over the new lands in Paraguay and Mexico, and north to the newer Mexico, and east to the Floridas, and then the long way south again—men like Cabeza de Vaca lived to look back and recall the bleak beginnings: the hunger and hardship on land, the suffering and death at sea in the storm that knows no mercy.

They traveled by ocean-going ships and coastwise vessels, by boats, barges, and rafts, on the backs of beasts of burden or seated in litters on the backs of the conquered, but mostly on foot.

And many were destined to be known by name and deed:

Coronado riding northward in armor of gold to the lands of the new Mexico; Hernando de Soto fighting beside Pizarro in Peru and then shifting his restless feet to the north; northward to the northern continent he trudged, to the Mississippi to die—but not before tramping up to a place that would some day be called Georgia, to be welcomed by some red folk there and their woman chief; Legazpi moving out of Mexico across the Pacific to the Philippines, founding Manila there for the swelling crown of Castile; Oñate pushing north to the lands of the Kansas; Olid riding south to Honduras; Niño looking over the coast of Nicaragua; Pedro Sarmiento sailing from Peru all the way to Magellan's Strait; and Sebastian Cabot, sailing now for the Spanish crown instead of the English, plumbing the lands up the Plate.

There were Juan de Garay making the third foundation of Buenos Aires on the silver estuary, the last that would be needed; Díaz de Solís having far less luck in his fatal move to found Montevideo on the wilder, eastern shore of the peaceful-looking Plate: Díaz de Solís with his party of fifty slain by the fighting Charúas.

North from the unconquered Uruguay, Portugal was holding fast to its world of treasure called Brazil, and the greater treasures waiting in the interior that would not awake until the coastal strip to north and south had become a country fully grown: the brightest, biggest jewel in the crown of Portugal.

Affonso de Sousa, meanwhile, starting the real job of founding and settling the towns, Coelho Pereira pushing the work forward, another Sousa laying out Bahia. And then the long treks beginning into the tangle of darkness, into the interior, under men like Cubas, Vasco de Caldas, Tourinho.

Spain in the continent of the north, and Spain in the south. But Portugal in between and spreading fast to the Castilian borders in the newly discovered world. Portugal in between, but Spain already pushing against her immense circling frontiers in the new-found lands. Spain pushing forward on all sides, and the Spanish ships still coming with conquerors seeking the mythical places in the south, as Ponce de León and the others had looked for them in Florida, The Flowery Land, in the north.

The ships kept coming, carrying the men that would step from their decks onto the western shore. Then onto the shore they stepped, onto the paths and into the virginal wilderness beyond, to search for the mysteries. Seeking the mysterious golden cities and the gilded men.

Seeking the gilded man—El Dorado was his name—on the heights above the isthmus shore where the two continents met, on the heights above the Magdalena, there trekked the lawyer turned soldier who seldom knew rest: Gonzalo Jiménez de Quesada. Also in search of the gilded man in the heights beyond the Andes of the equator, marched the conqueror of Quito, the man who called himself Benalcázar. Down the Magdalena he came. And up the Andes from the other side, from the lands of Venezuela came another: Nicholas Federmann of Ulm in Swabia. He had come to explore for the banking house of the Welzers. Up the Andes to the heights above the winding Magdalena, seeking El Dorado, the man of gold, came Nicholas Federmann: conquistador.

On the heights above the Isthmus, above the Magdalena, on the heights of the Andes, in the land of the Chibchas with the chief that was actually sprinkled with the sparkling dust of gold, in the land of the gilded man, El Dorado, on the high tableland cradled in light, Quesada sat down to rest—after losing three fourths of his men in the climb from the coast, after conquering the Chibchas with those that were left, after winning a treasure of gold that was neither a myth nor a mystery, after founding the city of Santa Fe de Bogotá on the heights that seemed like a shining heaven to him and his men. There on those heights, Quesada finally sat down to rest—but not for long.

There to one side of him, from west and south, came Benalcázar with his conquerors from Quito, from the Andes. And Federmann came from the opposite side, from the north and east, with his conquerors from Venezuela. On the heights above the Andes, above the Magdalena, the three men met. They might have fought and slain each other and each other's men. That was often the outcome where conqueror met conquistador in the disputed lands of the world being won in the west.

But Quesada was a shrewd lawyer as well as a man of peace before he was a soldier. He interrupted his rest, but not to fight. He interrupted the rest he seldom took, to greet them, to give them gold, to divide the wealth he had won—and win their agreement that the land and the conquest for Spain were his.

Up and down and across the two great continents of north and south that formed the western world, moved the conquering conquistadors. Although many were destined to be known by name or deed or both, many others were forgotten before they were cold. And many who were remembered forgot those who had served with them. But there were those like Quesada who could not forget the men or what they had done, how they had come into the land, and what was the fate of those who fought by his side and survived. A conqueror of the new lands and a conqueror of the hearts of men till his last days, Quesada remembered the men who had gone forever and the men who had gone to other parts. He remembered the men who had returned to Spain; he remembered the men who had stayed in the kingdom of New Granada, which he had founded, with its capital city of Bogotá resting on the zephyr-blown plateau.

He remembered the men:

Some are dead, and these are the most. Others are in Spain. With what they got here, they have gone to their lands, where they now live. Others left, in times gone by, for different parts of the Indies. There are others, who remained in this kingdom. Among these, also, there have been deaths since thirty years ago. So that, as this account is written, only fifty-three are living, whose names will be placed here. And as they are named in order, it should be understood that this is also the order of their merit—according to how they labored and served in the discovery and conquest of this kingdom, among those who are alive today.

Jiménez de Quesada Remembering His Comrades

Here will likewise be recorded what each one has and what he has received in reward for his services, and whatever else is needed for the understanding of this account—and all of it very brief, so that when someone repairs to Spain in search of payment for his services, it will suffice simply to see this account in order to know whether he is among the first conquerors; and if he is, to know by this account whether he was paid or not, and what he deserves.

Captain Juan de Céspedes is, among those living today, one of those who labored and served most in this discovery and conquest. He entered with me as captain, one of eight whom I brought with the people into this kingdom. He is a man of quality. He has three land grants in this city of Santa Fe on which there are more or less fifteen hundred Indians. The land grants are called Ubaque, Caquenza, Ubatoque. As things are in this kingdom, he eats well.

Captain Antonio de Olalla lives, and has food to eat, in this city of Santa Fe. He did not come in as captain with me, but he became so afterward—he came in with me as a second lieutenant of infantry. He has eight hundred or a thousand Indians on a good land grant called Bogotá. And so he eats well, as things are in this kingdom, and he is a man of quality.

Juan Valenciano, although he did not come into this kingdom as a captain, but as a corporal, labored and served much in this discovery. He has had some land grants, some of which through quarrels and some through other ways have been taken from him by those who governed— and also because of his absences and pilgrimages, among these one to Jerusalem. And so he has no land grant, nor anything to eat, though well deserving. And he is a man of some quality.

Captain Gonzalo Suárez is a man of quality. He came into this kingdom with me as a captain, and he is one of the eight. . . . He lives, and has food to eat, in the city of Tunja. He has three land grants, with three thousand Indians. He eats very well.

Captain Antonio Cardoso is a man of quality; although he did not come in as one of the eight captains who entered with me, he had been a captain before this discovery. He lives in Santa Fe, and eats well and plentifully on a land grant he has, which is called Suba and Tuna—on which there are nine hundred or a thousand Indians.

Captain Gonzalo García Zorro is a man of quality, and although he did not come in with me as captain, he did enter as a second lieutenant of cavalry. He eats reasonably well on a land grant which he has in the city of Santa . . . with about five hundred Indians.

Captain Hernán Vanegas, although he did not come in with me as a captain, but simply as a horseman, was made a captain later by those who governed, and he is a man of quality. He lives in Santa Fe. He eats very well on a principal land grant he has, called Guatabita, on which there are more or less two thousand Indians.

The sea swept in from the east, bringing the conquerors moving over the land now belonging to new nations, new kings, and new houses of finance, new men of conquest and their blood heirs. And the lands reverberated with the sound of the tramping feet of conquerors moving up and down the two continents, marching across the great chunks of land, advancing everywhere to take possession of soil and the stipulated number of Indians that went with it.

Some of the conquerors kept moving on to the sea beyond, sweeping on to the west, to the sea that led to the East, after all. But most of them stayed in the West, with its own fabulous wealth still to be won, along with the greater glory and power. They stayed to let their voices be heard, to let the stamp of their feet reverberate with the echo of shouted commands that only the few of noble blood had known before in the homelands back in the Old World.

The new lands began to shake to the echo of new, shouted commands, to the stamp of conquering feet, to the crack of the master's whip that had never been heard before. These were commands that shamed when they did not slay. And the wild cry for treasure, echoing day and night, climbed above the anguished moan of the people with flesh of the sun's own fire and eyes of the sun's own coal.

The sun's own folk were moaning already in the early morning of conquest, the sound climbing higher over the shores, the plains, the rivers, the mountains standing like silent mourners. The whole body of the land was shaken now out of the dream into nightmare, into terror of light; and the shame was sowed with steel and whip and torch—the conqueror descending upon her where she lay.

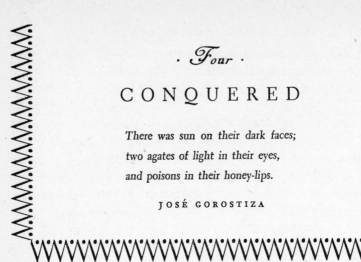

· *Four* ·

CONQUERED

There was sun on their dark faces;
two agates of light in their eyes,
and poisons in their honey-lips.

JOSÉ GOROSTIZA

THE SHAME AND THE DEATH

Before the long lament rose over the land, before the flight to a wilderness where beasts were kind by comparison, before the great bloodletting began, and long before the enslavement without end that was to follow, came the realization, quick as the hurricane, of what this conquest meant:

The white-skinned ones would feed on the toil of the conquered. The gold, the silver, the gems—all would be won by the work of the slaves for whom these conquerors hungered and lusted.

This was the dark revelation that burst upon the people of the land, striking and moving inexorably upon them as a tidal wave out of the night. Carried in the beat of the drums, from tribe to tribe the word went out. The word that warned of doom was relayed, and they told themselves it would be better to die.

Now throughout the islands of Hispaniola, Puerto Rico, Cuba, and the other jewels in the Carib sea where Columbus and the early ones had made their first landfalls, the red folk threw themselves off the sparkling cliffs, down on the rocks, down on the phosphorescent water. They slew each other, and there was gratitude in the eyes of slayer and slain alike. Women dashed their children against rocks and trees until the shining little bodies of fire turned to cold ash. And then they hurled themselves off the waiting cliffs.

To slay each other and to slay themselves, to die by friendly hands among familiar faces rather than submit to the shame and the death by torture and toil—this was the way they replied to the will of the conqueror.

There were those who fled to the wilderness away from the coast, knowing they fled to no safety, knowing the new masters would find them later, and there were also those who surrendered. Down the Caribbean, on the coast of Paria extending to the Venezuela gulf, there were some who gave up: hopeful in heart, choosing to stay to live with the men of conquest. And what they got was the life the conqueror gave:

This is also a known thing: that they never do transport Indians from these places but in their voyage they do pay the third part of them as a tribute to the waves—besides those that are murdered in their own houses. The cause of all these things are their own wicked purposes— that is to say, by the sale of the Indians to heap up treasure, yet furnishing the ships not with half provisions for the sustenance of those that they transport (because they would not be at too much charges).

Fray Bartolomé de Las Casas: The Tears of the Indians

And sometimes there are hardly provisions enough to suffice the Spaniards themselves—so that the Indians ready to die for hunger and thirst are immediately thrown into the sea.

And it was related to me for certain that a ship going from Hispaniola to the islands of Lucayos sailed thither without any compass: only by the carcasses that floated up and down the sea.

Afterwards when they are landed, where they are carried to be sold, there is no man that would not be moved with compassion to see both old and young, men and women, naked and hungry, drop and faint as they go along.

Afterwards they divide them like sheep, separating sons from fathers, wives from their husbands. And then, making up a company of ten or twenty, those that set out the ships and fitted them with necessaries presently cast lots for their shares.

And when the lot fell upon a company that had an old or a sick man, he to whom the lot fell was wont to break forth into these expressions: "Cursed be this old fellow, why do you give him me? To bury him? Why do you give me this sick man? To be his keeper?"

And thus let us consider in what estimation the Indians are among the Spaniards, and how the precept of charity on which the law and the prophets depends is observed among them.

There is nothing more detestable or more cruel than the tyranny which the Spaniards use toward the Indians for the getting of pearl. Surely the infernal torments cannot much exceed the anguish that they endure by reason of that way of cruelty. . . .

They put them under water some four or five ells deep, where they are forced, without any liberty of respiration, to gather up the shells wherein the pearls are. Sometimes they come up again with nets full of shells to take breath. But if they stay any while to rest themselves, immediately comes a hangman rowed in a little boat, who as soon as he hath well beaten them, drags them again to their labor.

Their food is nothing but fish (and the very same that contains the pearl) with a small portion of that bread which that country affords. In the first . . . there is little nourishment. And as for the latter, it is made with great difficulty—besides that they have not enough of that for sustenance.

They lie upon the ground in fetters, lest they should run away. . . .

Many times they are drowned in this labor, and are never seen again till they swim upon the top of the waves. Oftentimes they also are devoured by certain sea monsters that are frequent in those seas.

Consider whether this hard usage of the poor creatures be consistent with the precepts which God commands concerning charity to our neighbor, by those that cast them so undeservedly into the dangers of a cruel death—causing them to perish without any remorse or pity or allowing them the benefit of the sacraments or the knowledge of religion.

It being impossible for them to live any time under the water . . . this death is so much the more painful by reason that, by the pressure on the chest while the lungs strive to do their office, the vital parts are so afflicted that they die vomiting the blood out of their mouths.

Their hair also, which is by nature black, is . . . changed and made of the same color with that of the sea wolves—their bodies are also so besprinkled with the froth of the sea—so that they appear rather like monsters than men.

THE LESSON THEY LEARNED

Not all of the red folk who stayed to live in the conqueror's way of life were made the slaves and playthings of the new white lords. There were the Indian chiefs, for example, who were given privileges their people never could attain.

Some of the chiefs were more than willing to watch their people slave for the new conquerors. But others rebelled, knowing the fearful price. Then there were those who studied the faith the conquerors brought, studied the faith and watched the ways of the power of Spain or Portugal spread by the conquistadors who kept coming to conquer the folk in body and faith, now that the lands were mostly won. They watched the ways of the conquerors—but there were times when the lesson they learned was not the one they had been taught.

From the beginning there were the folk who fought the conquerors. They were the most, all the way from north to south across both continents. The people of the empires of the red folk fought the newcomers after trying to make friends with them, but the great nomad groups outside the empires fought the men of conquest again and again after each landfall, never offering the gifts of peace or expecting to receive them.

Then there were the wild tribes like the folk around the bulge of the land of Brazil, that finally cried welcome to the waiting voyagers. Crying welcome—but looking with a strange eagerness. And if the men who accepted the cry of invitation to land had included the noted traveller among them, the account might never have been written, the event never known, and the lands of the whole western world never have carried his name:

Amerigo Vespucci, native of Florence, sailing now under the Portuguese flag. Amerigo, the clerk and traveller with an eye for fact, with a pen not devoid of feeling for fancy or a flair for publicity. Amerigo whose name and not the name of one of the earlier ones would some day be stamped forever on the whole new world of the west.

Amerigo, whose name would unpredictably envelop the lands of each and every America, of the Americas in the north and the Americas in the south, of all America.

Signor Vespucci, meanwhile, meeting the folk still to be conquered. Meeting them from a fortunate distance:

It pleased God to show us a new land on the 17th of August, and we anchored at a distance of half a league, and got our boats out. We then went to see the land, whether it was inhabited, and what it was like. We found that it was inhabited by people who were worse than animals. But . . . we did not see them at first, though we were convinced that

A Letter from Amerigo Vespucci: Sighting the Coast of Brazil

the country was inhabited, by many signs observed by us. We took possession for that Most Serene King, and found the land to be very pleasant and fertile, and of good appearance. It was five degrees to the south of the equinoctial line.

We went back to the ships; and, as we were in great want of wood and water, we determined, next day, to return to the shore, with the object of obtaining what we wanted. Being on shore, we saw some people at the top of a hill, who were looking at us, but without showing any intention of coming down.

They were naked, and of the same color and form as the others we had seen. We tried to induce them to come and speak with us, but did not succeed, as they would not trust us. Seeing their obstinacy, and it being late, we returned on board, leaving many bells and mirrors on shore, and other things in their sight.

As soon as we were at some distance on the sea, they came down from the hill, and showed themselves to be much astonished at the things. On that day we were only able to obtain water.

Next morning we saw from the ship that the people on shore had made a great smoke; and, thinking it was a signal to us, we went on shore, where we found that many people had come, but they still kept at a distance from us. They made signs to us that we should come inland with them.

Two of our Christians were, therefore, sent to ask their captain for leave to go with them a short distance inland, to see what kind of people they were, and if they had any riches, spices, or drugs. The captain was contented, so they got together many things for barter, and parted from us, with instructions that they should not be more than five days absent as we would wait that time for them. So they set out on their road inland, and we returned to the ships to wait for them.

Nearly every day people came to the beach, but they would not speak with us. On the seventh day we went on shore, and found that they had arranged with their women; for, as we jumped on shore, the men of the land sent many of their women to speak with us. Seeing that they were not reassured, we arranged to send to them one of our people, who was a very agile and valiant youth.

To give them more confidence, the rest of us went back into the boats.

He went among the women, and they all began to touch and feel him, wondering at him exceedingly. Things being so, we saw a woman come from the hill, carrying a great stick in her hand. When she came to where our Christian stood, she raised it, and gave him such a blow that he was felled to the ground. The other women immediately took him by the feet, and dragged him towards the hill.

The men rushed down to the beach, and shot at us with their bows and arrows. Our people, in great fear, hauled the boats towards their anchors, which were on shore; but owing to the quantities of arrows that came into the boats, no one thought of taking up his arms.

At last, four rounds from the bombard were fired at them; and they no sooner heard the report than they all ran away towards the hill— where the women were still tearing the Christian to pieces.

At a great fire they had made they roasted him before our eyes, showing us many pieces, and then eating them. The men made signs how they had killed the other two Christians and eaten them.

A SUN GOD BURNS

They fought the conquerors. There were many who stood their ground till the ground rose up to take them, torn and bleeding, from their land forever. And there were many who turned and ran before the foe that fought with bursting fire and flying shot and four-footed beasts that maimed before their riders slew. Of those that fled, however, many returned, their numbers thicker than before, standing their ground this time, armed with little else than their naked will, chanting defiance.

They defied the foe that moved behind advancing iron. The people of the dead lord of the Aztecs, the people of the slain Inca of Incas, and the people of free tribes in the two continents, north and south, defied the fire that burst upon them where they stood gathered on their plains and plateaus. Bright with the plumes of the warriors, waving with the flags of the battle, the lands that were Aztec or Inca, or subject to independent chiefs, or maybe to no chief at all, continued to throb with the beat of drums, the sound of flutes and pipes, the cavernous call of the great conch-shells blowing defiance. The red folk by scores of thousands, month after month and year after year, still refused to bow.

From city to town to village to field to every stone that might serve as a shield for the moment, the earth rocked; the roar faded slowly, to rise once more, to fail, to surge forward again without fear, with new numbers upholding the fight and the sound of it: the pulse of the red folk resisting, knowing now there could be no rest—not even with surrender.

They knew that rest meant death of many kinds, and none of them noble. They knew now of the death by torture, or death by toil without respite that bowed the head and twisted the frames of red bodies shaped like the finest stalks of corn in the field; their bodies with limbs born of the wind.

Numberless as the grains of golden maize in their fields, they kept moving into the fight, unending, without quarter, with hatred growing, with their naked will against the potent foe.

Nowhere did the fight become more fierce than in the lands of the Quichés, south from Mexico, in the lands the conqueror called Guatemala, where the tribes first welcomed the conquering Pedro de Alvarado, the blond and ruddy captain sent by Cortés. They called him Tonatiuh, god of the sun. And the sun god was hailed—until they began to feel his burning breath upon them:

On the day 5 Ah was the eighth year of the first cycle. It was during this year—1524—that the Castilians arrived. Forty-nine years have passed since the Castilians came to Xepit and Xetulul. On the day 1 Ganel the Quichés were destroyed by the Castilians. Tonatiuh Alvarado, as he was called, conquered all the towns. Their countenances were previously unknown and the people rendered homage to sticks and stones. On their arrival at Xelahub, the Quiché nation was routed and destroyed. All of them had hastened there to oppose the Castilians. And there the Quiché nation was destroyed, in front of Xelahub.

Annals of the Cakchiquels: The Destruction of Their Nation

He then went to the city, Gumarcaah, and there came before him the chiefs, the king, and the next in rank. And tribute was paid by the Quichés. And the chiefs suffered many torments from Tonatiuh.

On the day 4 Qat three chiefs, the king and the next in rank, were burned alive by Tonatiuh. Nor was the heart of Tonatiuh satisfied with war. Soon a messenger from Tonatiuh came to the chiefs that they should send him warriors: "Let the warriors of the Ahpozotzils and Ahpoxahils come to the slaughter of the Quichés!" So spoke the messenger of Tonatiuh to the chiefs.

Immediately the words of Tonatiuh were published, and four hundred men went forth to the slaughter of the Quichés; but they were only those of the city, the other warriors refusing to obey the chiefs. Only three times did the warriors go forth to enforce the tribute on the Quichés; then we also were taken by Tonatiuh, O my children.

It was on the day 1 Hunahpu when the Castilians arrived at Iximche with their chief, Tonatiuh. The people went forth to meet Tonatiuh with the chiefs, Belehe Qat and Cahi Ymox. Good was the heart of Tonatiuh when he entered the city with the chiefs. There was no fighting and Tonatiuh rejoiced when he entered Iximche.

Thus did the Castilians enter of yore, O my children. But it was a fearful thing when they entered; their faces were strange, and the chiefs took them for gods. We, even we, your fathers, saw them when they first set foot in Iximche, at the palace of Tzupam where Tonatiuh slept.

The chief came forth, and truly he frightened the warriors. He came from his chamber and called the rulers: "Why do you make war with me, when I also can make it?" said he.

"Not at all. Why should so many warriors find their death? Do you see any pitfalls among them?" So replied the chiefs.

The word was then given. The chiefs gathered together all their metals, those of the parents and children of the king, and all that the chiefs could get from the people. While they were gathering the gold for Tonatiuh, a priest of the Demon showed himself:

"I am the lightning, I will destroy the Castilians!" So said he to the chiefs. "I will destroy them by fire. When I beat the drum, let the chiefs come forth and go to the other bank of the river. This I shall do on the day 7 Ahmak." Thus did this priest of the Demon speak to the chiefs.

Truly the chiefs thought that they should trust in the words of this man. It was when they were gathering the gold that we went forth. The day 7 Ahmak was that of the going forth. They deserted the city of Iximche on account of the priest of the Demon, and the chiefs left it.

"Yes, truly, Tonatiuh shall die," said they. "There is no more war in the heart of Tonatiuh, as he now rejoices in the gold given him."

Thus it was that our city was abandoned on the day 7 Ahmak on account of a priest of the Demon, O my children. But what the chiefs did was soon known to Tonatiuh. Ten days after we had left the city, war was begun by Tonatiuh. On the day 4 Camey began our destruction. Then began our misery.

We scattered in the forests. All our towns were taken, O my children. We were slaughtered by Tonatiuh. The Castilians entered the city, and they arrived as to a deserted spot.

From that time the Castilians were hated by the Cakchiquels.

And he went to the house of the chief, Chicbal. The Tonatiuh agreed to join the chiefs in their wars, and the chiefs said to him: "O thou god, we have two wars, one with the Tzutuhils, one at Panatacat." Thus spake the chiefs.

Only five days after, Tonatiuh went forth from the capital. Then the Tzutuhils were conquered by the Castilians. It was the day 7 Camey that the Tzutuhils were destroyed by the Castilians. Twenty-five days afterwards Tonatiuh went forth from the capital to Cuzcatan, going there to destroy Atacat. On the day 2 Qeh, Atacat was slain by the Castilians, with all his warriors. There went with Tonatiuh all his Mexicans to this battle.

On the day 10 Hunahpu he returned from Cuzcatan. He had been absent only forty days to make the conquest at Cuzcatan when he returned to the capital. Then Tonatiuh asked for a daughter of one of the chiefs, and she was given to Tonatiuh by the chiefs.

Then Tonatiuh began to ask the chiefs for money. He wished that they should give him jars full of precious metals, and even their drinking cups and crowns. Not receiving anything, Tonatiuh became angry and said to the chiefs: "Why have you not given me the metal? If you do not bring me the precious metal in all your towns, choose then, for I shall burn you alive and hang you." Thus did he speak to the chiefs.

Then Tonatiuh cut from three of them the gold ornaments they wore in their ears. The chiefs suffered keenly from this violence, and wept before him. But Tonatiuh was not troubled, and said: "I tell you that I want the gold here within five days. Woe to you if you do not give it. I know my heart." So said he to the chiefs. They made trenches, they dug pitfalls, that the horses might be killed, and war was waged by their men. Many men of the Castilians were slain, and many horses killed in the pitfalls. The Quichés and Tzutuhils were destroyed and all their villages ruined by the Cakchiquels. Only thus did the Castilians let them live, and only thus were they let live by all the villagers. . . .

The war continued with the Castilians. But the Castilians having received aid . . . at Xepau, carried on the war with such vigor that they destroyed the forces of the nation.

OUT OF RETIREMENT

In the continent of the north, they fought the conqueror without rest, returning again and again to the fight. And southward, in the continent below, they defied the conqueror, too, in a war where there was little time for fatigue except time to catch the final breath.

Far to the south, in the long and narrow strip that would be called Chile, a man was busy sowing the soil with the bones of the conquered and the seeds of new grain he had brought with his men and his drove of swine for the settlement. This man was Pedro de Valdivia, struggling now to win sustenance from soil that had granted no gold, planting the seed, for better or worse, before there was peace in the land.

He was faced by the fierce Araucos who sometimes fled, but never gave up. Skilled in their old ways of war, the Araucanians waiting now for an old captain and a young spy to show them a new way to wage war against new men who called themselves the sovereign masters of their soil.

When Valdivia arrived where the rebel Araucos were, he found twelve or thirteen thousand of them, with whom he had several desperate encounters in which the Spaniards were always victorious; and the Indians were so disheartened by the charges of the cavalry that they would not come out in the open plain, for ten horsemen would scatter a thousand Indians. They remained in the hills and woods, *Royal Commentaries of the Incas:* where the horses could not master them, and *The Slaying of Valdivia* thence they did all the mischief they could, refusing to listen to any terms that were offered to them, and obstinate in their determination to die rather than be servants of the Spaniards. Thus the two sides remained for many days.

These evil tidings spread each day into the interior of the Arauco country, until they were told to an old captain who had been famous in their wars, but was now retired to his own home.

He came out to see what wonder was this, that one hundred and fifty men could hold in check twelve or thirteen thousand warriors. This he was unable to believe, if these Spaniards were not devils or immortals, which the Indians thought at first. In order to undeceive himself on these points, he desired to join the war and see what passed with his own eyes.

He reached the top of a hill, whence he had a view of both armies, the line of his own people widely extended, and that of the Spaniards small and compact. He was considering for a long time what could be the cause that so few men could conquer so many. Having closely examined the situation, he repaired to the camp of his countrymen and called a council.

After long discourses on the events that had taken place up to that time, he asked these questions, among many others:

"Are the Spaniards mortal men like the Indians, or immortal like the Sun and Moon? Do they feel hunger, thirst, and fatigue? Have they the necessity for sleeping and rest?"

In short, he asked whether they were made of flesh and blood, or of iron and steel. He asked the same questions respecting the horses.

Having been told that they were men of the same appearance and habits as the Indians, he explained: "Let all now rest, and tomorrow we will see who are the better men, the Spaniards or ourselves." With that the council broke up, and at the first appearance of dawn next day he ordered a call to arms, which was sounded with much greater shouts and noise of trumpets, drums, and other like instruments, than was usual.

He armed thirteen squadrons of a thousand men each, and formed them in a thread, one behind the other.

The Spaniards came forth on hearing the shouts of the Indians, splendidly armed, with great plumes on their heads and on those of their horses, and with many breastplates hung with bells. When they saw the divided squadrons, they thought less of their enemies, as it seemed to them that they could more easily scatter many small squadrons than one very large body of men.

The Indian captain, seeing the Spaniards in the plain, said to the men of his first squadron: "Go, my brothers, and fight with the Spaniards. I do not say you will conquer them, but do your best for your country, and when you can do no more, fly, and I will succor you. But when you of the first squadron fly, do not mix with the second, nor the second with the third, but retire behind all the other squadrons, when I will direct what you should then do."

With these orders the old captain sent his men to fight the Spaniards, who attacked the first squadron, and, though the Indians did what they could in their defence, they routed them. They also scattered the second, third, fourth, and fifth squadrons with ease; but not so easily but that many on their side were wounded, and some killed, men as well as horses.

The Indian captain, as the first squadron fell back defeated, sent the others forward to fight, in their order. And in the rear of the whole army he had a captain who formed new squadrons out of the fugitive Indians, each of a thousand men, whom he ordered to be supplied with food and drink, and to rest until their turn to fight should come again.

Having defeated five squadrons, the Spaniards looked out to observe how many remained, and they saw another eleven or twelve before them. They had now fought for more than three hours; nevertheless they cheered each other on, and charged the sixth squadron and routed it, as well as the seventh, eighth, ninth, and tenth. Yet neither they nor their horses were as fresh as at first, since they had fought for seven long hours without ceasing for a moment. The Indians never gave them rest, one squadron having scarcely been defeated before another came to the attack, and the routed men fell out of the battle to rest and form themselves into new squadrons.

It was then that the Spaniards saw that their enemies still had ten squadrons ready to fight; yet, with indomitable courage, they prepared to renew the conflict, though they were worn and tired, both men and horses. Yet they continued the battle with as much vigor as possible, that their weakness might not be seen by the Indians. But the Indians from hour to hour recovered their strength, while the Spaniards were losing it; for they felt that their enemies no longer fought as they did in the beginning, or even in the middle of the day. Thus the two armies continued until two in the afternoon.

Then the Governor Pedro de Valdivia, seeing that there were still eight or ten squadrons to scatter, and that, though this were achieved, the Indians continued to form new ones; and considering that, in this new way of fighting, judging from the small respite there had been during the day, neither would there be rest at night; it seemed well to retire, before the horses were quite worn out.

His intention was to retreat to a narrow pass, which he had left about a league and a half in his rear, and he thought that if that point could be reached, he would be safe, as there the Spaniards, on foot, could defend the pass against the whole army of the enemy. Having taken this resolution, though tardily, he called to his men, and said that they were to retreat gradually to the narrow pass. This they did, forming in close order, and retiring little by little, with their faces always to the foe, but more with the intention of defending themselves than of attack.

At this moment an Indian who, from a boy, had been brought up by the Governor Pedro de Valdivia, named Felipe, his Indian name being Lautaru, a son of one of their chiefs . . . hearing the Spaniards calling to each other to retreat, and knowing their language from having been brought up amongst them, and fearing that his relations would be satisfied at seeing the Spaniards retreat and that they would allow them to retire unmolested, left the Spanish ranks, crying:

"Do not be faint-hearted, my brothers; these thieves are now flying, and they set their hopes on reaching the narrow pass. Think, therefore, of what is needful for the freedom of our country, and the death and destruction of these traitors!"

Saying these words, to animate his own people, he took up a lance from the ground and stationed himself at their head, to fight against the Spaniards.

The old Indian captain who had adopted these new tactics, seeing the road taken by the Spaniards, and hearing the warning of Lautaru, understood what the enemy intended to do and ordered the two squadrons which had not yet been engaged, to march with speed and diligence, and by short cuts, and occupy the narrow pass that the Spaniards wished to reach, and to remain there until they were joined by the rest of the Indians.

Having given this order, he advanced with the remaining squadrons in pursuit of the Spaniards, every now and then sending fresh companies forward to engage them and prevent them from getting any rest. This was also done that the Indians who were fatigued with fighting might retire from the conflict and refresh themselves for renewed efforts.

In this way they followed and pressed upon the Spaniards, until they reached the narrow pass, killing some, and never ceasing to fight for a moment. When they reached the pass, it was near sunset.

The Spaniards, on seeing that the pass was occupied and guarded by the enemy, gave up all hope of escaping death, and, in order to die like Christians, they called upon the name of Christ our Lord, of the Virgin, His Mother, and of the Saints for whom they felt most devotion.

The Indians, seeing that the Spaniards were so tired that neither they nor their horses could do more, rushed upon them, as well those who had pursued as those who guarded the pass, and gave the horses and their riders as many wounds as they could inflict on all parts of their bodies. They hurled them on the ground and killed them with all the rage and cruelty they could show.

They took the Governor Pedro de Valdivia, and a priest who accompanied him, alive, and fastened them to poles until the fight was over. ... The way in which the Governor Pedro de Valdivia was killed by the Indians was described in several ways. . . . Some said that his own servant, Lautaru, killed him. . . . Others said, and this was the most probable account, that an old captain had killed him with a club.

He may have been the same captain through whose tactics the victory was won.

They killed him hastily, lest their men should accept the offers of the poor Governor, and unfasten him from the pole to which he was tied. For the other Indian captains, trusting in the promises of Pedro de Valdivia, were inclined to liberate him. He offered to depart from Chile and to take with him all the Spaniards, and never to return again.

But that captain, seeing the inclination of the others and that they were ready to give credit to the Governor, rose up amongst them and suddenly killed the poor knight with a club, thus ending the discussion. He exclaimed: "Shame upon you for being so imprudent as to believe the words of a vanquished and bound slave. Tell me, will not a man in that position promise anything? But will he fulfill his promise when he is free?"

... From that time they adopted the plan of forming in many separate squadrons to fight against the Spaniards.

UNDER THE YOKE

The bones of Valdivia lay in the soil he settled before there was peace in the land. Across the Andes to the silver estuary of the Plate, lay Diego de Mendoza, another conqueror resting in unconquered soil. Up the Paraguay were the scattered bones of still another conquistador of people who would not give up. South to north lay the bones of those whom the folk of the land defied and fought in a struggle that would never quite come to an end.

But the struggle to hold back the tide of the well-armed conquerors from Spain and from Portugal was like trying to hold back the sea from which they poured in ceaseless, growing numbers. The red folk stood their ground to die, they fled only to come back to die, but they were yet to die a thousand deaths in the slavery they sought so desperately to stave from their lands and their lives. The great enslavement began, and it spread over most of the lands and most of the people living on them.

Even the small tribes who had their own captives serving them were doomed to fall under the dreaded yoke. Up the continent of the south, in the lands held by the Portuguese, the search for Indian slaves went on day and night, reaching into the dark interior:

These Tapajosos are a brave race and are much feared by the surrounding nations, because they use so strong a poison in their arrows that if once blood is drawn, death is sure to follow. For this reason the Portuguese themselves avoided any intercourse with them for some time, desiring to draw them into friendly relations. However, they received us very well and lodged us together in one of their villages, containing more than five hundred families, where they never ceased all day from bartering fowls, ducks, hammocks, fish, flour, fruit, and other things, with such confidence that women and children did not avoid us; offering, if we would leave our lands and come to settle there, to receive and serve us peacefully all their lives.

Enslavement of the Tapajosos, Recorded by a Friar

The humble offers of these Tapajosos did not satisfy a set of people so selfish as are those of these conquests, who only undertake difficult enterprises from a covetous desire to obtain slaves—for which object the Tapajosos were placed in a convenient position. Suspecting that this nation had many slaves in their service, they treated them as rebels, and came to attack them.

This was going on when we arrived at the fort of Destierro, where the people were assembled for this inhuman work, and though, by the best means I could, I tried, I could not stop them. . . . The *Sargente* mayor and chief of all, who was Benito Maciel, son of the governor, gave me his word that he would not proceed with his intended work until he had heard from his father. Yet I had scarcely turned my back when, with as many troops as he could get, in a launch with a piece of artillery, and other smaller vessels, he fell upon the Indians suddenly with harsh war, when they desired peace.

They surrendered, however, with good will, as they had always offered to do, and submitted to all the Portuguese desired. The latter ordered them to deliver up all their poisoned arrows, which were the weapons they most dreaded. The unfortunate Indians obeyed at once; and when they were disarmed, the Portuguese collected them together like sheep, in a strong enclosure, with a sufficient guard over them.

They then let loose the friendly Indians, each one of them being an unchained devil for mischief, and in a short time they had gutted the village, without leaving a thing in it, and, as I was told by an eye-witness, cruelly abused the wives and daughters of the unfortunate captives, before their very eyes. Such acts were committed that my informer, who is a veteran in these conquests, declared he would have left off buying slaves, and even have given the value of those he possessed, not to have beheld them.

The cruelty of the Portuguese, excited by the desire of these slaves, did not cease until they had obtained them. They threatened the captive Indians with fresh outrages if they did not produce their slaves, assuring them that if they obeyed, they should not only be free but be treated with friendship and supplied with tools and linen cloths, which they should receive in exchange.

What could the unfortunates do—themselves prisoners, their arms taken, their homes pillaged, their wives and children ill-treated—but yield to everything their oppressors desired? They offered to give up a thousand slaves whom, when they were attacked, they had placed in concealment. And not being able to find more than two hundred, they collected them and delivered them up, giving their words that the remainder should be found, and even offered their own children as slaves.

All these were sent down to Marañon and Pará, and I saw them myself.

The night of enslavement fell upon the children and their children's children. Wherever the tribes stayed to meet the conqueror, whether in friendly alliance against ancient foes, or with hatred and hostility, they were forced at last to kneel to the whip, to die from plagues brought by the whites.

There were tribes that kept moving farther back into the plains and the wilderness of mountain and jungle, and some of these never gave up the fight: the Araucanians in the strip that would be known as Chile, the people of the pampas rolling inland from the silver Plate, and northward the fierce warriors in the fastnesses of lands held by the Portuguese, and farther north in the high sierra of the middle lands that would be called Central America, and northward still among the wild roaming Otomís of Mexico, and their wilder kin, the Yaquis, the Comanches, the Seminoles even farther to the north in lands to be disputed for decades to come.

But in most of the territory won by the two masters from Iberia, the yoke of slavery descended. And the tribes and the nations with all their villages, towns and cities, with all their women and young folk, with all their live achievements and all their dying hopes, were harnessed to it. The people, and above all their energy and ability to labor, became a simple matter of property to be divided among the masters. Their bodies were booty of war, their soil a treasure-chest to be forced and plundered.

The crumbling walls of the Indian centuries began to fall, pulling down with them the great and positive accomplishments. Down went the high morals and clear-cut laws that enforced them, the intricate knowledge of astronomy and engineering and medicine, the vast performance in art and architecture and design. Down went the numerous large and small attainments. Not the least of these was the crystalline wisdom of the value they set on man as a source of joy and achievement. Man to them was neither a plaything nor an instrument for body-breaking toil.

The walls of their centuries were tumbling down. And only a shred would be left of the uniqueness of their way of life that reduced man's wants to a minimum—not out of indolence but out of regard for the creative force they found in leisure and kept alive in their works. Tiny vessels of clay, or temples of mammoth stone, their works were the proof of the power that lay in the time for contemplation that taught wisdom and beauty to the maker of things, even as, without haste, his hands moved in his work.

Down came the noble concepts, burying much of the beauty beneath them, burying the beauty along with the bones of both conqueror and conquered.

Down came the centuries. And over them rose the new tide of toil without respite, the pitiless tide of slavery surging over the whole body of the land:

Scattering the debris around her of all that was gone, the flood swept over her bed of soil of the two continents, the waters striking in fury against her, loosing her hold on the roots of the concept that grew into great fulfillment, tearing her agonized fingers from the precious roots that were vanishing in the new ways roaring upon the stricken body of the whole land, rushing now, for years and scores of decades to come, over her where she lay.

· Five ·

HEALERS

The ages gone and those to come
dismay me not, for I am born and shall be born:
I am one with all creatures

JORGE DE LIMA

MIRACLE ON TEPEYACAC

The men who brought the flood of conquest and slavery that overran the Indies of the West, scooping up the wealth as it lay before them, harnessing the people to the needs of the masters, also brought the healers:

With every contingent of conquerors came a man of the Cross, sent to heal the wounds of the conqueror's soul. With every boatload of conquistadors came a priest or friar, sent to see that the Cross of the holy mother church was planted beside the captain's sword wherever the conquered site was claimed for the crown. As soon as the site for a town was chosen, the plan of the church was laid; as the town took shape, so did the church; when the town was completed, there were the church doors, finished and carved by craftsmen from the Old World and the apprentices picked from among the cleverest slaves of the land. There were the church doors ready to be thrown open.

And just as the new towns were often built on the ruins of the old, so the churches were often built on the remains, sometimes even on the standing foundations, of the old pagan temples. Even the Holy Virgin chose to make her first appearance in the new world on the site where the folk of the Aztec empire still came to worship their goddess, Tonantzin:

On Tepeyacac, near the ruined city of Tenochtitlan where the new

capital of the Mexican land was going up—it was there on that sacred
hill that the Virgin Mary first set foot in the Indies of the West:

It happened that there was a poor Indian named Juan Diego—a native,
it is said, of Cuautitlan. With regard to spiritual things, everything was
still in Tlatilolco. It was Saturday, very early before dawn, and he was
on his way to divine worship. As he drew near the little hill called
Tepeyacac, it began to dawn, and he heard the sound of singing above
the little hill. It was like the singing of various
precious birds. At intervals the singers' voices
would grow still, and then it seemed as though
the mountain replied. The singing, very sweet and delightful, excelled
that of the *coyoltótotl* and the *tzinizcan* and other lovely birds that sing.

An Aztec Account of the Appearance of the Virgin at Tepeyacac

Juan Diego stopped to look, and he said to himself:

"Am I, perhaps, worthy of what I hear? Can it be that I am dreaming? Have I just awakened? Where am I? Perhaps in the earthly paradise which the old ones, our elders, talked about? Or am I already in heaven?"

He was facing the east, looking above the little hill, whence came the precious, heavenly singing, and when it suddenly stopped and there was silence, he heard them calling him from above the little hill, heard them call:

"Juanito! Juan Dieguito! Little Juan, little Juan Diego!"

Then he dared to go to where they were calling him. He wasn't frightened at all—on the contrary, he went climbing up the little hill very happily, to see where they were calling him from.

When he reached the summit, he saw a lady standing there, who told him to draw nigh. When he stood before her, he marvelled greatly at her superhuman greatness: her dress was radiant as the sun; the crag on which her feet rested, shot through with rays of light, was like an anklet of precious stones—and the earth shone like a rainbow. The mesquite trees, the cactus plants, and the many different little shrubs that grow there, were like emeralds, their foliage like fine turquoise, and their branches and twigs glittered like gold.

He kneeled before her and heard her word—very soft and courteous, as from one who attracts and esteems greatly. She said to him:

"Juanito, little Juan, the smallest of my children—where are you going?"

He answered: "My Lady and Virgin, I must reach your house in Mexico, Tlatilolco, to worship the divine things. . . ."

Then she spoke to him and revealed her holy will. She said:

"Know and understand—you, the smallest of my children—that I am the eternal Holy Virgin Mary, Mother of the true God who gives life; of the Creator through whom everything exists, the Lord of the sky and the earth. I desire most earnestly that a temple should be erected for me here, in order to show and to give all my love, compassion, aid and succor in it—since I am your pious mother: yours, and that of all of you dwellers on earth, and of all my other beloved ones who invoke me and trust in me. There I shall hear your laments and remedy all your misery, suffering, and pain. And in order to carry out what my clemency desires, go to the palace of the bishop in Mexico City, and tell him that I send you to inform him of what I greatly desire—that here on this plain a temple should be erected to me. Tell him exactly what you have seen and wondered at, and what you have heard. Rest assured that I shall be very grateful, and shall reward this act—because I shall make you happy, and you shall well deserve the reward for the labor and weariness which it will cost you to carry out my charge. Now you have heard my command—my son, the smallest of them all—so go now and do your best."

He kneeled down before her at once and said: "My Lady, I go now to perform your errand. For the time being, I take my leave of you—I, your humble servant."

Then he went down to perform the errand, and he came out on the highway that stretches in a straight line to Mexico City.

ST. ROSE AND THE DEVIL

In the land where the emperor of all the Aztecs had ruled, in the center of the land, at the very heart of the conquered empire of pagan folk toiling under the masters, the "Little Virgin" set her sacred foot. People gathered there from all parts of the empire, gathering there in that same spot to worship the "little mother," Tonantzin, the Aztec goddess who watched over the fields and took care of the crops. But Tonantzin was no longer there—the conquerors and the men in the long robes who went with them had already removed the idol that stood for the goddess —and the new Lady who had taken her place brought a message of hope to the poorest and humblest among them, who came to know her and portray her as the beloved Dark Virgin.

Our Lady of Guadalupe, patron of the Mexicans, she was called. And the power of all the miracles that she wrought rose with the power of the new masters and the men of the Cross who marched with them.

Southward marched the faith of the Cross brought by the whites. And in the very core of the empire that had been of the Incas, in the new capital city of Lima, which Pizarro himself had ordered to be built, another great miracle was wrought. It was there in Lima that the first saint of all the new lands in the west was born, to become the patron of Peru:

Rosa Flores, delicate daughter of a family as large as it was poor. Nimble with the needle, Rosa could spin a design in lace or embroidery as fine as the veins in the flower whose name she bore. Rosa of the sensitive hands, praying for guidance to help her family without harming her own soul. Rosa Flores, the fragile one with the discipline of iron, conquering the road to sainthood for the conquered lands of the west:

From the time that Almighty God appointed S. Catherine of Sienna to be her mistress, Rose had such frequent conversations with her that the features of this seraphic virgin seemed to have been transferred to her countenance—as it happened to Moses, who was completely transformed by God after he had spoken with Him on the mountain. For

The Virtues and Temptations of Saint Rose of Lima

she resembled her so perfectly that she passed, in the opinion of all the people, for a second S. Catherine of Sienna. She lived also in most familiar intercourse with her guardian angel; for when Jesus Christ, her dear Spouse, was a moment later than usual in visiting her at the ordinary time, she sent her guardian angel to seek Him.

She felt one night when in her hermitage the threatenings of a fainting fit, or some similar attack, and immediately returned to the house, for fear of being taken ill in that retired place where no one could help her. Her mother, seeing her much changed, and the perspiration on her forehead, thought she was going to die. She told the servant to run to the nearest confectioner's to buy some chocolate—which at Lima is commonly composed of cocoa, lemons, and sugar—to strengthen her.

But our Saint begged her mother not to buy it, assuring her that she should not have long to wait for it. Her mother grew angry and told the servant a second time to go immediately to the place she had named.

Rose, seeing her eagerness, told her to call her back and not to trouble herself, for some would be brought to her immediately from the house of the Receiver. Scarcely had she finished speaking when a servant entered the house and brought her a large silver cup, full of chocolate, from his Master.

Her mother, greatly surprised at so seasonable an assistance, ordered her, in virtue of her authority, to tell her how she knew that this remedy would be brought to her. Rose smiled, and confessed that, as her good angel always did what she asked him, she had sent him to the Receiver's wife to tell her of her illness and of her want of a little chocolate to restore her strength.

Her mother opened the garden gate every night before she went to bed, that her daughter might go to her room when she returned at midnight from her hermitage. She forgot it once. And when Rose was preparing to return, she saw from the window a white shadow fluttering, and apparently inviting her to follow it.

She thought at once that it was her guardian angel concealed under this form. She followed. And when they arrived together at the closed door, it opened of itself the instant the shadow touched it.

She was not only familiar with the holy angel that Almighty God had appointed as her own protector, but with those of others also, as she made known to one of her friends—a religious man who, having a long journey to take, came to recommend himself to her good prayers. He was fortunate at first, but when he had reached the vast plains of Truxillo, which is a fine town near the sea, he underwent great fatigue, and was twice in danger of losing his life.

On his return to Lima, he complained to the blessed Rose that she had not helped him in his perils as he had asked her before he left. She answered that these misfortunes happened by his own fault, as he was not then in the same state as when he came to say farewell to her. She then charitably mentioned to him some things which she could only have known through her guardian angel.

If the angels loved and respected her, the devils, on the other hand, had so great an aversion for her that there was nothing they did not attempt in order to make her feel the effects of their hatred and fury.

The devil attacked her once in her cell in the form of a giant. He tried for a long time to bite her. But being prevented by the power of God from tearing her in pieces, he seized her and dragged her furiously on the ground, till this chaste virgin entreated the protection of her Divine Spouse by these words of the royal prophet:

"Lord, do not abandon to the tyrannical fury of these hellish monsters those who hope in Thee."

Then the enemy immediately fled.

Nothing occurs more frequently in the history of her life than the insults she received from the evil spirit. He appeared to her one day, and when she showed no fear of his malice he gave her a severe blow on the cheek. Another time he threw a great stone upon her from above, which struck her, fainting, to the ground.

One night when she was praying at home in a corner, she saw the devil in a large basket, making a horrible noise to divert her from her application to God. She blew out the candle, and fortifying herself with the sign of the Cross, she courageously challenged him to the combat. He accepted the offer. And changing his form in a moment, he appeared in the shape of a prodigious giant.

He took hold of her by the shoulders, and shook her as if he would tear her in pieces. She did not lose courage, and though her bones were almost broken, and her nerves relaxed by these rough shocks, she laughed at him and reproached him with his weakness—that, appearing so strong, he could not even triumph over her firmness.

It was observed that she was very often engaged in combat with the enemies of her salvation, and that whenever she was obliged to defend herself from their temptations, she was so intrepid that she never seemed to fear them, though they assumed horrible shapes capable of freezing the blood in the veins of the boldest and most courageous persons. On the contrary, the more frightful they appeared, the more courageously did she attack them.

She was once, however, obliged to change her method of defence, and gain the victory by flight, on the following occasion:

The devil appeared to her one day in her garden, under the form of a beautiful young man. At the sight of this dangerous enemy, she retired without waiting or speaking to him, and by this flight she gained a complete and glorious victory. For taking a thick iron chain which she found, she gave herself a severe discipline.

HOSTAGES

Wherever the conqueror moved, the priest or the friar moved beside him. But from the beginning there was conflict between the two.

There was agreement on the need to perpetuate the faith and the church in the new conquered lands. There was sharp dissension when the man in the robe who marched beside the conqueror interpreted the need to perpetuate the faith as applying to the conquered as well as the conqueror. There was antagonism and even strife bordering on violence as the priest or friar attempted not only to convert the conquered folk to the Catholic Christian faith of the crown, but also to dispel their ignorance of the master's speech and the master's ways that kept them in slavery.

And there was martyrdom, too, for the men of the Cross who stubbornly sought to change those ways:

Once the friars of the Order of St. Dominick consulted about sending some of their Order to this island, to spread the light of the Gospel among the Indians for the salvation of their souls. Whereupon they sent a Licentiate, famous for his sanctity . . . to accompany him, to visit the country, converse with the inhabitants, and to seek out fit places for the building of monasteries. The religious persons, being arrived, were received as angels from heaven, ear being given to their words with all the attention, alacrity, and affection that they were able at that time—for they were ignorant of our language.

The Martyrdom of the Innocent Friars by the Innocent Indians

It happened afterwards, when the religious persons were gone, that there came a band of soldiers who, according to their wonted customs of fraud and impiety, carried away captive the prince of the province who . . . was called Alonso (for they delight to be called by the names of the Christians, and therefore before they are informed of anything else they desire to be baptized). By these soldiers was Alonso craftily seduced a-shipboard under pretense that they would give him a princely banquet.

With their prince there went seventeen other persons, for they had a confidence that the friars would keep the Spaniards from doing them any injury—for otherwise the said king would not have trusted them so far. But they were no sooner on shipboard but the Spaniards hoisted up their sails for Hispaniola—where they sold all the Indians for slaves.

Now all the region, being troubled for the loss of their king and queen, flocked to the religious persons, and had like to have slain them —who, perceiving the injustice of the Spaniards, were very much troubled. And I do believe that they had rather have lost their lives than that the Indians should have suffered such an injury to the hindrance of their salvation.

But the Indians were satisfied with the promises of the religious persons, who told them that as soon as any ships came to the island they would take the first opportunity to go to Hispaniola and endeavor to get their king and queen set at liberty. Providence sent a ship thither, to confirm the condemnation of those that governed, by which these religious persons sent to the religious persons of Hispaniola, but got no redress—for the Spaniards there were receivers of the prey.

When the religious persons who had promised to the Indians that their king should return within four months, saw that he did not come in eight months, they prepared themselves for death and to give up their lives to Christ to whom they had offered them before their departure out of Hispaniola.

And so the innocent Indians revenged themselves upon the innocent friars.

LIKE THE SAINTS OF OLD

Not all the martyrs were those who died at the hands of the innocent conquered folk. There were friars in every one of the new lands whose lives were a living martyrdom imposed by the will of the very same conquistadors beside whom they marched, whose Confessions they heard, and the wounds of whose souls they had come to heal.

There was Fray Bartolomé de las Casas, for instance—the great apostle of all these lands, who travelled and preached in both continents of the western world, who crossed the ocean sea ten times, and then five more, to plead for the freedom of the folk of the land. To plead and preach and cite the facts (along with his own exaggerations) and excoriate by written word and sermon—until the Laws of the Indies were born, until the people called Indians were freed at least in word, if not in deed.

But neither Fray Bartolomé nor the many like him who practiced what they preached, in the way the saints of old had done, had any intention of stopping there. They kept on fighting by word to make the new-won laws of freedom and benevolence for the conquered more than a meaningless word.

There were the men of the regular clergy and the men of the orders: Franciscans and Augustinians, Jesuits and Dominicans. And there were also the nuns: the Carmelites and the others. In Mexico and in the Caribbean lands, down to Brazil, to Patagonia, up through Chile, through Paraguay, and northward, there were the priests and friars of courage and zeal:

Friars like the fiery Dominican, Bernardino de Minaya, fighting even the great conquistadors by pen and sermon, fighting by the power of the word, by day and by night, making the pilgrimage to Rome itself to plead the Indians' cause with the Pope. Challenging the great Pizarro, and walking to Rome, and writing to His Catholic Majesty, Philip II, his king, to keep him informed and win his support to the cause:

I was accompanied by seven other ecclesiastics likewise moved by zeal for the conversion of those peoples to our holy faith. Arriving in Mexico, we were sent to various provinces, I going to Oaxaca, about eighty leagues from Mexico City. Here I erected a monastery and later raised others . . . in which I gathered groups of sons of the principal Indian chieftains. Having taught some three *A Memorial to the King from* hundred or more of these, I went to Soconusco *Bernardino de Minaya* and then . . . to the province of Nicaragua, baptizing the natives as I went . . . the Indians coming out to receive me with laurels of roses and with foodstuffs . . . and after being taught, they voluntarily burned their idols and temples. Having arrived in the city of Leon, Nicaragua . . . I began to teach many Indians, although Bishop Osorio and the Alcalde Mayor, Licentiate Castañeda, believed many of them incapable because they had said the *Ave Maria* was something to eat.

During Lent I remained there teaching the Indians and preaching to the Spaniards, and at Easter time I brought the Indians before the Bishop and Castañeda and proved that the Indians had the ability to become Christians. While in Leon, news came of the discovery of Peru.

When some Indians were sent to Panama to be sold as slaves . . . I notified Pizarro of Your Majesty's law against enslaving Indians even when they were the aggressors. He proclaimed the law but at the same time stopped giving me and my companions maintenance. Whereupon I told Pizarro take care what he did because the Emperor would disapprove what he was doing. . . .

I also proposed that we should explain to the Indians the reason for our coming: to make God known to them and not to rob them or despoil them of their lands. Pizarro responded that he had not come for any such reasons; he had come from Mexico to take away from them their gold, and he refused to do what I asked.

I straightway took leave of him with my companions. When he enquired whether I wanted to take my share of the gold won from the towns already subdued, I replied that I did not want any part of that gold; that it had been won unjustly and that I did not wish to lend approval by my presence to such robberies. And shortly afterward we arrived at Panama, suffering great hunger because the master of the ship refused us food. . . .

Later we arrived in Mexico where the Lord brought me at the very time that a law had arrived from Cardinal Loaysa in which he ordered captains to enslave Indians at their will. He was influenced to do this by a Dominican named Domingo de Betanzos who had stated before the Council of the Indies that the Indians could never become Christians despite all that the Emperor, the Pope, the Virgin, and all the celestial orders might do.

When the law which permitted the enslavement of the Indians arrived, Don Sebastián Ramírez, Bishop of Santo Domingo and President of the Audiencia in Mexico, called in all the ecclesiastics and bade them write to Your Majesty their true opinion of the ability of the Indians. The Franciscans wrote to you, but I wished to speak to the cardinal personally. . . . I embarked on a vessel bound for Spain with no preparation whatsoever, confident that the other passengers would help me.

Arriving at Seville, I went on foot, begging, to Valladolid, where I visited the cardinal and informed him that Friar Domingo de Betanzos knew neither the Indians' language nor their true nature. He replied that I was much deceived, for he understood that the Indians were no more than parrots, and he believed that Friar Domingo spoke with prophetic spirit and, for himself, would follow that friar's opinions.

When Dr. Bernal Lugo asked me what had happened at my interview with the cardinal, I told him, and added that I was determined to go to the Pope concerning this evil which so endangered the Christianity of the Emperor and the many souls in the Indies; that a more cruel judgment had been rendered against them than against the ancient Hebrews, and that, although merely a poor friar, I should not fear to oppose a cardinal on this matter if I could only get a letter of introduction to His Holiness from the Empress.

I will arrange this for you, said Dr. Bernal Lugo.

Then I went on foot to Rome with my letter of introduction, which I preserve to this day.

THE MOMENTOUS WORDS

Challenging the conquerors, challenging their own brethren of the Cross to face the facts and gather the strength to divulge them regardless of the risk, even challenging their superiors—the bishops, the archbishops, the cardinals—when it became necessary to do so, the good men of the cloth carried their crusade up and down the continents of the world that was new, and across to the old world where the final power lay, and back to the conquered lands again:

Reaching into the farthest and the wildest corners of the new world, learning the multitudinous native tongues, chronicling the ways of the numberless tribes, healing the heathen of the sicknesses of the land as well as the smallpox and the other diseases brought by the masters, healing their ills and comforting them in spirit, making death less painful by their patience and often merely by their presence.

Seeing the cruel conditions of the lives led by the conquered, and trudging back through the wilderness to appeal for aid. Challenging authority whenever authority grew callous and unjust. Pleading the cause of the Indians in the face of the threats from the greedy ones in the world of the new and the old. Affording no sleep to those in power who tried to shut their eyes to the plight of the poor and the downtrodden.

With humility in their hearts, but with zeal and valor never flagging, they laid bare the wounds of the conquered and oppressed before their king, bare and bleeding before the Pope. Until His Holiness Paul the Third—on the ninth day of June, in the fifteen hundred and thirty-seventh year of Our Lord—set down the momentous words declaring the Indians to be people:

Declaring them folk of reason, declaring them human beings in possession of mind and soul. Declaring them undeserving of slavery, whatever their faith might be. Declaring them free:

Truth itself, which can neither deceive nor be deceived, when it appointed the preachers of faith to the office of preaching, is well known to have said: "Go, teach all nations." He said *all* without any distinction, for all are capable of receiving the instruction of the faith. The enemy of mankind who always opposes good undertakings in order to bring them to nought, aware of this commission, and instigated by envy, invented a method hitherto unknown of preventing the Word of God from being preached to the nations that they might be saved. . . . He has excited some of his satellites who, eagerly desiring to satisfy their avarice, habitually presume to assert that the western and southern Indians and the other nations which in these times have come to our knowledge . . . should, like brutes, be brought under our servitude.

Pope Paul III: The Indians Are Declared Worthy of Freedom

And indeed, they are made slaves and treated with an inhumanity that their masters would scarcely exercise over the very brutes that serve them.

We, therefore, who, though unworthy, are the viceregent of our Lord upon earth, and who seek with our whole endeavor the sheep of his flock entrusted to us and who are outside of the fold, in order to bring them into the fold itself, reflecting that these Indians as true men are not only capable of the Christian faith, but also—as has been made known to us—that they embrace the faith with the utmost promptitude, and wishing to provide them with suitable remedies, decree and declare by apostolical authority:

That the above-mentioned Indians and all other nations who may in future come to the knowledge of Christians, though they be out of the faith of Christ, can freely and lawfully use, possess and enjoy their liberty in that regard. And that they ought not to be reduced to slavery. And that whatever may otherwise have been done is null and void.

Moreover, that those Indians and other nations are to be invited to the aforesaid faith of Christ by the preaching of the Word of God and by the example of a good life.

This decree is to hold good, notwithstanding any previous acts and whatsoever else to the contrary.

"YOU ARE ALL IN MORTAL SIN!"

By royal decree, duly signed, stamped, and sealed, commanding the conquerors and the authorities to obey the orders and proclaim them to the people of the lands. And by papal bull, bearing the written signature of His Holiness and the year of his pontificate. By the supreme authority of the crown and the cross—after countless pleadings from the missionaries, and after due deliberation concerning the expediency as well as the morals and the ethics involved in the issue—the people of all the lands in the new world held by His Catholic Majesty of Spain and the Most Serene King of Christian Portugal were declared to be free.

But year after year, from one decade to the next, there were amendments to the decrees, there were exceptions to the letter and to the spirit of the papal bull. So that the Indian's freedom remained a collection of fine phrases not meant to be heeded, or a question of rhetoric designed for debate or maybe merely applause: in any case, a matter of well-intentioned thoughts never intended to be turned into action. The cause of the Indian and his forbidden subjection became a "lost cause" to all but those scattered men of the cross carrying now the banner bequeathed by Fray Bartolomé and Fray Bernardino, by Father Montesinos and Father Pedro de Córdoba, by all the other courageous men of the missions that followed.

In the fast-growing lands of Brazil, continuing the great crusade begun by the Jesuit apostles before him—by Nóbrega, by Anchieta, called The Miracle-Man—there was Fray Antonio Vieyra, the scourge of the hunters and slavers of Indians:

Alexander and Caesar were lords of the world—but their souls are now burning in Hell and will burn there for all eternity. Who will tell me now how to ask Caesar and Alexander what it profits them to have been masters of the world, and if they find it has proved a good bargain to give their souls in exchange for it?

Alexander! Julius! Was it good for you to *Fray Antonio Vieyra: A Sermon* have been masters of the world and to be now *Against the Enslavers of Men* where now you are?

They cannot answer me—but answer me ye who can! Would any of you choose at this time to be Alexander the Great? Would any one of you choose at this time to be Julius Caesar? God forbid that we should! How? Were they not Masters of the World? They were so, but they lost their own souls . . . Oh, blindness! And it seems ill to you for

Alexander and for Caesar to have given their souls for the whole world—and it seems well to you to give your own souls for what is not the world, nor hath the name of it! . . .

At how different a price now does the Devil purchase souls from that which he formerly offered for them . . . I mean in this country? The Devil has not a fair in the world where they go cheaper! In the Gospel he offers all the kingdoms of the earth for a single soul: he does not require so large a purse to purchase all that are in Maranhão . . . It is not necessary to offer worlds, it is not necessary to offer kingdoms, it is not necessary to offer cities, nor towns, nor villages; it is enough for the Devil to point at a plantation and a couple of Tapuya Indians—and down goes the man upon his knees to worship him! . . .

Do ye know, Christians—do ye know, nobles and people of Maranhão —what is the fast which God requires of you this Lent? It is that ye loosen the bands of injustice, and that you set those free whom you hold captives and whom you oppress. These are the sins of Maranhão; these are what God commands me to announce: "Show My people their transgression!" Christians, God commands me to undeceive you, and I undeceive you on the part of God:

You are all in mortal sin! You are all living and dying in a state of condemnation, and you are all going straight to Hell! Many are already there, and you also will soon be there with them, except you change your lives! . . . Every man who holds another unjustly in servitude, being able to release him, is certainly in a state of condemnation. All men, or almost all men in Maranhão, hold others unjustly in servitude; all, therefore, or almost all, are in a state of condemnation. . . . Some are condemned for certainty, others for doubt, others for ignorance.

Those who were certain are condemned for not making restitution. They who were in doubt are condemned for not examining. They who were in ignorance are condemned for not knowing what it was their duty to know . . .

But you will say to me: this people . . . this state cannot be supported without Indians. Who is to bring us a pitcher of water or a bundle of wood? Who is to plant our manioc? Must our wives do it? Must our children do it?

In the first place . . . these are not the straits in which I would place you—but if necessity and conscience require it, then I reply, yes! And I repeat it—yes! You and your wives and your children ought to do it! We ought to support ourselves with our own hands, for better is it to be supported by the sweat of one's brow than by another's blood. O ye riches of Maranhão! What if these mantles and cloaks were to be wrung? They would drop blood! . . .

Let us resolutely overcome the cruel temptation which has carried so many from this land to Hell, and is carrying us also. . . . Let the world know, let the heretics and the heathen know, that God was not deceived when he chose the Portuguese for conquerors and preachers of His Holy Name. Let the world know that there is still truth, that there is still the fear of God, that there is still a soul, that there is still a conscience—and that interest is not the absolute and universal lord of all!

The men of the Cross appealed to the conquered as well as the conqueror, urging all throughout the new-won lands to heed the laws against slavery. For their pain and their persistence, for their implacable zeal, for holding the word and the deed of righteousness dearer than wealth, they were persecuted by the conquerors and settlers from their own homelands who craved and sought riches and ease in the New World at the cost of the conquered folk.

Abused and stoned and driven out of the towns and the settlements by the users of slaves, the missionaries moved on patiently through the wilderness. And if they escaped martyrdom by hunger or thirst, or at the jaws of beasts or reptiles or even cannibals, they found refuge among the friendly Indians. Day and night, in the furnace of the jungle, across the wastelands, up the savage streams, to the freezing heights, to the highest sierras, they preached their faith, they thundered against slavery and the shame of it. They never grew tired.

But there were times when they became weary of waiting for the word of justice to be enforced. There were the long hours and the grave moments when they knew that further delay in correcting the evil would bring disaster beyond repair upon the land and its folk, upon the Gospel of love they were trying to teach, upon the power of both the church and the crown they depended upon. And so there were times when the missionaries took matters into their own hands:

Setting up reforms that were more or less of their own decision, modifying the existing slavery of the conquered Indians that threatened to deprive the church of its converts and the crown of its subjects, and both of their revenues. Saving the conquerors in spite of themselves. Establishing the first real bonds of understanding with the Indians everywhere.

In Paraguay the bonds established by the Jesuit missionaries among the Guaraní and the other great tribes resolved themselves into a unique pattern of "reductions," where a communal system of recreation as well as labor was developed. Later these Jesuit-controlled "reductions" were to grow so powerful and independent that they constituted a state within a state, challenging the whole system of imperial profit and authority.

In time there were Jesuits and other missionaries whose deeds of true dedication to the most wretched among the enslaved and the conquered were known even in their own lifetime. In time there were future saints whose mortal remains drew the highest authorities of the land to pray and worship at their burial. In time there were men like Francis Solano, the Franciscan, who came from Spain to help the poor and heal the sick in the land Pizarro had won with torturing flame and murderous cord and steel.

There were men like Francis Solano, the friar in tattered robe, who was born in Andalusia, but was blessed in Peru.

These were the healers: the men of the Cross, the men of the hooded robes of black or brown or white, the men walking through the wilderness in their sandalled feet. Walking everywhere, settling down in the most remote and desolate corners where there were people needing attention.

These were the healers: closing the wounds of body and soul. Closing them to let new life grow over them when life was granted. Closing them in death as they closed the eyes of the stricken when all but death was denied. Extinguishing the burning pangs of sin and crime in the souls of the conquerors who slaughtered and enslaved the Indian folk and sacked their cities and soil. Extinguishing the pangs, but keeping this greatest wound open to show to the kings and the popes.

These were the priests: keeping the wound and the sin and the crime of enslavement of Indians open to show to the men of power and authority until atonement was made, in word, and slowly—very slowly and eventually, though not quite entirely—in deed, as well.

These were the men: opening new paths of communication through the wilderness, founding new settlements. All the while initiating new ways of enlightenment among the conquered. Establishing the first schools, not only instructing the people in the gospel of love, but also gradually spreading knowledge of the language, the arts and the sciences of the old world come to the new. Giving the conquered a first awareness of new concepts, an initial understanding and appreciation of new beauties hitherto hidden from them by the masters interested only in their labor and gold.

These were the men: teaching the Indians the unknown wonders of clear and detailed and inspiring communication by the written word, introducing them to the mysteries of vast learning suddenly laid open by the magic of the written word. Preserving the remains of the Indian cultures—the chants, the carved stones, the painted manuscripts —for the cause of future scholarship as well as for the immediate expediency of understanding the old ways in order to make their substitution by the new more lasting.

These were the healers, these were the priests, these were the men. Eusebio Kino in the Californias, followed by Junípero Serra and the others. Gante and Motolinia and Sahagún and many more in Mexico. Friar Ramón Pane who arrived with Columbus, and those who came after him to accompany the conquerors throughout the Caribbean. García de Palacio in Guatemala. And moving into the Amazon, Cristóbal de Acuña and all his brethren of the hood. Avila, Molina, Alvarez de Paz, with their multitude of colleagues in the Andes of Peru and all the adjacent territories.

The healing hand of these men and the many who began to follow in their soft, determined footsteps soothed the suffering, brought hope to the downcast and the despairing, and scattered the fresh seeds of enlightenment in the common world of conquered and conqueror that was barely beginning to form. They planted the seed in the night of enslavement while they struggled and prayed for the darkness to end.

But beyond the slow-fading night of Indian slavery, the horizon that loomed over the whole restless body of the land was not the hopeful light of liberation, or even the preface, or even the promise of it. Over the dazed and smitten land now slowly healing, over the land waiting and yearning for the sun that gave strength, over the whole land waking now and watching the night vanishing under the quieting hand of the healers, watching and staring expectant into the darkness into the sky holding the sun and its life-giving light—there rose instead the shattering clouds of another slavery:'

Rolling in from the ocean sea, in from the far, western shores of Africa, the iron clouds of black slavery moved in an endless chain over the great wearying body of the land—across Mexico and the whole Caribbean, across Peru, across Brazil. Across the darkening soil of her two continents. The black clouds bringing the cold and the weight of new oppression, bringing the strange people loaded down with shackles and sorrow, bringing the nightmare and the heavy reality of Negro slavery to the burdened land, still ailing where she lay.

· *Six* ·

SLAVES

No shining welcome will be made for you
In the dark land of dark men.

JACQUES ROUMAIN

THE PRICELESS HAND

Wherever the Indians had raised their great cities of empire, the conquered folk of the land continued to furnish much of the needed labor for the sustenance and enrichment of the masters. Whether as branded slaves or people freed in all but fact, the Indians—in most of the areas of Mexico and the lands to be known as Central America, in most of the Andes of Peru and the surrounding country, and in part of the region that would be called Colombia and Venezuela and where the Chibcha kingdom had flourished—remained the principal source of labor. And labor was beginning to turn the conquered lands into colonies from which wealth in every form was waiting to be wrested for the world across the sea.

But throughout many of the lands where the Indians had been of the wilder tribes, of the fierce nomads, of the hunting and fishing people, of the folk still roaming the shores and jungles, and throughout all of the lands where the Indians, exhausted from overwork and disease brought by the whites, were dying like fish in a flood—the priceless hand of labor came from over the sea. The hand to lift the colonial treasure from the roots of the soil where it lay waiting, the hand no price could measure, was purchased with shells and with slave-money from another continent:

From Africa, from its western coasts, from the very heartland of the old black continent that lay east, that lay south. From Africa's fields and from Africa's villages, from its mammoth market of slaves, the masters bought the men and the women to meet their feverish need for people of skill and people of endurance:

People who could turn metal, who could fatten the herds, who could make the soil golden with grain and green with sugar cane and greener with tobacco, who could fill the air with the perfume of coffee. People who knew the same burning sun. People who could toil from sun to sun.

To the twin colonies of Hispaniola that would be known as Haiti and Santo Domingo, to the large island of Cuba and the little island of Puerto Rico, southward around the bulge where the shores of Brazil were filling with people and sugar cane, and to the north and west from there, to the mainland coast of the south Caribbean, to the colonies springing up at Cartagena, at Santa Marta, to the waist of the isthmus joining the new world's continents. To the old mines and the new, to the shores being sown with plants from every world, went the ships loaded with slaves.

The ships bringing the miners, the peasants, the shepherds, the servants. Bringing the deft hands of the dark laborers to plant and care for the wealth waiting beneath the blazing sun. Bringing the Africans. Bringing their skillful hands of sorrow to tear the riches from the roots now spreading in the masters' soil:

Cartagena is one of the most considerable cities of America. The heats are excessive, the rains so frequent, the air so unwholesome, contagious disorders so common, that nothing but cupidity or zeal could make a residence there endurable. The soil, moreover, is so barren that most of the necessaries of life have to be conveyed thither from other countries. And, as the neighboring seas are very tempestuous, the inhabitants are often in want of everything, though surrounded with treasures of gold and silver. All these united inconveniences have not intimidated the avarices of men. The port of Cartagena is the general rendezvous where people from several nations repair for traffic, especially from Mexico, Peru, Potosí, Quito, and the neighboring islands.

Father Bertrand Fleurian: The Inhumanity of Black Slavery

Vessels laden with Negroes are constantly arriving there. It is they who do all the labor: they are employed in the mines and in all that is most painful. People there become rich only at the price of the sweat, and even of the blood, of these poor creatures.

Merchants purchase them on the coasts of Guinea, Angola, Congo, and will seek them even into the heart of Africa: they are originally purchased for about four crowns a head, and are resold for two hundred and sometimes more at Cartagena. They are in such numbers that not less than ten or twelve thousand are annually imported. . . .

It would be impossible to describe the miseries these poor slaves undergo in the course of their sea voyage. They are thrown one on another in the hold of the ship, without beds, clothing, and almost without food, loaded with chains, and plunged in their own filth.

All this, added to the heat and darkness of the place, and the unwholesome diet, produces complaints, wounds, and ulcers, which increase their natural infection to such a degree that they can scarcely endure themselves. Even cattle on board ship are not so ill used as are these miserable creatures. Hence, many of them fall into despair and prefer death by starvation to their deplorable state. It often happens that when old age or infirmity makes them unfit for work, they are cruelly abandoned, like beasts not worth caring for.

But what is still more deplorable, their souls are not more cared for than their bodies. The merchants who sell, and the masters who purchase them, take no further trouble than to order them to become Christians. And as fear and ignorance of what is exacted prevent them from resisting, advantage is taken of their silence, and they are baptized without precaution or instruction, not knowing either what they ought to believe or practise. Baptism, therefore, is to the greater number a mere ceremony, of which they understand nothing. The consequence is, with the mark and character of a Christian, they retain their pagan morals and idolatrous superstitions, so that they themselves can scarcely say what religion they belong to.

SHACKLES FOR ALL

They were people of many faiths and beliefs, with many rites of magic for many needs of their own. Like the conquered people of the lands they were to call their home, the Negro slaves were people of many tribes and many ways. They came from a continent called Africa, but the word meant little or nothing to them. They were folk of widely varying achievements, both general and specific, and high and low, that were destined to leave their lasting uniqueness on the land becoming colony.

The colony in time also becoming more than mere masters' soil, becoming even soil belonging to slaves—not by possession, but subtly by dint of their immense and gradual contribution. And this by reason of the inexorable growing need of the growing masters who had plucked them from their homelands' hearth across the southern Atlantic:

From the Congo and the lands of the Sudan. From Dahomey and Yoruba, Ashanti and Haussá. From the countries where the people spoke Bantu, where they spoke Fanti, where they talked in the Ibi tongue. From Guinea and from Mozambique. From the lands and the tribes and the shores of Africa, the masters plucked the people for their multiplying needs:

The enterprising Mandingas and the Minas, the Fuláhs and the Fula-Fulos. The Ba-Congos, the Balantas. The alert Nubians. The Banhaneca herdsmen, the Ambuelas who were miners, the Mozosuros who also were men of the mines. The Macuacuás, the Libollos and the Landins, all of them skilled in the pursuit of agriculture. And scores of thousands of folk from scores of other tribes speaking a multitude of tongues that would flavor the blend of the Portuguese or Castilian or French with the hundreds of Indian tongues of the folk of the land, flavoring the blend that was chaos again but that slowly resolved itself into powerful new idioms and a thousand newer ways and customs in the colonies of Brazil, of Cuba, of Hispaniola, the double colony, and of all the rest. The slaves in their infinite variety of language and custom and accomplishment, the slaves by their special aptitudes building an infinitely newer world in the new world of the west:

The world their hands were helping to create was a world unbounded in wealth and promise, but the hands wore shackles of iron. In Portugal's rising colony of Brazil there were shackles for all:

The lime of Rio is mades of shells scooped out of the Bay, and, of course, is in powder. See that *falua*—a light boat of one mast—riding at anchor some fifty feet from the Gloria Beach. She is charged with lime, and, dancing on the swell, is unloading her cargo. The slave on her bows,

keeping her head to the shore with a long bamboo, is captain; the other,
on the gunwale, raising the dust on the blade
Thomas Ewbank: Life in Brazil; of a hoe, is her deckhand. Observe those four
the Crippling Toil of the Slave blacks, with empty tea-chests on their heads,
wading toward her, and as many coming from her with their boxes filled.
How steadily they move, where the waves would take a stranger off his
feet! The water is at the arm-pits of him who is lifting his load from the
edge of the vessel—and see, as he turns and breasts that retiring swell, it
swashes over his eyes. Now he comes dripping out, ascends the bank
and, crossing the street, empties his chest on the floor of an establishment for the sale of building materials. As he does, so do eight or ten
more, keeping the hoe—used in place of a shovel—in constant motion. . . .

Some are, like the skippers on the craft, in shirts minus both sleeves
and skirts; others wear a petticoat that neither reaches the knees nor
meets behind; and two have aprons not one whit wider than aprons
usually are. White as their contents, the boxes contrast strongly with
their moving pedestals—while these increase in height as they near the
beach, and all but disappear at the *falua.* One, while his box was being
filled, plunged over head and washed himself; then tore off a part of his
pinafore, and fastened it over his shoulders, to protect them from the
caustic dust. . . .

I . . . continued on to the Campo—a spacious square, on the sides
of which several national buildings stand, including the Senate-house.
Covered with stunted grass, and the site of one of the principal foun-
tains, it is the city's great washing and bleaching establishment, and is
ever alive with *lavandeiras*—laundresses. More than two hundred are
now scattered over the field, exclusive of crowds at the fount. . . .

How busy all are, each in the center of a ring of drying garments! The
huge wooden bowl, which, in coming and returning, serves as a basket,
is now a washing-tub. . . . A single vestment with most suffices, and with
its purification the wearer winds up her labors. Some are Minas and
Mozambique girls, as evinced by their superior forms, and attentions
to attire. If others are naked to the waist, these are so seldom. Figures
graceful as any seen at the wells of the East occur among them.

With this business of the Campo the heavens sympathize: for, while
the grass is half concealed by garments bleaching in the sun, the blue
welkin is dappled over with snow-white patches, as if it was drying-day
above. . . . *Lavandeiras* have no saint assigned them, yet they deserve one
—were it only to relieve them once a year from the washing-tub. No
class have stronger claims upon the Church, nor on the saints them-

selves. A Mass cannot be performed nor a *festa* kept without them. *Festas* are hailed as blessings by all others, but what do they do for these? Drawing near, they demand additional toil, and in departing leave them naught but piles of dirty linen. . . .

I now turn down Rua San Pedro, a long and narrow street in which iron and copper smiths, hatters and guitar-makers were at work. . . . I emerged from the long avenue in Direita Street . . . where street-passengers have to run amok through piles of bales, barrels, packages, crates, trucks, and bustling and sweating Negroes. Here are no carts drawn by quadrupeds for the transportation of merchandise. Slaves are the beasts of draughts as well as of burden. The loads they drag, and the roads they drag them over, are enough to kill both mules and horses. . . . See— there are two slaves moving off with a cask of hardware on a plank of wood, with a rope passed through a hole at one end, and the bottom greased or wetted!

Trucks in every variety are now numerous. Some recent ones are as heavily built and ironed as brewers' drays, which they resemble, furnished with winches in front to raise heavy goods. Each is of itself sufficient for any animal below an elephant to draw—and yet loads varying from half a ton to a ton are dragged on them by Negroes. Two strain at the shafts and one or two push behind, or, what is quite as common, walk by the wheels and pull down the spokes.

It is surprising how their naked feet and legs escape being crushed, the more so as those in front cannot prevent the wheels every now and then sinking into the gutters, and whirling the shafts violently one way or the other. One acts as foreman, and the way he gives his orders is a caution to the timid. From a settled calm he in a moment rages like a maniac and seems ready to tear his associates to pieces.

A slave was chained to one heavy truck. He had been absent when it was wanted, and his enraged owner took this method of preventing him from losing another job. . . .

Neither age nor sex is free from iron shackles. I met this morning a very handsome Mozambique girl with a double-pronged collar on—she could not have been over sixteen. And a few evenings ago, while standing on the balcony of a house in Customhouse Street, a little old Negress, four fifths naked, toddled past, in the middle of the street, with an enormous tub of swill on her head, and secured by a lock and chain to her neck. . . .

With a friend I went to the Consulado, a department of the Customs having charge over exports. Gangs of slaves came in continually with

coffee for shipment. Every bag is pierced and a sample withdrawn—
while on the carrier's head—to determine the quality and duty. . . .
Every gang of coffee-carriers has a leader, who commonly shakes a rattle,
to the music of which his associates behind him chant.

The load, weighing 160 pounds, rests on the head and shoulders, the
body is inclined forward, and the pace is a trot or half run. Most are
stout and athletic, but a few are so small and slightly made that one
wonders how they manage to keep up with the rest. The average life of
a coffee-carrier does not exceed ten years. In that time the work ruptures
and kills them.

They have so much a bag—and what they earn over the sum daily
required by their owners they keep. Except four or five, whose sole dress
was short canvas shirts without sleeves, all were naked from the waist
upward and from the knees below. A few had on nothing but a towel
round the loins. Their rich chocolate skins shone in the sun. On returning, some kept up their previous chant, and ran as if enjoying the
toil. Others went more leisurely, and among them some noble-looking
fellow stepped with much natural grace.

A gang of fourteen slaves came past with enormously wide but shallow
baskets on their heads. They were unloading a barge of sea-coal, and
conveying it to a foundry or forge. The weight each bore appeared equal
to that of a bag of coffee—160 pounds.

This mode of transporting coal has one advantage: the material is
taken directly from the vessel to the place where it is to be consumed.
As with coal, so with everything—when an article is once mounted on
the head of a Negro, it is only removed at the place where it is to remain.

A couple of slaves followed the coal-carriers, each perspiring under a
pair of the largest sized blacksmith bellows—a load for a horse and cart
with us. A week ago I stood to observe eight oxen drag an ordinary
wagon-load of building stone for the Capuchins up the steep Castle hill.
It was straining work for them to ascend a few rods at a time. Today I
noticed similar loads of stone discharged at the foot of the ascent, and
borne up on Negroes' heads.

No wonder that slaves shockingly crippled in their lower limbs are
so numerous.

There waddled before me, in a manner distressing to behold, a man
whose thighs and legs curved so far outward that his trunk was not over
fifteen inches from the ground. It appeared sufficiently heavy, without
the loaded basket on his head, to snap the osseous step and drop between his feet. I observed another whose knees crossed each, and his

feet preternaturally apart, as if superincumbent loads had pushed his knees in instead of out.

The lamplighter of the Cattete districts exhibits another variety. His body is settled low down, his feet are drawn both to one side, so that his legs are parallel at an angle of thirty degrees. . . . It is the lower parts of the moving columns, where the weights are alternately thrown on and off the jointed thighs and legs, that are the weakest. These necessarily are the first to give way under excessive burdens; and here are examples of their having yielded and broken down in every direction.

WORSE THAN ANY ALLIGATOR

While their own bodies grew twisted from toil, and their own souls were maimed from neglect, the slaves laboring in the sun saw the roots of the colonial lands grow stronger in body and even in soul. They saw the fields blossom from their hands, the towns and cities rise from their dark and mighty heads. They watched the river of wealth go pouring from their arteries over the land, into the masters' mansions their hands and their heads and their blood had built, into the buildings of power and authority they had raised.

They stood in the sun and followed the course of that river of wealth out to the sea, watching the colonial river of plenty and ease carrying their sweat in its current, seeing it flow away to other worlds called Spain and Portugal, which they never saw, but knew to be riding to empire and glory on the full-flowing tide of the silver and gold and wood and grain and hides and sugar and all the other bounty to which their bones were shackled.

Most of the slaves stood in the sun and watched as they worked, finding some satisfaction in seeing the change and the beauty their hands had wrought from the roots, from the soil that was now a part of them. There was pride. But there was greater sorrow as they saw the chasm widening between them and the reward of the riches they begot. And soon there was a sense of injustice and resentment rising with that rise of wealth and leisure and authority and ownership upon their own dark shoulders.

Soon there were those who felt the unconquerable tide of hatred well-ing up within them, in the awareness of their exclusion from all but the smallest benefits and simplest joys of all the well-being that their hands and their heads and their hearts were helping to bring into life.

And soon there were those who fled from their owners, taking their hatred with them, taking their hatred along with their chains.

Many of the slaves who fled found freedom among the Indians who welcomed them and gave them soil of their own to till and women to wed and a place in the tribe: a place in the shade out of the sun.

Toiling and singing and loving beside the folk of the land, the slaves became peasants and craftsmen free to rest and to laugh as they liked when their work was done. They became husbands and lovers, and fathers of new red folk unafraid of the sun's blaze on their long and sinewy frames. And they became teachers:

Teachers of the skills they had brought from Africa and the newer skills they had learned or invented. Masters of a new music shaking the earth with the force they found and conjured from the calabash gourd and the long-necked drum. They became authorities in new medicine and new faith filling the air of the two continents with the voice and rumble of their African gods. They became respected carriers of wisdom and craft. They became men.

But many of the slaves who fled from their owners found only death in the wastes of the barren shores, in the desert, in the poisonous jungle among its beasts and insects, its giant snakes and hypnotic alligators. Others found death in the alien cold of the high plateaus and the mountain wilds.

And others who fled found a short-lived freedom that was worse than any alligator or any wind with teeth of ice:

With respect to the dogs, their general mode of rearing was latterly in the following manner:

From the time of their being taken from the dam, they were confined in a sort of kennel, or cage, where they were but sparingly fed upon small quantities of the blood of different animals. As they approached maturity, their keepers procured a figure, roughly formed as a Negro, in wicker work—in the body of which were contained the blood and entrails of beasts. This was exhibited before an upper part of the cage, and the

Marcus Rainsford: Of Dogs Trained to Hunt Men

food occasionally exposed as a temptation, which attracted the attention of the dogs to it as a source of the food they wanted.

This was repeated often, so that the animals with redoubled ferocity struggled against their confinement, while in proportion to their impatience the figure was brought nearer, though yet out of their reach, and their food decreased—till, at the last extremity of desperation, the keeper resigned the figure, well charged with the nauseous food before described, to their wishes. While they gorged themselves with the dreadful meat, he and his colleagues caressed and encouraged them.

By these means the whites ingratiated themselves so much with the animals as to produce an effect directly opposite to that perceivable in them towards the black figure; and, when they were employed in the pursuit for which they were intended, afforded the protection so necessary to their employers.

As soon as they were considered initiated into their business, the young dogs were taken out to be exercised in it, and trained with as much exactness as possible. In some instances this extended to a great length, but in general their discipline could not permanently retain them under the command of their leaders. The consequence is obvious.

The common use of them in the Spanish islands was in chase of runaway Negroes in the mountains. When once they got scent of the object, they immediately hunted him down—unless he could evade the pursuit by climbing up a tree—and instantly devoured him. If he was so fortunate as to get from their reach into a tree, the dogs remained about it yelping in the most dreadful manner, till their keepers arrived.

If the victim was to be preserved for a public execution of cruelty, the dogs were then muzzled and the prisoner loaded with chains. On his neck was placed a hoop with inverted spikes, and hooks outward, for the purpose of entangling him in the bushes or elsewhere. Should the unhappy wretch proceed faster than his wearied pursuers, or attempt to run from them, he was given up to the dogs, who instantly devoured him (with horrid delight the hunters sometimes preserved the head to expose at their homes as monuments of their barbarous prowess).

Frequently, on a journey of any length, these causes were, it is much feared, feigned for the purpose of relieving the keepers of their prisoners. And the inhuman wretch who perpetrated the act, on his oath of having destroyed his fellow creature, received the reward of ten dollars from the colony.

BEHIND THE MARGINS

Of the slaves who fled by the thousands, not all found life among the Indians or an end in the wilderness or death in the trained jaws of the masters' hounds. There were those who fled to find a new life and a very new freedom among themselves.

On the islands of Cuba and Jamaica, and on scores of smaller isles over the Caribbean, behind the margins of the southern coasts of Mexico, in the backlands of Brazil, on the mainland back of Cartagena, and in the interior of the Panama isthmus, the fugitive slaves founded their own settlements:

Building their own villages, erecting their own towns. Setting up their own councils and choosing their own chiefs for peace as well as war. Establishing their own lives, selecting their friends from among the foes of the enemy master, wherever they found them and whatever their color—even the hated white.

They had many names. But the best known and the most dreaded among the masters were the names they were known by everywhere in the Caribbean and the lands bordering on it:

Maroon! Cimarron!

By the Negroes in these frigates we were informed of the state of the town, and of a report that certain soldiers were daily expected from the governor of Panama for the defence of the town against the Cimarrons —a black people who fled from the Spaniards, their masters, by reason of their cruelty, and since grown into two kingdoms: the one to the east, the other to the west, of the way from Nombre de Dios to Panama. Our captain set those Negroes ashore, that they might join themselves to their countrymen, the Cimarrons, or at least that he might prevent their going to alarm the town with news of his arrival. . . . The Cimarrons, during our absence, ranged up and down the country to learn what they could for us. Now they bring us news that the fleet has arrived at Nombre de Dios. . . .

Cimarrons and Maroons: the Revenge of the Tortured

They have each two sorts of arrows—the one to defend himself and offend the enemy, the other to kill his victual. Those for fighting with are somewhat like the Scottish arrows, only somewhat longer and headed with iron, wood, or fish bones. But the arrows for provision are of three sorts: the first serveth to kill any great beast near hand, and hath an iron head of a pound and a half shaped like the head of a javelin, as sharp as a knife; the second for lesser beasts, and hath a head of three quarters of a pound; the third for all manner of birds, and hath a head of an ounce weight. These heads, though of iron, yet keep their edge long. For these and such uses iron is of more value here than gold—and he that can temper it well is most esteemed. . . .

The third day of our journey they brought us to a town of their own, situated upon the side of a hill near a river, encompassed with a dike eight foot broad, and a thick mud wall ten foot high. It had one long and broad street from the east to west, and two cross streets narrower. There were in it fifty or sixty households, which were so cleanly, that not only the houses but streets were pleasant. Their apparel is somewhat after the Spanish fashion. This town is distant from Nombre de Dios thirty-five leagues, and forty-five from Panama. It is sufficiently stored with beasts, fowls, and several fruits. . . .

They keep a continual watch in four parts within three miles of the town, for fear of the Spaniards—who sometimes by the conduct of some Cimarron captives . . . have come in upon them. We stayed there all night, during which time they related to us several broils betwixt them and the Spaniards. Particularly one:

A gentleman entertained by the governor of the country undertook last year with one hundred and fifty soldiers to put them, young and old, to the sword. Being conducted by one of them that had been taken prisoner, he surprised it half an hour before day, whereby many of the men escaped, but many women and children were killed.

But the same morning, by sun rising . . . the Cimarrons assembled themselves and behaved in such sort that they drove the Spaniards to such extremity that, partly by the disadvantage of the woods—having lost their guide—and partly by famine, not above thirty of them returned.

Their king dwelt in a city sixteen leagues southeast of Panama, wherein are supposed to be seventeen hundred fighting men.

NO EXIT

In the careful calculations of the Spanish and Portuguese masters, the slave from Africa was worth four times the enslaved Indian. This was not only because the Negro could knowingly perform four times as much work—but also because he could, though quite unwillingly, take four times as many beatings, four times as much torture, four times the score of frustration and hatred vented by the masters on the Indian and his vulnerable sensitivity to shame. But from the beginning, the Negro resisted.

Protecting his own vulnerable sense of outrage behind his intricate shield of indifference, the Negro resisted the old condition of his slavery surrounding him in a new life of abundance. He resisted the extension of the masters' ease—an ease without precedent that he knew to be primarily the product of his effort, of his enormous energy expended through the weeks and months, through the long crippling years.

He resisted by fleeing from his owners and building a braver life among his own fugitive kind. But most of all he resisted, hour to hour and minute to minute, while remaining under his master. He resisted even under the lash, under the other instruments of punishment, and under the torture. He resisted by pretending he felt no pain, or pretending the pain was unbearable. Pretending—whatever the punishment, whatever the pain. Pretending, and thus compelling the master to share the burden of shame. And he resisted by continuing to take his own ease at forbidden moments, by withholding his precious flow of energy, by mocking the masters and their ways of lust and indolence. He resisted from the very beginning, under the very first masters:

On the island of Hispaniola that was Haiti that was San or Santo Domingo, the Negro slaves resisted—watching the fear grow in the eyes of the master, watching the growing number of black slaves before him and of free blacks behind him in the slowly swelling margins held by the fearless maroons. The Negro slaves in front, and the cimarrons behind, watching the fear in the master's face turning its whiteness pale, making his limbs immobile. Watching him with his own shackles forged about him, with his own gates shut on himself:

There being among the Spaniards some who are not only cruel but very cruel, when a man occasionally wished to punish a slave—either for some crime that he had committed, or for not having done a good day's work, or for spite that he had towards him, or for not having extracted the

usual quantity of silver or gold from the mine—when he came home at
night, instead of giving him supper, he made
Benzoni's Chronicle: The Self- him undress, if he happened to have a shirt on.
defeat of a Policy of Oppression And being thrown down on the ground, he had
his hands and feet tied to a piece of wood laid across, so permitted under the rule called by the Spaniards the Law of Bayona—a law suggested,
I think, by some great demon.

Then with a thong or rope he was beaten until his body streamed with
blood. Which done, they took a pound of pitch or a pipkin of boiling oil
and threw it gradually all over the unfortunate victim. Then he was
washed with some of the country pepper mixed with salt and water.

He was thus left on a plank covered over with a cloth, until the master thought he was again able to work. Others dug a hole in the ground
and put the man in upright, leaving only his head out, and left him in
it all night—the Spaniards saying that they have recourse to this cure
because the earth absorbs the blood and preserves the flesh from forming any wound, so they get well sooner.

And if any die—which sometimes happens—through great pain, there
is no heavier punishment by law than that the master shall pay another
slave to the king.

Thus, on account of these very great cruelties in the beginning, some
of them escaped from their masters, and wandered about the island in a
state of desperation. They have gradually multiplied, however, to such
a degree that they have caused, and still cause, the Spanish population a
deal of trouble. . . .

When the Spaniards quarrel, the blacks make common cause among
themselves. Yet each nation recognizes its own king or governor, which
keeps the tribes separate—and from this cause they do not do the harm
to the Spaniards that they might if they were all united.

The presidents and auditors of the island, finally seeing that these
blacks multiplied and that all the Spaniards who fell into their hands
were made to die under every sort of torment, began to collect men together and send them into all parts of the island where the Negroes hid
themselves.

At first it turned out very favorable to the Spaniards. For, taking with
them some blacks—under promise of liberty—who knew the localities,
they used to attack them in the night. And finding the people asleep,
like a herd of animals without any fear of enemies, they captured and
killed a great many of them.

But in the sequel the runaways learned to keep watch and to be very vigilant, whereby the Spaniards often got the worst of it. Thus the blacks have now become so fierce and so numerous that when I was residing in the island, it was asserted that there were upwards of seven thousand.

And in the year 1545, while I was residing there, it was reported that the Cimarrones—for so the Spaniards in those countries called the outlaws—had joined in a general rebellion, were scouring over every part of the island, and doing all the mischief they could.

Whereupon the Admiral, Don Luis Columbus, the presidente and the auditors of San Domingo, sent some messengers to entreat and supplicate them to be content to live peaceably, for the Spaniards would do the same and would not annoy them any more—for they wished to be friends. And if they wanted priests or monks to instruct them in the Christian doctrine, they would willingly send some.

To these offers the answer was that they believed in the doctrine of Christ and wished for it, but would not accept of Spanish friendship— for they did not trust in their promises.

Many Spaniards prophesy for certain that the island in a short time will fall entirely into the hands of these blacks. Meanwhile the governors are very vigilant, when a ship sails for any other province, in preventing any Spaniards from embarking without permission, even if he be a merchant. . . .

When the licentiate, Ceratto, presidente of the island, brought liberty to the Indians, he allowed everybody to go where they chose. For which, being severely reproved by some citizens, he angrily answered:

"Since his Majesty the Emperor has given liberty to the Indians, it does not seem to me just that the Spaniards should—against his Majesty's will—be kept in slavery. Therefore, I only fulfill his royal will, and think it right to let them go freely where they like."

But when he learnt how thinly inhabited the island was becoming, and there being so few Spaniards that, at the most, they did not exceed eleven hundred men, while outlaws were becoming daily stronger— wherefore if an attack took place there were not Spaniards enough to defend themselves, so that there was danger of losing the island as well as their lives—he also was obliged to have recourse to restrictions and to shut the gates.

The gates were shut on the whole colonial empire of the Spanish and the Portuguese even in its beginnings. Not only the gates of freedom for master as well as slave—but also the gates of opportunity on which nature had set no limits. The gates of the two empires led into a colonial storehouse that could feed and enrich all the peoples of Europe and all the conquered and unconquered Indians and all the Negro slaves in all their towering strength and skill. But the gates were shut.

Fear of the slaves was only one of the fears that caused the masters to shut the gates. There were other fears among them that were equally great and even greater:

There was fear of the many surviving Indians—most of them hostile, many of them fierce. There was the ever-present fear of being betrayed by their own fellows envying them their slaves and their other wealth. There was the fear of interference from the powers at home: from the crown, from the church, from their host of officials and their faithful servants everywhere. And among the masters, but mostly among the powers at home and their authorities in the colonies, there was the constant and permanent fear of the envious nations coveting the wealth of the Spanish and the Portuguese empires. There was fear of the long arms of their rivals reaching out to steal the prize of the treasure they had won: fear of France and of Holland, fear of the English and their flair for trade.

Above all, there was the sleep-robbing fear that their miracle empires with all their riches from which power and plenty and glory and glorious ease flowed into their lives might vanish overnight. So that they snatched at every conceivable means they could find to gather the riches while they lasted, caring not whether the means they employed were intelligent or stupid, cruel or kind, diligent and efficient, or of waste beyond belief.

But the source of the riches they feared would slip from their grasp, leaving no trace behind it, was greater, far greater, than their own vision. In spite of the masters, in spite of the powers at home and the multiplying numbers of their agents and officials in the colonies, in spite of all their fears, the colonial wealth and the trade that followed its magical appearance burst in a shower without end over the whole fertile body of the land, scattering new riches over the opening soil and along the new roads and byways of the two gold and emerald continents of the whole land:

Bringing her new wealth of metal and gem, of wool and grain of the

highlands, of precious plants of the tropics. Dotting her busying mountains and shores with new towns become cities, become markets for
goods from across both oceans. Moving the goods from north and south,
eastward and back, by man and by burro, by ox-cart, by boat, on the
backs of horses from Iberia and on llamas of Peru. Down her zigzagging
trails, through her untrod wilds, across her pampas and plains. Carrying
the goods, transporting the utensils bought at the fair.

But mostly sending the treasure abroad, shipping the produce over the
sea, taking the commerce, the jewels, the gold and the grain far away
from the bountiful land, green and ripening where she lay.

Seven

TREASURE

Sweating and strong,
we shall go down to the bowels of the earth
to wrest new conquest

REGINO PEDROSO

GLASS BEADS

Trade was the goad that brought the empires searching westward for the gold and goods and spice of the well-worn ways of trade in the ancient East. Trade was the goad and treasure was the goal that brought them to the half-awakened land of the west. Treasure to enrich the homelands was the goal that brought the conquerors from Portugal and the conquistadors from Spain:

Treasure for the homelands hungering, as all Europe hungered, for spice for their drab dishes, for logwood for their rising towns, for dyewood for their plain clothes, for drugs for their ailing bodies, for old and new food and drink for their bodies young and old—for silver and gold and jewels to buy the health along with the wealth.

The pattern and purpose of the empires' commerce, multiplying through all the new discovered marts of their world growing big with commodities known and others whose existence had never been dreamed of, also served to open the eyes of the folk of the lands that had scarcely begun to know the meaning of barter and trade. The old world's hunger for new treasure, for old treasure, for treasure of all kinds, and for the trade that could germinate ever greater wealth from the treasures acquired, also became the new world's teacher as well as taskmaster from the beginning:

From the very first days, from the hands of Columbus, the Admiral of the Ocean Sea himself, on his own first voyage, the folk of the lands destined to become colonies of varying importance and, most important, of varying wealth, received the first lesson in the empires' intricate practice and simple procedure of—trading:

While in search of good water, we came to a village about half a league from our anchorage. The people, as soon as they heard us, all fled and left their houses, hiding their property in the wood. I would not allow a thing to be touched, even the value of a pin. Presently some men among them came to us, and one came quite close. I gave him some bells and glass beads, which made him very content and happy. That our friendship might be further increased, I resolved to ask him for something: I requested him to get some water. After I had gone on board, the natives came to the beach with calabashes full of water. . . . I ordered another string of glass beads to be presented to them. . . .

The Journal of Columbus: Trade with the Natives

All last night and today I was here, waiting to see if the king or other person would bring gold or anything of value. Many of these people came, like those of the other islands, equally naked, and equally painted: some white, some red, some black, and others in many ways. They brought darts and skeins of cotton to barter, which they exchanged with the sailors for bits of glass, broken crockery, and pieces of earthenware.

Some of them had pieces of gold fastened in their noses—which they willingly gave for a hawk's bell and glass beads. . . .

Yesterday at night the two men came back who had been sent to explore the interior. They said that after walking twelve leagues they came to a village of fifty houses, where there were a thousand inhabitants, for many live in one house. . . . They said that they were received with great solemnity, according to custom, and all—both men and women—came out to see them. They were lodged in the best houses, and the people touched them, kissing their hands and feet. . . .

There were great quantities of cotton gathered, spun, and worked up. In a single house they saw more than 500 arrobas [12,500 pounds] and as much as 4,000 quintals [400,000 pounds] could be yielded every year. It did not appear to be cultivated, and it bore all the year round. It is very fine, and has a large boll.

All that was possessed by these people, they gave at a very low price, and a great bundle of cotton was exchanged for the point of a needle or other trifle.

THE FAIR AT PORTO BELLO

Above all other riches, above and far beyond all other wealth—from the initial landfalls in the Caribbean, and even before the prize rewards that waited for them in Mexico and Peru were known—the treasure sought by the two Iberian empires expanding through the new land was the treasure of gold.

This was true of Portugal and truer of Spain—which had been granted most of the domains holding most of the gold and the silver.

From the earliest days of the conquest, Spain's conquering men of empire hungered for the element they felt could cure all of their ills of body and spirit. They hungered for gold, and their appetites knew no end. By day and by night, in every season and any weather, wherever they moved, from the strong or the sick or even the dying they demanded the gold that was already there, already shaped into ornaments, as well as the gold that was being mined. They demanded and got the gold along with the people to mine it.

Among the first seekers of gold to find it was Vasco Núñez de Balboa, who later found the Pacific and still later lost his head at the orders of his own scheming father-in-law who was made governor of the rich lands of the Isthmus which Balboa had found. Balboa chanced upon the Pacific, which led to the fabulous East—but his concern, his frantic search, was for the tangible and immediate gold that he, like all the other conquerors and explorers, knew to be the key to all the trade of the world:

Trade was the goad, and treasure the goal.

But the keys to both, the keys to empire, bursting the old bonds of scarcity everywhere, were the metals of permanent luster, the coveted metals of currency. The key was gold. The key was silver.

As the conquering empires lengthened their hold on the new lands becoming colonies, the production of commodities both old and hitherto unseen reached an intensity and multiplicity never known before. Stretching their hold farther over the land—over its hidden energies and over the visible, audible energies of its red and black people—the empires rose:

Upward with the shafts lifting from mines old and new, upward with the old-world wheat vertical over the first-ploughed, fresh-furrowed earth of the west. Upward the empires rose with the towns and the cities of wood and stone rising over the thatched huts over the folk of the land. Upward for three hundred years.

From the roots of the virgin world of the west, the settlers and the slaves tore the shining wealth. Most of it went over the sea to Spain, to Portugal, to all of Europe—by legal and all other means—growing fat and sleek upon it. Yet by the grace, and the considerable profit derived therefrom, of those privileged few who were authorized to serve as trading agents from the old world, a portion of the colonial wealth was also distributed in the colonies themselves.

There was the treasure, at long last: the colonial treasure from all the conquered lands. There was the treasure, won and waiting to be taken. And there were the trading ships: the intrepid galleons from the old world across the sea. Wherever the galleons called—at the few but stipulated points, at the yearly intervals—there was a rendezvous of vital concern to the fast-growing wealth and commerce of both the old world and the new. Such an event was the fair at Porto Bello on the Panama isthmus where only the two great oceans met during most of the year:

The town of Porto Bello, so thinly inhabited by reason of its noxious air, the scarcity of provisions, and the barrenness of its soil, becomes, at the time of the galleons, one of the most populous places in all South America. Its situation on the isthmus betwixt the south and north sea, the goodness of its harbor, and its small distance from Panama, have given it the preference for the rendezvous of *Ulloa and Santacilia: South* the joint commerce of Spain and Peru, at its *American Commerce* fair. On advice being received at Cartagena that the Peru fleet had unloaded at Panama, the galleons make the best of their way to Porto Bello, in order to avoid the distempers which have their source from idleness. The concourse of people on this occasion is such as to raise the rent of lodging to an excessive degree: a middling chamber, with a closet, lets—during the fair—for a thousand crowns, and some large houses for four, five, or six thousand.

The ships are no sooner moored in the harbor, than the first work is to erect in the square a tent made of the ship's sails, for receiving its cargo, at which the proprietors of the goods are present, in order to find their bales by the marks which distinguish them. These bales are drawn on sledges to their respective places by the crew of every ship, and the money given them is proportionally divided.

Whilst the seamen and European traders are thus employed, the land is covered with droves of mules from Panama, each drove consisting of above an hundred, loaded with chests of gold and silver, on account of the merchants of Peru. Some unload them at the exchange, others in the middle of the square. Yet, amidst the hurry and confusion of such crowds, no theft, loss, or disturbance is ever known.

He who has seen this place during the *tiempo muerto*, or dead time . . . must be filled with astonishment at the sudden change: to see the bustling multitudes, every house crowded, the square and streets encumbered with bales and chests of gold and silver of all kinds; the harbor full of ships and vessels—some bringing by the way of Rio de Chape the goods of Peru, as cacao, quinquina or jesuits' bark, vicuña wool and bezoar stones; others coming from Cartagena loaded with provisions. And thus a spot at all other times detested for its deleterious qualities becomes the staple of the riches of the old and new world, and the scene of one of the most considerable branches of commerce in the whole earth.

The ships being unloaded, and the merchants of Peru together with the *presidente* of Panama arrived, the fair comes under deliberation. And for this purpose the deputies of the several parties repair on board the commodore of the galleons, where, in presence of the commodore, and the *presidente* of Panama—the former as patron of the Europeans, and the latter of the Peruvians—the prices of the several kinds of merchandise are settled. And all preliminaries being adjusted in three or four meetings, the contracts are signed and made public, that everyone may conform himself to them in the sale of his effects. Thus all fraud is precluded. The purchases and sales, as likewise the exchanges of money, are transacted by brokers, both from Spain and Peru.

After this, everyone begins to dispose of his goods—the Spanish brokers embarking their chests of money, and those of Peru sending away the goods they have purchased, in vessels called *chatas* and *bongos*, up the River Chagres.

WHOSE NAME WAS LEGEND

Up the River Chagres and down the River Chape, down the Pacific and up the Caribbean. From Valparaiso in Chile across the Andes to Buenos Aires. From Buenos Aires fifteen hundred miles through the old heart of the continent up to the new silver mines, the new heart of the new cities in upper Peru. Up to the ports of Mexico from the ports of Peru, from the ports of the opening Plate. Up and down the two continents, into the new towns of the new world, into the old ports as well as the new of all the new-world colonies of Spain and Portugal—

Trade and commerce began to flow. And it flowed for three hundred years. It flowed from the early sixteenth to the early nineteenth century of Our Lord—from the start to the end of the long colonial years, the colonial trade went on:

But there was nothing easy or smooth about the way the commerce went by galleon or canoe, by mule-train or on the backs of slaves and Indians. There was little that the tempests and the rapids and the waterfalls did to make the flowing of the trade and commerce easy. There was little that the high cordilleras or the rocks and precipices and multiplying stretches of barren plain and cold plateau did to make the going smooth.

And there was even less that the crown and officialdom back in the homelands did to make trade in the colonies move as it might have moved if the weight of customs duties and taxes and other restrictions had been less of the leaden burden it was from the start.

There was the fair at Porto Bello in Panama, the fair at Cartagena in what would be Colombia, the fairs in Peru, the fairs at Vera Cruz and Acapulco in Mexico. And there were other fairs farther from those points where the galleons touched. But during most of the year, there were only the stagnant days, the atrophying weeks, the months of paralysis. During most of the year there was the time which the struggling merchants and all the other settlers in the colonies—growing slowly, yet still striving to survive—knew as the dead time.

When the galleons came, there were the European clothes and the countless other artisan-made luxuries now becoming necessities. There were the finished things from the old world to be traded mainly for the gold and the silver and gems of the new.

When the galleons had gone, there were the few things left in the shops and the warehouses to be traded for grain and other produce of the land. And when there was nothing else to buy or sell, there were always the slaves—there was always work that had to be done.

The work of mining the gold and silver went on throughout the year. Fair or no fair, galleon or no galleon, the job of mining the silver and gold continued through the rainy season and the dry. From this activity more and greater wealth arose, new towns sprang up. And new groups of prosperous people came into power all over the colonies—especially around the cities that had come into being almost overnight, clustering themselves around the booming silver mines of Mexico and Peru.

Of all of these, the most famous by far was the city in upper Peru that rose on the steep sides of the mountain of silver whose name was legend over the old world and over the new. The city where those who were free became owners of mines, became millionaires in a matter of months. The nugget of the Andes:

The city of Potosí!

The azogueros, or proprietors of mines, receive liberal advances from the government to enable them to carry on their works. These advances are $25,000 for every ingenio, or amalgamation work, which each azoguero shall establish, and some have two or three. This money is lent on the condition that the government receive one shilling on every ounce of silver produced by the azoguero. This class of *A Letter from Don Vicente Pazos, about Potosí, the City of Silver* men, whose capital is thus liberally augmented, have greatly increased the business, and added to the embellishments of the city. They live in the most profuse and princely style: it is not uncommon for them to possess gold plate, such as plates, goblets, spoons, forks, etc. They employ great numbers of clerks, and have numerous attendants.

This city is much frequented by strangers from different parts of the country; it is a place of great gayety and dissipation. There are no theatres, and the principal amusement for all classes is gambling; and faro-banks and billiard tables are scattered all over the city. The city is immensely rich in gold and silver; money is within the reach of everybody, and very abundant, as may be supposed, when more than $10,000 are coined every day, the year round.

The azogueros are extremely profuse in their expenditures, squandering their enormous wealth with the same liberal hand with which it is poured into their lap. As the source of their wealth is in their inexhaustible mines, and if poor today they may be rich tomorrow, their habits become essentially different from those of the merchant or manufacturer whose profits depend upon calculation and economy.

The manufactures of this city are in a wretched state, being confined principally to the making of leather, hats, and tools from imported steel, which is sold at an enormous price. The leather is made from goat-skins, which are of superior quality and very abundant here. Gold leaf is also manufactured in great quantities. This article is much used in the churches, and the candles even are gilded before they are lighted. And in the private houses of the rich, the leaves of the flowers which they have in great abundance in their drawing rooms, are often gilded with gold leaf.

There are no carriages in this city, and when the ladies take the air, it is on the backs of horses or mules, or in sedan chairs, which are very common. There are persons here whose profession it is to teach the mules and horses to travel with an easy gait, for the ladies. There is another mode of travelling which is curious: a chair is fixed on poles which are laid across the backs of two mules, and in which two or three persons frequently ride.

The Countess of Casa Real, a few years ago, attempted to introduce coaches into the city, but the first time her carriage was driven into the street, it was fairly run away with by the mules, and dashed to pieces against a church. This city is situated on the side of the lower part of the mountain, in the valley at the foot of it, and is altogether too steep and irregular to admit of wheel carriages.

In the other part of the town, called Ingenios, which lies northwest of the city, in the valley, are the mills or amalgamation works of the miners. The population of this part consists of Indians, kaachas or cholo miners, and other workmen, and amounts to about six thousand souls.

The Indians of the mita—which is a kind of annual conscription by which the Indians of several provinces in Upper and Lower Peru are obliged to work in the mines—present a most miserable and shocking appearance. They are employed in the hardest labor of the mines, such as stamping the ores, raising them from the mines, and attending to the trituration—which is done by the mills, and by which they are continually exposed to inhale the deleterious powders of the minerals. The price of their labor is fifty cents per day, and although experience shows that their labor is not useful as they are unfit for mining—and those mines are invariably worked the best in which the Indians of the *mita* are not employed—yet the infamous avarice of the mine-owners dooms them to these noxious employments . . .

The poor Indians are obliged to sleep in the open, cold air, on the bare ground. And from their exposure, the noxious inhalation of the mineral dust, and the hardships of their servitude, at least one third of every conscription die.

THE GRAND SCHEDULE

Spain's territories in the new world were famous for their riches almost from the beginning. Then little by little the old world also became aware that the trade waiting in the immense land of Brazil, held by Portugal, might gradually prove as profitable as that of Peru—and even more.

Even before the sensational discoveries of gold and of diamonds in Brazil, and in spite of the severe restrictions on immigration imposed by both Iberian empires to protect their conquests and, above all, their commerce—the colony of Brazil began to draw seekers of fortune from all over Europe:

Men from France and Holland, from the Italian nations, and even from England—Spain's most deadly rival—commenced to move into the "Indies of the West," owned and operated by Lisbon and Madrid. They were only a trickle at first, these new fortune-hunters, and most of them came surreptitiously.

By means of their slowly evolving trade and their accumulating commerce, the colonies were becoming a meeting-ground as well as a market for the world. Moreover, many of the finished cloths and other products brought from Cadiz and from Lisbon came, not from the Iberian countries where the making and the manufacturing of commodities by hand and by mechanical device were late in getting started because of the long Moorish domination. Most of the goods brought from the Spanish and the Portuguese ports came, in fact, from the countries of Europe where the skills and the crafts were more highly developed:

From France, from Holland, from England, where the workmen of skill could turn out the multitude of things needed for living and things needed for leisure—the capes of velvet along with the iron nails. So that the colonies were actually becoming a meeting-ground and a market for all of Europe.

And before long, when Spain and Portugal had taken possession of certain territories in the East—Spain in the Philippines, Spain on Guam, and Portugal in the East Indies and on tiny Goa off India itself—then the Iberian colonies in the hemisphere of the west became a mart for the whole world. By means of the traffic to the Pacific ports of Mexico and Peru, the new-world colonies of Spain and Portugal became the meeting-place for Europe and Africa—which kept providing the slaves—and the Asiatic kingdoms whose gold and silk and spice had drawn the Admiral to these western lands.

To the trading-ships from Europe, to the flotilla from Peru, was added a new messenger of spiralling wealth and spanning commerce, bringing still another world and its treasure to the western shores of the western lands: the galleon from the East bringing Cipango, bringing Cathay to the world whose discovery they inspired!

The galleon from Manila: bound for New Spain, for Mexico. Bound for Acapulco!

But it was becoming clearer all the time that the French, the Dutch, and especially the British were getting more of the natural wealth of the Iberian colonies, were selling more of their finished products to those same colonies—sometimes by fair means, but mostly by way of smuggling on a vast scale—than the two empire-owners themselves. That was the reality:

Spain in particular was gathering the New World's wealth and scattering it over the whole earth with a hand that was careless rather than generous. The Spanish crown sought, time and time again, to curb the carelessness, to organize the trade and make the commerce lawful. For three hundred years and more—throughout the colonial times—the crown of Spain sought, sporadically and with little success, to bring some order out of the frequent chaos, some national profit out of the private greed and corruption that muddied the flow of the empire's wealth over the world. And the symbol of all those grand but often futile efforts were the ships that were known in every port of the profiting world:

The ships that carried the treasures to and fro, the ships that served as convoys to protect the riches from pirates outfitted by the great rival nations of Europe, the special ships that were supposed to eliminate the deadly curse of smuggling from the rich but slowly dying economy of Spain—these were the symbol of elaborate effort doomed to perish, like the trapped scorpion, by the poison it carried in its own body. The ships from Spain, once the symbols of glorious empire that rode on their sails and their westward-pointed bows, became the symbols of wasting wealth:

The ships that had once stretched the sea-lanes of the world—the grand ships of Spain sailing now on their grand schedule:

The lawful commerce between Europe and Spanish America is entirely in the hands of the Spaniards, and absolutely subject to the direction of the Crown. . . . We shall speak of the galleons, the *flota*, the *flotilla*, register-ships . . . . A galleon is, properly speaking, a very large man-of-war, of three or four decks, built in a manner now altogether out of fashion, except in Spain. And the reason why it *An English Merchant Looks* is still used there is that it affords a great deal *upon Spanish Colonial Trade* of room for merchandise—with which the king's ships are generally so much crowded as to be in no condition of defending themselves.

That fleet which we call the galleons consists of eight such men-of-war. Of these, there are three very large ones . . . two others which are less . . . each of fifty guns, and an advice frigate of forty. The merchant-men which sail with this fleet, and purchase their licences at a very high rate, are in number from twelve to sixteen, and in size at least a third part bigger than is expressed in their respective schedules. These ships are intended to carry all that is necessary, either of warlike stores, or merchandise for Peru—and this is the specific difference between this fleet and the *flota*, which is intended for Mexico.

In time of peace, the galleons sail regularly once a year from Cadiz, at no set time, but according to the king's pleasure and the convenience of the merchants. From Cadiz the galleons steer directly for the Canaries where, if the *flota* sails with them—as it sometimes does—they anchor together in the haven of Gomera. Thence they bear away for the Antilles, and when they arrive at that height, the *flota* separates, and the galleons bear away for Cartagena.

As soon as they double Cape de la Vela, and appear before the mouth of Rio de la Hacha, advice is sent to all parts, that everything may be got ready for their reception. In the harbor of Cartagena they remain a month, and land there all the goods designed for the Audiencia of Terra Firma. Then they sail to Porto Bello, where they continue during the Fair which lasts five or six weeks; and having landed the merchandise intended for Peru, and received the treasure and rich commodities sent from thence on board, they sail again to Cartagena, where they remain till they return to Spain—which is usually within the space of two years.

When they have orders to return, they sail first to Havana, and having there joined the *flota* and what other ships are returning to Europe, they steer through the Gulf of Florida, and so to the height of Carolina where, meeting with the western winds, they shape their course then for the Azores. They take in fresh water and provisions at Terçeira, and thence continue their voyage to Cadiz.

The *flota* consists, as well as the galleons, of a certain number of men-of-war, and of a certain number of merchant ships. The former are seldom more than three. . . . The latter are usually about sixteen, in size between five hundred and a thousand tons.

This fleet sails about the month of August, that by the favor of the winds which reign about November they may the more easily pursue their voyage to Vera Cruz. In their passage they call at Puerto Rico, to take in fresh water and provisions, then pass in sight of Hispaniola, Jamaica, and Cuba; and—according to the season of the year and the nature of the winds—pass either by the coast of Yucatan or higher through the Gulf to Vera Cruz, which lies at the bottom of it.

The run of this fleet, according to the course we have mentioned, hath been thus computed. From Cadiz to the Canaries, two hundred and fifty leagues, in about ten days; to the Antilles eight hundred leagues in twenty days; to the most western point of the isle of Cuba, five hundred leagues in twenty days; to Vera Cruz, two hundred and sixty leagues in twelve days or thereabouts. In all, eighteen hundred and ten leagues in about sixty-two days.

As the *flota* is designed to furnish not only Mexico but the Philippine Islands also—as we have before remarked in speaking of the trade of Acapulco—with European goods, they are obliged to remain there for a considerable space. And when it is necessary, they winter in that port. The cargo with which they return is not so rich as that of the galleons. . . .

It is usually in the month of May that the *flota* leaves Vera Cruz, though sometimes it is detained in that harbor till August. Then the ships that compose it sail for Havana—for though the galleons and the flota seldom leave Spain together, yet they generally return together.

As soon as they are safely arrived in Havana, they detach a few of the lightest and cleanest ships to Europe, who, besides money and merchandise, carry also an exact account of the contents both of the galleons and flota. These ships are called by the Spaniards, with propriety enough, the flotilla—that is, the "little fleet." The principal reason of sending them in this manner into Spain, is to give the Court of Madrid an opportunity of judging what convoy may be necessary, in case of any alteration of affairs, to be sent to escort the Grand Fleet, as also to regulate the tax which may be levied on the merchants in proportion to their interest in the galleons and flota. . . .

What obliges this great fleet to remain so long at Havana? . . . Two causes may be assigned: namely, waiting for a wind, or for the register-ships which they are to convoy home.

A register-ship is so called from its being registered with all the effects embarked in Spain, in the books kept for that purpose in the Chamber of Seville. . . . A company of merchants having, as they conceive, just grounds to imagine that European goods are greatly wanted at some particular ports in the Indies, they draw up a memorial or petition containing these reasons in the clearest and concisest terms, and lay it before the Council of the Indies.

The prayer of this petition is, that they may have leave to send a ship of three hundred tons . . . or under to the port they mention. When leave is obtained, they pay a certain sum to the Crown, which is generally between thirty and fifty thousand pieces-of-eight, besides presents —and those no small ones—to the king's officers, from the greatest to the least. That this, however, may not induce any suspicion of fraud, they register their ship and cargo, that it may appear consistent with their petition and licence. And yet—such a fatality there attends on all Customhouse cautions—this ship of under three hundred tons generally carries upwards of six hundred tons of goods, and affords accommodation for passengers besides.

Copies from the register are transmitted to the governor and royal officers at the port to which the register-ship is bound. And such is their diligence, such their integrity, that when the ship comes to an anchor in the port, they make a very narrow inquiry. And yet there is seldom or never any fraud discovered—but, on the contrary, this ship of six or seven hundred tons returns into Europe with an authentic certificate from all the King of Spain's officers, that she does not carry quite three hundred, together with a bill of lading in the same strain of computation. By these register-ships there is sometimes a gain of two or three hundred percent, which enables the owners to pay so bountifully for cheating the king, having first got the money by robbing his subjects.

Behind the grand schedules and the elaborate regulations there was the reality of the graft and corruption from within menacing the very life of the two great empires, undermining the power of Spain and the sway of Portugal, challenging their hold on their great domains in the west. And there was the menace equally grave, and growing graver by the year, of the other powers of Europe extending their wealth and their influence to the very gates—and at times even within the gates—of the Portuguese and Spanish colonies in the new hemisphere. There was the threatening reality within, and there was the graver threat without:

The Pilgrims and the Puritans and other people from England began to settle the northern coasts of the hemisphere. To the north, to the same northern continent, went the Huguenots and the other French, and the Hollanders, and also the Swedes. Planting their own flags on the northern continent, and upon islands in the Caribbean, and even upon the north shores of the America of the south. Bringing their own ships and settlers with firearms and tools, moving into the interiors northward and westward—and southward, to the gates of the Spanish dominions and the Portuguese domain in the new American world.

By 1626 when the first Hollanders set their feet on new Dutch soil called New Amsterdam that would one day be known as New York, there was already a settlement in New England, there were already colonies established by the French. And by this time the Spanish and Portuguese territories were populous colonies with well-defined borders and thriving cities. They were colonies of wealth and achievement and fame—whose pride and position were threatened now along with the power of the empires that ruled them.

That threat to the colonies as well as the empires had begun, in fact, even before the rival settlements were raised by the rival powers in Louisiana and Florida, in Delaware called New Sweden, in New Amsterdam and New England, or down to the south in the settlements called Dutch Brazil. The threat to the colonies and the empires had arisen as soon as the promising extent of the treasure in the west had become known in Europe—as soon as the first gold from Panama and Mexico and Peru had commenced to circulate through Europe.

The threat to the colonies was born with the initial glimpse of their treasure among the rival powers in Europe. And the threat took ominous shape—first on the sea and then on the colonial soil itself. On the sea it bore the name of pirate. And on the soil its name was:

Buccaneer!

The name that was never spoken quietly, the name that was whispered in fear or shrieked as a cry of doom and warning over the whole body of the colonial land growing rich and helpless:

From the vulnerable shores of Mexico, through the hidden coves of the Caribbean, to the long coast on the west, and along the Spanish Main and down to the prospering ports of Brazil, the name that stood for rape and ransom, for torture and murder and pillage, for loss of life and home in an instant, rang over the land:

Buccaneer!

Bringing the new darkness and dread, the new and ever-present fear in the night. Chilling the warm blood and numbing the brain and the muscles of the whole body of the threatened land, cowering where she lay.

Eight

BUCCANEERS

. . . I wish you always health,
With quick return; and so much store of wealth
That Philip's regions may not be more stored
With pearl and jewels and the purest gold.

HENRY ROBERTS

REWARDS OF PARSIMONY

For three centuries there was the colonial trade. For three hundred years there was wealth beyond measure flowing into the world from the western empire of the Spaniards and the Portuguese. But during all those years, because all that treasure was prized by the other powers of Europe, there was the pitiless fight to capture those spoils—whatever the means and whatever the cost in effort and blood. Throughout the colonial years and decades, there were the wars, endless in their recurrence, between the empire-owners and the empire-challengers:

On the seas and on the soil of both hemispheres there was fighting with no quarter asked and less quarter given, between the Spanish and the Portuguese, trying to hold on to their domains and above all to the treasures that came from them, and the French and the Dutch and the British determined to win at least the wealth from those vast and sprawling colonies for themselves.

And while the powers who did the challenging spared no means to strengthen their ships and their arms and the men that manned them, those who did the defending were far less diligent in protecting either their ships or the men on whom the security and permanence of their abundant colonial wealth depended. Part of the carelessness and corruption in which the officialdoms of both empires were steeped was the parsimony often practiced in the outfitting of the vital fleets.

146

It was all part of the developing pattern of imperial greed and graft. And none was more familiar with that hated pattern than the man who sailed the ships for Spain and for Portugal through the waters of both oceans and the Caribbean where the sharks were feared less than the enemy pirates.

None was more familiar with that pattern of certain decay developing even in the beginnings of empire than the sailor who penned the piece he called "The Art of Stealing." The sailor from Portugal, maintaining his identity anonymous—and his anger eloquent:

The stores of the Indiamen, and of the galleons and ships which our Lord the King sends to Brazil . . . and other parts . . . are provided with rotten meat, stinking salt fish, biscuit of the worst quality, sour wine, and the lees of oil, because all this is laid in cheaper at first. But it turns out dearer in the end. For all the crew and passengers fall sick, half of them die, the voyage is frustrated, and all is lost. . . . What is the reason why no ship or galleon of ours, whether it goes alone or belongs to the fleet, carries any drugs or medicines of any kind, for the fevers of the line, nor for wounds received in battle . . . nor for anything else? It must be one of two reasons . . . either ignorance or parsimony.

A Portuguese Sailor Complains of Poor Rations

Ignorance I do not believe that it can be, because no person is ignorant that men are more liable to diseases at sea than on shore, and suffer more from them. It is parsimony, then—to save two or three thousand *cruzados* in things needful for the health and life of the crew and the soldiers, without which all is lost:

The people are lost—the most precious of all things, dying like mosquitoes, and cast into the sea in heaps. And everything is lost, because everything is left without anyone to preserve it against the dangers of the sea and the violence of the enemy.

Foreigners have much the advantage of us in these things. We often see medicines and instruments in their ships, for the sick and wounded, which are worth many thousand *cruzados*. . . .

The more we seek these nations—Holland and England—with embassies and overtures, the more insolent and unreasonable they show themselves, repaying our courtesy with rudeness and robbery, because such courtesy savors to them of cowardice, and they imagine that we are afraid of them, and plume themselves upon it. If they who are pirates and the *canaille* of Hell send no ambassadors to us, why should we—who are the Kingdom of God and Lords of the World—send any to them?

There can be no answer to this argument. And that which some politicians of the day give to it comes from raw cowards, who have not yet learnt that dogs must be tamed by blows.

But they will say we have not sticks with which to beat so many dogs. To this it may be answered that formerly a single galleon of ours sufficed to attack a large fleet, and spitting fire and darting thunderbolts, defeated and took the whole.

Seven of our sailors in a small boat were enough to attack two galleys, and they took the one and made the other sheer off. A few Portuguese ill armed, and eating the skins of their trunks and the soles of their shoes, sustained sieges against many thousand enemies, whom they overcame. For it was always our glory to conquer many with few.

NONE MORE DREADED

On sea and on land, the most dreaded of all the freebooting pirates and buccaneers were the English. And among these, none was more feared along the Spanish main and up and down the west and east coasts of the Spanish colonies than the man they called Draque or Drac—giving the "a" the broad sound, wide with fear.

He was a gentleman, a cavalier, high in the favor of Elizabeth of England when England was already emerging as Spain's most deadly foe—when England herself was busy building her own empire, half a century before the Pilgrims landed at Plymouth, on the spoils taken from the Spanish ships and the rich ports of the Spanish colonies. He sailed in style, thanks to the aid and encouragement of the dauntless queen of a determined England, for whose glory he sacked and slew.

In the colonies they frightened simpletons and children with the sound of the name of the man they called Francisco Drac. But to his own queen and among his own dear countrymen, that man was the brave and loyal captain of fame, Sir Francis Drake. The bane of the Spanish enemy, reaping rewards off Peru the morning after a capture:

On the following day, which was Sunday, in the morning, he dressed and decked himself very finely and had his galleon decorated with all its flags and banners. He also ordered that all the men on our ship be passed to another one of his—which he had taken on this same coast, and which had served for this purpose since he reached the coast of

A View of Sir Francis Drake by One of His Victims

Chile—where he had on his hands a ship laden with a large quantity of gold and many others laden with silver. He had entered the port of Callao de Lima and cut the cables of all the ships that were in port. As the wind was from the land, they all went out to sea, where he had time to sack them all.

Before he proceeded to do the same to ours, he said to me: "Let one of your pages come with me to show me your apparel."

He went from his galleon at about nine in the morning and remained until towards dusk, examining everything contained in the bales and chests. Of that which belonged to me he took but little. Indeed he was quite courteous about it. Certain trifles of mine having taken his fancy, he had them brought to his ship and gave me, in exchange for them, a falchion and a small brazier of silver, and . . . he lost nothing by the bargain. On his return to his vessel he asked me to pardon him for taking the trifles, but that they were for his wife. He said that I could depart the next morning, when the breeze would rise—for which I gave him thanks.

The next morning, which was Monday, he gave back to some of the passengers who were there, their boxes, and thus occupied himself until the hour for dinner. He ordered that this be served as the wind was rising. After this had been done, he said that he himself wanted to take me aboard. He ordered his sloop to be prepared and manned with two dozen archers. He had one of the artillery men called and ordered him to carry aboard half a dozen pieces of artillery. This done, he told me to embark with him, as all was in readiness.

I did so. And on arriving at our vessel, he boarded her first, and having all our sailors called together, he gave each one a handful of *reales*. He also gave the same to some other men who appeared to be the most needy. He commanded that one of those sailors should embark with him so as to show him where water was to be obtained.

All excused themselves, saying that they did not know where water was to be had. So he caused Juan Pascual to be put by force in his sloop, saying that he would hang him if he replied a word.

With this he took leave of me. And his last words were to beseech me earnestly to tell certain Englishmen who were in Lima that I had met him on April 6th and that he was well. From this it is to be inferred that he has spies in all this realm and in Peru. . . . Two or three of those who came in his service have already navigated where I have, on this route of New Spain. . . .

I understand that he carries three thousand bars of silver, and twelve or fifteen chests of pieces of eight, and a great quantity of gold. He is going straight to his country—and I believe that no vessel that went after him could possibly overtake him. . . .

This general of the Englishmen is a nephew of John Hawkins, and is the same who, about five years ago, took the port of Nombre de Dios. He is called Francisco Drac, and is a man about 35 years of age, low of stature, with a fair beard, and is one of the greatest mariners that sails the seas, both as a navigator and as a commander.

His vessel is a galleon of nearly four hundred tons, and is a perfect sailer. She is manned with a hundred men, all of service, and of an age for warfare. . . . Each one takes particular pains to keep his arquebus clean. He treats them with affection, and they treat him with respect. He carries with him nine or ten cavaliers, cadets of English noblemen. These form a part of his council which he calls together for even the most trivial matter, although he takes advice from no one. But he enjoys hearing what they say and afterwards issues his orders.

The aforesaid gentlemen sit at his table, as well as a Portuguese pilot . . . who spoke not a word during all the time I was on board. He is served on silver dishes with gold borders and gilded garlands, in which are his arms. He carries all possible dainties and perfumed waters. He said that many of these had been given him by the Queen.

None of these gentlemen took a seat or covered his head before him, until he repeatedly urged him to do so. This galleon of his carries about thirty heavy pieces of artillery and a great quantity of firearms with the requisite ammunition and lead. He dines and sups to the music of viols. He carries trained carpenters and artisans, so as to be able to careen the ship at any time.

Besides being new, the ship has a double lining. I understood that all the men he carries with him receive wages—because, when our ship was sacked, no man dared take anything without his orders. He shows them great favor, but punishes the least fault. He also carries painters who paint for him pictures of the coast in its exact colors. This I was most grieved to see—for each thing is so naturally depicted that no one who guides himself according to these paintings can possibly go astray.

THE WORD OF A PIRATE

The war without mercy, the war for spoils and trade with the wealthy colonies, the war for control of the treasure and the bartering of slaves from Africa, went on—through the seasons, on the seas and on the land. The war went on and the weapons were fire, and sword and cannon, and bribery and ransom. The weapons were also treason and rebellion—and even the betrayal of friends and allies, all in the name of the war that was seldom declared.

So that, if the word of a viceroy was often worth little and frequently nothing in that war, there were also numerous occasions when the word of a pirate was worth even less. Such as the word of the dreaded Sir John Hawkins, arriving off Rio de la Hacha on the Spanish Main, in the year of Our Lord, 1568, the event being recorded that same year by two royal officials anxious to apprise His Catholic Majesty of the loyalty of his harassed and suffering subjects:

On June 10 last, John Hawkins, English corsair, arrived off this port with ten warships, all well armed and supplied with artillery and fireworks and many other weapons and equipment suitable to so powerful an armada as his. He carried more than six hundred men very well armed and outfitted with corselets and arquebuses and pikes and crossbows and halberds and all other weapons that could be carried, suitable to attack. In good order they landed next day, about noon, half a league from this city. Their pinnaces and ships played many guns, for which reason Miguel de Castellanos, your majesty's general in command, was unable to prevent them from landing.

A Letter Concerning the English Corsair, John Hawkins

He went out to encounter them with as many as sixty men, whom he had succeeded in assembling—and with this, the small force he had, he offered as fine and valorous a defence as has ever been made in these Indies, and killed more than thirty of the enemy. He rendered such signal service that all were astonished at his great valor (both his adversaries and also the residents), for certainly it was a business that today, on looking back at it, fills with fright those who were present and those who hear it related.

In good order he withdrew this small force, without losing a man, whereas truly it seemed incredible that any should have escaped, and the English general took the town. Indignant to discover that your majesty's commander should have undertaken with so few soldiers to prevent him from taking it, and because certain gentlemen whom he much esteemed had been killed, he set fire to the town and burned nearly two thirds of it and blew up the government house.

This done, he began next day to march inland in very good order, his field-pieces in advance. Observing this, your majesty's general summoned what force he could and took up a position ahead of him, to prevent his advance in so far as possible, burning what houses were in the country and driving off the stock, that the enemy might not obtain possession of it. In doing this your majesty's general performed many valorous deeds and killed some of the enemy's men—seeing which the English general determined to return to the town from the point at which he had arrived, which was more than a league from the city. He retired in the same good order in which he had advanced. His intention was to march again into the interior at night, since he could not accomplish his purpose by day.

He dared to venture this because he had possession of a mulatto and a Negro, slaves of your majesty's general, who deserted to him and—that he might liberate them—offered to lead him to the place where your majesty's treasure-box was buried and where most of the people of this city were, with their goods.

With this in view they set out at midnight with these guides, and three hours before dawn arrived where your majesty's general had a tent with much property and where the said citizens were with their goods. The enemy captured a married man with his wife and children and other burghers and took all the goods and Negroes which were there.

The enemy having captured this booty, the burghers of the city and persons whom the Englishman had captured sent one of their number to your majesty's general that he might ransom them and their goods, for the Englishman had told them that unless they were ransomed, he would kill them and carry off all that he had taken from them. He repeated this threat often, and truly it inspired great pity to see them so afflicted and in such danger.

Seeing this, your majesty's general, moved by his great commiseration for the said burghers, resolved to ransom them from the Englishman, that he might not carry out his cruel threat. And so they and all their goods and the houses of the town which remained unburned were ransomed for four thousand pesos in gold.

Among those ransomed were the said mulatto and the Negro who had deserted to the enemy—for whom, had nothing else been redeemed, the said four thousand pesos would have been given, that they might be brought to justice. The English captain delivered them to your majesty's general, Miguel de Castellanos, and although they were his property, your majesty's general handed them over to the law that they might be punished according to it.

And so the mulatto was hung and the Negro quartered.

BEHIND THE COURTESY

In the continuing battle without quarter for the spoils from the Iberian colonies, friends were often sacrificed along with the foes. The ally along with the enemy, the old and the young became victims in the long conflict in which all the people of all the colonies were directly or indirectly involved.

After Hawkins and Drake, there were scores of other Englishmen leading the fight for plunder against the Spanish ships and the long and poorly defended coasts of the sprawling colonies. There were freebooters like Bartholomew Sharpe capturing La Serena in Chile and receiving ransom to release the city. There were the hated ravagers like Henry Morgan—taking the wealth and the women at Porto Bello and along the whole Spanish Main. There were those whose repeated assaults gradually enabled their country to keep some of the prizes permanently: to keep Jamaica, to keep Belize that would sometime be called British Honduras.

And there were the Dutch freebooters who also kept what they took from the Portuguese in Brazil and made their country at least the temporary proprietor of a colony contiguous to that of the Portuguese conquerors and slaveholders. Behind the courtesy pursued by the two colonial neighbors, the same relentless battle for spoils went on between the power that owned an empire and the power that was still but a challenger.

Rivaling the fame of Peter Stuyvesant, who was governor of Curaçao and later of New Holland far to the north, was that of the courteous governor of Dutch Brazil, Count Maurice.

But behind the courtesy there was the spying and the scheming for greater spoils.

There was always the fight to wrest the wealth from the two great empires and their colonies. One of the earliest powers to challenge the Iberians' position was the rising kingdom of France. And one of the bloodiest pirates known and hated throughout the Spanish colonies was the Frenchman, L'Ollonais.

Before him there was Sore, there was Florin, there were scores of others scattered over the Caribbean. And many more came after him— all of them cruel, most of them doomed to die by the violence they as well as their enemies practiced on sea and soil. Yet there was one among the later freebooters from France, Raveneau de Lussan by name, who lived to record his own exploits—the pleasantries along with the pathos and blood—off the prosperous colonies of Spain that looked out on the Pacific:

The best winter-quarters which we had met with in these seas—and that of longest duration—was that of the time of our sojourning upon this island of La Puna where, for the space of thirty-odd days that we stayed there, we lived mighty well. . . . Besides the victuals which the Spaniards brought us daily from Guayaquil, we had brought thither ourselves a great many refreshments. Neither did we want charms for our ears in this place, for we had all the music of the town among our prisoners, which consisted of lutes, theorbos, harps, guitars, and instruments I never saw anywhere else, wherewith they made a very fine concert.

The Reminiscences of the French Pirate, Raveneau de Lussan

Some of our men grew very familiar with our women prisoners, who, without offering them any violence, were not sparing of their favors, and made appear . . . that, after they once came to know us, they did not retain all the aversion for us that had been inculcated into them when we were strangers unto them. All our people were so charmed with this way of living that they forgot their past miseries and thought of no more danger from the Spaniards than if they had been in the middle of Paris.

Amongst the rest, myself had one pretty adventure. Among the other prisoners we had a young gentlewoman lately become a widow of the treasurer of the town, who was slain when it was taken. Now this woman appeared so far comforted for her loss . . . that she proposed to hide me and herself in some corner of the island till our people were gone, and that then she would bring me to Guayaquil to marry her: that she would procure me her husband's office and vest me in his estate, which was very great.

When I had returned her thanks for such obliging offers, I gave her to understand that I was afraid her interest had not the mastery over the Spaniards' recollections, and that the wounds they had received from us were yet too fresh and green for them easily to forget them.

She went about to cure me of my suspicion by procuring secretly from the governor and chief officers promises under their hands, how kindly I should be used by them. I confessed I was not a little perplexed herewith; and such pressing testimonies of good will and friendship towards me brought me, after a little consultation with myself, into such a quandary that I did not know which side to close with.

Nay, I found myself at length much inclined to close with the offers made me. And I had two powerful reasons to induce me thereunto— one of which was the miserable and languishing life we led in those places where we were in perpetual hazard to lose it, which I should be freed from by an advantageous offer of a pretty woman and a considerable settlement. The other proceeded from the despair I was in of ever being able to return into my own country for want of ships fit for that purpose.

But when I began to reflect upon these things with a little more leisure and consideration, and that I revolved with myself how little trust was to be given to the promises and faith of so perfidious as well as vindictive a nation as the Spaniards, and more especially towards men in our circumstances by whom they had been so ill used—this second reflection carried it against the first and even all the advantages offered me by this lady. . . . I was resolved, in spite of the grief and tears of this pretty woman, to prefer the continuance of my troubles (with a ray of hope I had of seeing France again) before the perpetual suspicion I should have had of some treachery designed against me.

Thus I rejected her proposals—but in a manner to assure her that I should retain, even as long as I lived, a lively recollection of her affections and good inclinations towards me.

NO GOOD EXAMPLE

Men like Raveneau de Lussan were the exceptions among the filibusters and the freebooters that ravaged the land of its riches. Most of the buccaneers showed little or no pity toward the men and the women they held for ransom.

Most of them were like the man who fell on Panama—overturning that coveted Cup of Gold with a single blow, spilling the gold and the silver, the laces and jewels, into his lap, carting it all away and leaving the country behind him a ruin of ashes and bone.

Born in Wales, this man had grown up in the hot Caribbean, where he would eventually become lieutenant-governor of Jamaica. He was conniving yet bold, as hard a drinker as he was a fighter, a being of lust and of lusty oaths. A man of unmatched cruelty, he was the scourge of the Spanish Main, otherwise known as Sir Henry Morgan:

Captain Morgan sent forth daily parties of 200 men to make inroads into all the country round about. And when one party came back, another went forth, who soon gathered much riches and many prisoners. These, being brought into the city, were put to the most exquisite tortures to make them confess both other people's goods and their own.

The Exploits of the Buccaneer, Sir Henry Morgan Here it happened that one poor wretch was found in the house of a person of quality, who had put on, amidst the confusion, a pair of taffeta breeches of his master's, with a little silver key hanging out—perceiving which, they asked him for the cabinet of the said key. His answer was, he knew not what was become of it, but that finding those breeches in his master's house, he had made bold to wear them.

Not being able to get any other answer, they put him on the rack, and inhumanly disjointed his arms; then they twisted a cord about his forehead, which they wrung so hard that his eyes appeared as big as eggs, and were ready to fall out. But with these torments not obtaining any positive answer, they hung him up by the testicles, giving him many blows and stripes under that intolerable pain and posture of body. Afterwards they cut off his nose and ears, and singed his face with burning straw till he could not speak nor lament his misery any longer. . . .

They spared, in these their cruelties, no sex nor condition—for as to religious persons, and priests, they granted them less quarter than others unless they could produce a considerable sum sufficient for ransom. Women were no better used, unless they submitted to their filthy lusts —for such as would not consent were treated with all the rigor imaginable.

Captain Morgan gave them no good example in this point. For when any beautiful woman was brought prisoner to his presence, he used all means—both of rigor and mildness—to bend them to his lascivious pleasure. . . .

Among the prisoners brought by the pirates from Toboga and Tobogilla was a gentlewoman of good quality, and no less virtue and chastity, wife to one of the richest merchants there. She was young, and so beautiful, as perhaps few in all Europe surpassed her, either in comeliness or honesty. Her husband then was from home, being gone as far as Peru about his commerce and trade. This virtuous lady, hearing of the pirates coming, had fled, with other friends and relations, to preserve her life from the cruelties and tyrannies of those hard-hearted enemies.

But no sooner did she appear before Captain Morgan, but she was designed for his pleasure. Hereupon he lodged her in an apartment by herself, giving her a Negro, or black woman, to wait on her, and treated her with all respect due to her quality. The poor afflicted lady begged, with many sobs and tears, to lodge among the other prisoners, her relations fearing that unexpected kindness of the commander might be a design on her chastity. But Captain Morgan would by no means hearken to her, but commanded she should be treated with more particular care than before, and have her victuals from his own table.

This lady had formerly heard very strange reports concerning the pirates, as if they were not men but, as they said, heretics who did neither invoke the blessed Trinity nor believe in Jesus Christ. But now she began to have better thoughts of them, upon these civilities of Captain Morgan—especially hearing him many times swear by God and Jesus Christ in whom, she thought, they did not believe. Nor did she think them so bad as to have the shapes of beasts, as had been related.

As to the name of robbers or thieves, commonly given them, she wondered not much at it, seeing, among all nations of the universe, their wicked men, covetous to possess the goods of others. . . .

This false civility of Captain Morgan towards this lady, as is usual to such as pretend and cannot obtain, was soon changed into barbarous cruelty. For after three or four days he came to see her, and entertained her with lascivious discourses, desiring the accomplishments of his lust. The virtuous lady constantly denied him with much civility, and many humble and modest expressions—but Captain Morgan still persisted in his base request, presenting to her much pearl, gold, and whatever he had that was precious and valuable.

But the lady, not willing to consent or accept his presents, showing herself like Susannah for constancy, he presently changed his note and addressed her in another tone, threatening a thousand cruelties and hard usages. To all which she gave only this resolute and positive answer: "Sir, my life is in your hands. But as to my body, in relation to that which you would persuade me to, my soul shall sooner be separated from it through the violence of your arms, than I shall condescend to your request."

Captain Morgan understanding this her heroic resolution, commanded her to be stripped of the best of her apparel, and imprisoned in a darksome stinking cellar. Here she was allowed a small quantity of meat and drink, wherewith she had much ado to sustain her life.

A few of the buccaneers like Henry Morgan lived to maintain a lively recollection of their exploits and those of their comrades-in-carnage. Some of them, like Raveneau de Lussan, even managed to return to their homelands to end their days in alien peace, among old women and little children.

But most of the pirates and buccaneers died by the very torture and violent death they were always quick to inflict on the Spanish and the Portuguese enemy.

There were also those who ran from the shores they had ravaged, ran inland to become masters of Negro slaves and rustlers of cattle originally brought by the settlers from Iberia. Those who fled to live thus on the island of Hispaniola—on the western part that would be known as Saint Domingue and then as Haiti—were the French buccaneers who lived on the cattle they rustled, roasting the meat on the boucans or spits, and selling it illegally to the clandestine foreign visitors: the English pirates and corsairs and the Dutch vry buiters as well as the French filibusters.

Out of this outlawed but expanding trade of the boucaniers in the western third of Hispaniola, grew the French claims to that area. And as the seventeenth century neared its end, the claims were finally recognized: by the Treaty of Ryswick in 1697 Haiti became the possession of France. The land of the buccaneers from France and of the slaves brought from Africa by the French, the English, and the Spanish, became the property of the French crown. The French became the masters of the dark slaves—new slaves and old—and of the dark soil of Haiti that was now their home.

France now had her foothold in the south as well as the north of the western world—as did Holland, as did England. And all three continued to reap the real rewards from the treasure that Spain and Portugal were gleaning from their vast colonies. With the gradual growth of the treasure, the power of the three great rivals of the Iberians had risen to new and greater heights. Until both Spain and Portugal had begun to realize that the only dependable power they could continue to hold lay in extending and strengthening their ownership of the colonial soil itself, in affirming their possession of the colonial subjects, in making their control over their colonial empire absolute.

In spite of their long battle with the other Old World powers for supremacy, the Spaniards and the Portuguese continued to own and operate the base on which the colonial empire was rising day by day: the soil itself, and the slave and other subjects that labored on it. In spite of their losing fight with the other powers to retain the wealth they drew from their own colonies, the Iberians held on to most of the soil, inscribing their pattern of absolute ownership upon the whole body of the divided and granted land:

From the very outset of the long colonial period, the crowns of Spain and Portugal began imposing their titled lords of the realm, some of them descended from the early conquerors, as absolute masters and feudal monarchs over every segment of the land—over the coastal plains and the mountainous plateaus, over the forests and jungles slowly being cleared. Soon the parts that were cleared became the cores of huge plantations and baronial holdings, some of them larger than the countries of Europe. The titled lords and their favorites became the lords of the very body of the land—of all of her, from San Francisco in the Californias down to the shining Plate. And the whole new land came under the ways and the will of the old-world large proprietor:

Dictating the manner that the land should be settled and worked, determining the life of the land, deciding her vocations and moods, establishing her daily and monthly and yearly routine. Allotting her benefits and distributing her hardships over the years and over the decades.

This was the control destined to outlast all the others—through the conquest and through the long colonial times and beyond. This was the most far-reaching domination of all, moving its grip over the land: the tightening grip of the large landholder stamping his feudal will upon the body of the whole agrarian land, held in serfdom where she lay.

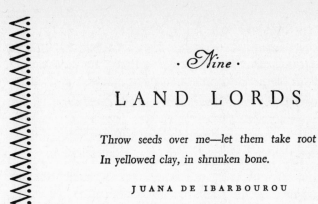

Nine

LAND LORDS

Throw seeds over me—let them take root
In yellowed clay, in shrunken bone.

JUANA DE IBARBOUROU

THE PRODIGAL HOSTS

Possession of the soil meant little or nothing in the colonial world of the southern Americas without the possession of Indians or Negroes, peons or slaves, to work the soil. The repartimiento or royal grant of land in the Spanish colonies meant little without the encomienda or royal grant of Indian slaves. From the two rose the vast plantation, the nucleus of the colonial land system, known as the hacienda.

The haciendas were the immediate source of the sugar and tobacco, bananas and oranges, coffee and cacao, maize and manioc, cattle and sheep, and hundreds of other products native to the new world or raised from plant and animal life transplanted from the old.

Many of the haciendas were self-sustaining, owned by a new and almost independent class of colonials: the large landholders, the hacendados.

They were strict masters, and they were often cruel toward their slaves and their peons—who were slaves in all but name, tied to the land they worked, tied through need, tied through the indebtedness that never ended. They were hard masters who claimed the rights of masters over their peons and frequently over the brides and wives and daughters of peons as well.

But to the men and women who were their social equals—to the lords and ladies, the viceroyal officials and their wives, the priests and lawyers, *the owners of mines, the military officers, to their fellow holders of huge tracts of land, and to whatever recommended visitors chanced to appear at the casa grande or big house of their enormous estates, the hacenda-dos surpassed all other colonial men of power in the generosity and the lavishness of the welcome they gave:*

Beyond Yautepec, the country is still more barren; the road lies over a stony mountain, covered with low brushwood. From the summit of this hill, we discovered the verdant plain . . . with numberless *haciendas*, towns, and villages. The sugar cane covers the valley to the foot of the mountain, and not a rood of land is lost. The first estates we come to are those of Calderón and Casasano, belonging

A Sketch of the Life of the Mexican Landowners

to the same proprietor; it is the largest in the country, and of immense income. We did not stop, but hastened onwards towards Santa Inés, where we arrived at about three o'clock.

We had a letter of recommendation from the proprietor, Don Angel de Michaus, to the steward, his relative, which, of course, procured us the best welcome he could give. Our equipage was well provided for, and the relics of the dinner brought forward for us. Our host, and some others of his party, had the politeness to keep us company while we despatched it.

But this was not a momentary affair, for although twenty-one persons of the house—besides about as many servants—had made their dinners before us, from the same ordinary daily provision, the dishes followed each other in such numbers that I am almost afraid to mention them. They were not less than a dozen, besides auxiliaries; and everything was excellent in the *mode du pays*. Coffee was handed afterwards—this was quite an innovation upon Spanish customs.

The party were on the terrace, where we joined them; and amongst them we recognized many of our Mexican acquaintances: the Marqués de Salvatierra, with his lady and family; the Marqués de Santiago, and his sister; miners, soldiers, lawyers—and priests, of course. Besides our worthy host, Don Antonio de Michaus, we made the number of his guests twenty-four, and for the most part they had come—like ourselves —*au hasard*, uninvited and unexpected, but sure of a hearty welcome and good fare.

One or two besides ourselves had arrived too late for beds in this hacienda. And they were sent to sleep at Cuautla, two miles off.

This is Spanish hospitality. Everybody may, at all times, command for himself anything that the house affords, besides the stated meals when all meet at one table: breakfast, à la fourchette, with coffee and chocolate, at ten o'clock; dinner at two, merienda at five, and supper at ten. And the wine—although twice as dear as in London—is consumed uncounted, like water. The expense of all this must necessarily be enormous. You will call it prodigality, and I believe it is unequalled.

We spent the afternoon in the shade on the terrace, chatting and smoking cigars, with the ladies—whose accomplishments and education I found very superior to what I have generally met with in the city. After merienda, the whole party set off for Cuautla. A long carriage holding twelve inside conveyed the ladies, and the gentlemen rode on horseback —forming a formidable cavalcade.

The object was, imprimis, a walk in the shady streets of Cuautla, among the groves of plantains; in secundis, billiards and chocolate, and rest at a house in the town belonging to the estate. And lastly: the theatre.

In the suburbs of the town, the small houses are overshadowed by the plantain and banana trees, which afford a delightful shade and fragrance—so particularly grateful in hot countries. And in these alleys, all the belles brunettes of the town appeared—to see the great folks from Santa Inés, and to be seen.

BY A DIFFERENT NAME

In Brazil, the Portuguese word that stood for the feudal ownership of the soil was different, but the system was almost identical. Here the great plantation was called the fazenda.

Hacienda or fazenda, the words stood for practically the same thing. In Brazil the owners of the large landed estates were called fazendeiros— these were the small but growing new class among the privileged few. These were the new gentry riding into power on the moving muscles of Negro slaves:

After breakfast, I attended the weekly muster of all the Negroes of the fazenda. Clean shirts and trousers were given the men, and shifts and skirts to the women, of very coarse white cotton. Each, as he or she came in, kissed a hand, and then bowed to Mr. P——, saying, "Father, give me blessing," or "The names of Jesus and Mary be praised!"—and were answered accordingly, either "Bless you," or "Be they praised." This is the custom in old establishments. It is repeated morning and evening. . . . As each slave passed in review, some questions were asked concerning himself, his family, if he had one, or his work; and each received a portion of snuff or tobacco, according to his taste.

Lady Calcott's Description of Plantation Life in Brazil

Mr. P—— tells me that the creole Negroes and mulattoes are far superior in industry to the Portuguese and Brazilians—who, from causes not difficult to be imagined, are for the most part indolent and ignorant. The Negroes and mulattoes have strong motives to exertion of every kind, and succeed in what they undertake accordingly. They are the best artificers and artists. The orchestra of the opera-house is composed of at least one third of mulattoes. All decorative painting, carving, and inlaying is done by them; in short, they excel in all ingenious mechanical arts.

In the afternoon I attended Mr. P. to see the Negroes receive their daily allowance of food. It consisted of farinha (flour), kidney-beans, and dried beef, a fixed measure of each to every person. One man asked for two portions, on account of the absence of his neighbor, whose wife had desired it might be sent to her to make ready for him by the time he returned. Some inquiries which Mr. P—— made about this person induced me to ask his history.

It seems he is a mulatto boatman, the most trusty servant on the estate, and rich, because he is industrious enough to have earned a good deal of private property, besides doing his duty to his master. In his youth—and he is not now old—he had become attached to a creole Negress, born, like him, on the estate. But he did not marry her till he had earned money enough to purchase her, in order that their children, if they had any, might be born free.

Since that time, he has become rich enough to purchase himself, even at the high price which such a slave might fetch. But his master will not sell him his freedom, his services being too valuable to lose, notwithstanding his promise to remain on the estate and work. Unfortunately these people have no children—therefore, on their death their property, now considerable, will revert to the master. . . .

STILL THE SAME

In the French colony of Saint Domingue or Haiti, they had another name for the large plantation and the whole system of ownership and power that went with it. The plantation was called habitation. And the master was known as the colon.

The words differed greatly from the terms used in Portugal's Brazil or Spain's domains in the Americas. But the system denoted by the words in French differed hardly at all from the others.

In Saint Domingue the new class that had come to take the place of the old buccaneers and filibusters from France was the twin class of grands blancs—grand whites—and petits or little whites. They were grand or they were little according to the size of their holdings of land and all that went with it. They were the whites, and the whites were the holders of land. They were the planters.

Gradually a small number of affranchis or offspring of free blacks and mulattoes also became planters and even holders of a few slaves. But the affranchis were small in number and even smaller in the little power or privilege they were permitted to wield in their native Haiti.

Favorites of the crown of France, or friends and relatives of the royal favorites, the grand whites who were the grand planters ruled their slaves with an iron hand. And from the heritage of sweat handed down by the first slaves from Africa to their descendants in Haiti, the plantations rose, rich with sugar and logwood, rum and chocolate, tafia and indigo, and the coffee that would be prized through the colonial decades and long after.

The words were different: habitation, grand blanc, colon. But the growing agrarian system they denoted—the system based on large holdings of land and slaves—could scarcely be told apart from the hacienda and fazenda that prevailed in the colonies of Spain and Portugal. In Haiti, as in Mexico, as in Brazil, there was the planter and there was his "property." And there was the planter's philosophy regarding the worth of his "property" and how it should best be managed:

It is necessary . . . to turn this our property to the best account. We must exact from the Negro all the work he can reasonably perform, and use every means to prolong his life. If interest directs the first, humanity enjoins the second, and here they both go hand in hand. Happy accord! —the consciousness of which forms the whole philosophical and political system of the planter: all the magic of the supreme power of one chief, and of that entire submission of the many. . . . Several planters are desirous of working their estates with Negroes accustomed to the country, and to accomplish this they pick them up singly as they find them—and more frequently in towns—or they purchase entire small gangs. Where there is a proper choice, I have no objection to this; but it is not an easy matter to effect in general. In the second instance there is a paltry mixture of children or of decrepit invalids. In both cases there must be a motley compound of opposite habits and dispositions, where vices will meet and ferment together.

A Coffee Planter's View of His Human Property

I have advised to begin with Negroes ready made because, in the hardships of a first settlement, they are better able to shift for themselves. It was partly for that reason that I recommended beginning with a small number. I also advise that a mason, a carpenter, a shingle planer, and a saddler be procured, if any of good character can be found. For want of these, young Negroes are placed as apprentices with artificers. But these will not be ready in less than three years, and then they sometimes will be found to have acquired bad habits and not even to have learned their trade.

I should prefer, in many respects, to form a gang of young Guinea Negroes of the best choice. And even when there is a sufficient number of men full-grown for the labor, I would advise to purchase only boys and girls of fourteen and fifteen. Guinea Negroes require, in the beginning, to be gently worked and well attended. Some may be lost in the seasoning to climate, but to counterbalance this, they are formed and disciplined according to the master's own ideas, and it is the surest means to make a good and beautiful gang.

In the choice of Guinea Negroes, the planter ought to attend to the following circumstances: youth, an open cheerful countenance, a clean and lively eye, fresh lips, sound teeth, a strong neck, a broad and open chest, sinewy arms, dry and large hands, a flat belly, strong loins and haunches, round thighs, dry knees, muscular calves, lean ankles, high feet and lean; an easy and free movement of the limbs; and a middling stature, or rather small.

The Congo, Arada, and Thiamba are the best nations. Women in general do not admit of so much nicety of choice in this respect because, all over the coast of Guinea, women are accustomed to work for the men.

A gang ought to be, as much as possible, composed of the same nation. I preferred the Congos. They are docile, and work pretty well, provided they are well fed.

As soon as Guinea Negroes are purchased, the first care is to have them well bathed with warm water—in order to take off the palm oil with which they are rubbed on shipboard. This is necessary as it intercepts perspiration. They must next be clothed as the climate requires. It is likewise extremely necessary to cause them to drink, for the space of a fortnight, a sudorific potion (as the dock water) to forward the eruption of cutaneous distempers which the ship surgeons have often barbarously repressed and which produce fatal consequences. If direct suspicion of this is entertained, it is better to reproduce the itch and then to cure it methodically.

They ought to be christened also as soon as possible. Some planters stand godfathers for all their Negroes—to keep them free from the superstitious and abusive power of godfathers and mothers of their own color.

I prefer setting Negroes to work as soon as they arrive. But this must be done by degrees, avoiding exposure at first to cold rains and dews, because the climate to which they have been accustomed is different from that of the mountains of St. Domingo. . . .

The planter who wishes to work at ease, to execute all his works properly, and to spare his Negroes, ought to have a fifteenth part more than is absolutely necessary for the labor of the estate. But I own this happens seldom—ambition, and the facility of extending the plantations, being great temptations to cause deviations from this rule. . . .

The driver or chief of the Negroes and mules—employed in carriage—should be faithful, sober and attentive to the care and good plight of his beasts. He ought to know to cure their wounds and ordinary distempers. In journeys he must have, over the Negroes under him, the same authority as the drivers in the field. To conduct twelve mules, six Negroes are necessary—of whom three should be sufficiently strong to lift and carry the bags of coffee. . . .

I pass now to the gang in general; and in the first place, to what relates to the important article of population:

It cannot be denied but that a number of children occasion great loss of labor in the mothers, which perhaps overbalances the actual benefit.

But it must be considered that these children are bonds of love which bind the Negroes to the soil and to the master. And nothing evinces so strongly the satisfaction, happiness and welfare of this class of people as a great population—which, besides, will one day or other furnish recruits for the field. . . .

But though population is desirable, it is not always an easy matter to attain it. Sometimes women have an aversion to a situation which checks their amours, and they consequently endeavor to prevent pregnancy, or to procure abortion by forced means. It is then that strict watchfulness is necessary. On the one hand, encouragements to favor pregnancy, on the other severity to prevent voluntary and early miscarriages, must be tried. Beware of this: if women come to the hospital with sudden flood-ings, and particularly if, in remote places, you find the alligator-pear trees and others of that kind stripped of their bark.

I was witness to an instance where every method failed, till such time as the women were bound to declare their situation every month, which was verified and registered. And an iron collar was fixed upon those who miscarried, till their ensuing pregnancy was well ascertained.

"LE HAUT MONDE"

The ways of the planters stamped themselves on the very roots of the new pattern of life beginning to spread through the colonies in the southern Americas. The influence of these ways was most powerful and most permanent among the dominant groups of the colonial society.

In the colonies of Spain the alta sociedad or high society reflected the influence of the hacendados in a thousand new forms. In Brazil the ways of the fazendeiro were becoming the ways of the whole colony—but especially of the men and women of privilege.

And in the French colony of Haiti or Saint Domingue the ways and manners of the colon or master were fast being transformed into a set pattern of attitudes among the several groups that ran the colony. These constituted the haut monde:

As all are, or pretend to be, planters, it is extremely natural that each should dwell on what interests him most. . . . They have scarcely ceased to speak of their Negroes, their cotton, their sugar, and their coffee, ere they begin anew on their coffee, their sugar, their cotton, and their Negroes! For a stranger who lands here with a view of acquiring infor-

Baron de Wimpffen's Observa- mation in the succinctest way, nothing can be
tions on Leisure among the so desirable as these eternal conversations. It
Planters is not always that the opinions coincide. It may

sometimes happen that both parties are equally wrong. . . . You will readily imagine that each brings to the meeting his proportion of claims.

But on what do you suppose them to be founded? On the extent of his possessions? On the advantages cultivation has derived from his wisdom and experience? On the reputation his conduct has obtained amongst his neighbors?

No, sir, on none of these—but on the species of commodity he raises! So that the cultivator of coffee never fails to return to the cultivator of cotton the contempt with which he is heard by the cultivator of sugar.

The number of Negroes, too, has no inconsiderable influence on the degree of consideration to which it is permitted to aspire, since they reckon by Negroes here as they do by tons of gold in Holland:

"He has one—two—*three* hundred Negroes!"

This is saying everything. The wit of man can add nothing to this eulogium.

The free intercourse of sexes, which forms in the old world one of the first charms of society, when neither of them usurps the characteristics of the other, adds nothing here to its pleasures. The European ladies seldom see the Creoles but to ridicule them, especially when they have not been educated in France, and these, in their turn, see little in the others but creatures of affectation and folly—while the men, who seldom find (and above all in the former) the degree of sensibility on which the mulatto ladies pique themselves, leave both to lament amongst themselves the decline of the ancient good breeding and the depravity of the tastes of our sex.

The languor which this monotonous mode of existence flings on the commerce of life is neither relieved by instruction, nor by talents, nor even by a love of reading. Several of the colonists, to excuse in some measure their ignorance, have had the disingenuity to give out, on their return to France, that it is impossible to preserve books in Saint Domingue. . . .

I have here a variety of books, bound and unbound, which are as free from injury now as they were on the day of my arrival. It is true I took care of them; but this care is necessary everywhere, since everywhere books which are carelessly thrown aside and left in the dirty corners of garrets and cock-lofts, a prey to dust and moisture, become—as they do here—the food of moths and worms. In fine, the true way to preserve books here, as well as elsewhere, is to read them.

PRINCE OF GAUCHOS

In the older colonies—in Mexico and the rest of New Spain, in Peru and New Granada and Brazil and Saint Domingue—many of the large landholders were men who had won their position by inheritance or by royal favor. But in the newer colonies such as the lands of the Plate, which had been settled more slowly, where there had been no real empire or existing treasure waiting to be taken, and where the growth and development were proceeding against greater odds, more than one of the owners of vast lands and great quantities of wealth in peons and cattle and produce belonged to a new group gradually leaving its impress on the colonial roots:

These were the gauchos—the cowboys or herdsmen—who had become small ranchmen largely through their own initiative, and then, by dint of untiring energy and ruthless defiance of all obstacles, had risen to the estate of large landowners. They were the entrepreneurs of their class, and while they were to be found in the hinterlands of all the older colonies, it was in the newer provinces, such as Buenos Aires and the other lands bordering the Plate that they were attaining positions of real importance with greatest rapidity.

One of the most famous of these successful gauchos was also one of the most typical. Francisco Candioti was his name—a man of tangible achievements who could afford a few tangible luxuries and even a boast or two:

I had often heard of Candioti—who had not, that had ever been in that country? He was the very prince of gauchos: lord of three hundred square leagues of territory, owner of two hundred and fifty thousand head of horned cattle, master of three hundred thousand horses and

mules, and of more than half a million of dollars laid up in his coffers,
in ounces of gold imported from Peru. Just re-
W. P. Robertson's Portrait of
Señor Candioti
turned from one of his excursions into that
country, there he sat, on a sleek and powerful
bay gelding, the finest animal, decidedly, I had seen in the country. Anything half so splendid as horse and rider, taken together, and with reference to the gaucho style of equipment in vogue, was certainly not to be
found in South America.

When the family congratulations on meeting, after a six months'
absence, were over, I was introduced to Señor Candioti, and made my
bow with all the deference due to so patriarchal a potentate. His manners and habits were alike primitive; and his mode of carrying himself
towards others was as unostentatious and courteous as were his claims
to superiority in wealth and station universally admitted.

This prince of the gauchos was a prince in nothing more than in that
noble simplicity which characterized his whole deportment. He was too
high in his own sphere of action to fear competition; too independent
to condescend to civility for mere personal advantage; and too ingenuous
to admit into his breast a thought of acting the hypocrite.

He continued sitting on his horse, and kept up a familiar chit-chat
with all around. Every now and then he lighted his cigar by striking fire
with a flint and steel on tinder kept in a polished tip of horn, which was
embossed with silver, and had a gold chain attached to it, by which the
lid, or rather extinguisher, depended, while the horn was in use. As I
looked at him I could not but admire his singularly handsome face and
dignified mien.

His small mouth and strictly Grecian nose, his noble forehead and
fine head thinly strewed with silver locks, his penetrating blue eyes and
countenance as hale and ruddy as if he had spent his days in Norway,
instead of riding over the pampas, were all remarkable. Then, for his
attire, according to the style and fashion of the country, it was magnificent. His poncho had been made in Peru, and beside being of the
richest material, was embroidered on a white ground in superb style.
Beneath it he wore a jacket of the finest India cloth, covering a white
satin waistcoat—which, like his poncho, was beautifully embroidered,
and adorned with small gold buttons, each depending from a little link
of chain of the same metal. He had no cravat, and the collar and front of
his shirt displayed, upon fine French cambric, the richest specimens
of tambouring which could be furnished in Paraguay.

His lower vestment was of black velvet, open at the knees, and, like the waistcoat, adorned with gold buttons, depending also from little links of chain, evidently never intended for connection with the button-holes. From under this part of his dress were to be seen the fringed and tamboured extremities of a pair of drawers, made of the fine Paraguay cloth. They were ample as a Turkoman's trousers, white as the driven snow, and hung down to the calf of the leg, just far enough to show under them a pair of brown stockings, manufactured in Peru from the best vicuña wool. The potro boots of Señor Candioti fitted his feet and ankles as a French glove fits the hand, and the tops of them were turned over, so as to give them the air of buskins. To these boots were attached a pair of unwieldy silver spurs, brightly polished.

To complete his personal attire, the princely gaucho wore a large Peruvian straw hat with a black velvet band around it, while his waist was girded with a rich crimson sash of silk, serving the treble purpose of riding-belt, braces, and girdle for a huge knife in a morocco sheath, from which protruded a massive silver handle.

Gorgeous as was the apparel of the rider, it was, if possible, outdone by the caparison of his horse. Here all was silver, elaborately wrought and curiously inlaid. The peaks of the saddle, and the complicated head-piece of the bridle, were covered with the precious metal; the reins were embossed with it; and in the manufacture of the stirrups there must have been exhausted all the ingenuity of the best Peruvian silversmith, with at least ten pounds of plata piña—or virgin silver—to work upon.

Such, in character and person, was Candioti, the patriarch of Santa Fé. . . . I must give you some idea of his extraordinary and successful career in life, of how he became possessed of such a vast extent of terri-tory. . . .

Having in his youth, with a few mules for sale, made a short excursion into Peru, at a time when the mines of Potosí and other parts of that country were yielding a vast produce, Candioti saw how inadequate to the demand was the supply of those useful animals for the purpose of conveying ores and merchandise—as well as passengers—over a rocky and arid country. Increasing numbers of them were also required for the purpose of carrying the produce of Paraguay to Córdoba, Mendoza, San Luís, Tucumán, Salta, and other towns.

Returning to Santa Fé, the sagacious speculator and observer invested the ten thousand dollars earned by his trip in the purchase of an estate in the Entre Ríos, about thirty leagues from Santa Fé, on the opposite side of the river, Paraná. He determined to give his chief attention to the breeding of mules for exportation to Peru. From this time forward he made an annual journey to that country, and every year a more successful one than that which had preceded. As he returned periodically to his native town, he regularly invested in new estates, contiguous to the old ones, and in cattle upon them, the whole profit of his year's adventure.

At that period of superabundance of land in South America, and indeed up to a much later period, the mode of purchasing an estate was not by paying so much a rood, an acre, a mile, or even a league for it—but simply by paying so much a head for the cattle upon it, and a trifling sum for the few fixtures (such, perhaps, as half a dozen mud huts, and as many corrals in which to shut up the livestock). The general price then paid for each head of horned cattle was two shillings, and for each horse sixpence.

An estate of five leagues in length by two and a half in breadth—that is, of twelve and a half square leagues—might have upon it, generally speaking, about eight thousand head of horned cattle, and fifteen thousand horses. The price of it, at the above-mentioned rates, would be . . . for the stock and fixtures, 1,275 Pounds, leaving the estate of twelve and a half square leagues—or thirty-seven and a half square miles—as a bonus to the purchaser.

Now, if it be considered that Candioti's journeys to Peru, becoming every year more profitable, enabled him at last to buy in the year three or four such estates as that described above, it will soon be seen how his landed possessions must have extended; how his horned cattle, his horses, and his mules must have increased and multiplied; and how the man himself must have waxed "exceeding great."

Many other families of Santa Fé followed, at a distance, the example of Candioti; and at length the town came to supply all Peru with mules. It became, too, the emporium and port of transit for the produce of Paraguay destined for Chile and Upper as well as Lower Peru. And it extended its influence and increased its wealth by the acquisition of many estates on the Banda Oriental—the Eastern Shore of the Uruguay—and Entre Ríos, where most of the mules for exportation were bred.

Candioti's mode of journeying to Peru with his annual caravan, and with five or six thousand mules, was this: having brought them from his estates on the east side of the Paraná, by making them swim, under the direction of many herdsmen, over that stream, he collected them into potreros, or large paddocks, in the vicinity of Santa Fé, till he had got together the number he required. He then loaded thirty or forty huge wagons with the merchandise most wanted in Peru; and taking with him, under the guidance of his own vigilant eye, five hundred tame oxen to serve as relays in the drawing of these wagons, and his six thousand mules driven, *en masse*, by forty or fifty *gaucho* peons, he set his face to the plains, and commenced his journey towards Santiago, Tucumán, and Salta, leaving Córdoba to the left.

The country, covered with grass, and copiously irrigated by streams, afforded sustenance for his cattle wherever he chose to make halt; and he had to encounter, on his journey, the obstruction of neither ditches nor fences, any more than he had to incur the expense of a single far-thing for the maintenance of his numerous cavalcade. Beside his draught bullocks, he had with him a sufficient number of others for daily slaughter as he proceeded; and neither himself nor his men thought farther provision necessary, than beef, *maté* (Paraguay tea), salt, water, and watermelons. None of these, except the salt and *maté*, could be said to cost Candioti anything; and these were very cheap.

The peons . . . had their luxury—equally cheap—of tobacco. But even that was deducted from their wages.

Whenever the caravan came to a halt, the bullocks, being loosed from their yokes, were let out to pasture on the plain. The herd of mules, too. And while half the cortege of peons were riding round and round them, to keep them together, the other half were busied in lighting fires upon the sward, roasting beef, boiling water, eating melons, or stretching themselves out under the shade of the wagons for repose.

At a given hour the refreshed party was sent off to relieve the work-ing one. And when man and beast were sufficiently rested and fed, off again marched the cattle and caravans. In fine moonlight they travelled from evening till morning, and rested during all the hours of solar heat. But when the nights were dark, they necessarily stopped, kindled their fires, and kept . . . watch over their herds of cattle—as wandering at large, under the inspection of the peons, they grazed within sight of the numerous fires kindled to prevent their straying far from the spot of encampment.

Candioti was of course the presiding genius of the journey. Sleeping less than any one of his peons, he was ever the last to lie down and the first to rise. He invariably got up at midnight, and at some other hour of the night or morning, to see that the watches were properly relieved, and the cattle kept compactly together. The whole discipline of this moving camp was not only in accordance with his own precise regula-tions, but was seldom infringed, because so vigilantly superintended. He would pardon drunkenness in a peon, impertinence (upon an apology made for it), absence, gambling, and even theft. But never was he known to forgive a man whom he once caught asleep when he ought to have been awake. . . .

He came at last to think it a sort of disgrace that it should be known he slept at all; and every servant he ever had was ready to aver that he had never seen his master sleep. That his wife might not bear testimony against his being guilty of so great a weakness, Candioti had always a bedroom separate from hers.

Two friends of his endeavored to take him by surprise, by calling upon him, the one at two and the other at three o'clock, on different mornings. "Señor Don Francisco," said the first, as he knocked at his door, "are you asleep?"

Candioti was nearly asleep—for, in spite of all his exertions, he did require a little of that refreshment. But with ears as quick as those of a hare, the moment his friend's first tap saluted them, "No," replied he, "I am thinking what it can be that keeps that last herd of mules so long after their time from arriving." He instantly struck a light from his yesquero, or tinder-box, lit a candle, and, with a cigar in his mouth, opened the door to his friend. He gave him a cigar, asked him to be seated, and—without the least remark upon the hour at which he had called—began to talk as a matter of course on the topics interesting to both. . . .

The second friend . . . knocked and said, "Señor Don Francisco . . . are you asleep?"

"Nada de eso—not at all," replied the prince of the gauchos, "walk in."

When his friend walked in, accordingly, Candioti told him that he had just got up to order his horse to be saddled, and that he was going to the potrero to see if the mules and peons were ready for a start the following day.

By his wife Candioti had only one child, a daughter, and she the heiress of all his property and estates. But his illegitimate progeny was so numerous, that most of his estancias were managed by one or more of his sons.

I dined with him one day when four of his natural—but not unacknowledged or dishonored—children were present. Our dinner was most plentiful. The slaves who attended us were numerous. Every article in the house, where silver could be used, was made of it: plates, forks, dishes, salvers, ewers, all were of that ore.

And yet there was not a carpet in the whole house. The chairs were common rush-bottom chairs; the tables were of deal, not even painted. The beds were stretchers, with hide bottoms; curtains to them, or sashes for the windows, there were neither. And in the very drawing-room, or *sala*, there stood upon a horse-rack the whole of Candioti's horse-gear. The patio of his house was continually filled with *capataces*—overseers— calling for orders, or with peons bearing messages, and leaving or taking away horses.

In his habits of eating and drinking Candioti was very abstemious. He seldom drank anything but water and *maté*, and was moderate at his meals—unless it were occasionally, on the plains, when the irresistible *carne con cuero* (beef roasted in the skin of the animal) was placed before him. He never seemed precisely in his element unless when on horseback, and he contrived, whether at home or on his travels, to pass sixteen hours of the twenty-four in his favorite way.

He smoked and talked all day, seldom took up a pen—except to write his signature—and never, even by chance, looked into a book. He used to say he knew nobody but priests and lawyers who had any business to do that—and he was not at all sure that we did not owe much of the litigation and religious strife in the world to the propensity observable in those two classes of men to pore over books, which he believed to be generally filled with legal cavils and polemical controversy.

Not all the proprietors of the class of small ranchers were men of the class of Candioti. Most of the little landowners, like most of the big ones, showed slight interest in the enormous and necessary job of turning the rich soil of the colonies to serious productive use. Their indifference led to neglect of the land throughout the colonies in the southern Americas and through the three slow centuries of the colonial period.

But in spite of the contempt for the great task of cultivating the soil that prevailed among the small number of hacendados and fazendeiros and colons that owned the soil and the Indian serfs and the Negro slaves, in spite of their neglect and the waste that caused much that was garnered to rot, and in spite of the many arid areas that spotted the New World soil—agriculture throughout the colonies thrived and began to reach greater heights of productiveness and to expand into bright new planes of variety.

The feudal lords were contemptuous, but they introduced the cattle and the plough. And the soil responded to the new instruments that took the place of the old planting-stick of the Indians with a bounty of crops that had never been known before. Crops of the old world and crops of the new: wheat of Castile and maize and maguey of Mexico, pigs of Portugal and manioc of Brazil, citron of France and coffee of Haiti.

The new lords of the soil improved on the old methods of cultivation, just as they perfected their Old World system of latifundio, or large landed estates, on the existing feudal structures of the Aztec and Inca empires in the new world. This was the process and the pattern in Mexico, in the Guatemala provinces and south to the Isthmus, and in the Andes where the Incas had ruled. And where they failed to find those existing feudal societies, as in Brazil and the islands of the Caribbean, they proceeded to establish a similar pattern of the few owning the many with the use of the imported Negro slaves and their descendants.

Even before the colonies were a hundred years old from the date of the Admiral's arrival, all of the soil and the serfs and the slaves throughout that conquered world were owned by only a few thousand masters—all of them Europeans. Yet most of the Europeans in the colonies were landless, slaveless, serfless, because they were too poor to pay the price and lacked the proper friends who might obtain favors for them from the crown, which disposed of the soil and the people to work it as the royal officials saw fit. And none of the common people were permitted to own or acquire property.

So that the purchases of soil and serfs and slaves kept going to the rich and privileged few, the largest landholders—whose holdings and riches and privileges multipled. Whose rise to power outdistanced all others.

But soon the power of the land lords was challenged. From the beginning, in fact, and sporadically through the long colonial years, it was challenged first by the church—which was itself to become one of the largest holders of soil and other riches—but principally by the royal crown and its high officialdom everywhere in the colonies:

Over the whole body of the land held in the colonial grip of the feudal lord, there rose the competitive challenge from the other dominant groups seeking to break the master's hold on her ploughed soil, rich with produce and rich with people laboring in field and town, laboring in serfdom and slavery. The challenging groups sought to curb the narrowing control and fierce affirmation of the feudal owner's hold on the colonial land with measures of law and gestures of force—

Until the challenge turned to tangible threat, turned to the actuality of spanning violence and riots and bloodshed, turned to the intermittent civil wars that tore at the whole colonial body of the land, possessed and fought over where she lay.

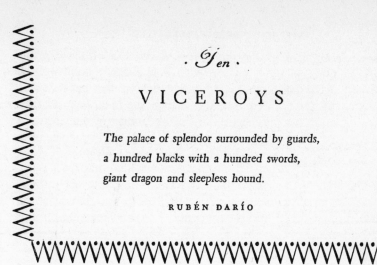

· *Ten* ·

VICEROYS

The palace of splendor surrounded by guards,
a hundred blacks with a hundred swords,
giant dragon and sleepless hound.

RUBÉN DARÍO

ENTRY INTO LIMA

Pitted against the multiplying power of the landholders in the colonies was the power of the kings who had granted them titles of nobility along with their estates, and the more threatening and immediate powers of the kings' many representatives in the colonies. From the very first conquests and the very first settlements in the southern colonial lands of the new world—especially in the territories owned by Spain and by Portugal—the chief threat to the power of the conquerors and settlers becoming the lords of the soil and its serfs and slaves was the plethora of officials sent by the fearful crown to watch over the landowners and over each other.

In theory and sometimes in practice the principal role of the numerous officials in each of the four Spanish viceroyalties—New Spain, Peru, New Granada, La Plata or Buenos Aires—was to administer the laws, collect the taxes, maintain order. The highest symbol of these delegated royal powers was the office of viceroy, the personal representative of the king. And the theory and the symbol of that colonial system of government found elaborate expression in each viceregal court.

Most particularly it found its expression in the ceremonies that were held to celebrate the arrival of a new viceroy in the great colony of Peru, as noted by two of the king's special as well as secret representatives, Don Antonio de Ulloa and Don Jorge Juan y Santacilia:

179

Of all the solemnities observed in America, the public entrance of the viceroy is the most splendid; and in which the amazing pomp of Lima is particularly displayed. Nothing is seen but rich coaches and calashes, laces, jewels, and splendid equipages, in which the nobility carry their emulation to an astonishing height. . . . On the landing of the viceroy at Paita, two hundred and four leagues from Lima, he sends a person of great distinction, generally some officer of his retinue, to Lima, *The Elaborate Celebration of the Public Entrance of the Viceroy* with the character of an ambassador; and, by a memoir, informs his predecessor of his arrival, in conformity to His Majesty's orders, who had been pleased to confer on him the government of that kingdom. On this ambassador's arrival at Lima, the late viceroy sends a messenger to compliment him on his safe arrival; and on dismissing the ambassador, presents him with some jewel of great value, and a jurisdiction or two which happen at that time to be vacant, together with an indulgence of officiating by deputy, if most agreeable to him.

The *corregidor* of Piura receives the new viceroy at Paita, and provides litters, mules, and every other necessary for the viceroy and his retinue, as far as the next jurisdiction. He also orders booths to be built at the halting places in the deserts; attends him in person, and defrays all the expenses, till relieved by the next *corregidor*.

Being at length arrived at Lima, he proceeds, as it were incognito, through the city to Callao, about two leagues and a half distant. In this place he is received and acknowledged by one of the ordinary alcaldes of Lima, appointed for that purpose, and also by the military officers. He is lodged in the viceroy's palace, which on this occasion is adorned with astonishing magnificence.

The next day all the courts, secular and ecclesiastical, wait on him from Lima, and he receives them under a canopy in the following order: the *audiencia*, the chamber of accounts, the cathedral chapter, the magistracy, the *confulado*, the Inquisition, the *tribunal de Cruzada*, the superiors of the religious orders, the colleges, and other persons of eminence. On this day the judges attend the viceroy to an entertainment given by the alcalde, and all persons of note take a pride in doing the like to his attendants. At night there is a play, to which the ladies are admitted veiled, and in their usual dress, to see the new viceroy.

The second day after his arrival at Callao, he goes in a coach provided for him by the city, to the Chapel de la Legua, so called from its being about half-way between Callao and Lima—where he is met by the late viceroy. And both alighting from their coaches, the latter delivers to him a truncheon as the ensign of the government of the kingdom. After this, and the usual compliments, they separate.

If the new viceroy intends to make his public entry into Lima in a few days, he returns to Callao, where he stays till the day appointed. But as a longer space is generally allowed for the many preparatives necessary to such a ceremony, he continues his journey to Lima, and takes up his residence in his palace, the fitting up of which on this occasion is committed to the junior auditor and the ordinary alcalde.

On the day of public entry, the streets are cleaned and hung with tapestry, and magnificent triumphal arches erected at proper distances. At two in the afternoon the viceroy goes privately to the church belonging to the monastery of Montserrat, which is separated by an arch and a gate from the street, where the cavalcade is to begin. As soon as all who are to assist in the procession are assembled, the viceroy and his retinue mount on horses, provided by the city for this ceremony, and the gates being thrown open, the procession begins in the following order:

The militia; the colleges; the university, with the professors in their proper habits; the chamber of accounts; the *audiencia* on horses, with trappings; the magistracy, in crimson velvet robes, lined with brocade of the same color, and a particular kind of cap on their heads, a dress only used on this occasion. Some members of the corporation who walk on foot, support the canopy over the viceroy; and the two ordinary alcaldes, who are in the same dress, and walk in the procession, act as equerries, holding the bridle of his horse. This part of the ceremony, though prohibited by the laws of the Indies, is still performed in the manner I have described—for the custom being of great antiquity, the magistrates have not thought proper to alter it, that the respect to the viceroy might not suffer any diminution, and no person has yet ventured to be the first in refusing to comply with it.

This procession is of considerable length, the viceroy passing through several streets till he comes to the great square, in which the whole company draw up facing the cathedral, where he alights, and is received by the archbishop and chapter. *Te Deum* is then sung before the viceroy, and the officers placed in their respective seats. After which he again mounts his horse and proceeds to the palace gate, where he is received by the *audiencia*, and conducted to an apartment in which a splendid collation is provided, as are also others for the nobility in the antechambers.

On the morning of the following day he returns to the cathedral in his coach, with the retinue and pomp usual in solemn festivals and public ceremonies. He is preceded by the whole troop of horse-guards, the members of the several tribunals in their coaches, and after them the viceroy himself with his family, the company of halberdiers bringing up the rear.

On this occasion all the riches and ornaments of the church are displayed; the archbishop celebrates in his pontifical robes the Mass of thanksgiving; and the sermon is preached by one of the best orators of the chapter. . . . In the evening of this, and the two following days, the collations are repeated, with all the plenty and delicacy imaginable. To increase the festivity, all women of credit have free access to the halls, galleries, and gardens of the palace, when they are fond of showing the dispositions of their genius, either by the vivacity of repartees, or spirited conversations, in which they often silence strangers of very ready wit.

This show and ceremony is succeeded by bull-feasts at the city's expense, which continue five days: the three first for the viceroy, and the two latter in compliment to the ambassador who brought advice of his arrival, and the great honor conferred on him by the sovereign in the government of this kingdom. . . . The bull-feasts are succeeded by that ceremony in which the university, the colleges, the convents and nunneries acknowledge him as their viceroyal protector. This is also accompanied with great splendor, and valuable prizes are bestowed on those who make the most ingenious compositions in his praise.

THE SYMBOL AND THE STRIFE

The office of viceroy was the highest symbol of the king's power in the colonies of Spain and Portugal, as the office of governor was the symbol of the royal authority in the French colony of Haiti. But from the earliest days of the colonies, there was strife that rose in word and deed against the symbol and the power it stood for. And the strife often overshadowed the symbol.

In the Spanish and the Portuguese colonies the gravest threat—as grave as the external challenge of the encroaching arms of the enemy buccaneers and other foreign foes—came from the conquerors and their descendants, and from the other feudal lords who had also gained political as well as military power with their possession and control of the people and the provinces, the monies and the municipalities. The threat to the crown's authority came from the belligerent and pioneering spirit *itself* of the Spanish conquistador and the Portuguese bandeirante or banner-bearer in the new-world wilderness.

Out of that spirit of the challenging conqueror and pioneer rose the threat that smoldered into the long conflict of three centuries and that sometimes flared into bloody civil war. In Peru, for instance, there was the long war without quarter between the factions of Almagro and the Pizarros, which cost the lives of hundreds of men, including Almagro and Don Francisco the Conqueror himself. And then there was the war between Gonzalo Pizarro and his forces and the viceroy who attempted to enforce the New Laws of the Indies that would curb the powers of the feudal lords over the Indians and over the land.

There were even times when the conflict burst into open rebellion against the king. In the earliest days of the colony of Peru, when the land was still being conquered and the wilderness was barely being opened, there were fierce and violent conquistadors turning their swords against their captains, turning the steel against their own countrymen.

There were men of turmoil like Lope de Aguirre—daring to defy the king's authority by written word as well as sanguinary deed:

King Philip, native of Spain, son of Charles the Invincible: I, Lope de Aguirre, thy vassal, an old Christian, of poor but noble parents, and native of the town of Onate in Biscay, passed over young to Peru, to labor lance in hand. I rendered thee great services in the conquest of the Indies. I fought for thy glory, without demanding pay of thy officers, as is proved by the books of thy treasury. I firmly

Aguirre's Letter of Defiance to Philip II, His King No More

believe—Christian King and Lord, very ungrateful to me and my companions—that all those who write to thee from this land (America) deceive thee much because thou seest things too far off. I recommend to thee to be more just toward the good vassals whom thou hast in this country. For I and mine, wearied of the cruelties and injustices which thy viceroys, thy governors and thy judges exercise in thy name, are resolved to obey thee no more.

We regard ourselves no longer as Spaniards. We make a cruel war on thee because we will not endure the oppression of thy ministers—who, to give places to their nephews and their children, dispose of our lives, our reputations, and our fortunes.

I am lame in the left foot from two shots of an arquebus, which I received in the valley of Coquimbo, fighting under the orders of thy marshal, Alonzo de Alvarado, against Francisco Hernández Girón, then a rebel—as I am at present and shall be always. For since thy viceroy, the Marquis of Canete—a cowardly, ambitious, and effeminate man— has hanged our most valiant warriors, and I care no more for thy pardon than for the books of Martin Luther.

It is not well in thee, King of Spain, to be ungrateful toward thy vassals; for it was while thy father, the emperor Charles, remained quietly in Castile that they procured for thee so many kingdoms and vast countries. Remember, King Philip, that thou hast no right to draw revenues from these provinces, the conquest of which has been without danger to thee except insofar as thou recompensest those who have rendered thee such great services.

I am certain that few kings go to heaven. . . .

The Marquis of Canete sent to the Amazon Pedro de Ursua, a Navarrese—or rather a Frenchman. We sailed on the largest rivers of Peru, till we came to a gulf of fresh water. We had already gone three hundred leagues when we killed that bad and ambitious captain.

We chose a *caballero* of Seville, Fernando de Guzman, for king; and we swore fealty to him, as is done to thyself. I was named quartermaster-general, and because I did not consent to all his will he wanted to kill me. But I killed this new king, the captain of his guards, his lieutenant-general, his chaplain, a woman, a knight of the order of Rhodes, two ensigns, and five or six domestics of the pretended king.

I then resolved to punish thy ministers, and the counsellors of thy *audiencia.*

I named captains and sergeants. These . . . wanted to kill me. But I had them all hanged.

THE ROYAL SERVICE

In Spain there was the Council of the Indies, responsible to the king and charged with making the laws for the colonies. In the Spanish colonies there were the powerful audiencias or judicial and administrative councils made up of oidores or judges who were sometimes strong enough to constitute themselves the highest body of government— higher than the captains-general or military chiefs, higher than the governors of provinces, and occasionally even higher than the viceroy himself.

There were also the royal visitadores or inspectors who could and would suddenly appear in a colony, to review and challenge the record of viceroy and audiencia alike. And there was a host of other officials vying with each other for influence in the colony and at the court of the viceroy as well as at the court of the king across the sea.

The same plethora of officialdom characterized the top-heavy Portuguese administration of Brazil, not only during the sixty years, from 1580 to 1640, that Portugal was under Spanish rule, but throughout the colonial decades. The Portuguese officialdom was the curse of the colony —especially of the free settler compelled to share his profits with the crown. So that the failure to discover gold or diamonds or emeralds in a given province in Brazil, as they were being discovered in other parts of the colony, was sometimes interpreted as a blessing in disguise:

How many royal Ministers, and how many Officers of Justice, of Property, and of War, do you suppose would be sent here for extracting, securing, and remitting this gold or silver? If you have experienced so many times that one alone of these powerful men is sufficient to depopulate the state, what would so many do? Do you not know how far the name of the royal service extends, contrary *A Sermon on the Blessings of* to the intention of the kings themselves, how *Being Without Gold. 17th Century* violent it is, and how insupportable? How many Administradores, how many Proveedores, how many Treasurers, how many Almoxarifes, how many Secretaries, how many Accountants, how many Guards by sea and by land, and how many other Officers, of new names and jurisdictions, would be created and founded, for these mines, to confound you and to bury you in them!

What have you got, what do you possess, what do you cultivate, what do you raise, that will not be necessary for the service of the King, or of those who make themselves more than kings, with this specious pretext! In that day you will begin to be factors, and not lords, of all your own property. Your own slave will not be yours, your own canoe will not be yours, your own cart will not be yours, and your own ox will not be yours —only to feed it and to serve with it.

They would embargo your harvest for the maintenance of the mines. They would take your house for lodging for the officers. Your cane field

would have to remain uncultivated because those who should cultivate
it must go to the mines. And you yourself would not belong to yourself,
because they would distress you for what you had, or for what you had
not.

And your *engenhos* alone would have much to grind, because you and
your children would have to be ground!

"WHEN JUSTICE WOULD BE NO FATHER . . . "

One of the main functions of the viceroys and governors was to watch
the movements of the enemy pirates and freebooters and the smugglers
of the realm who were allied with them. The Spanish and Portuguese
officials watched the French and the English and the Dutch coming
closer and sporadically descending on their frontier settlements. And
they built forts along the coasts and inland to protect the colonies from
that aggression.

They also watched and garrisoned the frontiers where the Indian
tribes were still far from being pacified, or where runaway Negro slaves
had established hostile camps that fell on the settlers whenever the opportunity arose.

The Spanish and Portuguese officials watched their enemies. And
while they also watched each other in their conflict for control of the
long frontier separating their dominions, and while they vied with each
other for the trade with the Indians, they often accepted bribes from
each other, shutting their eyes to the threat aimed at their own king's
colony and particularly shutting their eyes at the consequent omission
of the royal fifth which the king demanded as his share in all colonial
transactions.

But there were also representatives of the crown in the colonies of the
southern Americas who showed enterprise as well as intelligence in matters other than those dealing with the presence of rival or enemy agents
and forces in their provinces. There were some officials who took a real
interest in the development of the domains under their care. There were
men like the Marquis of Lavradio, who promoted agriculture and trade
in Brazil where he was the king's own viceroy.

There were viceroys and other high officials who were New World
pioneers in their own way:

There were representatives of the king in the New World colonies who served with shrewdness and sagacity. There were some who served with honesty. There were a few who even performed their offices with wisdom. The term served by a Spanish viceroy was fixed at only six years, and then at only three. But on more than one occasion an appointment was renewed—and more than once this was all to the good as far as the colony's welfare was concerned.

But there were also viceroys who were not free from the bribery and other corruption that characterized the rule of local and provincial officials in most of the colonial realm. There were viceroys who even dared to flaunt their favoritism for men engaged in selfish enterprises that struck a blow at the everyday lives of the common people.

Against this recurrent threat of the viceroy's power combining with the power of men of money and privilege, there rose the challenge from that puissant source that was the first to defy the rule of the feudal overlord of the New World's soil and the new soil's slaves:

Against the intermittent violation of the rights of settlers as well as slaves by the officials and agents of the crown, there rose the defending arm of the rising strength of the Church. Against the actions of a certain Count of Gálvez, Viceroy of New Spain, and his favorites, there rose Don Alonso de Zerna, the Archbishop himself.

Don Pedro Mexía of the Indians bought at the price he list their maize. And the wheat of the Spaniards he bought it according to that price at which it is taxed by the law of that land to be sold at in time of famine —which is at fourteen reales a bushel . . . at which price the farmers and husbandmen, knowing it to be a plentiful year, were glad and willing to sell unto him their wheat, not knowing *Thomas Gage Records the Downfall of a Conniving Viceroy* what the end would be. And others fearing to gainsay him whom they knew to be the Viceroy's favorite. Thus Don Pedro Mexía filled all his barns which he had hired about the country, and himself and the Viceroy became owners of all the wheat. He had his officers appointed to bring it into the markets upon his warning, and that was when some small remnants that had escaped his fingers were sold, and the price raised. Then hoisted he his price, and doubled it above what it had cost him.

The poor began to complain, the rich to murmur, the tax of the law was moved in the Court of Chancery before the Viceroy. But he being privy to the monopoly expounded the law to be understood in time of famine, and that he was informed that it was plentiful a year as ever had been, and that to his knowledge there was as much brought into the markets as ever had been, and plenty enough for Mexico and all the country. Thus was the law slighted, the rich mocked, the poor oppressed, and none sold wheat but Don Pedro Mexía, his officers for himself, and the Viceroy.

When justice would be no father, the people go to their mother the Church. . . . Don Alonso de Zerna, the Archbishop, who had always stomached Don Pedro Mexía and the Viceroy, to please the people granted to them to excommunicate Don Pedro Mexía, and so sent out bills of excommunication to be fixed upon all the church doors against Don Pedro: who not regarding the excommunication—and keeping close at home, and still selling his wheat, raising higher the price than it was before—the Archbishop raised this censure higher against him, adding to it a bill of cessatio a divinis, that is, a cessation from all divine service.

This censure is so great with them that it is never used but for some great man's sake, who is contumacious and stubborn in his ways, contemning the power of the Church. Then are all the church doors shut up (let the city be never so great), no Masses are said, no prayers used, no preaching permitted, no meetings allowed for any public devotion or calling upon God. Their Church mourns as it were, and makes no show of spiritual joy and comfort, nor of any communion of prayers one with another, so long as the party continues stubborn and rebellious in his sin and scandal, and unyielding to the Church's censure.

And further, whereas by this cessation a divinis many churches and especially cloisters suffer in the means of their livelihood . . . therefore this censure or cessatio a divinis is so inflicted upon the whole Church . . . that the party offending or scandalizing, for whose sake this curse is laid upon all, is bound to satisfy all priests and cloisters which in the way aforesaid suffer, and to allow them so much out of his means as they might have daily got by selling away their Masses for so many crowns for their daily livelihood.

To this would the Archbishop have brought Don Pedro Mexía, to have emptied out of his purse near a thousand crowns daily. . . . And secondly, by the people's suffering in their spiritual comfort and non-communion of prayers and idolatrous worship, he thought to make Don Pedro Mexía odious to the people.

Don Pedro, perceiving the spiteful intents of the Archbishop and hearing the outcries of the people in the streets against him, and their cries for the use and liberty of their churches, secretly retired himself to the palace of the Viceroy, begging his favor and protection. . . . The Viceroy immediately sent out his orders, commanding the bills of excommunication and cessation *a divinis* to be pulled from the church doors, and to all the superiors of the cloisters to set open their churches, and to celebrate their service and Masses as formerly they had done.

But they disobeying the Viceroy through blind obedience to their Archbishop, the Viceroy commanded the Arch-Prelate to revoke his censures. But his answer was that what he had done had been justly done against a public offender and great oppressor of the poor, whose cries had moved him to commiserate their suffering condition, and that the offender's contempt of his first excommunication had deserved the rigor of the second censure—neither of the which he would or could revoke until Don Pedro Mexía had submitted himself to the Church and to a public absolution, and had satisfied the priests and cloisters who suffered for him, and had disclaimed that unlawful and unconscionable monopoly wherewith he wronged the whole commonwealth and especially the poorer sort therein. . . . The Viceroy, not brooking this saucy answer from a priest, commanded him presently to be apprehended and to be guarded to San Juan de Ulua, and there to be shipped for Spain.

The Archbishop having notice of this . . . retired himself out of Mexico to Guadalupe with many of his priests and prebends, leaving a bill of excommunication upon the church doors against the Viceroy himself, and thinking privily to fly to Spain, there to give an account of his carriage and behavior.

But he could not flee so fast but the Viceroy . . . with his sergeants and officers pursued him to Guadalupe. Which the Archbishop understanding, he betook himself to the sanctuary of the church, and there caused the candles to be lighted upon the altar, the Sacrament . . . to be taken out of the tabernacle, and attiring himself with his pontifical vestments, with his mitre on his head, his crozier in one hand, in the other he took his God of bread, and thus with his train of priests about him at the altar, he waited for the coming of the sergeants and officers. . . . The officers coming into the church went towards the altar where the

Bishop stood, and kneeling down first to worship their God, made a short prayer; which being ended, they propounded unto the Bishop with courteous and fair words the cause of their coming to that place, requiring him to lay down the Sacrament and to come out of the church and to hear the notification of what orders they brought unto him in the King's name.

To whom the Archbishop replied, that whereas their master the Viceroy was excommunicated, he looked upon him as one out of the pale of the Church, and one without any power or authority to command him in the house of God, and so required them as they tendered the good of their souls to depart peaceably and not to infringe the privileges and immunity of the Church . . . and that he would not go out of the church unless they durst take him and the Sacrament together.

With this the head officer, named Tiroll . . . called to the altar a priest whom he had brought for that purpose, and commanded him in the King's name to take the Sacrament out of the Archbishop's hand. Which the priest doing, the Archbishop unvested himself of his pontificals, and (though with many repetitions of the Church's immunity) yielded himself. . . .

Some of the city of Mexico in private began to talk strangely against the Viceroy, and to stomach the banishment of their Archbishop, because he had stood out against so high a power in defence of the poor and oppressed. And these their private grudges they soon vented in public with bold and arrogant speeches against Don Pedro Mexía and the Viceroy—being set on and encouraged by the priests and prebends who, it seems, had sworn blind obedience to their Arch-Prelate. . . . Then began a fire of mutiny to be kindled. . . .

The rude multitude . . . being now set on by two or three priests who were joined with them . . . began more violently to batter the palace gates and walls, having brought pikes, and halberds, and long poles. Others had got a few pistols and birding pieces, wherewith they shot, not caring whom they killed or wounded in the palace.

It was wonderful to see that none of the better sort, none of the judges, no high justice, no inferior officers durst or would come out to suppress the multitude, or to assist the Viceroy. . . . Nay, I was told by some shopkeepers who lived in the marketplace that they made a laughing business of it, and the people that passed by went smiling and saying: "Let the boys and youngsters alone, they will right our wrongs, they will find out before they have done both Tiroll and Mexía and him that protects them."

But amongst them was much noted one priest, named Salazar, who spent much shot and bullets, and more his spirits, in running about to spy some place of advantage which he might soonest batter down. They found, it seems, the prison doors easier to open, or else with help within they opened them, and let out all the malefactors—who joined with them to assault the palace.

The Viceroy, seeing no help came to him from the city, from his friends, from the judges of the Chancery, from the King's high justices, nor other officers for the peace . . . set up the royal standard and caused a trumpet to be sounded to call the city to aid and assist their King. But this prevailed not, none stirred, all the chief of the city kept within doors. . . .

The day drawing to an end, the multitude brought pitch and fire, and first fired the prison, then they set on fire part of the palace, and burnt down the chief gate. . . . Many got into the palace, some fell upon the Viceroy's stables, and there got part of his mules' and horses' rich furnitures. Others began to fall upon some chests, others to tear down the hangings. . . . Others searched about for Don Pedro Mexía, for Tiroll, and the Viceroy.

None of them could be found, having disguised themselves and so escaped. Whither Don Pedro Mexía and Tiroll went, it could not be known in many days. But certain it was that the Viceroy disguised himself in a Franciscan habit, and so in company of a friar went through the multitude to the cloister of the Franciscans, where he abode all that year —and there I saw him the year after—not daring to come out until he had informed the King and Council of Spain with what hath happened, and of the danger himself and the city was in.

Against the arrogance of the crown and the cruelty of the large holders of soil and slaves, there rose the militant power of the Church and its zealous bishops, defending the cause of the colonists and the weal of the serfs as its early saints and healers and missionaries had done.

The wealth of the Church grew greater, its possessions of soil and other holdings multiplying into vast domains, its range of influence encompassing city and town and village, carving out virtually independent provinces for itself in the enormous interiors of Brazil and Paraguay and the other colonies. With its greater wealth and its spanning and spiraling influence, the Church gradually acquired even greater power—

Until the control of this power and all that went with it became the goal of achievement of men of crass ambition, of men of perverted zeal, of acquisitive men skilled in chicanery:

Of men who were among the wealthiest owners of soil and serfs in the colonial realm, but who still coveted greater riches. Of men in the service of the crown greedy for further authority. Of men in the service of the Church itself, fanatical and determined to establish their power over the Church and the Church's power over everything that could be surveyed.

Out of the covetousness and greed, out of the fanatical ambitions, out of the cliques steeped in chicanery and gluttonous for wealth and for power—and out of the frantic struggle, too, to preserve the colonies intact and subservient to the crowns of Portugal and Spain—came the cruel institution whose shadow hung for three hundred years over the whole body of the great colonial land:

Over the whole land already subjected, from New Spain down through New Granada, down through Brazil, down through the Viceroyalty of Peru that included Chile, down through the colony of the Plate, hovered the long and dreaded shadow of the Inquisition!

The Inquisition, known as the Holy Office, but against which even the long defending arm of the good men among the powerful, in the Church as well as without, were helpless to protect the land pleading for mercy in tears and flame. The fearful shadow, whose shape was an Inquisitor's cowl, bent relentlessly over the body of the tortured land, broken and burning where she lay.

Eleven

INQUISITORS

There is a place in the world, my brothers,
There is a place in the world beyond the burnings.

JACINTO FOMBONA PACHANO

HOLY OFFICE

From the beginning of the conquest, the priest went with the conquistador. With the marching power of the conqueror and the power of the crown, marched the power of the Church.

From the moment the site for a city was laid, the priest was there to see that the Church shared the power as well as the possession of the soil and the people claimed by the conqueror in the name of the crown.

During most of the colonial period, the highest symbol of Church power was the Jesuit order and its numerous missions scattered over the land, from Sonora in New Spain down to the Paraguay and the Plate. In the heart of the southern continent—in Brazil as well as in Paraguay—the Jesuits had entire provinces with thousands of natives under their exclusive control.

The work of the Jesuits was eulogized by some men of power. But most of the gentry and the officialdom feared the Jesuit aggressiveness and opposed its expansion over the colonies. These men fought the Jesuit power by invective, by bitter complaints to the crown, and by violent deeds—to the point where the populous provinces occupied by the Jesuit missions with their independent armies of Indians in the southern continent became a no-man's-land of frequent skirmishing. From the colonial settlements in Brazil, for instance, where there was constant need of more slaves and serfs for the growing towns and spreading fields, raids were launched against the Jesuit missions that lay between the settlements and the frontier of free Indians beyond. In the fighting, thousands of the mission Indians themselves were captured and enslaved, and many blamed their former Jesuit guardians for their suffering.

Before long the men of the rich and militant order that had first been founded in Rome as a defense against Protestantism found themselves in an even worse position than ever before as far as their vast colonial powers were concerned. The Jesuits became the chief source of friction between the power of the Church and the authority of crown and landholder. And the friction grew worse, becoming a challenge to the whole colonial rule, becoming another threat of civil war on a scale that could pulverize the slowly crumbling power of the two Iberian empires themselves.

But among the colonial people in general, there was not more fear of the Jesuit order than of that other institution established in the new world by the crown and known variously as the Holy Office, the Holy Tribunal, the Inquisition. Whatever the name, it was seldom even whispered. It was rarely mentioned in private; it was never mentioned in public.

The Inquisition was feared mainly because it operated in secret and because not even the viceroy could challenge its power—derived directly from Madrid and Lisbon where it had been set up as part of the crown's political drives against the Moslems and the Jews in the larger war to end the Moorish domination. But with the rise of the Reformation and the rapid climb to power of England and Holland and the other enemy nations strongly influenced by the new teachings, Protestantism also became the target of the Holy Office in the new world as it was in the old:

Protestantism stood for piracy, the monster that menaced the imperial sway of Spain and Portugal, and piracy had to be purged:

The chief Inquisitor visited me every Saturday during three months, pressing me every time to abjure my religion; but I would neither hearken nor obey to his urging solicitations. They proceeded then to give me such violent sort of victuals, which turned my head and brains in such a manner that I knew not what I either did or said—insomuch

The Examination of Louis Ramé by the Inquisition of Mexico
that in one of these fits I had like to have thrown myself out of a window. This lasted a whole year, during which I pulled to pieces a pair of silk stockings which I had, and with the silk and some of the boards of my bed I contrived a sort of harp—which I having been heard to play upon, they took it from me.

After this I contrived another way how to divert myself and pass away the time. I undid another pair of stockings which I had with me, and with part of the worsted, made myself a cap and with the rest of it I made galloon. I made a sort of needle, to weave my cap with, out of some boards of my bed, which I cut out with a piece of the lock of my trunk, having sharpened it for that purpose upon bricks. Some days I made almost three yards of galloon, and then undid it again, and so on, to divert my melancholy thoughts.

The second year being at an end, they carried me before the Tribunal, where, instead of seeing the Inquisitor and the Fiscal, as I had before, I found a great many ecclesiastics and lawyers. A Jesuit, who was the nearest to me, began to speak, and bestowed on me the title of "brother" —telling me that God had made use of all these ways to open my eyes, and had brought me into their power for the salvation of my soul.

I answered him that it had been God's will to let all these punishments and afflictions fall upon me in order to awaken me, and to make me consider the many sins which I had committed against his Divine Majesty, and to try in a greater measure the resolution and constancy which I had shown at the same time that others had abjured their religion, for the sake of some conveniences of this world—and that I prayed God to fortify me in this trial.

He repeated then several passages of the Holy Scripture, which he pretended made against me. After this, another began his discourse and said: "Is it possible, my son, that your heart can be so hardened as not to consider the wonders of God, who has brought you before the Holy Tribunal, that you might therein find the salvation of your soul?" After which he brought the parable of the vineyard, and said that God had sent to seek for laborers for his vineyard both in the morning, noon and evening; and several other things which I am not capable of forming into a discourse, and which it is impossible for me to relate in the same style.

To this I answered: "Your Reverence will forgive me if I speak here my sentiments, this Tribunal having granted me the liberty of speaking.

Therefore, I say that our Savior Jesus Christ called the people to him by his preaching and admonishing of them, and that he never made use of secret prisons, fetters, etc. . . ."

The others began to talk and run down the Protestant religion, saying that it had been invented by one Calvin, who was a very ill man, and had been whipped, etc. To which I answered that I knew of no such religion as the religion of Calvin, but that my religion was that of Christ.

They went on with their discourses, and called me blind. . . . They named to me four attorneys and bid me to choose one to defend my cause. . . . I named one, who presently began to argue with me after the lawyer's way, representing to me, by a great many fine words, the goodness and charity of the Holy Tribunal in condescending and offering to receive and forgive me, but that instead of taking hold of this happy opportunity to save both my body and soul, I still continued obstinately and blindly to run on to my entire ruin both here and hereafter. I told him he preached in vain. After which he desisted from my cause, and I begged to die.

After all this they sent me back again to my secret prison, where I immediately kneeled down, returning God most hearty thanks for his assistance in my past trials, begging at the same time the continuance of it in those which I was likely still to undergo. After which I sang a psalm.

The chief Inquisitor, Don Juan de Miel, came to visit me every Saturday, and always asked me how I did. I generally answered him, as well as I could in this place.

"Do you want anything?" said he.

I told him, "Yes, I want the patience of Job, the virtue of Joseph, the wisdom of Solomon, the resolution of Tobit, the repentance of David, justice from your Tribunal, and a quick expedition."

He answered me, that as soon as the verification was made, I should have justice done me.

In this manner did I pass the third year, being pretty well used in the beginning. But afterwards they gave me such unwholesome food that it bought upon me a violent and continual looseness, which lasted between three and four months, and I became as lean and as dry as a red herring. I sang, cried, and fought with the Fiscal—as if he had been with me—telling him that he was worse than an infidel. However, I escaped these three years without falling sick. I was troubled with the toothache, and I had one tooth pulled out.

The fourth and last year passed with very little solicitation from my enemies, the Inquisitors, but with great torments caused by the bad victuals which were given me during five months.

In the month of November, they carried me before the Tribunal, where the first Inquisitor said to me: "By virtue of the oath which you have taken of speaking the truth, I command you to tell me whether you continue in the same mind and sentiments as before."

I answered, yes I did, with tears in my eyes, believing that the time of my death was at hand. After which my sentence was read in these words; viz.:

"We have found that we ought to condemn, and we do by this actually condemn, the aforesaid Louis Ramé, to be banished out of this Kingdom of New Spain, and to that effect he shall be delivered into the Officer of War's hands, and put into the Royal Prison."

. . . After the sentence being read, the first Inquisitor said to me: "Do you promise by the oath you have taken not to divulge anything of what has been done or said to you here, under the penalty of two hundred lashes?"

To which I answered that, whilst I continued in the dominions of the King of Spain, I would say nothing of it, but that when I should come to France, I must of necessity tell it, because it would be asked me where and how I had been all this while. And upon this they made me take a fresh oath.

After this they carried me into another prison in the first court, from whence I could see the people that walked in the street. And they gave me good victuals during seven or eight days in which time my sight became stronger—having almost lost it before through the ill food which they had given me. I was then carried into the aforesaid Royal Prison. As soon as I came there, they clapped fetters upon my legs.

The next Sunday after, at the Mass-time, for which purpose there is a chapel in the said prison, all the prisoners were brought out of the dungeons and other places, and carried into a great hall joining to the said chapel. When the gaoler came to me, I told him that none of my religion did go to Mass. He gave notice of it to the Tribunal, and I was put in a room by myself—as if they feared that I should breed an infection—where I remained during three months, very ill used.

The Viceroy with all the Judges came to visit the prisons at Christmas. I begged of him that I might have some ease from the hardships I endured, telling him at the same time how much I had suffered, and the extreme want of necessaries I was now brought to.

After this I was transferred from the Royal Prison to Mixcoac, which is a village about four or five miles from Mexico City. I was put there in a manufacture of cloth, which is the place where all the thieves and malefactors that are condemned by the justice, are bought and sold. . . .

From this manufacture I was carried back into the Royal Prison, where I continued six months longer with fetters on. . . . After these six months they took me out of the prison, and sat me on a mule, to carry me to Vera Cruz, having two guards along with me, and fetters on which weighed at least five and twenty pounds. They made me get up and down with all this weight, and the mule was so vicious and full of tricks that I believe they gave it me in hopes that she would break my neck.

About this time I had the news of Don Martín de Soto the Inquisitor's being dead. It was him that had threatened to have me burnt.

CHAMBER OF TORMENT

Frenchmen, Englishmen, and Dutchmen who fell into the hands of the crown officials in the Spanish and the Portuguese colonies were nearly always turned over to the Inquisition at once for torture and trial. Those who escaped death by strangling—to say nothing of those like the Frenchman, Louis Ramé, who was banished and even lived to tell his story to his own countrymen—were very few and very far between.

The story was almost the same where the Jews and "New Christians" who had managed to come to the colonies, especially Brazil, were concerned. Many had been permitted to come with the first groups of settlers. But later they and their descendants were denounced by competitors and rivals and personal foes. They were ferreted out by the Holy Office. And most of them were doomed to die at the stake—

But even these were not exempt from the preliminary ordeal of the chamber of torment:

Half of the rooms contained alcoves in which they slept; but as there was scarcely room enough for three persons, and as double that number were often shut up in each chamber, the most robust were obliged to sleep on the ground—where they had scarcely as much room as is usually appropriated to the dead in their graves.

Llorente's Description of the Tortures of the Inquisition

The chambers were so damp that the mats which were granted to these unfortunate beings in a short time decayed. The other moveables in the dungeons consisted of a few earthen vessels, which were removed only once a week—a circumstance which obliged them to live in an atmosphere so unhealthy that the greatest part died, and those who went out were so disfigured that they were taken for walking corpses.

But it was not enough to put men in places so close and infected: they even prohibited them books and everything else which could for an instant make them forget their unhappy situation. Complaint was even interdicted; and when an unfortunate prisoner uttered any groans, they punished him by gagging him for a number of days, and by scourging him cruelly the whole length of the corridor if the first measure was not sufficient to force him to silence.

The same punishment of whipping was inflicted on those who made a noise in their chambers, or who disputed among themselves—in the latter case they considered the whole company as guilty, and scourged them all. The punishment was inflicted on all, without distinction of age or sex—so that young ladies, nuns, and ladies of distinction were disrobed and beaten unmercifully.

Such was the state of the prisons of the Holy Office, and the treatment which the prisoners suffered, towards the end of the fifteenth century. Since then some meliorations have successively taken place in the interior of the prisons. But the fate of the prisoners has been almost always the same, and many of these unfortunate persons have voluntarily given themselves up to death to put an end to their sufferings.

Others—more worthy of pity—were taken from their prisons to be conducted into the chamber of torment. There they found the inquisitors and the executioners. There every person accused, who had refused to declare himself guilty, received trial.

A subterranean vault, to which they descended by an infinity of windings, was the place appointed for the application of the torture. The profound silence which reigned in this chamber of torment, and the terrible appearance of the instruments of punishment—feebly seen by the vacillating light of two flambeaux—must necessarily have filled the mind of the victim with a mortal terror. Scarcely had he arrived before the inquisitors and executioners, who were clothed with long robes of sackcloth, and their heads with a hood of the same stuff—pierced with holes for the eyes, mouth and nose—seized and stripped him even to his shirt.

Then the inquisitors, joining hypocrisy to cruelty, exhorted the victim to confess his crime. And if he persisted in denying it, they ordered that the torture should be applied in the manner and for a length of time which they deemed proper. The inquisitors never failed, in case of injury, death, or fracture of limbs, to protest that the act was to be imputed to the accused alone.

There were three modes of making trial: the cord, fire, and water.

In the first case, they tied the hands behind the back of the patient, by means of a cord passed through a pulley attached to the roof, and the executioners raised him up as high as possible. After having left him some time thus suspended, they loosened the cord, so that the unfortunate prisoner fell suddenly within a half a foot of the ground. This terrible jar dislocated all the joints; and the cord cut the wrists and entered often into the flesh, even to the very sinews.

This punishment, which was renewed every hour, left the patient without power and without movement. But it was not until after the physician of the Inquisition had declared that the sufferer could no longer support the torture without dying, that the inquisitors remanded him to prison. There they left him, a prey to his sufferings and to despair, till the moment that the Holy Office had prepared for him a torture still more horrible.

This second trial was made by means of water. The executioners stretched their victims in a wooden instrument of torture, in the form of a spout, fitted to receive the body of a man, without any other bottom than a stick which traversed it, and on which the body, falling backwards, was bent by the effect of the machinery and took such a position that the feet were higher than the head. It resulted from this situation that respiration became very painful, and that the patient suffered the most dreadful agonies in all his limbs, in consequence of the pressure of the cords, the knots of which penetrated into the flesh and caused the blood to flow even before they had employed the bands.

It was in this cruel position that the executioners introduced at the bottom of the throat of the victim a piece of fine linen, wet, a part of which covered the nostrils. They afterwards turned the water into the mouth and nose, and then left it to filter so slowly that one hour at least was exhausted before the sufferer had swallowed a drop, although it trickled without interruption.

Thus the patient found no interval for respiration. At every instant he made an effort to swallow, hoping to give passage to a little air. But as the wet linen was so placed as to prevent this, and to cause the water, at the same time, to enter by the nostrils, it will be perceived that this new combination must necessarily place great difficulty in the way of the most important function of life. Thus it often happened that when the torture was finished they drew the fine linen from the throat all stained with the blood of some of the vessels which had been ruptured by the struggles of the unfortunate victim.

It ought to be added that every instant a powerful arm turned the fatal lever, and at each turn the cords which surrounded the arms and the legs penetrated even to the bones.

If by this second torment they could obtain no confession, the inquisitors afterwards had recourse to fire. To make this trial, the executioners commenced by tying the hands and feet in such a manner that the sufferers could not change their position. They then rubbed the feet with oil and lard, and other penetrating substances, and placed them before the fire—until the flesh was so roasted that the bones and sinews appeared in all parts . . .

Things were carried to such lengths by the inquisitors that the council of the Supreme was obliged to prohibit their applying the torture more than once to the same person. But the coldhearted and barbarous monks immediately found means to elude this prohibition, and . . . when they had tortured a victim during an hour, they remanded him to prison, declaring that the trial was "suspended" until they should judge proper to continue it.

It was thus they left their prisoners, and forced them almost always to confess themselves more guilty than they really were. Fatigued with suffering, death appeared to them a relief. Many gave themselves up to it in the prisons, and others saw without pain the preparations of the auto de fe, which should deliver them to the flames.

THE SINGULAR PROCESSION

Torture by water and fire and the cord. Slow starvation in the stench of a dark dungeon. The sting of the lash at any hour of the night or day. And through it all, the ceaseless cry of the Inquisitors exhorting the accused to confess and to repent.

These, and a hundred other deaths-in-life which the accused and their relatives and friends were forced to undergo in varying degrees throughout the colonial years, were sometimes but the painful prologue to a longer story of suffering and persecution written with the blood of men and women charged with being witches or heretics, Jews or "Judaizers" —some of them high in the roster of high colonial officials. The story of such victims was most satisfying to the Holy Tribunal when it could be told with the grand ending:

The auto-da-fé!

The place selected was the town hall, being in the principal square of the city, where was ordered to be erected a sumptuous seat. Its base was on a level with the balustrade of the balcony, which formed a running cornice, with curious mouldings, in the clear of which they placed the seat, raised in form of a dais, with sufficient room for the chairs of the Viceroy, Inquisitors and the Town Council, above which was the canopy of the tribunal—which, with its silk curtains and the beautiful worked and rich carpets spread all over the spaces and flooring of the dais, made a most majestic appearance.

Fray Juan de Torquemada: An Auto-da-fé in Spanish America

It was quite a marvelous thing to see the people who crowded to this celebrated and famous auto (they were in the windows, and every place, which they filled, and even to the house and floors of the Holy Office) and to see the singular procession and accompaniment of the "relaxed" and penitentials who came out with ropes about their necks and pasteboard caps on their heads, with flames of fire painted on them; in their hands they held a green cross and each had a monk by his side who exhorted him to die well; they had also familiars of the Holy Office for a guard.

The reconciled Jews with *sambenitos*, those twice married with caps, upon which were painted objects signifying their crimes. Those accused of witchcraft with white caps on their heads, candles in their hands, and ropes about their necks. Others for blasphemy, with gags in their mouths, half naked, their heads uncovered, and with candles in their hands, all in order, following one after the other—those for lesser crimes going first and in the same order the rest, the "relaxed" following behind, and the dogmatists and teachers of the law of Moses as captains or leaders, the last with their trains on their caps, rolled up and twisted to signify the false doctrines they taught.

And in this manner they proceeded towards the places erected for them, which were in front of the seats for the tribunal, at the foot of which were also seats in the form of steps, upon which were seated the familiars of the Holy Office, each according to his seniority.

As for the scaffold, or framework for the seats of the condemned, it was marvelous. . . . In the middle of it was a half pyramid, surrounded by semicircular steps up to the top. Upon these were seated in their order the "relaxed," the dogmatists upon the highest steps, and the others in gradation. And in this order also were the effigies of those who were "relaxed," but who were either dead or absent. The reconciled and other penitentials were seated upon low benches in the open space of the scaffold.

The head jailor of the Holy Office had a chair placed for him at the base of the scaffold. A pulpit was also placed upon the right of the Holy Office, from which a sermon was preached by the Archbishop of the Philippine Islands, Don Fray Ignacio de Santibáñez, of the order of my glorious father San Francisco.

Two other pulpits were placed, one on each side of the tribunal, from which were read by the reporters the sentences of the condemned. . . . It will be enough to say that there were many of those obstinate Jews, who each one might have been a Rabbi of a synagogue.

All this was celebrated with great majesty, the immense majority of the people not being a little astonished at the rites and ceremonies.

THE LARGER SPECTACLE

The people were not a little astonished at the ritual and the burning. But all during the colonial period few people dared to express more than astonishment at the spectacle of the autos-da-fé—which, compared to the burnings in Spain and in Portugal, were few in number and few in the number of victims consumed. And very few people in the colonies dared to express even so much as astonishment at that larger and more enduring spectacle pervading their lives:

The day-to-day spectacle of the Inquisitors' vise holding them and most of their fellows in the omnipotent grip of intimidation and terror. Holding their lives in its ubiquitous grip. Policing their bodies and policing their minds:

Policing the books:

Such is the vigilance of the Inquisition that this regulation concerning the policing of books is more rigorously executed both in Europe and America than any other regulation appertaining to the Spanish regime. From whatever part books may come, in whatever language they may be written, neither the entrance, circulation, nor use, are permitted, until

The Censorship of Books under they have been judged orthodox by the com-
the Inquisition missaries of the Holy Office. Every bookseller in the Spanish dominions is bound to furnish, in the first two months of every year, an inventory of the books he exposes for sale. To this must be subscribed his oath that he has no others than those contained in the inventory.

He is forbidden to purchase or sell any book prohibited by the Inquisition, under penalty, for the first offence, of interdiction from all commerce in books for two years; banishment, during the same term, to twelve leagues distance from the place in which he was established; and a fine of two hundred ducats to the profit of the Inquisition. Repetitions of the offence are proportionally punished.

The book forming the substance of the crime may have been already sold, and in the hands of a third person; but the declaration of the purchaser suffices to subject the bookseller to all the penalties specified.

Every bookseller must have in his store a catalogue of the books censured by the Inquisition, under penalty of forty ducats. It is even necessary that the catalogue should be his own—for if it is borrowed, he is equally liable to the fine, as if he has none.

No bookseller may proceed to the inventory, estimate, purchase, or sale of private libraries, without furnishing to the commissary of the Inquisition a statement containing the names and surnames of the authors, the titles of the books, the subject matter, and the place and year of the impression, under penalty of fifty ducats.

Every person who enters the country with books, must make a declaration detailed and sworn to, which is sent to the tribunal of the Inquisition or its commissaries, who have the power to permit their introduction or to seize them. The omission, or imperfect execution of this declaration, occasions a confiscation of the books, and a cost of two hundred ducats for the expenses of the Holy Office.

When books, as most frequently happens, are deposited at the custom-house with other effects or merchandise, the officers of the customs cannot release the books but by express permission of the commissary of the Inquisition—which he does not grant till he has previously examined them.

Catalogues, which Spaniards may receive from abroad for the selection of books, must, before any use is made of them, be sent to the Holy Office, which may retain or restore them.

Whoever may have the temerity to elude the vigilance of the Inquisition is not, therefore, in peaceable possession of the proscribed books he has received. He remains exposed to those domiciliary visits, which the commissioners of the Inquisition have a right to make at any hour either of day or night.

By day and by night, whatever the hour and whatever the place or the person, the Inquisitors' hunt went on. The hunt went on for anything that might resemble heresy in thought if not in deed, because it might fail to endorse in full the status quo of imperial power over the colonial domains and over their people and the thoughts of their people.

The Inquisitors' hunt went on. Not against the Indians, who were considered innocent pagans who could be saved by catechizing. But against all others known or suspected to be other than orthodox believers and followers of the Church and the authority it shared with the crown and the gentry. The hunt went on—but the prey of unorthodoxy was small. The Inquisitors' hunt seldom stopped for rest—but still the prey was small. The prey was scattered and sparse in the long stretching years of the slowly evolving people of the whole colonial land:

From St. Augustine in Florida down to Santiago in Chile the people were engaged in a quiet struggle, for three long and lingering centuries, to adapt themselves to the inexorable bonds of colonialism imposed on them and their thoughts and feelings and all their efforts at expression. With pleasure or pain, or insensible to both, the colonial people—the hunted ones along with those who were not hunted but whose colonial freedom was still a hazardous quantity subject to caprice or sudden suspicion—were slowly and gradually learning the orthodox patterns of thinking and doing brought from the old world.

And they were slowly and gradually changing those patterns to fit the ways of their provincial and local American lands.

Out of the conflict and the blending of the Old World ways with the new, their own colonial patterns were emerging. In the process the Old World ways were dying as the Indian ways before them had begun to die. The two ways were dying—but from their slowly expiring energies, as from some mammoth wild plant covering the whole land, runners were subtly spreading through the colonial subconsciousness:

Runners of feeling and thought from which the new roots of behavior and custom were to come to life. And the new roots lay deep in the hard subsoil of colonialism. Deep and spreading relentlessly through the sub-surface, the colonial roots were shaping the pattern of life in the southern American lands that would last, for better and for worse, for years and decades to come.

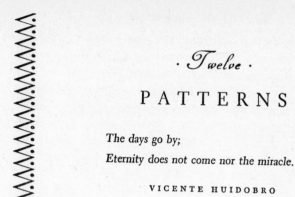

· *Twelve* ·

PATTERNS

The days go by;
Eternity does not come nor the miracle.

VICENTE HUIDOBRO

INDIAN LAMENT

What was left of the Indian centuries was dying, giving way through the colonial decades. But it was dying and giving way slowly.

In many parts of the land there was little apparent change in the Indians' lives except the substitution of the Christian priest for the pagan, the replacement of native master and official and captain of arms by the Spaniard or the Portuguese. The change was slight in appearance—but it was great in fact. It was great because the hard pagan core of their cultures was gone and because the Indians as a whole had fallen low in the strict social hierarchy of the colonial system:

The Indians had become a class of serfs.

But they were serfs with a long memory. They were people slow to forget the events that had made them vassals of new conquerors. Throughout the colonial years and after—they recalled those events in song and dance and pageantry of their own making. And remembering, they wept—as their ancestors had wept in remembering the deeds of earlier conquerors over the land.

Among those who now remembered most keenly and most poignantly were the descendants of the Inca rulers and the Inca people in the colony of Peru. The colony was second in riches only to New Spain. And the Indians' portion of that wealth was as poor as their memory was rich:

While in Huamalies I was twice entertained with the representation of the death of the Inca. The plaza or square had a kind of arch erected at each corner, adorned with plate, flowers, ribbons, flags made of handkerchiefs, and whatever could be collected to ornament them. Under one of these sat a young Indian, with a crown on his head, a robe, and other emblems of monarchy. He was surrounded by his coyas or princesses, who sang to him in the Quechua language. Presently several Indians came running from the opposite corner of the plaza, and after prostrating themselves, informed the Inca of the arrival of the viracochas— white men, or children of the sun. At this time drums and trumpets were heard, and Pizarro, with about a dozen Indians dressed as soldiers, made his entry on horseback, and alighted at the arch opposite to that of the Inca.

The Indians Recall the Fateful Arrival of the White Men

An ambassador was now sent to the Inca by Pizarro, requesting an interview, and the Prince immediately prepared to visit him. A kind of litter was brought, which he entered, and, surrounded by a number of Indians and his coyas, he was carried to where Pizarro stood, and waited for him.

Pizarro first addressed the Inca, promising him the protection of the king, his master; the answer was the acceptance of the promise. Pizarro then told him that he must become a Christian, but to this he objected —when he was immediately seized by the soldiers and carried to another corner of the plaza.

Pizarro followed him, and ordered him to deliver up all his treasures. He now took from him his crown, sceptre, and robes, and then ordered him to be beheaded. The Inca was dragged to the center of the plaza, and laid on the ground, which one of the soldiers struck with an axe, and a piece of red cloth was thrown over the head of the Inca. The Spaniards then departed, and the Indians began to wail and lament the death of their king. . . .

The plaintive ditties—yarabis—sung by the coyas, particularly after the death of their beloved Inca, were, to a feeling mind, superior to the sweetest warblings of an Italian cantatrice. The surrounding scenery, the view of the Cordilleras, the native dresses, the natives themselves, and the very earth which the Inca had trod on . . . were well calculated to rouse sympathy and compassion. . . . After three centuries have elapsed, the memory of the ancient monarchs of this country is kept alive by the annual representations of the cruel and unmerited death of the last of the race.

FEAST OF FOOLS

There was gaiety as well as sorrow in the lives of the colonial people. In the privileged lives led by the whites—whether they were Europeans or whether they were Creoles born in the land, or whether they were part European and part Creole—there was plenty of gaiety and hearty mirth.

Throughout the colonies, the Creoles were gradually outnumbering the Europeans, whom they now sometimes referred to in uncomplimentary terms—such as the Brazilian settlers' term of "feather-legs" applied to the Portuguese colonists. In their habits both of leisure and of occupation, the Creoles were far less restrained than the Europeans who came after the great flood-tide of the sixteenth century with its conquest and settlement and pioneering in thought and in deed.

The Creoles, though white and therefore highest in the social scale—alongside or just below the European—were also the new people of the backland frontiers. Many who lived in the towns and the cities still had traits of the plainsmen and cowboys and of the pioneers of the jungle. And there was little restraint in their ways of work or play toward the Europeans, or toward each other or the Indian serfs or the Negro slaves around them. In the colony of Brazil their favorite feast was the Feast of Fools:

For a week past I have noticed colored balls exposed here and there on plates for sale. The green ones might be taken for small apples, the yellow for oranges and lemons. Some are formed like pears, others like melons. An acquaintance made with some this morning has banished the indifference with which I have passed by them. Another article has also been pressed upon my attention. It is native starch—not granulated like ours, but an exceedingly white and fine powder, put up in paper cylinders six inches long and half an inch in diameter. When used, one end is opened and the contents shaken out.

Intrudo-*day in Brazil, Described by Thomas Ewbank*

While sitting at breakfast, S—— passed behind J——'s chair and, to my amazement, emptied a couple on his head and shoulders. The operation was performed so quietly, and the dust fell so lightly, that he knew not what was going on till a handful was applied to his face and ears. He sputtered, sprang up, and half-blinded, was saluted with liquid shots from a long-necked cologne bottle. Half in anger, and amid much laughter, he made a quick retreat, dressed, and went to the city.

While wondering what this could mean, a particle or two dropped from my forehead. Raising a hand, I found my own hair had also been powdered—a discovery that elicited a general screech. I rose to decamp, but this had been foreseen, and the only door through which escape was possible was locked. Now beset by a host of female foes, I dodged and ran till well-nigh exhausted, in trying to evade incessant volleys of starch and water.

At length I protested if the unrighteous war was continued I must and would come to close quarters, and, *vi et armis*, capture and play their own ordnance upon them. This was received with fresh peals of merriment and fresh broadsides. But at last an armistice—to endure through the day—was agreed on. I now was told that the *Intrudo* begins tomorrow, when all classes, indoors and out, dust and sprinkle one another—and that it is usual to do a little, by way of preface, the day before.

I retired to change my dress, but had not taken five paces ere I was overtaken by a storm of colored balls, charged with some liquid, similar to those I had noticed in the city. Surprised at this open breach of faith, and at the red and blue fragments with which I was bespattered, I lost no time in reaching my room and securing the door. I took from the shelf an old Portuguese dictionary for information.

It derives *Entrudo*, or *Intrudo*, from the Latin *Introitus*—Entrance, or Beginning—and describes the festival as one in which people, like Bacchants, romp, feast, dance and frolic indoors, and play all manner of tricks out, wetting and powdering one another. . . . The *Intrudo* occurs in the latter part of February and lasts . . . three days, invariably beginning on the Sunday previous to Ash-Wednesday. . . . Throwing dust and water is its special characteristic, the most conspicuous of its rites.

Intrudo-balls—for so the colored shot are named—instead of fruit, which they resemble, are mere shells of wax filled with water. They are sufficiently tenacious to retain the liquid, to bear gentle handling, and to be thrown to a considerable distance. Like more fatal bombs, they explode when they strike: the wax is shivered, and most of it sticks where it hits. I received a present of specimens of a superior kind, formed like bottles or decanters, and decorated with paint and gilding.

The necks were closed in imitation of corks sealed over. When used, they are charged with cologne or other scented waters. . . .

This is *Intrudo*-day. On rising, my friend R—— found the lower extremities of his pants sewed up. It is not unusual to lodge half a dozen balls in each leg; but as he is rather unwell, these singular marks of affection and foot-baths were spared him. In the act of shaking hands, I had one or two balls crushed in mine.

At breakfast one had his coffee without sugar, another found it sweetened with salt, a third began to pick threads out of his mouth, which caused fresh explosions of laughter—of two plates of toast, fine thread had been drawn through and through every piece, so that the teeth became unavoidably entangled in the meshes.

Some foreign merchants came up, on their way to the Botanic Garden. T—— invited them in. The simpletons! Their riding-costumes were soon like bathing-dresses. One got out without his hat, and actually rode off bareheaded! He returned in the afternoon with a slave bearing a large basket of the cereal missiles, and, quietly entering the rear, repaid his foes with interest.

The vicar came, and was saluted with cologne; they spared his *sutain* the infliction of the starch. He mentioned instances where he had been half drowned after receiving the most solemn pledges that he would not be molested. That I can fully believe. And turning to some ladies, I asked how they could—and on a Sunday too—tell such ——.

"Oh!" they replied, "*Intrudo* lies are no sin."

There is no believing anyone while it lasts. The padre wisely took his departure. He did not dare to stay for dinner, lest his rooms should be robbed by friends sending, in his name, for every valuable in them. Doña F——, by a ruse of this kind, obtained a dozen bottles of porter from J——'s carpenter, who had charge of them. He himself tricked the vicar last year; and, by the aid of a slave, deprived a friend of a turkey and fowls, upon which the owner and his family dined as guests, without dreaming of having contributed to the feast.

It used to be a custom to set before guests joints of wood, pies of sand, custards and puddings of kindred inedibles, dishes out of which leaped frogs, etc. But the *Intrudo*, like other festivals, is not kept up as formerly.

Señor F—— rose to depart, but was induced to drop again into his seat, on which a neighbor had slipped a quantity of flour and water balls. He sprang up as these nest-eggs crushed beneath him, while the mischief-loving projectors were in convulsions. Nor was the tumult one whit lessened by his manner of relieving the parts affected. Finding it impossible now to remain, he good-humoredly waved an adieu with one hand, and with the other placed his hat upon his head—and snatched it off again. It had been lined with the current ingredients of the day. Two extremities of his person were now in the condition of Quixote's head when he suddenly called for his helmet at an inconvenient moment for Sancho to deliver it.

Retiring to my room, I found a strange lady writing at the table. I paused and addressed her. No answer or motion. I advanced. The intruder was a bolster, furnished with sleeves, skirts, bonnet, shawl, etc., very artistically got up. Opening the drawers, I found the sleeves and neck of every shirt sewed up, and other garments hermetically sealed, so as to require both time and patience to get into them.

Both sexes are expert in calming a person after an attack, and throwing him off his guard. Ladies will show their open palms, rub them down their sides to prove that they have no concealed missiles, sit down by you, express fatigue, and say that a little frolic is well enough but this excess is foolish and very vulgar, look innocent as Madonnas, and conclude with:

"No more *Intrudo!*"

Your suspicions are lulled. But, ten to one, that same moment a couple of waxen wash-balls are applied to your face in the manner of soap and water, and a paper of cassava starch emptied on you. Your fair enemy springs from you with a shriek, and your surprise now takes another turn. She draws from her person ball after ball, and paper after paper, till you are ready to conclude she is made of them or has some machine about her producing them.

Employing parties on fool's errands is practiced. An unsuspicious person is sent on what he imagines a confidential matter of great moment to his friend—to borrow money on an emergency perhaps. The substance of the letter he carries is "Send the fool to Señor B—— and ask him to forward him with a like request to others."

An example has been given of a family being feasted on their own victuals. A reverend sweet-tooth revenged himself for a similar trick played on him by indulging largely at a neighbor's table. His hilarity became more enhanced when a splendid cake was brought in and placed before him. With sparkling eyes he cut deep into it. And when three fourths had disappeared, some hint was dropped which caused him to rise, stand aghast, and pray for patience—the cake (a highly valued present from a female friend) had been filched from his own larder!

I walked out toward the Passeio, and saw a few individuals molested. One gentleman in a new suit received two or three balls, and was quite indignant: he addressed some remarks to me and pointed to the window whence the shots came. It is useless to get vexed—those who do are sure to have their anger cooled by a fresh shower.

SOME LADIES OF JAQUEMEL

The hardihood and heartiness of the Creole was assimilated in part from the Indians and mestizos and mulattoes and Negroes beneath him.

In the colonies where the Creoles were surrounded by thousands of Negroes and mulattoes, the Creole's capacity for fullness in fun as in work was derived in part from the men and women of that lowest social class—many of them slaves, doing most of the work that had to be done, furnishing the skill and the power for the white's leisure. The slaves supplied the leisure and the joy to fill it, too:

In the French colony of Haiti, not only the Creoles but also the European whites could seldom resist the overpowering influence of the dark-skinned people around them:

These female mulattoes, who dance so exquisitely . . . are the most fervent priestesses of the American Venus. They have reduced voluptuousness to a kind of mechanical art, which they have carried to the highest point of perfection. In their seminaries Aretino himself would be a simple and modest scholar. They are, generally speaking, above the middle size, perfectly well formed, and so extremely supple in their limbs that they appear as if they had a swinging in their gait. They

Baron de Wimpffen Comments on the Charms of Certain Ladies

join to the inflammability of nitre, a petulance of desire which, in spite of every consideration, incessantly urges them to pursue, seize, and devour pleasure—as the flame devours its aliment—while on every other occasion these furious Bacchantes . . . scarcely seem to have strength enough to drag along their limbs or articulate their words.

It is from these women that the housekeepers are usually taken—that is to say, the acknowledged mistresses of the greatest part of the unmarried whites. They have some skill in the management of a family, sufficient honesty to attach themselves invariably to one man, and great goodness of heart. More than one European, abandoned by his selfish brethren, has found in them all the solicitude of the most tender, the most constant, the most generous humanity, without being indebted for it to any other sentiment than benevolence.

Their conversation, when it is not licentious, is insipid, which is not so much their fault as that of the men who frequent them. Susceptible of delicate feelings, they want nothing, perhaps, to be completely amiable but the degree of instruction necessary to enable them to turn to the advantage of the genius and the heart, that excess of sensibility which they abuse for want of knowing how to vary its use. . . .

The female mulattoes are adroit, but indolent. Those who join a spirit of economy to their other talents seldom fail of acquiring a fortune. They will employ a whole month in making a shirt—but then it will be the perfection of needle-work.

They love expensiveness in dress. It is a tribute to their beauty. But you must not implicitly trust to the enthusiastic encomiums you will sometimes hear on their magnificence. Their favorite coiffure is an India handkerchief, which is bound round the head. The advantages they derive from this simple ornament are inconceivable; they are the envy and despair of the white ladies—who aspire to imitate them, and who do not see that it is impossible for strong and glaring colors . . . to harmonize with the alabaster and the roses of Europe.

CASTE BY COLOR

The blending of white, Indian, and Negro, and the blending of the resultant blends with each other, continued without interruption in the Spanish, French, and Portuguese colonies—where the customs of their Old World combined with the climate of the New, the scarcity of white women, and the natural attractiveness of many of the dark-skinned folk, to break down whatever barriers might have impeded the blending.

There was some blending of the races through marriage, but most of it proceeded through the years without formal ceremony of any kind. The result was a vast range of new physical types, new mental and emotional attitudes, new talents, new aspirations that found some expression in the cultural contributions of the times: in the significant works of art and architecture as well as in the rich additions made by the Indian and the Negro influence to the developing language and speech in the colonies and to the literature and music of their growing cultures.

Yet these slowly opening horizons in human achievement and human promise meant little in the basic scheme of life under colonial rule, which whittled down the vast new range of human specimens with all their new potentialities to a few carefully labelled categories:

Old World or Creole white, Indian, Negro. And the varieties in between. These were the categories that dictated the position and power, the leisure and labor, the distinctions and deprivations, of every person in every one of the colonies. And the real criterion—for cultural as well as political and economic purposes—behind the setting-up of those social categories, and behind the determination to squeeze the sprawling colonial population into them, was a simple one:

The lighter the color the higher the rank.

That was the official criterion that largely predetermined the position of every man, woman, and child in every one of the colonies. That became the chief criterion of a person's social and cultural position, as it was already the prime factor that had fixed his economic and political place. And the criterion prevailed in the colonies where the laboring classes were mainly Negro as in the colonies where the hand of labor was predominantly the hand of the Indian:

The Mexican population is composed of the same elements as the other Spanish colonies. They reckon seven races: The individuals born in Europe, vulgarly called Gachupines; the Spanish Creoles, or whites of European extraction born in America; the Mestizos, descendants of whites and Indians; the Mulattoes, descendants of whites and Negroes; the Zambos, descendants of Negroes and Indians; the Indians, or copper-colored indigenous race; and the African Negroes. Abstracting the subdivisions, there are four castes: the whites, comprehended under the general name of Spaniards; the Negroes; the Indians; and the men of mixed extraction, from Europeans, Africans, American Indians, and Malays—for from the frequent communication between Acapulco and the Philippine islands, many individuals of Asiatic origin, both Chinese and Malays, have settled in New Spain. . . .

Baron von Humboldt Catalogues the Colors and Castes of New Spain

The son of a white—Creole or European—and a native of copper color, is called *Mestizo*. His color is almost a pure white, and his skin is of a particular transparency. The small beard and small hands and feet, and a certain obliquity of the eyes, are more frequent indications of the mixture of Indian blood than the nature of the hair. If a *Mestiza* marry a white man, the second generation differs hardly in anything from the European race.

As very few Negroes have been introduced into New Spain, the *Mestizos* probably compose seven-eighths of the whole caste. They are generally accounted of a much more mild character than the *Mulattoes*, descended from whites and Negresses, who are distinguished for the violence of their passions and a singular volubility of tongue. The descendants of Negroes and Indian women bear at Mexico, Lima, and even at Havana, the strange name of *Chino*. . . . On the coast of Caracas, and, as appears from the laws, even in New Spain, they are called *Zambos*.

This last denomination is now principally limited to the descendants of a Negro and a female Mulatto, or a Negro and a Chinese female. From these common *Zambos*, they distinguish the *Zambos prietos*, who descend from a Negro and a female *Zamba*. From the mixture of a white man with a Mulatto comes the caste of Quadroons. When a female Quadroon marries a European or Creole, her son bears the name of Quintroon. A new alliance with a white banishes to such a degree the remains of color that the children of a white and female Quintroon are white, also. . . .

The mixtures in which the color of the children becomes deeper than that of their mother are called *Salta-atrás*, or back-leaps.

In a country governed by whites, the families reputed to have the least mixture of Negro or Mulatto blood are also naturally the most honored. In Spain it is almost a title of nobility to descend neither from Jews nor Moors. In America, the greater or less degree of whiteness of skin decides the rank which a man occupies in society.

A white who rides barefooted on horseback thinks he belongs to the nobility of the country. Color establishes even a certain equality among men, who—as is universally the case where civilization is either little advanced or in a retrograde state—take a particular pleasure in dwelling on the prerogatives of race and origin. When a common man disputes with one of the titled lords of the country, he is frequently heard to say: "Do you think me not so white as yourself?"

This may serve to characterize the state and source of the actual aristocracy. . . .

It often happens that families suspected of being of mixed blood demand from the high court of justice—la audiencia—to have it declared that they belong to the whites. These declarations are not always corroborated by the judgment of the senses. We see very swarthy Mulattoes who have had the address to get themselves "whitened"—this is the vulgar expression. When the color of the skin is too repugnant to the judgment demanded, the petitioner is contented with an expression somewhat problematical.

The sentence then simply bears "that such or such individuals may consider themselves as whites."

MAN OF LEARNING

The social categories were as rigid in New Spain as anywhere else in the colonial Americas. But New Spain was the richest colony of all. It had able and willing patrons of art and of culture in general. And it was there, in Mexico, that most of the intellectual advances of those times were made.

It was there that the first printing press in the New World had been set up early in the sixteenth century. It was there, in that same century of achievement for Spain and her colonies, that one of the first universities in the Americas had been founded.

Even in the lagging seventeenth century, when the British colonies in New England and the French colonies in New France and the Dutch colonies in the New Netherlands were barely getting underway, New Spain was the center of growing intellectual activity and the origin of real contributions to the art and literature and learning of both worlds.

Intellectual pursuits in New Spain as in the rest of the colonies were confined to the small lettered class of whites—most of them Creole. And their reading and thinking, influenced if not always supervised by the Church, were concerned largely with questions of dogma. Yet little by little, matters of other interest, and the ideas that went with them, were taking hold—science and secular writing, mathematics and medicine.

Even before the eighteenth century's rising wave of enlightenment

over the Old World and the New, even before the interminable discus-
sions and writings on theology had begun to lose their listeners and
readers, intellectuals and artists of real stature arose in the southern
colonial Americas—especially in Mexico:

Artists like the brilliant Creole nun, Sor Juana Inés de la Cruz, whose
verse was esteemed in Europe as well as the colonies. Intellectuals like
her contemporary, Don Carlos de Sigüenza y Góngora: also a Creole and
also a poet, as well as an antiquarian and an explorer—but above all, a
man of learning:

Don Carlos, the scholar, recording his scientific observations along
with his portrait of the times:

The swollen condition of Lake Texcoco on the 22nd of July caused the
faint-hearted to raise the cry that Mexico City was being flooded. This
alarm was followed by a swarm of proposals and schemes to avoid such
an eventuality. Although, so far as the whole city was concerned, there
seemed to be no danger at that time—because the lake was far from
being filled up and because the ground where
Don Carlos de Sigüenza Writes the most important buildings are located was
of a Flood and an Eclipse. 1692 still a vara and a half (about four feet) above
the level reached in the flood of 1629—the Viceroy gave considerate attention to all these propositions. He did this because it was his desire
to satisfy everyone and to do the right thing.

He pretended not to notice how vexatious was one individual who
suggested that there was some opening into the lake through which the
water was at present entering and who volunteered to point out its location. To cheer the Viceroy up he asserted that within a short time the
whole lake would be dried up again. To this suggestion the Viceroy
listened with great patience.

Although I had already talked to His Excellency about this matter,
relating to him in great detail all that I know about it . . . he appointed
Sr. Doctor D. Juan de Escalante y Mendoza, fiscal of His Majesty in the
Criminal Court of the City of Mexico, as commissioner of this operation. The Viceroy did this in order that that meddling individual might
not feel hurt and also in order that a failure to consider this scheme
which, in the circumstances under which it was offered, was worthless,
might not later be construed as neglect on the Viceroy's part in what
concerns the welfare of Mexico City.

His Excellency ordered me to accompany this man, the cost of arrangements being at his expense. Inasmuch as this fellow not only knew nothing about the lake, but had not even seen it until we set him upon it on this occasion and later ones in which the same measure was repeated at the further request of this man and His Excellency, nothing was found.

A similar result attended another proposal (if the crack-brained fancy of a priest of Mexico City deserves this name). Neither in Mexico City nor in the Council of the Indies where he also presented it was it acceptable. After being imprisoned for several months, he still persisted in it. His Excellency now listened to it with patience. It was just another "drain." He assured him of what he wanted for its discovery and, having been conducted with all kinds of comforts and attentions to the place where he indicated, he pointed out a hill (who ever saw water run uphill!). They dug and, after having pulled a big tree out by the roots, instead of a drain they found a spring!

Although these laughable incidents are hardly in harmony with the gravity of the matters which I am relating to you, I wanted to give space to them in this letter in order that you may infer from them the zealous manner in which His Excellency applied himself. . . .

While these things were happening, the 23rd of August arrived—the date on which, as the almanacs and prognostication had foretold, there was an eclipse of the sun. If Your Grace understood something about astronomy, I would here recount to you with proper terms a thousand wonderful and beautiful things that I observed that day, for it was not only a total eclipse but one of the greatest that the world has ever seen.

It happened that very shortly after 8:45 in the morning we were in not a "good night" but a "bad night," because there can never have been any night more awful in comparison with the darkness in which we found ourselves for the period of almost a quarter of an hour. Since such blackness as this was not expected, at the very moment that the light failed and the shadows fell the Indian women and children, abandoning their stalls where they sold fruits, vegetables, and other small wares, and with the dogs howling, went shrieking and flying at full speed to get inside the cathedral. At the same time the bells for prayer were rung, not only in the cathedral but also in the majority of churches in the city. Such was the sudden confusion and excitement brought on by all this that it struck terror.

In the meantime I stood with my quadrant and telescope gazing upon the sun, exceedingly happy and thanking God repeatedly for having granted me the privilege of beholding what only happens very rarely in one given place and about which there are so few observations in the books.

The sun lay between Mercury which, about five degrees away toward the east, could be seen with the telescope—since the Moon was in quadrature—and the Heart of the Lion was to the west. Farther on lay Venus greatly cut off. The sky was everywhere covered with stars but only those of the First, Second, and Third Magnitude were visible to the south, perhaps because the Moon then had some apparent northern latitude.

Against what some declare, I noted some atmosphere on the Moon during the period of total obscuration. And lastly, from 8:30 to 9:30 the air was as cold and as intemperate as in the winter—which verifies the maxim of the astrologers attributing this condition to eclipses, particularly eclipses of the sun.

SCHOOL FOR CRIMINALS

From wealthy New Spain came the leisure and funds that furthered the spread of colonial culture which was also making slow but lasting headway in Peru and Chile and other parts of the empires in the west. And soon the progress was no longer confined to the southern colonies. Soon it began to move at an even swifter pace over the growing colonies in the northern continent—over New France, over New Holland. Especially over the British colonies where towns and cities were rising all along the north and middle Atlantic from Newfoundland, from Maine, down through Massachusetts and Pennsylvania and Virginia, down to the frontier facing Spain's own Florida—with new numbers of British colonials pushing westward, ever westward, and south, to the Mississippi and the larger frontiers bordering the great domains that belonged to France or to Spain.

From wealthy New Spain that extended all the way from those northern borders of Texas and New Mexico and California, down through Mexico and the central Americas, down to the Isthmus, also came the silver that was shipped as the situado—the pirates' favorite prey—to other parts of the empire for their support. To such poor but vital colonies as Puerto Rico went the situado.

And to that island fortress in the Caribbean were also shipped many of the criminals from the other colonies and even from Spain itself:

The presidios (or, according to the usual phraseology, the galleys) of Puerto Rico, are divided into two departments. The first, which is the criminal galley, is for the punishment of the greater offenders—for men who have committed murder and robberies in Spain, or in the island of Cuba—and also for soldiers belonging to the regiment in garrison of the city of San Juan, who have offended against military law. . . . The second place of punishment is the correctional presidio (or galley), where persons—generally natives of the island—are sentenced for terms varying from a month to a year, for petty offences and misdemeanors. . . .

Col. George Flinter: Conditions in Colonial Puerto Rico

Whoever for a moment seriously contemplates a presidio, must be forcibly struck with its inadequacy as a place of punishment, and with the state of moral and physical degradation to which it invariably subjects its wretched inmates. The villain who has committed deliberate murder, the homicide, the highway robber, the domestic thief, the incendiary, and the political delinquent, the perpetrators of every variety of crime of which human wickedness is capable . . . are blended and promiscuously associated together. . . .

They are alike exposed to the public view as criminals of the same stamp. They all drag a chain. They work together. They eat and sleep together. They have continual intercourse with each other. They all march forth in the morning to the public works, exhibiting by their filthy and squalid appearance all the extremes of human misery, clanking their iron chains to excite the compassion of the spectators, and uttering expressions in their wickedness or despair, revolting to the ear of modesty.

They are escorted by a guard of soldiers. They work or loiter out the day, little interested in the performance of a task which is stimulated by no hope, and carries with it no reward. They only watch for a favorable opportunity to elude the vigilance of the guard—and should they escape, they are sure to find an asylum among the people, who look on them with compassion and forget their crimes in the contemplation of their sufferings. They also receive news from their friends and accomplices who are at liberty, and who spare no pains to favor their escape.

At sunset the convicts are marched back to the prison through the town, exhibiting again the same scene—clanking of chains, profanity, and wretchedness.

The rooms where they sleep are generally so crowded as to produce an atmosphere physically unwholesome and disgusting in a high degree, and at the same time adapted to promote the debasement of every moral sentiment. . . . Young lads for the first offence, perhaps for concealing the value of two dollars of goods from the customhouse officers, share the same dark fate, and are mingled indiscriminately with hardened and aged villainy.

Their food is bad and scanty, so that the vigor of the most robust is soon reduced, and sickness and disease prey upon their physical strength. The administration of their miserable rations is as corrupt as cold, un-feeling avarice can make it. Those who supply the provisions purchase them by wholesale of the worst description—and by that villainous sys-tem of peculation which too often pervades public employments when not filled by honorable men, they deal them out to the convicts, di-minished in weight and measure, while they make government pay at the retail prices, thus preying on the subsistence of the wretched prisoner and defrauding government by a system of knavery. . . .

The convicts, accommodated with a blanket merely, sleep on the bare ground. They soon learn to brave exposure and to disregard privation. They are at once objects repulsive to the senses, and present a deplorable exhibition of moral depravity. . . .

So notorious is the demoralizing nature of these institutions, so gen-erally do those liberated from them come out more vile and corrupt, and more skilful in the various modes of depredation than when they en-tered—without shame, feeling, or remorse—that they may be termed the schools of crime, the seminaries of vice, where villains are tutored and instructed to sally forth and prey on mankind.

ODYSSEY

If the colonial way of meting out justice was often a school for criminals, the colonial system in general was not conducive to the encouragement of high morals or broad education. No class or group was exempt—least of all the privileged whites—from the corrosion of the times or the gradual decay that was eating through the entire fabric of colonialism.

It was a phenomenon well understood by some men of education, however, who were scattered through the colonies. Among those who saw its cancerous core were men like Don Miguel José Sanz of the colony of New Granada. He was a gentleman of the law who framed a code for Caracas, the capital of his home province of Venezuela, and his written words summed up the whole rotting system:

"Everyone wishes to be a gentleman, to lead an idle life."

The social organism of the colonies was becoming more and more complex, and increasingly unstable, by the time the first half of the eighteenth century had ended. To the warm antagonisms between the free whites on the one hand and the dark-skinned slaves and serfs on the other, there was now added the hot resentment of the Creole whites toward the European whites, who still monopolized the top colonial powers and privileges.

In spite of the thickening problems of colonial rule, the empire-holders still managed to encourage some work of further exploration into the vast interiors of their new-world domains. New groups of bandeirantes or banner-bearers moved farther into the great Brazilian backlands: the sertão. And in the little-known hinterlands of the Spanish colonies, the natives began to witness the arrival of even some foreigners—travelers and scientists expressly invited to study those lands:

Men like the great German, Baron Alexander von Humboldt, who would write volumes opening the way to a later understanding of the whole colonial system in the new world;

Men like the eminent French scientist, M. de La Condamine, and his colleagues, traveling over South America and recording their observations in the wilds of mountain and forest and jungle with cool precision. One of them, Monsieur Godin, dropped his coolness for the moment to write of a certain woman's odyssey through those wilds—

The certain woman being Madame Godin, his long-lost wife:

The Spanish governor of the province of Maynas and Omaguas, informed of the approach of Madame Godin, politely sent to meet her a canoe stored with refreshments, such as fruit, milk, etc., which reached her a little distance from the town of Omaguas. But to what misfortunes, what a horrible situation, was she not exposed before that happy moment! She left her residence at Riobamba with her escort on the 1st of October, 1769, and with these she reached Canelos, the spot at which they were to embark, situated on the little river Bobonasa, which empties itself into the Pastaca as that last does into the Amazon. M. de Grandmaison, who preceded them a month on the way, found the village of Canelos well inhabited, and immediately embarked, continuing his journey, to prepare everything necessary for the transport of his daughter at each stage of her way. As he knew that she was accompanied by her brothers, a physician, her Negro, and three female mulattoes . . . he proceeded on to the Portuguese missions.

From M. de La Condamine's Narrative of Travels

In the interval, however, between his journey and the arrival of my wife, the smallpox, an European import, more fatal . . . in this part than the plague, which is fortunately here unknown, is to the people of Levant, had caused the village of Canelos to be utterly abandoned by its population. They had seen those first attacked by this distemper irremediably carried off, and had in consequence dispersed among the woods, where each had his own hut, serving as a country-retreat.

On her departure my wife was escorted by thirty-one natives to carry herself and baggage. You know . . . that this road . . . is impracticable even for mules, that those capable effect the passage on foot, but that others are carried. The natives who escorted Madame Godin, who were paid in advance according to the bad custom in this country, a custom founded on mistrust, at times but too well founded, scarcely reached Canelos before they retraced their steps, either from dread of the air being infected, or from apprehension of being obliged to embark, a matter obnoxious in extreme to individuals who had perhaps never seen a canoe in their lives but at a distance.

Nay, such excuses are possibly superfluous, for you well know how often we are abandoned by them on our mountains, on no pretence whatever. What, under such circumstances, was to be done? Had my wife been able to return, yet the desire of reaching the vessel awaiting her, together with her anxiety to rejoin a husband from whom she had been parted twenty years, were incentives powerful enough to make her, in the peculiar circumstances in which she was placed, brave even greater obstacles!

In the village, only two Indians remained free from the contagion. These had no boat, but they engaged to construct one and pilot it to the mission of Andoas—about twelve days' journey below, descending the river Bobonasa, a distance of from one hundred and forty to one hundred and fifty leagues. She paid them beforehand.

The canoe being finished, they all departed from Canelos. After navigating the river two days, on the succeeding morning the pilots absconded. The unfortunate party embarked without anyone to steer the boat, and passed the day without accident. The next day at noon, they discovered a canoe in a small port adjoining a leaf-built hut, in which was a native recovering from illness, who consented to pilot them. On the third day of his voyage, while stooping over to recover the hat of Mr. K——, which had fallen into the water, the poor man fell overboard and, not having sufficient strength to reach the shore, was drowned.

Behold the canoe, again without a steersman, abandoned to individuals perfectly ignorant of managing it! In consequence, it was shortly overset, which obliged the party to land and build themselves a hut. They were now but from five to six days' journey from Andoas. Mr. R—— proposed to repair thither, and set off with another Frenchman of the party and the faithful Negro belonging to Madame Godin, taking especial care to carry his effects with him.

I since blamed my wife for not having dispatched one of her brothers to accompany Mr. R——, but found that neither of them, after the accident which had befallen the canoe, were inclined to trust themselves on the water again, without a proper pilot. Mr. R——, moreover, promised that within a fortnight a canoe should be forwarded to them with a proper complement of natives.

The fortnight expired, and even five and twenty days—when, giving over all hopes, they constructed a raft on which they ventured themselves, with their provisions and property. The raft, badly framed, struck against the branch of a sunken tree, and overset, all their effects perishing in the waves, and the whole party being plunged into the water. Thanks to the little breadth of the river at this place, no one was drowned, Madame Godin being happily saved, after twice sinking, by her brothers.

Placed now in a situation still more distressing than before, they collectively resolved on tracing the course of the river along its banks. How difficult of effect was this enterprise, you . . . are well aware, who know how thickly the banks of the rivers are beset with trees, underwood, herbage, and lianas, and that it is often necessary to cut one's way. They returned to their hut, took what provisions they had left behind, and began their journey.

By keeping along the river's side they found its sinuosities greatly lengthened their way—to avoid which inconvenience, they penetrated the wood. And in a few days they lost themselves. Wearied with so many days' march in midst of woods, incommodious even for those accustomed to them, their feet torn by thorns and brambles, their provisions exhausted, and dying with thirst, they were fain to subsist on a few seed, wild fruit, and the palm cabbage.

At length, oppressed with hunger and thirst, with lassitude and loss of strength, they seated themselves on the ground without the power of rising, and waiting thus the approach of death, in three or four days expired one after the other.

Madame Godin, stretched on the ground by the side of the corpses of her brothers and other companions, stupefied, delirious, and tormented with choking thirst, at length assumed resolution and strength enough to drag herself along in search of the salvation which providentially awaited her. Such was her deplorable condition she was without shoes, and her clothes all torn to rags. She cut the shoes off her brothers' feet, and fastened the soles on her own.

It was about the period between the 25th and 30th of December, 1769, that this unfortunate party . . . perished in this miserable manner. The date I gather by what I learn from the only survivor, who related that it was nine days after she quitted the scene of the wretched catastrophe described before she reached the banks of the Bobonasa. Doubtless this interval must have appeared to her of great length, and how a female so delicately educated and in such a state of want and exhaustion could support her distress though but half the time, appears most wonderful. She assured me that she was ten days alone in the wood—two, awaiting death by the side of her brothers, the other eight wandering at random. The remembrance of the shocking spectacle she witnessed, the horror incident on her solitude and the darkness of night in a desert, the perpetual apprehension of death, which every instant served but to augment, had such effect on her spirits as to cause her hair to turn grey.

On the second day's march, the distance necessarily inconsiderable, she found water, and the succeeding day some wild fruit and fresh eggs —of what bird she knew not, but which, by her description, I conjecture to have been a species of partridge. These with the greatest difficulty was she enabled to swallow, the esophagus, owing to the want of aliment, having become so much parched and straitened. But these and other food she accidentally met with, sufficed to support her skeleton frame. . . .

It was on the eighth or ninth day, according to Madame Godin, after leaving the dreadful scene of the death of her companions, that she found herself on the banks of the Bobonasa. At daybreak she heard a noise at about two hundred paces from her. Her first emotions, which were those of terror, occasioned her to strike into the wood. But after a moment's reflection, satisfied that nothing worse could possibly befall her, than to continue in her present state, and that alarm was therefore childish, she proceeded to the bank of the river, and perceived two native Americans launching a boat into the stream.

It is the custom of these people, on their landing to pass the night, to draw their canoe either wholly or partially on shore, as a security against accidents, for should it be left afloat, and the fastening tackle break, it would be carried away by the current and leave the sleepers on shore in a truly helpless state. The natives, perceiving Madame Godin, advanced towards her—on which she conjured them to transport her to Andoas.

They had been driven by the contagion prevalent at Canelos to withdraw with their wives to a hut they had at a distance, and were then going to Andoas. They received my wife on board with kindness truly affectionate, showed every attention to her wants, and conducted her to that village.

Here she might have stopped some days to rest herself and recruit her strength (and well may it be conceived she had great need of rest). But, indignant at the conduct of the missionary at whose mercy she was left, and with whom for that reason she was obliged to dissemble, she resolved on making no stay at Andoas, nor would even have stopped a single night had it been possible to be avoided. . . .

Madame Godin, with the canoe and crew from Andoas . . . reached Laguna, where they were received with the greatest politeness by Dr. Romero, the new chief of the missions who, by his kind treatment during six weeks that she remained with him, did much towards re-establishing her health, but too much impaired, and making her forget her misfortunes. . . . When Madame Godin was somewhat recovered, M. Romero wrote . . . to the governor, acquainting him that he had represented to Madame Godin, whose courage and piety he could never sufficiently admire, that she was yet merely at the beginning of a long and tedious voyage, and that, though she had already travelled upwards of four hundred leagues, she had yet four or five times that distance to pass before she reached Cayenne; that, but just relieved from the perils of death, she was about to incur fresh danger; concluding with offering, if she chose to return, to cause her to be escorted back in perfect security to her residence of Riobamba.

To these he added that Madame Godin replied she was surprised at his proposals; that the Almighty had preserved her when alone amid perils in which all her former companions had perished; that the first of her wishes was to rejoin her husband; that for this purpose she had begun her journey; and, were she to cease to prosecute her intention, that she should esteem herself guilty of counteracting the views of Providence, and render useless the assistance she had received from her two dear Americans and their wives, as well as all the kindness for which she was indebted to him and for which God alone could recompense them. My wife was ever dear to me, but sentiments like these add veneration to tenderness. . . .

Hearing . . . of the approach of Madame Godin, I left Oyapok on board a galliot belonging to me, in view of meeting her; and, on the fourth day of my departure, fell in with her vessel opposite to Mayacare. On board this vessel, after twenty years' absence, and a long endurance on either side of alarms and misfortunes, I again met with a cherished wife whom I had almost given over every hope of seeing again.

Thus the patterns were impressing themselves relentlessly in the hard sub-surface of colonial life, impressing themselves on the rigid system of class and of caste by color. These were the patterns: the luxuriant roots of new and multiple ways spreading from the runners of decay; the intricate roots merging in spite of all the restrictions—merging and twining through the entire awakening subconscious of colonial life. These were the patterns: the inevitable meeting of white and Indian and Negro across the strict but artificial barriers.

Out of the social decay, the long irrepressible runners of a new society were shooting through the subsoil of colonialism, stirring the energies in the face of all the obstacles, slowly laying open the existent colonial surface, gradually opening the newer and greater trails to thought.

Out of the colonial decay came the lengthening runners and new-born roots tearing open the way for the human forerunners with their bold ideas that would fire the people of the whole land:

The giant forerunners with the impassioned ideas and the urge to act who were already looming over the land.

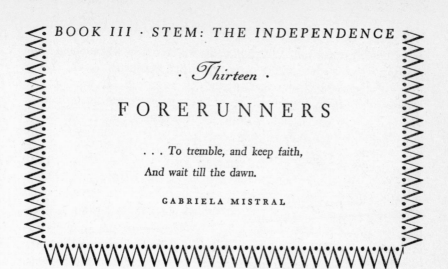

· *Thirteen* ·

FORERUNNERS

. . . To tremble, and keep faith,
And wait till the dawn.

GABRIELA MISTRAL

THROUGH BOLTS AND BARS

Over the southern American lands straining to ease the empires' hold on the minds and bodies of men and institutions, loomed the great forerunners of greater thoughts and deeds to come.

These were the intellectual heirs of the earlier and the current European forerunners whose plain new precepts were already shaking the whole world of the 18th century by the roots. In the plain but puissant thoughts written and spoken by such men as the Frenchman Rousseau, laying down the clear line that all true government derives from the consent of the governed, the eventual doom of rule by monarchy could be glimpsed.

In the utterances of Rousseau and in the bold statements of rationalist, liberal principles based on investigation and logic and made by renowned men of the calibre of the Conde de Aranda and Padre Feijoo in Spain, Lavoisier in France as Descartes before him, as Leibnitz before Christian Wolf in Germany, as Hobbes and Locke and Newton before Hume in England, as Spinoza before no one in Holland. In the statements of men like these and other men like Pombal in Portugal and Malaspina who, like that other Italian three centuries earlier crossing the uncharted sea, was in the service of Spain. In these and many more, the ultimate substitution of science for superstition could be discerned.

They were the glimmer of fresh thought, the new hale spirit of speculation and experimentation. And the glimmer was gradually growing into powerful rays of light shooting across the world from Spain and Italy and Portugal and Russia and England and even from the maturing British colonies in North America that were soon to show the old world how the good pupil surpasses the master. The rays of reason were shooting out over the world from all of Europe. But especially from France:

From Rousseau and the other Encyclopedists bent on guiding opinion against the institutions of crown and church: from Diderot and Voltaire and Montesquieu and D'Alembert and Chateaubriand, and all the other writers and philosophers and scientists steeped in the new materialism of the times and demanding proof and still more proof why the teachings of divine law and the divine right of kings should not be tossed on the junk-heap of history along with the archaic and unjust systems of the ancient world.

The horizons of thought were opening again, trapping the stubborn remnants of feudalism everywhere. It was the second half of the 18th century, aroused and glowing at last after the centuries of slow stagnation and the slower growth. It was the Enlightenment: the age of reason and the rights of man.

But it was also the age of despots of crown and church alike turning benevolent in a frenzied effort to save their precarious powers. In 1767 the Jesuits, who had set up theocratic states in Paraguay and other parts of Spanish America, were expelled from the colonies and all their wealth of goods was confiscated. And already the Inquisition was being driven into oblivion. Even among the Inquisitors in La Plata and other colonies, "forbidden" books expounding the new materialist principles of science and the rationalist ideas of government based on the general will were being preserved and read in secret and occasionally in the lecture room.

In the same spirit of belated benevolence and as part of the same program to save the order of empire and monarchy and feudalism that was rocking now at its very foundations, there were fewer restrictions on colonial trade, there was an easing-up of taxation, there was the granting of a few human rights and privileges to the Negro slaves, there was a greater margin of local political rights offered to the Creoles and even to some of the freemen descended from slaves. But all the new concessions granted to the colonials everywhere in the Americas by the tottering empires at home could not hold back the tide.

The time for concessions was past, and the tide of enlightenment seeking full freedom for human thought and existence rolled on.

From Jean Jacques Rousseau and his Social Contract and his exaggerated but welcome praise of the "noble savage" roaming the forests in comparative freedom, and from the general and specific appeals to reason as opposed to blind faith and blinder superstition made by all the other materialists of the time, came the fructifying seed that was exploding already into the American and the French revolutions:

Against monarchy and for republicanism, against bigotry and for freethinking of every kind, against the restrictive power of clergy or king and for secular, political democracy. Against fear by superstition. For boldness by reasoning in all fields of human endeavor. Against the old. And for the new.

In the realization of the American and then the French revolution, the word became deed. No longer had men been satisfied to speak or write against oppressive forms in thought and government: they had taken up arms and struck those forms down, and they were still striking at them. The word had become deed once more, and with it a new conscience and a new social morality were born in the world.

Throughout the colonies of the southern Americas, out of the earlier irrepressible need there now arose a new urgency, and out of the urgency a new determination, to reshape the colonial patterns into a whole new life. In every colony, every province, every city and every hamlet of the reawakening lands, the new determination was felt in a thousand different ways. It was felt with greatest force where the cracks in the long-pounded dike of empire were widest and the holes were deepest:

It was felt, for instance, in the Spanish colony of New Granada:

This colony, which would later become Colombia and Venezuela, embraced the top of the South American continent and was the passageway from that continent to all of Central and North America—and in many instances to Europe as well. Yet it was a weak spot in the Spanish dike for both political and geographical reasons. It was difficult to reach from the two strongest viceroyalties—Mexico and Peru. And with its broad face to the Caribbean and the Atlantic, it was a fresh first haven for the ships and the men bringing the explosive new ideas and the news of newer events from a republican France and an American democracy.

Through this vulnerable point in the rotting, sagging dike of Spanish empire in the Americas, the mighty thoughts from the two rising republics poured like a giant waterfall, roaring out the sound of the doom of empire everywhere. And the thunderous sound went echoing through the whole colony of New Granada:

Through its capital city Bogotá. Through the public buildings and the private homes. Through the cellars and through the prohibited gatherings reading the French Assembly's principles of the Rights of Man that had been translated into Spanish and distributed by a man of Bogotá:

Antonio Nariño by name:

Student, scholar, writer, and statesman to be. Agitator and pamphleteer, and future general. Absent for the moment from the cellar gatherings and from his clandestine press, but still the burrowing mole—

Antonio Nariño, stilling his raging heart the better to guide his fearless quill:

On the 20th of December, at three o'clock in the afternoon, I was again arrested at the home of the priest, the curate of that city, and I was led, with considerable pomp and by the governor himself, to the military barracks, where I was locked in a dark cell with my son—after strong bars had been installed in the only window there, and a pair of shackles had been hammered onto each of us. I still *Antonio Nariño: His Account* cannot come to this passage in my life without *of Imprisonment* a shiver. Upon arriving at the cell, I saw, in the middle of the room, two chairs—and this sight announced to me the cruelty that was about to be practised. They ordered me to sit in one chair and my son in the other. The jailor came in carrying three or four pairs of shackles, and we were fitted with those which struck him as being best.

The clerk immediately began to search my son to remove all that he had on him. Indignation, rage, and tenderness, followed each other rapidly in my heart, and when he was about to do the same on my person, I caught his hand to stop him, telling him not to add this fresh insult to my misfortune—and handed him the purse he had come to seek, a watch, and a small wallet, which was all I had on me. He left, satisfied with his booty.

Leaving us in this same position, they drew the bolt, and we found ourselves in the midst of darkness, immobile and immersed in thought. Let all sensitive souls place themselves in my predicament for a moment! The wishes of my enemies have been fulfilled, I said to myself—they have managed to add a new victim to their fury, and to my own heart a new torment to finish me. My unhappy wife will never survive this blow—she will die. And what is my crime? I am ignorant of it, and I cannot even imagine the pretext that may be given by my iniquitous judges. Suddenly I felt my son's head against my chest. Merciful heavens! —but my feelings are leading me away from the purpose of this petition.

Twelve days later I was sent in chains to Cartagena, without having had my money returned to me, and with such wretched treatment that in San Estanislao—where the ailments which I still suffer first began—I had to sell my handkerchiefs in order to purchase some fowl. When we arrived at Cartagena, my shackles were changed for others weighing thirty-six pounds, and I was placed in a cell of the kind used to lodge notorious criminals who have been condemned to death. It is built over one of the large conduits of the common toilet in those barracks—covered only by a few boards and surrounded with filth.

I can say, without the least exaggeration, that I was deprived of all movement, of bread, of water, and even of air to breathe. The government did not furnish me even with a daily piece of bread, the shackles weighed me down, and the stench around me was so great that even the soldiers, when they entered, were compelled to leave the door open in order to breathe.

By the third day, one of my legs would no longer fit into the shackles, and Governor Montes ordered the shackles removed, leaving only those on the one leg—but with seven varas (about twenty feet) of chain added. Thus I remained for fifteen days, while the arch of the castle of San José de Bocachica was made fast with two gratings consisting of bars of lignum vitae, and new doors and bolts were installed—even in the little skylight, the only one it has.

MAN OF IMAGINATION

Behind the bolts and the bars, a new age was being born. Typical of its birth was the man whom posterity would know as "The Precursor." His library was filled with the works of the finest thinkers of the time—colonials as well as Europeans. He traveled over Europe and he traveled to the United States. Earlier he had even visited George Washington and his men encamped at Valley Forge. The Precursor:

Don Francisco de Miranda of Caracas, capital of the province of Venezuela, which was also part of that weakening segment of Spanish empire
known as the colony of New Granada.

Miranda the unorthodox, steeped in new dreams and new theories of
life and government. Miranda striving always to turn his thoughts into
action, organizing the first serious expedition aimed at overthrowing Spanish rule on the southern continent. Miranda the man of imagination, the
man of projects, faithfully portrayed by one of the two hundred Americans who sailed with him from New York in the Leander on the daring
but ill-fated expedition:

His imagination and feelings were an overmatch for his judgment. He is
more rash and presumptuous in projects, than dexterous in extricating
himself from difficulties. In religion he is reputed skeptical—but in our
hearing he never derided subjects of this nature. He used formerly to
talk infidelity to the offence of the serious; experience has taught him
caution, or he has changed his sentiments. It is
Mr. Biggs's Portrait of Miranda, said upon good authority that he partook the
the Revolutionist sacrament at Coro. He is too much of an en-
thusiast in his favorite objects to allow his means to be enfeebled by
moral scruples. I am willing to believe he has as much conscience as the
impetuous passions of such men generally admit.

I make a few remarks on his person, manners, and petty habits.

He is about five feet ten inches high. His limbs are well proportioned;
his whole frame is stout and active. His complexion is dark, florid and
healthy. His eyes are hazel colored, but not of the darkest hue. They are
piercing, quick, and intelligent, expressing more of the severe than the
mild feelings.

He has good teeth, which he takes much care to keep clean. His nose
is large and handsome, rather of the English than Roman cast. His chest
is square and prominent. His hair is grey and he wears it tied long behind with powder. He has strong grey whiskers growing on the outer
edges of his ears, as large as most Spaniards have on their cheeks.

In the contour of his visage you plainly perceive an expression of per-
tinaciousness and suspicion. Upon the whole, without saying he is an
elegant, we may pronounce him a handsome man.

He has a constant habit of picking his teeth. When sitting he is never perfectly still; his foot or hand must be moving to keep time with his mind, which is always in exercise. He always sleeps a few moments after dinner, and then walks till bedtime, which with him is about midnight.

He is an eminent example of temperance. A scanty or bad meal is never regarded by him as a subject of complaint. He uses no ardent spirits; seldom any wine. Sweetened water is his common beverage. Sweetness and warmth, says he, are the two greatest physical goods; and acid and cold are the greatest physical evils in the universe.

He is a courtier and gentleman in his manners. Dignity and grace preside in his movements. Unless when angry, he has a great command of his feelings, and can assume what looks and tones he pleases. In general his demeanor is marked by hauteur and distance. When he is angry he loses discretion. He is impatient of contradiction. In discourse he is logical in the managements of his thoughts. He appears conversant on all subjects. His iron memory prevents his ever being at a loss for names, dates, and authorities.

He used his mental resources and colloquial powers with great address to recommend himself to his followers. He assumed the manners of a father and instructor to the young men. He spoke of the prospect of success, and of the preparations made for him with great confidence. The glory and advantages of the enterprise were described in glowing colors. At another time he detailed his travels, his sufferings and escapes in a manner to interest both their admiration and sympathy.

He appeared the master of languages, of science and literature. In his conversations he carried his hearers to the scenes of great actions and introduced them to the distinguished characters of every age. He took excursions to Troy, Babylon, Jerusalem, Rome, Athens and Syracuse. Men famed as statesmen, heroes, patriots, conquerors and tyrants, priests and scholars he produced, and weighed their merits and defects. Modern history and biography afforded him abundant topics. He impressed an opinion of his comprehensive views, his inexhaustible fund of learning, his probity, his generosity and patriotism.

After all, this man of renown, I fear, must be considered as having more learning than wisdom; more theoretical knowledge than practical talent; too sanguine and too opinionated to distinguish between the vigor of enterprise and the hardiness of infatuation.

LIKE A DESERT

Nariño and Miranda in New Granada, and other men of the pen-turning-to-sword in other provinces of other colonies in the dying western empires.

There were Lizardi in Mexico, exposing the corruption of crown and church in pamphlets and in his full-grown satire called The Scurvy Parrot; Peralta in Peru, corresponding with the vigorous Academy of Sciences in the newborn French Republic; José Antonio Rojas of Chile, traveling as far as St. Petersburg in Russia and shipping back forbidden books to the homeland. And scores of other men of reason, assimilating and adding to the ideas of the world's new thinkers.

There were teachers and writers like Espejo in Quito, and Mariano Moreno in Buenos Aires, and Villaurrutia in Guatemala. These and many more speaking out in every province. These and the multiplying numbers of members of banned societies, such as the Freemasons and the Jacobins, advocating and furthering the principles of rationalism and liberalism. There were these and there were all the carriers of the developing precepts of freedom emanating from the first republic of the Western Hemisphere, the first democratic republic of the modern world: the United States of America.

There were the great inanimate but eloquent carriers: pendants and buttons bearing the red-white-and-blue colors of the republic of the north and smuggled into the awakening colonies of the south, thousands of copies of the American Declaration of Independence translated into Spanish and printed and scattered in secret over the southern Americas. And the simple but shattering ideas of a certain Benjamin Franklin, whom the stirring colonials of Spanish and French and Portuguese America now saw as the great symbol of the new American rationalism and the new American democracy.

There were all these and the animate carriers, too—the men of many talents, like Hipólito Unanue of Peru, physician and teacher and scientist and pleader for free trade; like the priest, Fray Juan Pablo Viscardó y Guzmán, pleading for full independence from Spain even before the French Revolution. And there were other men, interested in effecting the combination of action with idea—and paying dearly for the successful experiment:

Men like Tupac Amaru, descendant of the Inca chiefs, who led thousands of Indians in a powerful rebellion—only to be taken by the Spanish authorities in Peru, where, before the eyes of his family, he was tied to four horses and torn into four parts, all because he was a daring man and a patriot.

Men like Ubalde, joining Lanzas and Rodríguez, who led the people of La Paz, the future capital of a future country, in a later attempt against the Spanish power. Ubalde, the martyr:

Ubalde, whose execution I witnessed . . . died with the serenity of a philosopher, without denying his principles, or the causes which led him to engage in the revolution. . . . On the contrary, while seated on the scaffold, he said that his death could not stop the progress of a cause which had been so long preparing by the corruption of the government; that the independence of South America was not far distant, and that, although he was going to the grave without the satisfaction of seeing that glorious day, yet his mind was brightened with the hope that his friends who survived him would enroll his name among the martyred heroes of his country; that Providence had decreed that a period should be put to the sufferings of the people of South America, the extent and magnitude of which he well knew from the situations which he had held in the public administration; that, although he should soon cease to be, and should leave behind him a wife and children exposed to the ignominy and disgrace which always attach to a rebel family, he felt a consolation in the reflection that he should die in the same place where the most illustrious Americans had died before him.

Don Vicente Pazos Recalls the Fate of La Paz

This address, pronounced by a man like Ubalde, so beloved as he was in Cuzco, drew tears from every eye. . . .

Events proved that Ubalde knew the real state of the country, as five years did not pass away after his execution before a new revolution broke out in La Paz. . . . They deposed the Spanish authorities in the country, held meetings of the people, erected a government under the name of *Junta Tuitiva*, and published a manifesto to the world in which they asserted the right of governing themselves. . . .

The people of La Paz organized all the departments of the public administration and raised an army to oppose the Spanish authorities, who at the same time rose up to destroy the unhappy city. . . . The leaders of La Paz were natives—and therefore were marked as traitors and devoted to destruction. An armed force was dispatched by Cisneros, Viceroy of Buenos Aires, under the command of Marshal Nieto, which was to form a junction with other troops which were dispatched by the Viceroy of Lima, and commanded by Goyeneche.

This assassin of his country—for he was a native of Peru—had the glory, if it may be called such, of entering La Paz before the arrival of Nieto. The unhappy city, after a stout resistance, was taken by storm, and for several days the savage barbarity of the conquerors sent to the scaffold, without discrimination and without trial, great numbers of the principal inhabitants, to appease the vindictive wrath of the monster, Goyeneche.

After the first flush of victory was over, it was deemed proper to give some formality to the bloody business. The opinion of Cisneros was consulted upon the fate of those who were not yet executed, and then it was that this Viceroy imbrued his hands in the blood of men to whom their country owed a crown. . . .

La Paz became like a desert after such desolation, and a few of the miserable inhabitants who remained alive, inspired by that stubborn valor which adversity strengthened but could not subdue, fled to the forests of Yrupana—whither they were instantly pursued by a strong division of the royal troops, and fell in battle, or expired by famine, in preference to surrendering to their enemies.

UNDER A SCORCHING SUN

Ubalde in La Paz, and the many other giant forerunners in the hundreds of other cities and towns and villages of the Spanish colonial provinces in the Americas. And in Portugal's Brazil there were men like the devout young officer and ex-dentist nicknamed "Tiradentes": "The Toothpuller."

Tiradentes and men like him sowed the dying imperial wilderness of Brazil with their blood, showered their new ideas of freedom and their new belief in republicanism upon the neglected, expiring growth of empire in the west. Tiradentes and men like him scattered their convictions over the cities of Rio and São Paulo and Minas Geraes and over the great sertão, the backlands, in the knowledge that they would ultimately penetrate to the hidden soil underneath; in the knowledge that gardens of liberty would eventually rise and flourish from that feracious soil beneath the dying growth of empire.

Knowing all this, and more, men like Joaquim José de Silva Xavier (Tiradentes, the toothpuller) led the conspiracy at Minas Geraes. Tiradentes, the puller of teeth from the jaws of empire, went to his death calmly under the scorching Brazilian sun:

The death sentence was commuted—for all the accused except Tiradentes—to deportation for life to places in Africa. And if they should ever return to America, they were to die irrevocably, by hanging. . . . Tiradentes, finally judged to be the seducer in the conspiracy, was tied by hands and feet. He observed this unexpected development, then, as strong-headed as he was contrite, told his spiritual father that now he would die full of joy, inasmuch as he would not take with him the many unfortunate souls he had contaminated . . . and that this is what he himself had always asked: that only he should be made a victim of the law. . . .

Description of the Last Moments of Tiradentes

It was the dawn of the twenty-first day of April, the day that was to open the doors of eternity for him. The hangman entered his cell to dress him and to ask him the customary pardon for having to execute him, saying that it was justice and not his own will that would move his arm. Tiradentes turned to him calmly and said:

"Oh my friend, let me kiss your hands and feet."

He did this to show his humility. And then he removed his shirt and put on the bag-like *alva* and said that his Redeemer was also undressed when He died for him. . . .

There was the gay sound of martial music. The local troops, wearing their dress uniforms, left their barracks and lined up at their previously determined positions. The Moura regiment was drawn up along the entire street of the prison, on both sides. Then came the artillery regiment, extending to the Barreira de Santo Antonio square which is also called the Campo da Lampadoza. Patrols moved over this square continually amid the thick, increasing crowds.

The remaining regiments were deployed in a triangle, leaving an empty space where the gallows was set up—very high, so that the stairway leading to the platform consisted of more than twenty steps. These

columns reinforced the others bordering the street and the ones marching behind the group that followed the condemned man. The troops
stood with their backs to the gallows, their bandoleers provided with
powder and shot.

The commander was Brigadier Pedro Alvez de Andrade, who had
ordered this deployment of the troops. . . . Riding on a beautiful, well-
appareled horse, the Brigadier reviewed the square, observing the align-
ment of troops. Next to the Brigadier, also mounted, was Dom Luiz de
Castro Benedicto, aide-de-camp to his father, the Viceroy. The escort
was composed of two cavalry soldiers and two master-sergeants, also
mounted on good horses. They accompanied the aide-de-camp on all
necessary expeditions.

In front of the prison stood the troops that serve as the viceregal
guard, formed of the two aforementioned companies. The army was
in charge of the prison. When the Irmandade da Misericordia—the
"Brotherhood of Mercy"—arrived, the procession started. Although an
execution is a sorrowful event, on this day the proceedings were brilliant
and sumptuous.

The procession was preceded by the first company of the guard, followed by the churchmen, the members of the Brotherhood, and finally,
the religious folk surrounding the unfortunate Tiradentes and singing
psalms appropriate to the occasion.

There was admiration for the firmness displayed by the condemned
man. . . . The swift, courageous way he walked, the way he talked while
holding the crucifix in his hands, filled those attending him with great
consolation.

The ministers of justice formed a respectable and majestic group.
Court officials guarded the condemned man. They were followed by the
judge, mounted on a fiery horse with silver trappings, its mane braided
with pink silk ribbons. A special judge rode on another horse whose
trappings competed in splendor with those of the horse bearing the regular judge. The supreme judge towered over all the others; he sat on a
horse wearing a harness of gold-plated silver and liveried in scarlet velvet
with gold frayings. The procession came to an end with the second company of the guard, followed by a cart bearing the hangman's appliances.

At eleven o'clock, under a scorching sun, the condemned man, the
judges, the members of the Brotherhood, and the priests and churchmen
entered the empty space through a corner guarded by the troops.

Tiradentes climbed the stairs to the gallows lightly. And without re-
moving his eyes from the crucifix, without trembling at all, he eased the

task of the executioner by requesting him three times to hurry with his work. . . .

As the attending priest repeated the Credo, the . . . condemned man was swung from the gallows. . . .

The windows of the houses looked as though they were about to be torn apart, they were filled with so many women, each one vying with the next in spruceness of appearance. Providence did not, however, permit curiosity to dominate the spirit of the spectacle—for the people's pity toward the condemned man and his unhappy life in this world was so great that they voluntarily offered money for Masses to be held to help him in his eternal life.

A FIRE IS LIGHTED

The wood of imperial neglect and oppression was dry and waiting in Brazil and in the Spanish colonies. And the kindling of all the new ideas of all the new freedoms from Europe and from the infant republic of the United States was there, too, waiting for the tinder to light the fire.

But the indispensable spark of all-consuming hatred toward the old order that was needed to light the fire of general revolt, was still missing in the colonies belonging to Spain and to Portugal. It was to appear first in the colony where the imperial neglect and oppression were at their very worst—where most of the colonials were Negro and mulatto slaves held in bondage by a few white owners and their families. It was to appear in the colony belonging to the newborn French Republic itself!

Even before the last embers of the 18th century were out, the first great fire of revolt was being lighted by the colonials with slaves' blood in their veins. The spark was being supplied by certain angry men from the westerly portion of the island of St. Domingo. The tinder-box was the little French colony of Haiti, the immediate carriers its Negro deputies seeking vainly to be heard in the National Assembly of republican France:

When I was at Paris . . . I dined occasionally with General Lafayette. It happened on one of these occasions that the deputies of color, who had then just arrived from St. Domingo, had been invited to dine there also. . . . We met—with about fifty others—in the same room. The general introduced me to them, and when we took our seats at the dinner table, he placed me between two of them: M.

An Englishman Writes of His
Meeting with Ogé

Raymond, a mild, gentlemanlike man, and another whose name I have forgotten. In the course of conversation I learnt their errand, and they learnt mine—which was . . . to get the subject of the slave-trade introduced into the National Assembly, if possible, whilst I was at Paris. . . .

In the course of three or four days Raymond, Ogé, and the four others, called upon me at my hotel. It was a mere visit of compliment, in consequence of having dined together at General Lafayette's. I wished to return the compliment, but was prevented in consequence of not knowing their address. I was told that they did not lodge together, but had separate lodgings of their own in different streets.

In about a week after this, a mere accident brought us together again. They were going in a body—six of them—to consult their advocate, M. Jolie, and it so happened that in their way thither they passed near the street in which I lived. At this moment one of them proposed calling upon me, and the rest agreed. They came, they said, to inform me that they had been admitted the day before into the body of the National Assembly to prefer their claims, and that the president had assured them they might take courage, for that the assembly knew no distinction between whites and blacks, but considered all men as having equal rights. They hoped soon to be admitted there as deputies. They did not stay more than ten minutes with me, and then left me—apparently all of them in high spirits.

At another time I received a message from M. Raymond to say, that he had something to communicate to me, and that he would bring one or two of his friends with him to see me, if it were agreeable. They came accordingly. He then said that the liberal speech of the president of the Assembly, which had given them last week so much pleasure, had called forth an host of the bitterest enemies against them:

The white planters resident in France, and the white planters usually resident in the colonies but then at Paris, supposing that they, the deputies—who had slaves' blood in their veins—were to have a seat in the Assembly and equal rights and privileges with themselves, had been worked up by that speech to a feeling bordering upon madness. They held nightly meetings. They had sent to them—the deputies—anonymous letters, threatening their assassination if they persisted in their claims.

They said, too, that they had reason to think that these white colonists had a design upon my life, also, and they wished to put me upon my guard. I replied that I had received letters to the same purport, but that I should still go on as before. I had determined, however, by way of precaution, to change my hotel, and to go to another, to be near to General Lafayette for protection, and not to stir out at night.

I saw nothing more of the deputies for a fortnight, when they proposed a visit, to which I immediately assented. All the six were present. They complained bitterly of the white colonists in Paris. Some of these, whose faces they had before seen at Cap Haitien, had insulted them—and particularly Ogé—in the streets. But what was worse than all, they had spread terror among many of the members of the Assembly, so as to make them believe that the welfare of the mother country would be endangered by hearing their claims.

They appeared to be quite disheartened. They were now sure that they should not be able to make a head against their intrigues. Day after day had been fixed for the hearing of their cause—day after day it had been deferred. They were now weary with waiting. Ogé could not contain himself, but broke out with great warmth:

"I begin," says he, "not to care whether the National Assembly will admit us or not. But let it beware of the consequences. We will no longer continue to be held in a degraded light. Dispatches shall go directly to St. Domingo, and we will soon follow them. We can produce as good soldiers upon our estates as those in France. Our own arms shall make us respectable and independent. If we are once forced to desperate measures, it will be in vain that thousands will be sent across the Atlantic to bring us back to our former state."

On hearing this I entreated the deputies to wait with patience. I observed to them that in a great revolution like that of France, the Assembly would have a thousand things to attend to at home before they could think of anything abroad. France would first take care of herself—she would then, I had no doubt, extend her care to the colonies. Was it not reasonable to conclude that this would be the case when they, the deputies, knew that they had almost all the first men in the Assembly—such as the Duc de Rochefoucauld, Lafayette, Mirabeau, Grégoire and others—in their favor? I entreated them therefore to wait patiently, as well as upon another consideration—which was, that by imprudent conduct they might not only ruin their own cause in France, but bring indescribable misery upon their native land.

They all seemed to listen to what I said—except Ogé, whose mind seemed to have been so violently stirred up that its emotions, like the waves of the sea after a storm, could not be stopped at once. . . .

I began now to think of returning to England, and concluded at length that my stay in Paris should not exceed another week. During this time I fell in with Ogé in one of the streets. He seemed to be very gloomy. He revived the subject spoken of at our last meeting: namely, the wicked and barbarous conduct of the white planters at Paris towards the deputies, but more particularly towards himself. We exchanged . . . but few words. . . .

I met him again by accident as I was walking in the garden of the Tuileries. We stopped and talked. He appeared to me to be in an agitated state of mind. He said that the cruel treatment of the deputies of color by the white colonists at Paris was not to be borne. From the white colonists at Paris he then went to the white colonists at St. Domingo. He said that the people of color there were men of property as well as these—that they were men of education as well as these—that they had mind and intellect as well as these—that they had souls as magnanimous and courageous as these—

He was going on, when I beseeched him to be more tranquil. And to pacify him, I told him that if he and his colleagues would call upon me in the evening, I would be at home to receive them.

At the time appointed, Ogé and three others came to me; the other two were indisposed. They seemed now, all of them, to have caught the infection, for they all complained bitterly. I heard what they had to say most patiently, and told them again and again that I sympathized with them in their distress. After some farther conversation I bade them adieu, as I was to leave Paris in two days; and recommended to them, in the most earnest and impressive manner I could, moderation and forbearance as the best legacy I could leave them. And I entreated them rather to give up their seats in the Assembly than to carry their anger home, for that with patience their cause would ultimately triumph.

They replied that I had prescribed to them a most difficult task, but that they would endeavor to follow my advice.

There was, however, evidently a spirit of dissatisfaction in their countenances, which nothing but a redress of their grievances could subdue. And it appeared clear to me that if the white colonists should persevere in their intrigues, and the National Assembly in delay, a fire might be lighted up in St. Domingo which could not easily be extinguished.

Over the length and breadth of the southern Americas, the fire was being lighted. Over Haiti and Brazil and nearly all of the lands belonging to Spain in the Americas—over Venezuela and Peru, Mexico and Guatemala. From the shining silvery Plate to the "big river," the Rio Grande of the north, and somewhat beyond, the new winds of hatred for the oppressive imperial order and its colonial pattern of death were ready to carry the flames of protest.

The winds of hatred were ready to fan the tender flames of protest into the great roaring fire of revolt that would burn for two decades and more. The winds of hate and furious determination to break the Old World's power in the New forever were beginning to blow—were fanning the flames everywhere, turning the sporadic outbursts into the long and steady upheaval, turning the skirmishes into battles and the battles into the fierce and bloody war for independence about to envelop all of the southern Americas.

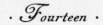

Fourteen

LIBERATORS

And marching down the golden day
I hear the countryside exclaim:
A man of mourning, a man of gloom,
Lighting the way in a blaze of noon!

JUAN MARINELLO

"I HAVE AVENGED AMERICA"

Where the fire of independence was first lighted, there it burned most fiercely. Over the little French colony of Saint Domingue, over its green hills and valleys, over the whole shore that was the profile of a giant jaw —there now rose the black smoke of the masters' plantations burning through the day and night.

Over the hard but ever verdant landscape of the land that was once known as Haiti and would be so again, rose the black smoke from the plantations fired by the black slaves rising together at last. And beneath the blackness, the red flames of fury, shooting upward and spreading over the hills and down into the farther vales of all that was Haiti, roared out the end of the long colonial nightmare, the end of the dungeon of slavery.

Freedom! roared the fire, the smoke, the black slaves moving over the land to the swift pounding of the vodoun drums that were painted red to please the vodoun gods of war. Liberty! was the message relayed by the drums, and it went beating through the air of Haiti to the long-awaiting blacks and mulattoes, to the people of the interior as well as the people in the coastal towns, to men and women alike, to the slaves on the plantations, to the few who had been freed, and to the many who had fled to the hills to join the armed maroons.

Up and down the coast shaped like a huge reaching jaw, from rocky

Cap Haitien to the south, and deep into the hinterland to the borders of the Spanish colony of Santo Domingo that was the eastern part of the same island—the fighting commenced. And with it began the long war that would be the war for the liberation of all the colonies of the southern Americas, all the New World's lands of the south that were known as Spanish America and Portuguese America and French America, and would be known separately by many names, and eventually would be known together as Latin America. The long war for full independence began:

Overnight, slaves and former slaves with skins dark as the mahogany forests of Saint Domingue arose to stop the enslavement, arose to halt the massacres of their kin, arose to carry the torch and drive the knife and speed the bullet into the homes and the hearts of the enemy they hated more than death: into the blanc, the white, the French owner of soil and slave.

Over the slain white masters and the burning green plantations rose the black smoke writing the end of slavery in the Saint Domingue sky. Over the dead and dying slavery rose the blood-red flames writing the birth of liberty and independence in the sky that was now Haiti. And the black and the red writing in the sky formed the names of all the slaves who had risen to make the land free, and of the earlier and the later slaves and free descendants of slaves—the affranchis—who led the way:

After Bauvais and Lambert—who had fought in the war for American independence—and after the other affranchis who led the fight for political rights, there were still other men of Haiti whose names and deeds would never be lost.

After the martyred Boukman there were his fellow vodoun priests who enabled the slave and the armed maroon to meet and join hands in a common cause by means of the vodoun offerings left in the woods in open daylight and before the very eyes of the French vigilance.

After the great Toussaint L'Ouverture had been betrayed by the French who gave him lingering death in a damp dungeon cell in France instead of the freedom in his own native land they had promised—there was still Pétion, the bold mulatto officer who had quit Leclerc's army to side with the rebels. There was still Henri Christophe, the "Black Emperor" in the north. Above all, after Toussaint's martyrdom, and during the height of Napoleon's rise to power in France and Europe and his determination to crush the Haitian movement with some of his finest troops commanded

by his own brother-in-law, Leclerc, and then by the cruel Rochambeau—
there was still Dessalines:

There was Dessalines, the boldest and most daring of all the rebel leaders. There was Dessalines, the former slave and ex-maroon and late officer in the French army who followed Pétion's example and went over to
the patriot cause. There was Dessalines, stronger than ever, in fact, and
recognized by Pétion and the other leaders as the commander-in-chief:

Jean Jacques Dessalines—raising the torch of liberty and independence
high over the land, reaffirming the people's will to be free. Dessalines
proudly recalling the shattering defeat of Napoleon's army in little Haiti
and warning the world that his people meant to stay free from that time
on—from that first year of freedom, 1804:

Crimes, the most atrocious, such as were hitherto unheard of and would
cause nature to shudder, have been perpetrated. The measure of their
cruelty overflowed. At length the hour of vengeance has arrived, and the
implacable enemies of the rights of man have suffered the punishment
due to their crimes. My arm, raised above their heads, has too long de-
layed to strike. At that signal, which the justice
of God has urged, your hands, righteously
armed, have brought the axe to bear upon the
decrepit tree of slavery and prejudice. In vain had time, and more especially the infernal politics of Europeans, defended it with triple brass.
You have stripped it of its armor, and have placed it upon your heart,
that you may become (like your natural enemies) cruel and merciless.

Dessalines on the Free Negro
Government in Haiti

Like an overflowing and mighty torrent that bears down all opposition, your vengeful fury has swept away every obstacle to its impetuous
course. Perish thus all tyrants over innocence, all oppressors of mankind!

What then? Bent for many ages under an iron yoke, the sport of the
passions or the injustice of men, and of the caprices of fortune, mutilated victims of the cupidity of white Frenchmen; after having fattened
by our toils these insatiate blood-suckers, with a patience and resignation
unexampled, we should again have seen that sacrilegious horde attempt
our destruction, without any distinction of sex or age! And we—whom
they call men without energy, of no virtue, of no delicate sensibility—
should not we have plunged in their breast the dagger of desperation?

Where is that Haitian so vile, Haitian so unworthy of his regeneration, who thinks he has not fulfilled the decrees of the Eternal by exterminating these blood-thirsty tigers? If there be one, let him fly: indignant nature discards him from our bosom. Let him hide his infamy far from hence. The air we breathe is not suited to his gross organs—it is the air of liberty, pure, august, and triumphant.

Yes, we have rendered to these true cannibals war for war, crime for crime, outrage for outrage. Yes, I have saved my country; I have avenged America.

The avowal I make in the face of earth and heaven constitutes my pride and my glory. Of what consequence to me is the opinion which contemporary and future generations will pronounce upon my conduct? I have performed my duty, I enjoy my own approbation—for me that is sufficient.

But what am I saying? The preservation of my unfortunate brothers and the testimony of my own conscience are not my only recompense: I have seen two classes of men, born to cherish, assist, and succour one another—mixed in a world, and blended together—crying for vengeance and disputing the honor of the first blow. Blacks and yellows, whom the refined duplicity of Europe for a long time endeavored to divide—you, who are now consolidated and make but one family—without doubt it was necessary that our perfect reconciliation should be sealed with the blood of your butchers.

Similar calamities have hung over your proscribed heads. A similar ardor to strike your enemies has signalized you. The like fate is reserved for you, and the like interests must therefore render you forever one, indivisible, and inseparable. Maintain that precious concord, that happy harmony, amongst yourselves: it is the pledge of your happiness, your salvation, and your success. It is the secret of being invincible.

It is necessary, in order to strengthen these ties, to recall to your remembrance the catalog of atrocities committed against our species: the intended massacre of the entire population of this island, meditated in the silence and sang-froid of the cabinet. The execution of that abominable project to me was unblushingly proposed, when already begun by the French, with the calmness and serenity of a countenance accustomed to similar crimes. . . .

Sooner or later Divine Justice will unchain on earth some mighty minds, above the weakness of the vulgar, for the destruction and terror of the wicked. Tremble, tyrants, usurpers, scourges of the new world! Our daggers are sharpened, your punishment is ready!

Sixty thousand men, equipped, inured to war, obedient to my orders, burn to offer a new sacrifice to the names of their assassinated brothers. Let that nation come that may be mad or daring enough to attack me. Already at its approach, the irritated Genie of Haiti, arising from the bosom of the ocean, appears: his menacing aspect throws the waves into commotion, excites tempests, and with his mighty hand disperses or dashes fleets in pieces. To his formidable voice the laws of nature pay obedience: disease, plague, famine, conflagration, poison, are his constant attendants.

But why calculate on the assistance of the climate and of the elements? Have I forgot that I command a people of no common cast—brought up in adversity—whose haughty daring frowns at obstacles and increases by dangers? Let them come, these homicidal cohorts!

I wait for them with a firm and steady eye. I abandon to them freely the shore and the places where cities have existed—but woe to those who may approach too near the mountains! It were better for them that the sea received them into its profound abyss than to be devoured by the anger of the children of Haiti.

"War, even to death, to tyrants!" This is my motto. "Liberty! Independence!" This is our rallying cry. . . .

I have been faithful to the promise I made to you when I took up arms against tyranny; and whilst the last spark of life remains in me I will keep my oath. Never again shall a colonist, or an European, set his foot upon this territory with the title of master or proprietor.

THE PEACEFUL BEGINNING

In the colonies owned by Spain and in Portugal's Brazil, the beginnings of the long battle for independent nationhood were far more peaceful than they had been in blood-drenched Haiti, which was no longer part of France, no longer part of the prevailing system of black slavery.

Yet the sparks of unrest and change carried by the ships from France, carried by the news from Haiti, were the main sparks—carried also by the fresh winds of progress blowing from the young United States, and carried also by the winds of the times crying that life was not life without liberty—that lit the fires of the independence struggle in the rest of the southern Americas.

In France the flood-tide of revolution and war, raised first by the establishment of the French Republic and then by Europe's ambitious man of the hour, Napoleon Bonaparte, poured across the French borders into the rest of the old world—wiping out the rule of older dynasties and challenging the role of outmoded forms, doing away with the old borders, ending the status quo in most of Europe. Ending it in the Iberian peninsula:

Napoleon's assumption of power in Spain and Portugal by means of his brother, Joseph, nullified the imperial authority of Madrid and Lisbon as far as their New World colonies were concerned. Ferdinand VII, the weak and corrupt king of Spain who had allowed himself first to be taken to France and was later to become the oppressive instrument of outworn feudalism after regaining the throne, was the personification of the Spanish crown's crumbling authority over the colonial empire in the west.

The old norms and the old forms were cracking wide open.

Haiti was free. Haiti had shown the way, and Napoleon himself was the unwitting catalyst compelling the rest of the southern Americas to follow in Haiti's burning path.

Slave and other uprisings had already occurred in Peru, in Mexico, in Venezuela, and in almost all the other colonies. Their course had been bloody; the aftermath of massacre and other reprisals had been even worse. But the actual beginnings of the full independence struggle in the Spanish colonies and in Brazil were peaceful enough:

Five and a half years after Haiti had won her independence, the start on the road to sovereignty in Spanish America was made in the newest viceroyalty of all—in the robust colony of the peaceful Plate.

May was the month, late Fall the season in that south-temperate zone, when the good start was made in that city of good winds—Buenos Aires—that fateful year of 1810:

Castelli, a lawyer of reputation in Buenos Aires, made his country-house the rendezvous for the secret meetings of the revolutionists. There they met, eluding the vigilance of the governmental spies. They took care to gain to their interests the soldiery in Buenos Aires, who were at that time four thousand strong. Of these, one thousand were the regiment,

Pazos on the Argentine Declaration of Freedom

Patricios, from the city, under the command of Colonel Saavedra; another regiment, Arribanos, or Highlanders, commanded by Colonel Ocampo; and the cavalry, composed of Creoles, under the command of Rodríguez. These were by far the best troops, and took part with the revolutionists.

Those who remained attached to the interests of the Viceroy were the regiment "del Fixo," the dragoons, and the other European corps.

Already had the revolutionists conciliated the good wishes of the citizens, and were waiting a favorable opportunity to strike a decisive blow, when an English vessel from Gibraltar arrived at Montevideo bringing the information of the dissolution of the *Junta Central* in Spain and the passage of the French troops through the pass of Sierra Morena. The Viceroy immediately issued a proclamation announcing the disastrous state of Spain—and thereupon the revolutionists compelled the *cabildo* or municipality to ask permission of the Viceroy to call a public meeting of the citizens. . . . The Viceroy, perceiving that his power was undermined and that he could not prevent the meeting, allowed it with the best grace he could.

In this public assembly, in which were present all who held employments under the Spanish government—in order to neutralize as much as possible the influence of the Creoles—the question for discussion was, whether after the dissolution of the *Junta Central*, the authority of the Viceroy ceased (and consequently, whether the people could proceed to protect their own rights and those of King Ferdinand).

After a warm debate which continued through the day . . . Castelli with his popular eloquence confounded the Europeans who mingled in the debate, and convinced them that they could not contend with the orators of the people—who, besides the superiority of their talents, were supported by a body of armed citizens, called *Manolos*, who were posted at a short distance from the public square to see that no harm befell the friends of the people.

At length a majority of the assembly decreed that the authority of the Viceroy was at an end, and that it should be resumed by the *cabildo*, which immediately proceeded to appoint a governing council, *Junta Gubernativa*—leaving the Viceroy, however, president of the Junta. Scarcely were the people made acquainted with the establishment of the new government than a new disturbance broke out, and a memorial was addressed to the *cabildo* stating that it was not the will of the people that the Viceroy should hold any place in the new government.

A new Junta of nine persons was thereupon established. . . . This new government was established on the 25th of May, 1810, and covered with mourning all the European Spaniards, who saw that the measure would put an end to the Spanish domination in South America.

YOUNG WOMAN WITH A CIGAR

In Brazil, where the beginnings of independence were also peaceful, the power of Portugal was also nearing its end.

With the entry of Napoleon's forces into Portugal in 1808, the royal Braganzas, who ruled that ancient land, had fled to Brazil—Portugal's chief colony became her seat of empire:

Rio de Janeiro was made the provisional center of the whole Portuguese empire ruled by the Regent, João VI. The rich colony that had given Lisbon and the rest of Europe its precious brazilwood and other wealth was now raised to the status of kingdom. More and more, Rio grew to resemble the capital of a sovereign state.

During the thirteen years following the blue-blooded Braganzas' first landing at Bahia, the great tide of political progress, begun with the American and the French revolutions, moved over the Americas. The United States was a thriving republic, gaining in strength day by day. Haiti was free—free as a nation and free as the first American land to put an end to slavery. Haiti was even helping Bolívar and other future leaders in the spreading movement to free the Spanish colonies. And soon those colonies were in the midst of their long war to win their place as independent nations in the changing world.

Throughout Brazil now—in the larger centers of Rio and São Paulo and Minas and Bahia, as well as in the great and endless sertão behind those earlier settlements—people talked openly of the need to follow the example of the other peoples fighting to end colonialism in their own American lands. Their talk grew louder and more vehement. Their talk was of full and sovereign independence by the time their journals showed the year to be 1821.

It was the year João VI was finally able to sail back to Europe freed of Napoleon, to assume the throne at Lisbon once more. Behind him he left his son, Dom Pedro, as Regent of a Brazil still tied to the Portuguese crown. But within a year, when Lisbon's political onslaught against most of Brazil's recently won rights as a Portuguese kingdom was already underway and the protests from Brazil could be heard in all Portugal, Dom Pedro faced the choice of his life:

Should he return to Portugal to take his place as heir at the court of his father, as his father had ordered him to do? Or should he follow the advice whispered by some of his own counsellors, and remain in Brazil to become the head of an independent empire—which might otherwise transform itself into a nation without monarchs, as the Americans had done at Philadelphia, and the Haitians at Gonaives, and as the Spanish-Americans were doing or had already done all the way from Buenos Aires to the City of Mexico and beyond?

On the side of the hill at Ypiranga, in that year of 1822, Dom Pedro heeded the advice of his counsellors. Remembering especially the counsel of his tutor and friend, the scientist, José Bonifacio de Andrada, he made the momentous decision. On the seventh day of September of 1822, having just been apprised of Portugal's latest-planned measures of repression against the Brazilians' new-won rights, Dom Pedro stood on the hillside near São Paulo, waving his hat to the assembled group, and shouting the three decisive words:

"Independence or death!"

And Dom Pedro, the Portuguese heir and regent of Brazil became Pedro I, emperor of the sovereign, independent, new-born Empire of Brazil. In spite of the threats from some of the Portuguese garrisons stationed in Brazil who swore to carry him back to Lisbon by force if necessary, Dom Pedro remained to declare Brazil free and to become the constitutional emperor and the symbol of its sovereignty. The beginnings were peaceful enough, but it was not long before the peacefulness of the beginnings in Brazil—as in the Spanish colonies, from the northern Rio Grande down to the southern Plate, where the struggle for independence had long since turned into a cruel and lengthy war—was at an end. In Bahia and in other parts of Brazil, the war of the Reconcave began: the Portuguese and their followers began the bloody war against the Brazilians who supported Dom Pedro and recognized him as emperor of a free Brazil.

Instead of peace, there was torture and killing, there was massacre without mercy. And the war spread into the vast interior, into the great Brazilian wilds known as the sertão:

The war spread, waking the wilderness with the sound of guns, with the sight of settlements put to the torch, with the more muffled noises of death: the quick stab of the knife, the guerrilla's bullet finding its mark in the desolate hour at the lonely spot. The pitiless fight went on, *drawing into it women along with the men. Drawing into it women with the spirit of untamed creatures of the wilds, with a fierce love for their land. Drawing into it women said to be descended from the mythical Amazons. Some, indeed, came from the Amazon, but there was nothing mythical about them or their descent. There was nothing mythical about Dona Maria de Jesus:*

Today I received a visit from Dona Maria de Jesus, the young woman who has lately distinguished herself in the war of the Reconcave. Her dress is that of a soldier of one of the Emperor's battalions, with the addition of a tartan kilt, which she told me she had adopted from a picture representing a highlander, as the most feminine military dress.

Lady Calcott's Picture of a Brazilian Rebel

What would the Gordons and MacDonalds say to this? The "garb of old Gaul," chosen as a womanish attire! Her father is a Portuguese, named Gonsalvez de Almeida, and possesses a farm on the Rio do Pex, in the . . . sertão, or backlands. . . . Her mother was also a Portuguese. Yet the young woman's features, especially her eyes and forehead, have the strongest characteristics of the Indians. . . .

The farm of the Rio do Pex is chiefly a cattle farm, but the possessor seldom knows or counts his numbers. Senhor Gonsalvez, besides his cattle, raises some cotton—but as the sertão is sometimes a whole year without rain, the quantity is uncertain. In wet years he may sell 400 arobas, or 10,000 pounds . . . in dry seasons he can scarcely collect above 60 or 70 arobas—1500 to 1750 pounds. . . . His farm employs twenty-six slaves.

The women of the interior spin and weave for their household, and they also embroider very beautifully. The young women learn the use of firearms, as their brothers do, either to shoot game or defend themselves from the wild Indians.

Dona Maria told me several particulars concerning the country, and more concerning her own adventures. It appears that, early in the . . . war . . . emissaries had traversed the country in all directions, to raise patriot recruits, that one of these had arrived at her father's house one day about dinner time. . . . Her father had invited him in, and . . . after their meal he began to talk on the subject of his visit.

He represented the greatness and the riches of Brazil, and the happiness to which it might attain if independent. He set forth the long and oppressive tyranny of Portugal; and the meanness of submitting to be ruled by so poor and degraded a country. He talked long and eloquently of the services Dom Pedro had rendered to Brazil; of his virtues, and those of the Empress, so that at the last—said the girl, "I felt my heart burning in my breast."

Her father, however, had none of her enthusiasm of character. He is old, and said he neither could join the army himself, nor had he a son to send thither. And as to giving a slave for the ranks—what interest had a slave to fight for the independence of Brazil? He should wait in patience the result of the war, and be a peaceable subject to the winner.

Dona Maria stole from home to the house of her own sister, who was married and lived at a little distance. She recapitulated the whole of the stranger's discourse and said she wished she was a man that she might join the patriots.

"Nay," said the sister, "if I had not a husband and children, for one half of what you say I would join the ranks for the Emperor."

This was enough. Maria received some clothes belonging to her sister's husband to equip her; and as her father was then about to go to Cachoeira to dispose of some cottons, she resolved to take the opportunity of riding after him—near enough for protection in case of accident on the road, and far enough off to escape detection. At length, being in sight of Cachoeira, she stopped; and going off the road, equipped herself in male attire, and entered the town.

This was on Friday. By Sunday she had managed matters so well that she had entered the regiment of artillery and had mounted guard. She was too slight, however, for that service, and exchanged into the infantry—where she now is. She was sent hither, I believe, with dispatches, and to be presented to the Emperor, who has given her an ensign's commission and the order of the cross, the decoration of which he himself fixed on her jacket.

She is illiterate, but clever. Her understanding is quick, and her perceptions keen. I think with education she might have been a remarkable person. She is not particularly masculine in her appearance, and her manners are gentle and cheerful. She has not contracted anything coarse or vulgar in her camp life, and I believe that no imputation has ever been substantiated against her modesty. One thing is certain—that her sex never was known until her father applied to her commanding officer to seek her.

There is nothing very peculiar in her manners at table, excepting that she eats farinha (flour) with her eggs at breakfast and her fish at dinner

—instead of bread—and smokes a cigar after each meal. But she is very temperate.

A TOWN IS ERASED

In the Spanish colonies as in Brazil, the war for independence from the old world's domination was led mainly by the Creoles—the whites born in the new world, the whites whose position and power vied most keenly with those of the more favored European whites. But from the less favored classes—from the Negroes and the Indians and the multitudinous mixtures in between—the people also rallied round the patriot cause, forming its fighting core.

In Mexico a Spanish priest of Guanajuato began the big revolt on the sixteenth day of September, 1810, with the cry of death to the Spaniards! And behind him rose the Creole and the other leaders: Iturbide, who left the royalist army to join the fighters for independence, Morelos, the mestizo who abandoned the priesthood to help the battle against colonialism.

Behind the priest with the name like a live river—Miguel Hidalgo y Costilla—rose all the other new leaders of a new Mexico being born in the rising flood of rebellion: Allende, Guerrero, Mina. The lone mountain-lion who called himself Guadalupe Victoria. And all the many other patriots and martyrs to the independence cause. Behind the priest, Hidalgo, rose the Indians of Guanajuato—

But against them, against their leaders, came the reprisals declared and executed by many of the Spanish royalist generals. Against the people in Guanajuato—as in the rest of Mexico and all the rest of embattled Spanish America—rose the terror, proclaimed and carried out with no pity and no quarter by generals like the royalist commander in Mexico who signed his orders briefly under the name of F. Calleja:

It is decreed that the Indians of Zitácuaro and its department shall be deprived of their property, as well as of those immunities and privileges which the extreme beneficence of the government had granted them. This forfeited property, as well as that of those South Americans who have taken part in the insurrection, who accompanied the rebels in their flight, or who left the city at the entrance of the king's troops, to be placed in the public treasury. If those who are included in this decree will present themselves to me, giving proofs of repentance, and of willingness to contribute to repair the roads, etc., they shall receive their pardon. But property cannot be restored.

General F. Calleja: A Decree to Destroy a Rebel Village

The capital of this department is to be transferred to Marabatio, where a military government is to be established, and the people are to be compelled to arm, equip, and support companies of infantry and cavalry for the defence of this department.

Monarchical government being hated by the inhabitants of this criminal town, who have supported three engagements against the king's forces, and having found the heads of many of our chiefs—who sacrificed their lives for the public good—placed on poles at the entrance of the town, we decree that every building in Zitácuaro shall be razed to the ground, or destroyed by fire.

Every inhabitant to leave the town within six days. And as a proof of mercy, I permit them to take their moveable property.

Every inhabitant to receive from the government a written testimonial of his name, family, and day of his departure. Any person remaining in the town after the time fixed for departure, or not having provided himself with the requisite testimonial, to be put to death.

All arms to be given up to the government, under the penalty of death.

The clergy to be sent to the Bishop of Valladolid.

An absolute prohibition is made against rebuilding the town of Zitácuaro, or any other town which may in future be destroyed to punish rebellion.

Any town or village admitting either of the three members of the insurgent junta, or any of their delegates, or who shall refuse to surrender them to the king, or attempt to resist the king's troops, are subjected to the above-mentioned penalties.

The Count of Casa-rul is intrusted with enforcing this decree.

PALAVER

Not all the Indians in the colonies were on the side of the patriots. Some fought with the royalists. And some, seeing little or no difference be-

tween the European and the Creole white, seeing the independence war
as a war of rivalry between different groups of masters, went to the side
that offered the biggest bribe. Such were the Pehuenches of the lands
between the Argentine and Chilean provinces.

Few knew their ways better, however, than a certain fox of the southern Andes, leading the patriots' war as none had led it before and few
would lead it later. Few knew the ways of war or the ways of the
Pehuenches as they were known by José de San Martín, commander of
the independence forces in the south of South America, where the future nations of Argentina and Chile were being born.

And there were those, fortunately, who knew the ways of San Martín
as he knew the ways of the Indians. There were the volunteers from
England and the United States and other countries who came to fight
with the different patriot leaders of South America. Among these was
General William Miller, late of the United States, who learned a thing
or two about his commander-in-chief and took the trouble to write it
down while the picture of San Martín and his clever use of the Pehuenches was still fresh in his mind:

The patriot general (San Martin) hoped to be enabled by a ruse of war
to cause Marcó—royalist captain-general and presidente of Chile—to divide his forces. For this purpose—when every preparation to march was
nearly completed—San Martín caused a conference to be held with the
Indians of Pehuenche, for the ostensible object of soliciting leave to
march unmolested through their territories for
the purpose of attacking the Spaniards from the
pass of el Planchón. On the day before that
fixed upon for an interview with the Indians, San Martín caused to be
sent to the fort of San Carlos, on the river Aguanda, one hundred and
twenty goatskins of aguardiente or grape brandy, three hundred skins of
wine, a great number of bridles, spurs, all the old embroidered or lace
dresses that could, with great diligence, be collected in the province,
hats, handkerchiefs of an ordinary kind, glass beads, dried fruits, etc. for
presents—an indispensable preliminary to success in any Indian negotia-
tion.

At eight o'clock on the morning of the —— of September, 1816, the
caciques approached the esplanade in front of the fort, with all the

From the Memoirs of General Miller: San Martín's Ruse

pomp of savage life, each at the head of his warriors, their wives and children bringing up the rear. Polygamy being practiced, the wives were very numerous. The men wore their hair unconfined and long; their bodies, naked from the waist upwards, were painted with different colors. Their horses were also stained precisely in the same manner as when they go to war. . . .

Each cacique was preceded by a small party of patriot cavalry, sent by the general for the purpose of keeping up an irregular fire of blank cartridges from their pistols as the tribe advanced. This mode of ushering the Indians to the presence of Christians is a compliment with which they never dispense.

As the tribes arrived on the esplanade, the women and children filed off, and took their station on one side, without dismounting. When all the tribes had arrived, the warriors of one tribe commenced a sham fight, during which they kept the horses at full speed, or made them turn on their hind legs, curvet, caper, and prance about in the most extraordinary manner. During the exhibition, a gun was fired every six minutes from the fort. The Indians answered the salute by slapping their mouths and making the most frightful noises, in token of satisfaction. . . .

The palaver commenced in the *place d'armes*, where the governor of the fort had provided a table covered with the cloth of the chapel pulpit, and benches for the caciques and war-captains, who were the only persons admitted to conference with the general. The Indians outside remained formed and mounted, keeping themselves on the alert, until the result should be made known.

Upon arriving at the *place d'armes*, the chiefs took their seats according to seniority: the caciques first and then the war-captains. San Martín, the governor of the fort, and the interpreter, placed themselves on a bench at the head of the table. The general, as a matter of courtesy, proposed a friendly glass previous to proceeding to business—but all declined, assigning as a reason that if they drank, their heads could not be firm to give proper consideration to the matter they had assembled to discuss.

The interpreter—Father Julián, a Franciscan friar, an Araucanian by birth, and brought up by a Creole family from the age of ten—then commenced an harangue. He reminded them of the good understanding which had subsisted between the Pehuenche Indians and the general-in-chief, who relied with confidence upon a continuation of the harmony so happily established, and who had convened them in solemn palaver to compliment them with drink-offerings and gifts, and to request that the patriot army might be permitted to pass through the Pehuenche territory, in order to attack the Spaniards. . . .

A dead silence followed . . . for a quarter of an hour. . . . At length the senior cacique, named Ninconyancu, broke silence. He was nearly eighty years of age, his hair was snow-white, and his appearance venerable in the extreme. Directing his discourse to his brother chiefs, he calmly asked if they were of opinion that the proposals just made by the Christians ought or ought not to be accepted.

The debate which followed was carried on in a manner exceedingly interesting. Each chief in his proper turn declared his sentiments with the utmost tranquillity, and without the slightest interruption, or sign of impatience, from the rest. Having agreed upon the answer proper to be given, Ninconyancu addressed himself to the general, and informed him that the Pehuenches, with the exception of three caciques—whom the rest knew how to restrain—accepted his proposals. All then rose from their seats—except the three caciques who did not concur in opinion with the majority—and in testimony of their sincerity embraced the general.

Without losing a moment, the cacique Milyagin stepped out and communicated to the Indians on the esplanade that the proposals of the Christians were such as could be accepted. They instantly unsaddled, and delivered their horses to the militia to turn them out to feed. They next proceeded to deposit their lances, hatchets, and knives . . . in a barrack-room, not to be returned till after the conclusion of the revels which invariably follow a palaver. . . .

Two thousand persons, including women and children, were seated in circles upon the esplanade. One of the first subjects of conversation was their own feats, or the deeds of their ancestors. Some were affected to weeping in relating family history. As soon as the liquor exercised its influence all talked together, and shouted, and yelled with deafening din. Quarrels ensued, as a matter of course, and many fought—when, in the absence of weapons, they bit and kicked each other and tore out hair by handfuls. . . . Towards midnight the revels subsided into the silence of the grave. Men and women were stretched upon the ground as if in a lethargy, or in the arms of death, except a very few who still retained the power to crawl or roll a few paces—but the greater part were perfectly motionless. . . .

A day was set apart for the exchange of gifts. Each cacique presented the general with a poncho, the manufacture of his wives. . . . Some of the ponchos accepted by the general were by no means contemptible as specimens of native manufacture, particularly in the liveliness of the pattern and the permanence of the colors. What the Indians appeared to prize most highly of the gifts they received were the hats, and the embroidered or lace dresses, which were put on and worn the instant they came into their possession. The distribution of presents was made on the fourth day. . . .

On the sixth day, San Martín received despatches from General Pueyrredon, who was marching from Salta to Cordova—where San Martín proceeded to meet him . . .

The Pehuenches remained at San Carlos eight days longer, on account of some dealers having appeared from Mendoza with spirits, and bartered them away for most of the presents which the Indians had received from San Martín. The Pehuenches departed at the end of a fortnight, so highly gratified by the entertainment that they declared that such a splendid palaver was not known in the annals of tradition. . . .

As San Martín foresaw, they soon sold the secret—that the patriots intended to invade Chile by the southern passes—to Captain-General Marcó, who instantly divided his forces by transferring the greater part from the north to Talca and San Fernando in the full conviction that Chile would receive the first blow from one of the southern passes of the Andes. . . . To keep up the illusion, San Martín sent guerrillas to make demonstrations towards the south.

DECISION IN CHILE

By ruse and stratagem, and the clever use of guerrillas; by all that was irregular and unorthodox in the European ways of war; but above all by the unquenchable and all-consuming fire of their determination that their lands must be free of foreign domination, the patriot leaders throughout Spanish America advanced their cause nearer and nearer its goal.

In the face of superior numbers of men and arms; in the face of hunger and painful wounds and torturing illness and death on the parching desert or the freezing mountain-passes; in the face of frequent betrayal of themselves and their persecuted dear ones; in the face of every obstacle raised by the enemy with or without the support of nature —the leaders carried the patriot banners closer and closer to victory.

After the successful declaration of independence issued by a congress of patriots assembled at Tucumán in Argentina, the first lasting decision by arms in Spanish America came in Chile. The decision came when the Spanish forces were gaining ground everywhere on the continent. It came in the dark year of 1817:

The leaders were San Martín and a Chilean leader with his ragged army resting for the moment on the Argentine side of the Andes under the protection and care and encouragement of José de San Martín. The leaders were San Martín and the illegitimate son of an Irish immigrant who had risen to become the viceroy of Peru: Bernardo O'Higgins, the bold rebel son of the man who ruled the Viceroyalty of Peru, of which Chile was a part. Bernardo O'Higgins, disciple along with San Martín of Francisco Miranda, the Precursor, whom they had known in England. Bernardo O'Higgins and his fellow-patriot leading their army of starving stragglers for twenty-one days and twenty-one nights over the raw heights of the Andes—instead of marching through the southern passes as the Spaniards had expected them to do. O'Higgins and San Martín!

They led their men over the freezing top of the southern Andes to fall on the enemy where the first decision by arms would come. The men of O'Higgins and of San Martín forgot their exhaustion, finding their strength in the surprise of the Spanish enemy looking up to see his foes rushing upon him from the slope of the Andes they had crossed— the Spanish enemy, staring up to see defeat rushing upon him in the year of 1817, at the place called Chacabuco, where the first decision came.

February 4th, Don Miguel Atero, chief of the royalist staff, informed the government of Santiago that the enemy had surprised the guards of the Andes, placed about twelve leagues in advance of Santa Rosa . . . and that of seventy-five men, thirteen only had escaped, bringing with them the news that the enemy was advancing. At the same time, Major Vila

The Defeat of the Spaniards at Chacabuco—from a Spanish Diary reported to the government that the advanced guard at the Paso de los Patos had reconnoitred the enemy and requested a reinforcement. Atero immediately sent a company of Talavera infantry, and then re-treated with the division of the army stationed at Santa Rosa, to Chacabuco, leaving behind him two pieces of artillery, ammunition, baggage, and warlike stores. The force stationed at Santa Rosa amounted to about four hundred men.

· February 5th, the Captain-general Marcó ordered Colonel Quintanilla to join the army at Chacabuco, with the battalion of carabiniers. They arrived on the 6th, when Quintanilla immediately advanced to the convent of Curimon to reconnoitre the enemy in Villa Vieja, and having reported to Atero that their number did not exceed six hundred, an attack was immediately ordered, which took place on the morning of the 7th.

The cavalry engaged that of the enemy in a place called De las Comas; the crafty enemy retired towards the Cordillera, and halted at Putendo, where they were joined by an ambuscade of a hundred horse. Our infantry did not advance with the cavalry, so that as soon as they were overpowered by the enemy they fled in the greatest disorder towards our infantry for support. On their return, to their great surprise they found that the infantry also was in a disordered retreat, without having taken part in the action, and also that the commander-in-chief, Atero, had fled.

Colonel Quintanilla now took the command and collected the dispersed soldiers. He placed the infantry in the center and flanked it with the cavalry, although harassed in the rear by the enemy in his retreat. Having at length reached Villa Vieja, a council of war was held by the officers, and it was resolved to continue their march to Curimon. On their arrival they learnt that the enemy was about to renew the attack —on hearing which, Colonel Marqueli, to whom Atero had given the command, continued his march to Chacabuco.

The victorious army took up its quarters in Villa Vieja. Our loss was about thirty carabiniers. There is no doubt that the whole of our loss is to be attributed to Atero, who, observing a party of the enemy's cavalry on an eminence to the right, exclaimed, "We are cut off!"—when he immediately mounted his horse and fled.

At ten o'clock at night the news arrived at Santiago, and the greatest confusion began to prevail. On the morning of February 8th, the two judges, Pereyra and Caspi, and the general of brigade, Olaguer Feliu, fled to Valparaiso. On the 9th, Colonel Barañao arrived at Santiago with Colonel Eloriga and 360 hussars. On the 10th, Lieutenant-colonel Morgado arrived with 450 dragoons. At ten o'clock at night Brigadier-general Maroto was appointed by Marcó to take the chief command. Our whole force consisted of 1000 cavalry and 1100 infantry.

On the 12th, at six o'clock in the afternoon, an officer arrived at

Santiago with a verbal communication from General Maroto, declaring that he had suffered a total defeat. This was confirmed on the 13th by the arrival of Maroto and Quintanilla. Marcó had left the city with about 1500 men, and resolved on renewing the attack. But after more private conversation with Maroto, he returned to the capital, and summoned a council of war. After a long conference, nothing was determined on, and the sub-inspector-general, Bernedo, the judge advocate, Lescano, and the commandant of artillery, Cacho, fled to Valparaiso.

From the 13th at noon to the evening of the 14th, officers, soldiers and civilians continued to arrive at Valparaiso, where they embarked on board several vessels then at anchor in the bay, and fled to Lima. But it was not known till our arrival at Callao that the *presidente* Marcó was left behind at the mercy of Bernardo O'Higgins—to whom the insurgents owe their victory, and we our disgrace.

A FORCED MIGRATION

Behind San Martín and O'Higgins lay the decision at Chacabuco, the subsequent entry into the capital, Santiago, the freeing of Chile. Even farther behind lay the freeing of the Plate and the Argentine. All that lay behind.

But what lay before them was only this: not peace or even rest, but the inescapable need to march to the north and the west, to march to the very heart of royalist power in South America—to the country Pizarro himself had conquered.

Before O'Higgins and San Martín rose the challenge from the northwest. Before them rose Peru, the fortress of Spanish power on the continent. Before them lay Peru, where the head of the dragon of Spanish power still breathed in fire and smoke, still intact and ready to strike at any time to recover its lost domain.

Other patriot leaders in the north were also turning their eyes to Peru. But first they had to finish the job of liberation in their own provinces, as San Martín and O'Higgins had done. There in the north, throughout the colony of New Granada, which would be Venezuela and Colombia, the fighting had started, the skirmishes and battles were growing fierce— but the war was still to be won.

The war in the north was still to be won. And the odds were great, the odds were long—

Even under the fiery leadership of that young man of Caracas, the scion of a well-to-do Creole family, who drowned his deep sorrow over the loss of his young wife not so much in French wine as in the stronger wine of French republican ideas. The odds against victory in the north were still great, even with the small but determined hands of that high-strung former officer in the Spanish army holding the reins, even with the will of iron ringing loud within the skinny frame of that short man with the long head, even with the sure hands of that restless man, who broke with all conventions, guiding the reins as he whistled the French republican airs and tapped out the rhythm with a nervous foot:

Even under the ruthless but inspired command of Simón Bolívar himself, chief of the patriot forces in the north of South America—even under the great Bolívar, the odds in the fight for freedom were hard. The odds were long:

Bolívar . . . escaped unhurt, flying to Caracas with the greatest speed, reaching it in twenty-four hours. He caused a proclamation to be immediately issued, ordering, under pain of death, that men, women, and children should emigrate. This peremptory order, together with the terror occasioned by the advance of the *llaneros*—the outlaw "cowboys" —excited an alarm and confusion difficult to be described: the ringing of the bells; the fugitives who escaped the slaughter of the preceding day, covered with dust, galloping through the streets; soldiers running from house to house, with drawn swords, to see that the order was carried into execution. The old and the young, the lame and the blind, men and women, were running up and down in confusion, packing up as much clothes as they could carry in their hands. Great numbers who resolved on not abandoning their homes, but to wait patiently their fate, took refuge in the sanctuary of the churches and convents. Mothers, with all their children clinging to them, were seen imploring the protection of those who had mules to carry them—but every feeling of pity was absorbed in the contemplation of their own danger, and the distresses of others was a consideration of secondary importance.

Colonel George Flinter: On Bolívar's Retreat from Caracas

The whole cavalcade moved forward, some on mules, with their wives and daughters behind them; others galloping forward to save themselves. Some were laughing, unconscious of the dangers that hovered over them, whilst others, awake to the horrors of their situation, lamented the hard fate that should have forced them to abandon their property and their homes. Others bitterly deplored the loss of a father, a brother, or a lover, who had fallen in the preceding battles, or shuddered, reflecting what would be the fate of some relative who, through age, sickness, or infirmity, was left in the city to the mercy of the savage *llaneros*.

These ill-fated emigrants had to traverse a tract of desert country of more than three hundred miles, over steep and rugged mountains and unfordable rivers, without any habitation to shelter them from the inclemency of the weather during the night; no place from whence they could derive subsistence, except from the precarious food, supplied by the trees of the forest, or the wild animals, which they might take by chance.

The first morning of their departure went on very well, and everyone seemed to have forgotten their sufferings, in the contemplation of the romantic scenery of the country, and the warbling of the birds. But towards noon, when the heat had overpowered those who were on foot, particularly the women who had to carry their children, and the young girls whose tender feet were not accustomed to walk on the rough precipices of the mountains—their thin shoes and dresses being torn to pieces by the bushes, and their feet streaming with blood—presented a most distressing scene. Some of the horsemen used to take the children and place them before them. But in general, a sense of self-preservation drowned every other feeling—for the *llaneros* were fast pressing on the rear.

When night came on and clouded every surrounding object in darkness, those who loitered behind or lay down through fatigue would be either killed by the *llaneros* or devoured by the tigers. They durst not even light fires, for fear of discovering their line of march to the enemy. The dawn of morn disclosed one of the most affecting sights that can be imagined:

The *llaneros* began to overtake those in the rear, whilst every individual, anxious for his own safety, pushed on, spreading in every direction, through the woods and mountains, to escape being taken. Some—unable to move forward, and overcome by fatigue—in an agony of despair threw themselves on the ground to wait the approach of the *llaneros* to end their sufferings. Others, as if devoid of every sentiment of maternal tenderness, abandoned their infant children to destruction in the woods, the better to enable them to proceed. But some, less inhuman, resorted to a stratagem which nothing but self-preservation could have justified: when crossing a river they would supplicate the horsemen to carry their children to the other side, and when they had taken the children, they would have either to support the incumbrance or to destroy it—for the mothers would instantly disappear amongst the crowd.

Every moment some one would drop down, through hunger and fatigue, never to rise again. It is supposed that upwards of six thousand souls perished in this emigration.

NATURE ROSE UP

The fight for liberty was growing more ruthless on every side. More than once, nature itself took sides against the fighters for freedom.

Two years after the great crossing of the Andes in the south brought the first lasting decision at Chacabuco, nature rose up to smite Bolívar and his heroic band, still battling to crush the Spanish power in their own northern lands. Nature with all her ruthless weapons arose to smite Bolívar's rabble army of native patriots and volunteers from England and the United States.

In the territory that was waiting to become Colombia, waiting for the second lasting decision to come at the end of another great crossing of the Andes, nature struck: Against Bolívar and his daring band determined to free the very heart of New Granada, that would be Colombia, and thus insure the freedom of the freshly won province of Venezuela. Against that motley band of Creoles, foreigners, mestizos, mulattoes, Indians, and Negro slaves freed by decree of the patriot leaders. Against that intrepid band intent on executing the next-to-impossible plan drawn up by Bolívar and his chief aides (with their only camp-chairs the bleached skulls of the cattle eaten by their famished men). Against Bolívar and his dying band of two thousand men struggling across the Granadian Andes in the far north of South America. Against that diminishing band of men dragging themselves in pain and final fatigue over the wind-swept bleak plateau of Pisba, thirteen thousand feet above the sea. Against Simón Bolívar—known too soon, for his own mind's comfort, as the Liberator—and against his little band:

Nature struck with all her fury!

Our road lay across minor rivers, whose streams were so swollen and currents rendered so strong and rapid by the falls of rain, that in fording them numbers of the men, from their excessive debility, were unable to bear up against their force. The footing once lost, all is over—the rush of waters bears the body down with the rapidity of a shot, dashing it in its course against stumps of trees, jutting rocks,

With Bolivar, Crossing the Granadian Andes

and loose stones, until life is extinct, and the sweeping tide is stained with blood. We had also several mountains to pass. And the waters winding round their diversified forms, produced—according to the number of passages between them—so many different streams for us to wade through. . . . In one day the same piece of water, owing to its various windings, may be crossed more than ten times.

The excessive fatigue of exertions so unremitting, under circumstances which were otherwise very afflictive, soon broke down many of the already reduced troops, and above four hundred of the British perished, besides natives. And even those who escaped the death which lay in wait for them at every step, were so wretchedly enfeebled that even death itself was earnestly wished for.

Their shoes, from being constantly saturated with water, became so enlarged that they were continually escaping from the feet. And to add to their misery, the surfaces of the mountains were chiefly composed of sharp-pointed stones, resembling in color broken Scotch granite—but harder, and in some parts approaching to the appearance and quality of white flints. By this latter species of stones, the edges of which are so keen and hard that the poorer Indians use them as knives and hatchets, the feet of the men were so shockingly lacerated that on the more elevated and dry rocks their course might have been tracked by the bloody marks of their footsteps. The deep gashes thus made were soon filled up by the cutting brittly sand, which is lodged between the acclivities, and which caused an inconceivable degree of torture—again heightened as they approached the plains of Maturin, by the intrusion of myriads of insects named chiggers, from which their feet had no protection. . . .

In the numerous woods through which we passed, our ears were incessantly assailed by the screams of the flying monkeys, who united to express their indignation at our trespass on their peaceful seclusion. Part of these were shot and eaten—but owing to their extreme sagacity, they were but few, and those of the youngest. Their flesh is like that of the wild rabbit in appearance, but somewhat sweeter to the taste.

At night, the different sounds of these and other animals, united with the howlings of the storm, the creepings of the number of lizards over the troops as they reposed, and the consciousness of being surrounded not only by snakes in abundance, but by the small kinds of lions and tigers with which these woods are plentifully stocked, all conspired to banish sleep, and to keep the mind completely alive to the horrors of the situation. Nor were these horrors lessened by the melancholy indication which the roars of the last-mentioned carnivorous brood afforded, of the fate of the remains of the poor fellows who were continually falling martyrs to their sufferings, which for the most part found a grave in the entrails of these savage beasts of prey.

The precaution and comfort of having fires round the camp could not be taken, as the descent of the rain, which resembled the burst of a waterspout, extinguished them as soon as kindled. At the same time, the ground on which we lay was covered with water to the depth of from six to nine inches, so that we were obliged to prop up our heads with anything we could procure, to avoid suffocation.

During our progress we necessarily passed many standing pools of water—which, as we approached the plains of Maturin, where the lands being so much higher were not inundated, became more frequent. At these the soldiers, at first, were in the habit of stooping to assuage their thirst, until several of them were found dead at the margin of these receptacles for small alligators and snakes of the most poisonous description.

When it happened that one of these pools, which were sometimes of vast extent, lay directly across our path, so as to render it necessary to march a long way round, many of the most fatigued and reckless of existence among the troops preferred wading through them. In several of such instances, a species of fish, called the raya, oftentimes seized their thighs and the calves of their legs, and tore large pieces from them, leaving those who survived altogether incapable of further service. Some of the men so bitten were obliged to be left behind, as they could not walk—and the mules, which were engrossed by the general, were not allowed to carry them. These unhappy persons would earnestly implore their comrades to shoot them, instead of abandoning them to starvation —and certainly a speedy death in such dreary instances would have proved a blessing.

Many of the troops had ulcers which deprived them of their toes— one of the many disagreeable consequences of low living and unwholesome food. And others were lamed by the thorns of the sensitive plant, which penetrated the soles of their feet. Ulcers were also produced on various parts of the body by the sudden transitions from heat to cold, occasioned by the scorching rays of the sun on the mountains, after being so long saturated in the waters of the lowlands. . . .

Upon the whole, a more horrible complication of evils has seldom been inflicted by military incapacity than that which in this dreary march was encountered by our ill-fated band. . . .

We continued our irksome journey until we came near the branch of the cordillera of the Andes, which stretches across the route from Cumana to Maturin. Its cloud-capped summits towered before us abruptly, just as we had emerged from an extensive wood which we had been traversing for three nights and three days. We had previously deemed our progress sufficiently calamitous, and had never contemplated this new and stupendous difficulty—to surmount which the little strength we had left seemed wholly inadequate. . . .

A spirit of despondency spread over the whole party. And many, but for the laudable efforts of their officers, would have laid themselves down to perish without another exertion.

THE TURNING POINT

Out of the pain, out of the final weariness of their fevered heads and frigid limbs, out of their last hard gasping for breath on the hostile highland at the end of their trek—there might have come only death to those who remained, as it had come to those who fell by the way. Only death might have come at the end of that long and cruel trek—if Bolívar and the survivors of his band had not seen the fear in the eyes of the surprised Spanish enemy as they descended upon him at Socha.

Out of the stark terror they saw in the eyes of their startled foe, the tired Bolívar and his enfeebled and ailing men drew the strength and the sudden resolve and the success of the initial engagement that seemed like a miracle.

But while the patriots were strengthened more in heart than in force or numbers by the successful skirmish at Socha or the fresh enrollment of new recruits, the royalists moved to effect a strategic and powerful junction of their two main forces at the nearby capital, Bogotá. The big battle of the north was shaping up, and it could not be long in coming—

It came sooner, in fact, than the royalist general, Barreiro, wanted it to come. Before he could reach Bogotá to join his forces with the seasoned army under the Viceroy of New Granada himself, his strategic flight was cut short by Bolívar. As Barreiro and his forces rushed toward a certain bridge that had to be crossed, they found Bolívar already there with his men drawn up to meet them.

Bolívar and his men stood on that bridge and on the heights behind it and on the road before it. They stood on that bridge that crossed the River Boyacá and forced the Spaniards to fight them there. It was around that bridge that Bolívar forced the big battle which was destined to be the turning point of the war of independence in the north of South America. This was Bolívar's great challenge:

The Battle of Boyacá!

At dawn yesterday the advance guard of our army reported that the enemy was moving down the Samacá road. The army took up its arms and—as soon as it was evident that the enemy's intention was to cross the Bridge of Boyacá in order to open up his direct communications and establish contact with the capital—marched down the main road to

Communiqué of the Army of Liberation, 8 August 1819

halt the enemy in this, or force him to engage in combat. At two o'clock in the afternoon the first enemy division was drawing near the bridge when our cavalry reconnaissance appeared. The enemy, who had not yet succeeded in discovering our army, and who thought that the opposing force was a body of scouts, attacked with his riflemen to drive it off the road, while his main force continued to advance.

Our divisions accelerated their march, and to the enemy's great surprise our entire infantry appeared in column formation on a height dominating his position. The enemy's vanguard had gone up part of the way in pursuit of our reconnaissance, and the rest of his army—a force of three thousand men—was in a hollow one quarter of a league from the bridge.

The Cazadores battalion of our advance guard sent out a company in guerrilla (or scattered) formation, and with the remainder in columns attacked the enemy's riflemen, forcing them to retreat hastily to a large wall—from where they were also dislodged. They crossed the bridge and took up positions on the other side. Meanwhile, our infantry kept moving down the hill, and our cavalry continued to advance up the road.

The enemy attempted to launch a movement from his right, and he was opposed by our "Rifles" and a British company. The first "Barcelona" and the *Bravos de Páez* battalions, together with a squadron of cavalry from the upper plains, moved down the center. The *Nueva Granada* line battalion and the *Guías* rear guard joined the *Cazadores* battalion to form our left. The *Tunja* and *Socorro* columns were held in reserve.

At this moment action began along the entire front.

General Anzoátegui commanded the operations of the center and the right. He ordered an attack on a battalion which the enemy had spread out in guerrilla formation in a canyon, and he forced it to retreat to the main enemy body which—drawn up in columns upon a height, with three pieces of artillery in the center and two cavalry corps on its flanks —awaited our attack.

Our troops of the center, ignoring the fire coming from enemy formations on their left flank, attacked the enemy's main force. The enemy's fire was terrible, but our troops, in most daring movements carried out with the strictest order, surrounded all enemy formations.

Our squadron of cavalry from the upper plains charged with its customary bravery and, from that moment, all the efforts made by the Spanish general were fruitless: he lost his position.

The enemy's company of mounted grenadiers (made up entirely of Spaniards from the Peninsula) was the first to abandon the field of battle in a cowardly manner. The enemy infantry attempted to re-form its lines on another height, but it was destroyed immediately. A corps of enemy cavalry which had been held in reserve awaited our charge with drawn lances and was broken to pieces by our own lances.

And the whole Spanish army, in complete rout and surrounded on all sides, after having suffered heavy casualties, surrendered its arms and gave itself up as our prisoner.

Almost simultaneously, General Santander, who directed the operations of our left and who had met with fearful resistance from the enemy's advance guard—to which he had opposed only his *Cazadores* battalion of riflemen—charged with several companies from the line battalion and the *Guías* of the rear guard, crossed the bridge, and completed the victory.

The enemy's entire army fell into our hands.

General Barreiro, Commanding General of the Army of New Granada, was taken prisoner on the field of battle by Private Pedro Martínez of the First Rifles. The general's second in command—Colonel Jiménez—

and almost all the commanders and chiefs of corps, as well as a multitude of lesser officers and more than sixteen hundred men, were also captured, together with their arms, ammunition, artillery, cavalry, etc.

Scarcely fifty men escaped, among them some cavalry chiefs and officers who fled before the battle ended. General Santander with the advance guard and the Guías of the rear, immediately set out in pursuit of the fleeing enemy, while General Anzoátegui remained all night on the battlefield with the rest of the army.

The advantages won by the Republic as a result of the glorious victory of yesterday are incalculable. Never before had our troops obtained a more decisive triumph, and seldom before had they fought against such disciplined and well-commanded troops.

Nothing can compare with the intrepidity with which General Anzoátegui, at the head of two battalions and a cavalry squadron, attacked and subdued the enemy's main corps. It is to him that the victory is in large part due.

General Santander directed his movements with precision and firmness. The Bravos de Páez and first "Barcelona" battalions and the cavalry squadron from the upper plains fought with astounding courage.

When the battle was over, the Tunja and Socorro columns joined on the right.

In short, His Excellency (Simón Bolívar, the commander-in-chief) is highly satisfied with the conduct of all the chiefs, officers, and men of the Army of Liberation in this memorable one-day's feat.

Our losses consist of thirteen dead and fifty-three wounded. Among the former are Lt. of Cavalry N. Pérez and the Reverend Father Miguel Díaz, chaplain of the advance guard; among the wounded are Top-Sergeant José Rafael de Las Heras, Captain Johnson, and Lieutenant Rivero.

ON THE PLAIN OF AYACUCHO

His Excellency, the Liberator, was highly satisfied with the outcome of the battle at Boyacá. But there could be no ease of body or mind until the head of Spanish power in the hemisphere was smashed. There could be no rest until the threat of the dragon's return to authority on the American continents was ended. There could be no peace until Peru was snatched from the dragon forever.

Pounded by sea from the patriot ships, harried and cut by the liberating armies that had come with San Martín and O'Higgins from Argentina and Chile—still the dragon of Spanish power held the stronghold of Peru:

Until the year 1824 was nearing its end.

Five years after the turning point at Boyacá, the year being 1824, the date December 9, and the hour precisely ten o'clock in the morning— the final battle began, the final decision approached, on the plain of Ayacucho in the stronghold of Peru.

The man of the day, the man of the single furious hour the battle would last, was already known as the young liberator of the land that would be known as Ecuador: Antonio José de Sucre it was who led the united patriot army against the Viceroy's forces, led his army of freedom against the Spanish forces in Peru that were nearly twice the size of the patriot army in numbers and more than twice its strength.

Sucre, the youngest and most modest of all the great independence leaders, noted the dark contents of the dispatch from Bolívar himself in Peru advising the trapped Sucre that he could expect no reinforcements. Sucre took his tired men out of the trap overnight, hoping to turn imminent defeat into impossible victory. Sucre prepared to force the long-postponed decision. Sucre and his weary men without cannon or food, faced the Viceroy and his powerful force:

Antonio José de Sucre, face to face with the dragon at last, on the Ayacucho plain:

Quinua, an Indian village, is on the western extremity of the plain of Ayacucho, the shape of which is nearly square, about a league in circumference, and flanked right and left by deep, rugged ravines. In the rear of the plain, or towards the west, is a gradual descent of two leagues to the main road from Guamanga to Guanta, which runs along the base

General Miller's Memoirs of the Battle of Ayacucho

of a mountain range that rises like a wall with no apparent outlet. The eastern boundary of the plain is formed by the abrupt and rugged ridge of Condorkanki—which gigantic bulwark, running north and south, overlooks the field of Ayacucho.

A little below the summit of this ridge was perched the royalist army. The liberating army was drawn up on the plain, in front of the Spaniards, at an interval of about a mile, having Quinua in the rear, each corps being formed in close column, to await the attack of the royalists. . . .

During the night of the 8th, a brisk fire was maintained between the royalist and patriot outposts. It was the object of Sucre to prevent the royalists' descending in the night. For this purpose the bands of two battalions were sent with a company near to the foot of the ridge, and continued playing for some time whilst a sharp fire was kept up. This feint had the desired effect, for the royalists did not stir from their lines.

The Viceroy's position in the night of the 8th was very much exposed. His infantry, occupying the front of the ridge of Condorkanki, was within musket-range of the foot of the hill. The fire from two or three battalions, deployed into line, might have obliged the royalists to abandon their position. As it was, a lieutenant-colonel and two or three men, within the Spanish encampment, were killed, as they sat round their fires, by chance balls from the patriot company at the foot of the hill.

The night of the 8th was one of deep and anxious interest. A battle was inevitable on the following day, and that battle was to decide the destinies of South America. The patriots were aware that they had to contend with twice their own numbers, and that nothing but a decisive victory could save them and their country from ignominious servitude. The patriot soldier might indeed expect to escape with life, reduced to the condition of a slave. But with the patriot generals and officers, it was only a choice between death and victory. They knew full well what would be the cruel policy of the Spaniards if they proved victorious. . . .

The morning of the 9th dawned particularly fine. At first there was a chillness in the air which seemed to influence the minds of the men, but when the sun rose above the mountain, the effects of its genial warmth became manifest in the renovated spirits of the soldiers. The men on both sides were observed rubbing their hands, and exhibiting every token of content and satisfaction.

At 9:00 A.M. the division, Villalobos, began to descend. The Viceroy, on foot, placed himself at its head. . . . The files wound down the craggy side of Condorkanki, obliquing a little to their left. The division, Monet, forming the royalist right, commenced at the same time to defile directly into the plain. The cavalry, leading their horses, made the same movement, though with greater difficulty, between the infantry of each division.

As the files arrived on the plain, they formed into columns. This was a moment of extraordinary interest. It appeared as though respiration were suspended by feelings of anxiety, mingled with doubts and hope.

It was during this operation, which had an imposing effect, that Sucre rode along his own line, and, addressing a few emphatic words to each corps, recalled to memory its former achievements. He then placed himself in a central point and, in an inspiring tone of voice, said that upon the efforts of that day depended the fate of South America. Then, pointing to the descending columns, he assured his men that another day of glory was about to crown their admirable constancy.

This animating address of the general produced an electric effect, and was answered by enthusiastic viva's.

By the time that rather more than half the royalist divisions, Monet and Villalobos, had reached and formed upon the arena, Sucre ordered the division, Cordova, and two regiments of cavalry to advance to the charge. The gallant Cordova placed himself about fifteen yards in front of his division, formed into four parallel columns with the cavalry in the intervals. Having dismounted, he plunged his sword into the heart of his charger, and turning to the troops, exclaimed:

"There lies my last horse. I have now no means of escape, and we must fight it out together!"

Then, waving his hat above his head, he continued:

"Adelante, con paso de vencedores — onward with the step of conquerors!"

These words were heard distinctly throughout the columns, which, inspired by the gallant bearing of their leader, moved to the attack in the finest possible order. The Spaniards stood firmly and full of apparent confidence. The Viceroy was seen, as were also Monet and Villalobos, at the head of their divisions, superintending the formation of their columns as they reached the plain.

The hostile bayonets crossed, and for three or four minutes the two parties struggled together, so as to leave it doubtful which would give way. At this moment the Colombian cavalry, headed by Colonel Silva, charged. This brave officer fell, covered with wounds, but the intrepidity of the onset was irresistible. The royalists lost ground, and were driven back with great slaughter. The Viceroy was wounded and taken prisoner.

As the fugitives climbed the sides of Condorkanki, the patriots, who had deployed, kept up a well-directed fire, and numbers of the enemy were seen to drop and roll down, till their progress was arrested by the brushwood or some jutting crag.

The Spanish enemy rolled down the steep sides of the mountain. And after that last great battle, Royalist resistance rolled downward to despair and surrender. And soon all the Spanish Americas—except the island of Cuba, which was not yet ripe for independence, and the isle of Puerto Rico, which was also still unripe and which had served as a haven for fleeing royalists from the other colonies—were free and sovereign nations.

All the way from California, which had been part of New Spain and was now part of free Mexico, down to Tierra del Fuego, independence was no longer a thing to be dreamt about or a something to fight toward. Independence was no longer a dream or a vision or even a goal. By 1825 independence was a hard-won fact.

There was Mexico, stretching from California down to the Isthmus, and then only down to the Guatemalan borders after the five new states were born more or less peacefully out of the southernmost provinces:

The five points of the star of federation they formed for the moment were called the Central American States—Guatemala, Honduras, Salvador, Costa Rica, and Nicaragua.

Far to the south there was that other free federation of former provinces on the Plate that would soon be known as Argentina—a power gradually to be reckoned with. On her borders there was Chile, and there was Paraguay—where independence had come quietly but ominously through a man named Francia, who was still to be heard from. On her border, too, there was embattled Uruguay.

On the eastern shore of the Plate there was little Uruguay, whose sovereignty had to be won by the tenacious Artigas and his rough-riding Gauchos, and then by the patriot band known as the Immortal Thirty-three. There was Uruguay, long to be known as the State of the Eastern Shore, having to fight not only the Spaniards but also the Portuguese, not only the Brazilians but the Argentines as well, in order to be free.

At the top of the southern continent, there was the new state known as Gran Colombia, out of which Colombia and Venezuela and Ecuador would soon emerge. And, finally, in what had been the strongest and the richest viceroyalty in South America, there was, besides the independent land of Peru, a new mountainous nation named after the Liberator: there was Bolivia.

There were all these nations where before there had only been Spanish America. There were these new nations and the great sovereign state of

Brazil, the immense heart of the whole continent of the south. There were these new states and there was free and independent Haiti.

Out of the sprawling colonies of the west owned by Spain and Portugal and France, all these new American nations had been born. Out of the Old World's dead and withering rule, nations aspiring to be truly free had sprung into the living world. And most important—out of those birth throes of Latin-American independence, leaders in every field appeared from among the most downtrodden groups:

"Who could have imagined," exclaimed one of the British volunteers who crossed the Andes with Bolívar, "that men whose fathers had been treated like wild beasts of the field . . . could all at once display that intensity of feeling and those high and lofty purposes which are only expected from individuals who are nurtured in the bosom of a free and civilized community!"

Who could have expected it? Yet out of the upheaval which had shaken the whole of society to its roots, new leaders were rising everywhere from the new lands. Some of the leaders were taking the road of liberation and enlightenment opened by the independence struggle. But others were moving into the dark ways of new tyranny. Who could have expected this—

Yet in the very midst of the struggle for independence, there were new leaders who showed their fear and hatred and hostility to the concept that liberty for the nation also meant freedom for the people!

Even in the midst of the heroic wars for independence, new despots were already rising over the new-born Latin-American lands.

Fifteen

DESPOTS

How could I fail to see the prowling brute
In their long stride,
And in their eyes the savage beast of prey?

RAFAEL ARÉVALO MARTÍNEZ

GOVERNMENT BY PENSION

Where the fires of independence were first lighted in Latin America, they had burned most fiercely. But where they had burned most fiercely—in the new republic of Haiti—despotism first began to choke them off before they could consume the old decay and thus consummate its revolutionary course.

In Haiti, where Dessalines had risen to lead the people to freedom from foreign tyranny and freedom from slavery, the same Dessalines made himself emperor with the aid of Pétion and the other military leaders of the independence struggle. The meaning of what was happening in Haiti even before the independence wars were launched in the rest of Latin America was clear—but it was clear only to a very few at first, and most of these were anonymous. And most of these were inevitably martyrs who fell before the rise of the new despotism which they defied because they saw its ultimate direction. Yet the meaning was there, to be remembered later and still later.

The men who had led the people lacked the full faith in man and in man's ability to understand his new-won freedom and to extend it to every part of his life, for his country's good as well as his own. Out of the leaders' lack of faith in the people's need to understand in order to grow, the new forms of despotism were born.

Not only in Haiti, but all over the southern Americas, instead of govern-

ment based on republicanism and democracy, there rose government based
on personal power and the will to hold and to stretch that power farther
and farther over the free but still illiterate and groping people and over
the independent but barely waking nations. Against the rising freedom of
people and nations, there rose caudillismo—rule by military chiefs, the first
of whom had all sprung from the very struggle for independence.

Throughout the new-found nations of Latin America, the caudillos, or
military chiefs, fearful of losing the power they had just gained, soon began
to subject not only their own people, but the people of neighboring territories, to their rule by force. From the beginning, these caudillos found
their ready and eager backers among the Creole whites—in Haiti among
the lighter-skinned mulattoes—and among the high clergy and the other
men who formed part of the new groups of property and authority that
had risen to displace the European. And from the beginning, the men and
the forces around them that had become despots over their own people
lost little time in projecting their brutal powers into the bordering territories of other people.

From the beginning, caudillismo over one people and one nation went
hand in hand with dreams and deeds of conquest over other people and
other nations.

Thus Haiti had its General Boyer, who, as early as 1821, invaded the
neighboring territory of Santo Domingo where the people were already
preparing to achieve complete separation from Spain. Santo Domingo was
forced for the time being to accept a flag that was not its own, and an
enmity sprang up between the two nations and the two peoples that would
last for more than a century, long afterward to smolder into massacre.

Haiti had its Boyer, and Mexico had its Iturbide.

General Agustín Iturbide, the Creole officer who had helped to lead the
patriots to victory, but who began to betray the basic principles of that
struggle before the bodies on the battlefield of liberty were cold—this
patriot general became emperor and tyrant. This fighter for sovereignty
turned into the oppressor of both Mexico and the neighboring Central
American countries, which he futilely tried to retain as part of what had
been New Spain.

His more or less self-appointed Majesty, Agustín I, briefly administered
his short-lived government—chiefly by means of the system of bribery that
bore the respectable name of "pension":

The session of the congreso instituyente was opened this afternoon by a speech from the throne, and we set out immediately after dinner to witness the ceremony. The hall fitted up for congress had been formerly a church of the Jesuits. The galleries are spacious, and were well filled; but the hall, with seats to contain two or three hundred persons, looked empty and deserted, with only forty members scattered over it. We were provided with seats in the gallery in front of the throne. About six o'clock His Majesty entered, preceded by a crowd of attendants bearing lights, and accompanied by the counsellors and ministers of state. He was received by a committee, and conducted to the throne, where he remained seated, and read a long speech, in which he gave his reasons for dissolving the late congress, and insisted upon the necessity of retracing the steps taken by that body and of being governed by the plan of Iguala and treaties of Cordova.

J. R. Poinsett's Notes on Mexico—and on Iturbide

He gave a short exposé of the state of the nation, insisting that, as it had supported in 1816 an army of thirty-five thousand men, troops of the line, when there was a large insurgent force feeding on the resources and destroying the revenues of the country, there ought to be no difficulty in maintaining the present civil and military establishment. He dwelt at some length on the situation of the army, and attributed their miserable condition, their want of clothing and of pay, to the neglect of the late congress.

After he had concluded his written speech, he addressed the members for a short time, recapitulating with some force and eloquence what he had before read to them.

The secretary of the hacienda (treasury) then ascended the tribune and read a statement of the finances—but in so low a tone of voice that I found great difficulty in hearing him. I understood him to have said that the receipts into the treasury of the last year amounted to eight millions and the expenses exceeded thirteen.

The deduction of His Majesty—of what the country is capable of supporting, from what it has supported—is not very logical. Their resources have been exhausted by that very effort. From this report of the secretary, and from what I was told this morning, I believe the finances of the country to be in a very wretched condition. No one knows the exact truth, and the refusal of the executive to account for monies expended was one cause of difference between him and congress.

I was presented to His Majesty this morning. On alighting at the gate of the palace—which is an extensive and handsome building—we were received by a numerous guard, and then made our way up a large stone staircase, lined with sentinels, to a spacious apartment where we found a brigadier general stationed to usher us into the presence.

The emperor was in his cabinet and received us with great politeness. Two of his favorites were with him. We were all seated, and he conversed with us for half an hour in an easy unembarrassed manner, taking occasion to compliment the United States, and our institutions, and to lament that they were not suited to the circumstances of his country. He modestly insinuated that he had yielded very reluctantly to the wishes of the people, but had been compelled to suffer them to place the crown upon his head to prevent misrule and anarchy.

He is about five feet ten or eleven inches high, stoutly made and well proportioned. His face is oval, and his features are very good—except his eyes, which were constantly bent on the ground or averted. His hair is brown with red whiskers, and his complexion fair and ruddy, more like that of a German than of a Spaniard.

As you will hear his name pronounced differently, let me tell you that you must accent equally every syllable: I-tur-bi-de.

I will not repeat the tales I hear daily of the character and conduct of this man. Prior to the late successful revolution, he commanded a small force in the service of the Royalists, and is accused of having been the most cruel and bloodthirsty persecutor of the Patriots, and never to have spared a prisoner. His official letters to the Viceroy substantiate this fact.

In the interval between the defeat of the patriot cause and the last revolution, he resided in the capital, and, in a society not remarkable for strict morals, he was distinguished for his immorality. His usurpation of the chief authority has been the most glaring and unjustifiable; and his exercise of power arbitrary and tyrannical.

With a pleasing address and prepossessing exterior, and by lavish profusion, he has attached the officers and soldiers to his person. And so long as he possesses the means of paying and rewarding them, so long he will maintain himself on the throne. When these fail, he will be precipitated from it. It is a maxim of history—which probably will be again illustrated by this example—that a government not founded on public opinion, but established and supported by corruption and violence, cannot exist without ample means to pay the soldiery and to maintain pensioners and partisans.

TYRANT ON HORSEBACK

The early "empires" of Haiti and Mexico soon gave way to the rawer, native patterns of despotism. These were framed in the borders of a republicanism that was still—and would long remain—more false than true. But the frame—in Haiti and Mexico as in all the other countries of Latin America except the empire of Brazil—would continue to be the republic save for sporadic periods of invasion by foreign powers.

In Brazil the frame of government would long continue to be the empire founded by the Portuguese house of Braganza. The pattern of government in Brazil was, nevertheless, that of a constitutional monarchy—especially after the native landholders and slaveowners forced the absolutist Pedro I to abdicate in 1831, scarcely ten years after independence had been won. And the monarchy became even more liberal after Pedro's young son and heir succeeded to the Brazilian throne in 1840 as Dom Pedro II. It was largely the liberalism of Pedro Segundo that insured the life of that monarchy for nearly another half century.

In spite of the more enlightened policy pursued by the Brazilian ruler within his country's borders, even before he assumed the throne, the empire was launched into a program of expansion and aggrandizement by the men around him, ostensibly to safeguard their interests and power against the real, rising threat of the young Argentine nation to the south, which was also beginning to expand. The rivalry and conflict between the two great expanding powers of South America would go on—steadily, quietly, yet with intermittent outbursts of open violence—for decades to come. And the nations between them would suffer most.

Meanwhile, in the Argentine there rose the most sanguinary despot the continent had yet known. He was the pink and shining apple of the wealthy landholders' eye: Juan Manuel de Rosas, the Gaucho caudillo. Rosas the Tyrant they called him, the curse of the pampas. The hated Rosas, who would turn the Plate red with the blood of his own countrymen:

Buenos Aires is the most powerful of the Provinces which constitute the Argentine Republic, as it is called. . . . The greater part of the country—denominated by a local term, gauchos—consists of Indians. . . . From the suburbs of the city to the Andes, over the vast plains called *pampas,* roam the *gauchos* who, strictly speaking, are in the incipient stage of civilization—a pastoral people watching the immense herds of cattle, horses and sheep which feed on these plains. Untaught either in letters, manners, religion or morals, always mounted, they never quit the back of the horse except to throw themselves on a hide to sleep. They hear Mass and hold their convivial meetings on horseback. In some respects they are the most efficient cavalry in the world. Dismount them, they are nothing—for they are scarcely able to walk. Constantly engaged in ham-stringing and slaughtering cattle, they have engrafted the ferocity of the butcher on the simple habits of the shepherd, and are both ignorant and cruel.

A Dispatch from the U. S. Chargé d'Affaires at Buenos Aires

A nation in this situation, with a population nearly divided between two classes with usages, habits and moral discipline so totally unlike, will always be liable to feuds and civil dissensions; and the power of the government will be wielded by such as can unite the greatest and most efficient mass of physical force. And the *gauchos* can give the preponderance to either contending party in the city, for they can always be united under a favorite leader or chief, while the city, containing many who aspire to be leaders, will inevitably be divided into parties and factions. . . .

The present parties are . . . Federalists and Unitarians. . . . The Unitarians predominated many years. It was their object to create a strong central government and a close union or rather a consolidation of the provinces. . . . Rivadavia, the chief of the Unitarian Party, possessed a bold original mind. . . . He formed schemes of improvement on a grand scale and would have effected in a year the work of half a century. He was determined to abolish what he called ancient abuses, and his schemes involved the overthrow of the priesthood. . . .

His open attacks on sacerdotal power gave him for opponents a united and powerful body whose influence with the people he found he had greatly underrated—and he also united against him many old and wealthy men who could not be swerved from habits which almost made a part of their natures. . . .

The present Governor and Captain General of the Province—Rosas—at this period was in the country where he has large possessions. This gentleman was in the prime of life and closely connected with the Anchorenas (the wealthiest men of the province), to whom he had acted in the capacity of a steward or overseer and managed their extensive possessions in the country.

His education had been very slight, but he had certain qualities which gave him a commanding influence with the gauchos. He possessed much personal beauty, having a large commanding figure and a fine face. And he was a rubio—you must understand that this term is applied to those with florid complexions and light eyes, indicating a descent from the pure Gothic race (the ancient Lords of Spain), without any intermixture of Moorish or Jewish blood. . . . In addition, he was inimitable in all athletic exercises: he could manage a horse and throw the lasso with as much dexterity as the most thoroughbred gaucho.

At his estancia in the country he received all the discontented who flocked to him from the city. And he soon gathered under his banners all the gauchos of the plains. . . . Aided by the funds of the Anchorenas and other wealthy Federalists . . . after much fluctuation of fortune, he, with his wild followers, approached the city.

The citizens, alarmed at the prospect of the irruption of such an horde who threatened them with universal pillage and slaughter, were determined that a convention should be made and the city saved. An arrangement was finally effected, and Lavalle (who had been a Unitarian) and his principal friends were finally compelled to go into exile. . . .

Rosas is now the Chief of this "Republic" of Buenos Aires, and by a decree of the Legislature is invested with dictatorial powers. He has no knowledge either of international or even municipal law, and no acquaintance even with the common forms of public business. Reared amongst the cattle and the gauchos, it is his influence over the latter— and the patronage of the Anchorenas—which has elevated him to his high station.

His disposition, in my opinion, is not bad, and his intentions are honest (but in this opinion I differ from many intelligent Americans here)—but the tremendous power with which he is clothed would transform a patriot into a tyrant and an angel into a demon. He can shut up the Courts of Justice; suspend criminal and civil processes; imprison the people by his own authority. And the press is already in fetters—no voice can issue from that mighty engine in free governments but the voice of adulation.

Shortly before my arrival, he caused sixteen persons to be shot in one day without even the form of a trial. . . . Three hundred women were seized lately in the night and sent off to the frontiers without any notice or investigation of their offences. All the severe and oppressive practices of the Romish Church are in a course of restoration—and perhaps the Inquisition itself. . . .

The two brothers Anchorenas have a commanding influence over the Governor. They are facsimiles of the old Spaniards: proud, bigoted, narrow-minded, and oppressive, hating all foreigners—especially Protestants.

THE LIFTING MASK

In the very cradle holding all the aspirations toward freedom that were born with the heroic wars for independence—the deadly serpents of new oppression were already showing their fangs. The old colonial evils—autocracy and bigotry and suppression of the people's yearning for light and liberty—had merely shed their serpent skins for the new ones they had found in the dark neglected corners, the warm and hidden corners, of the cradle of liberty itself. And now the renovated serpents of power were showing their fangs.

In the bright land with the dark and brooding past, in the green land where the shadow of earlier men of ruthlessness had shut off the sun from the people's lives—in Paraguay, of the many flowing streams and rivers, where the Jesuits had once tried to hold back the flow of time around the singing Indian lives they had controlled by day and by night, the shadow of a single man now arose to turn the luminous days into strange night.

Over independent Paraguay, almost at the moment of its birth of freedom, loomed the shadow of the mysterious man who would insulate his country and its people from the rest of the South American continent. Over the hushed land of Paraguay and its frightened and bewildered people, the looming shadow of power was that of the very man whose sudden bold words and defiant gesture had ended the rule of Spain in his land. Over Paraguay now rose the absolute power of the man who would even take the land from the Spanish owners and make it the property of the whole nation—but would still keep the people under his autocratic rule. Over Paraguay and over the Indian lives of its people, loomed the ubiquitous shadow of the brooding, black-clothed man of mystery—the man who called himself Doctor Francia.

On occasion of the installation of the junta which superseded, in Paraguay, the authority of Spain, the question was agitated by a number of the first citizens convened for the purpose in the Government House, as to whether the government of the country should be carried on in the name of Ferdinand VII. Francia, whose mind was made up that it should not, entered the hall of deliberation at *J. P. and W. P. Robertson:* the warmest period of the debate. Walking up *A Portrait of Dr. Francia* to the table and taking his place beside several government functionaries, he calmly laid a pair of loaded pistols before him, and said:

"These are the arguments which I bring against the supremacy of Ferdinand VII."

From so daring and practical an argument there was no appeal. And Francia, thus—as it were, at the cannon's mouth—forced his countrymen into the first direct declaration in South America, of absolute independence of Old Spain.

No sooner, by the tumultuous and unanimous voice of Congress, was Francia seated in the First Consular chair, than his air gradually gathered more of austerity. His measures were more divested of conciliation. His address became more abrupt, his tone more imperative. And it was evident to me, as well as to many others, that he was already beginning to lift the mask which he had too long reluctantly allowed to cover his ambitious projects and designs.

One ominous feature of despotism began now to display itself in Paraguay: every man feared to open his lips to another on politics.

Among the first of Francia's legislative enactments was one of singular degradation to the Old Spaniards. There had been some vague rumors, when the Consul was living in retirement, that he was less inimical to the Spaniards than was generally supposed. These rumors were circulated by his political opponents; and in order not only to silence them on this subject but to teach the Spaniards how little reason they had to congratulate themselves on the report that he was their friend, he decreed that within the territory of Paraguay they should not be allowed to contract marriage, except with Negresses and mulattoes.

If bitterly to mortify the proud natives of Old Spain—men who had hitherto looked down upon the best American blood as only uncontaminated in so far as it was mixed with their own—were Francia's aim, as doubtless it was, the plan he selected was most effectual. The decree —or *bando*—published by sound of drum and fife, came upon them like a thunderclap. Nor was it the least part of their punishment that, keenly as they felt this attempt to degrade them, they were forced to restrain every expression of indignation or even of chagrin.

Nor were the white . . . ladies of Asuncion less mortified than the Spaniards—for not only were many marriages with them on the tapis, but it had ever been considered by the highest-bred damsels of the place a much greater honor to be wedded to a Galician shopkeeper than to a Paraguay gentleman.

Meantime, my intercourse with the Consul not only continued, but increased. I had frequent citations to attend him at the Government House, or, as it was officially styled, "Palace."

Our interviews were always in the evening, and were sometimes protracted till eleven o'clock. Francia's greatest pleasure consisted in talking about the "War Department." . . . On one occasion the gunsmith came in with three or four old muskets repaired. Francia held them up one by one to his shoulder, and pointing them, as in the act of firing, drew the trigger. When the flint struck good fire, the Consul was charmed, and said to me:

"What do you think . . . will my muskets carry a ball to the heart of my enemies?"

A HERO'S FAREWELL

Dictators in the north and dictators in the south. Many if not most of them were the very liberators of yesterday—even O'Higgins in Chile; even San Martín who wanted monarchy in South America, but who had the grace and the unselfish heart to retire rather than precipitate war over his differences with Bolívar. And even the great Bolívar himself showed some fatal flaws where his faith in the people was concerned.

He believed, for instance, that presidency for life was the best way to guarantee sovereignty and stability for the new-born American nations of the south—on the grounds that they had not yet sloughed off the Spanish colonial attitude of accepting authority only when it stemmed from power that was more or less permanent. He argued stubbornly for this idea of permanency, until finally he reaped hostility and hatred from many people who had previously given him their love and loyalty. Only death, generous death in this tragedy of the liberators, prevented the greatest liberator of them all from sailing away to end his days in gnawing exile, as San Martín and others were doing.

But among the men who had led the people of Latin America to independence and sovereignty, there were still a few who held to their uncompromising confidence in the ability of the people to govern themselves by republican and even democratic principles. Among the very few who wanted none of the power for himself, but all of the power for the people, was the young hero of the last decisive independence battle, the fight at Ayacucho; the man who had helped to bring the new and free nations of Ecuador and Peru and Bolivia into being.

Among the very few leaders whose modesty was as true as his courage, and who never lost faith in the people—not even as he said farewell— was Antonio José de Sucre:

I take leave, gentlemen, of you and of Bolivia, and I am certain that it is forever, because I am sure that you will at once convoke the Constitutional Congress. . . . I believe that you will use the time of your sessions well, and that they will be guided by dignity, firmness and patriotism, with . . . wisdom, moderation and philanthropy. . . . Upon leaving, I have to make a frank declaration which shall serve as an example to my successors. Since I have been in charge of the Government of

Antonio José de Sucre: His Farewell Message. 1828

Bolivia, I have subordinated my feelings to my duty towards her. Even in relations with our neighbors, I have never used any other language than that required by my public position, and on this account my personal inclinations have been silenced. Following the principles of an upright man, I have adhered to the belief that in political life there is neither friendship nor hatred, nor any duty to fulfill except making the people happy, preserving their laws, their independence, and their freedom. My hatred and my love during my administration have been only for the enemies of Bolivia or her friends. Even this document, which is my last public report, follows the same line of conduct. . . .

The Constitution makes me inviolable. No responsibility may follow me for acts of government. I beg that this prerogative be taken away from me, and that my conduct be scrupulously examined to determine whether any transgression of the law can be proven against me. . . . If the Constitutional Congress finds cause for a trial of the Cabinet, I shall return from Colombia to submit myself to the decision of the laws. . . . On departing I ask this reward from the representatives of the nation, and if through respect of the law they refuse it to the President of

Bolivia, let them not refuse it to its first citizen, who has so devotedly served her and who asks this as a protection to shield him against those accusations with which slander and envy will seek to stain him.

I shall also ask another reward of the whole country and of her rulers: not to destroy the work I have created, to preserve the independence of Bolivia through all dangers, and to prefer all misfortunes and even the death of their children to the loss of the sovereignty of the Republic which was proclaimed by the people and which was obtained as a reward for their generous sacrifices in the revolution.

For the rest, gentlemen, it is enough remuneration for my services to return to my country after an absence of six years employed in serving Colombia's friends with honor. And although as a result of foreign instigations I carry broken the arm which put an end to the war of American independence at Ayacucho, which broke the chains of Peru and gave life to Bolivia, I feel comforted, knowing that in the midst of difficult circumstances my conscience is free from crimes.

Upon crossing the Desaguadero I found a group of men divided into murderers and victims, slaves and tyrants, eaten up by hatred and thirsty for vengeance. I reconciled all these spirits, I have formed a country which has its own laws, which is reforming its colonial education and customs, which is recognized by its neighbors, which has no foreign debt, which has only a small domestic debt that was acquired for its own benefit, and which will be happy if a wise government rules it.

When I was called by the General Assembly to take charge of Bolivia, I was told that the independence and organization of the State were based on my labors. In order to obtain these benefits in the midst of party agitations which lasted fifteen years, and desolated the country, I at least have not caused suffering to any Bolivian. No widow or orphan mourns because of me. I have spared many condemned men from punishment, and my government has been distinguished by clemency, tolerance and kindness.

It might be said that this mildness is the cause of my own wounds; but I am glad of them if my successors with equal kindness will accustom the Bolivians to follow the law without any need that bayonets constantly threaten life and put snares in the way of freedom. From my seclusion I shall view my scars and shall never be sorry for them, for they will remind me that in order to create Bolivia I preferred the empire of law to the tyranny of the sword.

EVEN IN THE BLEAK RETREAT

Against the rise of empire and dictatorship in Latin America, there rose men who saw and felt things largely the way the heroes like Sucre felt and saw them. And with their understanding went the deep compulsion to show how they felt—through the power of action as well as the wonder of the word.

In Uruguay, where the people's sovereignty and liberty were threatened by the converging force of the two main conflicting powers on the continent—the empire of Brazil and the growing republic of Argentina—men like the "Thirty-three Immortals" took the lead in the new fight for freedom. They fought as the since exiled patriot Artigas had fought before them, until Uruguay's independence was secure.

The extending battle against the spanning aggressiveness of the new native systems of tyranny in Latin America attracted newer patriots at home to its slowly swelling ranks. Soon it also began to attract some of the more ardent lovers of liberty from other lands, as the independence wars had done before. These new volunteers in the cause of liberty came from different parts of Europe to participate in this new struggle for fuller freedom against the new despotisms that were rising in the New World as they were in the Old. And among them came a certain Italian patriot and revolutionary:

He came to join the rebels in one section of Brazil, and then to join the people of Uruguay in their fight against the Brazilian Empire and its oppressive ways. He came from struggling Italy to join his vast energies and his undying belief in liberty to the new fight for freedom in South America. And he came to find that cause his own—to find a woman in that cause becoming his own wife, to find comradeship among his fellow-fighters in the New World as he had found it among his fellow-fighters in the Old. Even in the midst of the privations and sorrow and suffering, even in the midst of retreat, there was the comradeship:

The retreat, undertaken in the winter, over the precipitous mountain-paths, amid almost unceasing rain, was the hardest and most terrible that I ever saw. We drove along with us, for all provision, a few haltered cows, as there were no animals on the steep tracks we had to pass, rendered still more difficult by the rains. The numerous rivers of the Serra,

From the Autobiography of
Giuseppe Garibaldi

running high in flood, rolled over men, arms, and baggage. We marched in the rain without food; in the rain we encamped. In the interval between one torrent and the next, those whose turn it was to remain in the neighborhood of those unlucky cows had meat—the rest went without. The poor infantry especially suffered terribly, being in want even of horseflesh, which the cavalry were in the habit of using when they had no other.

There were scenes to make one shudder. Many women, as is the custom in that country, accompanied the army, and indeed made themselves extremely useful, being employed to look after the spare mounts, which they did on horseback, being thoroughly accustomed to this exercise. With the women there were, naturally, children of all ages. Of the younger ones, not many got out of the forest alive. Some few were picked up and carried by the riders of the horses we contrived to save. But many mothers, as well as children, remained behind, dead or dying with hunger, hardship, and cold.

There are forests in the lower part of the province where the climate is almost tropical; and here we could find wild fruits in abundance which are edible and nourishing, such as the guava, the arassá, and others. But in the forests of the high Serra, into which we had penetrated, there were no such fruits to be found. And scarcely could we get taquara leaves, a poor kind of fodder for animals and insufficient to save the lives of the two mules carrying my poor baggage—for now that I had a wife and child, I had been obliged to provide myself with a tent and some other articles.

Anita, my wife, was in constant terror at the thought of losing our Menotti—and indeed it was a miracle that we saved him. In the steepest parts of the track, and when crossing the torrents, I carried him—then three months old—slung from my neck by a handkerchief, trying to keep him warm against my breast and with my breath.

Of a dozen beasts, my own property, which I had brought with me into the forest—some for riding, and others to carry baggage—I had only two horses and two mules left. The rest had foundered, and been left behind. The guides, to complete our misfortunes, had mistaken the track, and this was one of the causes which made it a matter of difficulty for us to cross that terrible forest. . . .

As we went on and on, never finding the end of the path, I remained

in the forest with the two mules, which were now quite worn out, and
sent Anita on with my assistant and the child—so that, riding our two
remaining horses in turn, she might make an attempt to get out into
the open country, and there find some food for herself and the infant.
These two horses, and her own high-hearted courage, were the means of
saving what was dearest to me on earth. She got to the end of the
piccada, and found some of my soldiers round a fire—a thing we had not
been able to obtain, on account of the rain which had continued to fall
in torrents and the poor condition to which we were reduced.

My comrades, who had succeeded in drying some rags, took the child
—a favorite with them all—wrapped him up, warmed and revived him,
when the poor mother almost despaired of the tender little life. With
the kindest care, the good fellows then tried to find some food to restore
the strength of my dear wife and her first-born.

I labored in vain to save the mules. Remaining with the poor exhausted beasts, I cut as much sedge and young bamboo as I could to
feed them. But it was no use. I was obliged to leave them, and try to
get out of the forest myself—on foot, and nearly famished.

Out of the liberating struggle for independence came the new caudillos
and other despots trying to keep that struggle from reaching its full
fruition of freedom for the society and the individual as well as the
nation.

Against the despotism of the caudillos and the support of that despotism that came from many of the high clergy and from the new Creole
and other landed proprietors, there sprang the defiance of the people.
There rose the people's determination to achieve the goal of genuine
freedom they knew would have to be achieved if the independence they
had won was not to become a meaningless and an empty thing.

Against these new patriots, then, rode new tyrants on horseback, new
inheritors of the will and power to oppress that had been handed down
by Iturbide and Rosas and the others.

In Mexico a man named Santa Ana came galloping from behind a
cloud of patriotism to recover and strengthen the tyrannical powers that
had been lost by the exiled and later executed Iturbide. In Paraguay, the
two Lopez dictators rose—from the Inferno, people said—to lead their
country into decimating wars that would make the land a "land of
women."

In Uruguay there was Fructuoso Rivera. In Bolivia, Melgarejo. There was the tyrant, Flores, in Ecuador, and there was Mosquera in Colombia. Paez made the blood of good men run in Venezuela, as Carrera, "the Butcher," did in Guatemala. These and the many more destroyers and the multiplying successors to their power and urge to annihilate arose in every part of Latin America in the years and decades following independence.

But with the rise of new patriots and the attraction of foreign volunteers to the new horizons of liberty, other pioneers began to arrive, too. These were the explorers who were less interested in the political and social turmoil of the Latin American nations than in their virgin wildernesses. These were the men of science, the men of adventure and study, the men of new initiative—and they came, seeking a new store of knowledge. They came, seeking the knowledge and the virginal resources for the world's new undertaking—power-driven industry. They came as pioneers.

· *Sixteen* ·

PIONEERS

Where does he go? What ecstasy leads him on?

OLEGARIO VICTOR ANDRADE

THE WAYS OF THE "GUANACO"

The horizons in Latin America were opening. While those countries had been fighting to the death to become free and sovereign nations, another vast upheaval—of lasting importance in the affairs of men everywhere—was already underway in other parts of the world whose course of development was henceforth inextricably linked with the growth of the new American nations.

In Europe and in the United States—the young republic that was also the oldest sovereign nation in the New World—the industrial revolution was being forged.

Taking part in the momentous beginnings were men of many nations, but primarily men of the still-expanding empire of trade and commerce that had its center in the little island of England, as well as men of that empire's own independent and equally trade-conscious offspring: the United States of America. Taking part were men from all ranks of society: scholars and scientists, technicians and explorers, financiers and poor workingmen who had flocked to the rising urban centers and who only yesterday were peasants and poor farmers evicted from the soil by the rising land monopolies.

All were entrepreneurs in the great new undertaking that was evolving from the new century's need—from the overpowering need of the fast-growing nineteenth century—to find speedier and more fruitful ways

296

to fill the many fresh-born wants of men and women and children no longer bound by the shackles of feudal power and feudal fears.

The power which the people wanted now was not the power of kings or bishops. The power they wanted was the power derived directly from nature and its laws. The power they wanted, and the power they got, was derived directly from those natural laws and man's growing understanding of them. Combining science and its new discoveries with the earlier and still prevalent use of simple mechanics, applying the principle of the distribution of labor to the bursting need for greater productiveness to meet the many new wants of men, the entrepreneurs at length evolved the means for man's eventual and full liberation:

Machine-power!

The machine was born in a huge cloud of the element whose potent properties had recently been discovered: the machine was born of a cloud of steam. That was the first power picked by men to do much of the work that men had had to do. Steam was the power that was transforming the life of men and nations. England and the United States were already the heart of the age of steam that was ushering in with giant strides the never-ending age of machine-power.

Harnessed to an engine, steam was beginning to turn wheels and cogs of the new iron machines of industry—whose pace and scope already promised productiveness beyond men's wildest dreams. Steam was pushing wheels that spun cotton into thread, steam was pulling the thread to other wheels, steam was turning those other wheels that wove the thread into cloth of all kinds: for all kinds of people—in all kinds of lands. Steam was industrializing man's creativeness while creating new industry.

Out of the use of steam to manufacture textiles, came the need for great quantities of cotton and other raw materials required in the making of cloth, and in the making of the machines to make the cloth, and even in the making of tools to make the machines. Out of the very beginnings of machine-power came the need for still other machines required for the making of still other products and still other machines. Out of the early beginnings of power-driven industry came the need for greater supplies of steel and iron that were being tempered and molded into machines. And out of the new gigantic need for steel and iron grew the need for greater varieties and greater reserves of fuel—the need for coal, the need for waterpower.

Out of all these needs, finally, and out of all the earlier basic needs of men as well, there was born the realization that with this new greater expenditure of natural energy, new means and new sources for obtaining energy had to be found: new supplies of raw materials had to be found. And new ways of conserving energy through the means and the sources already at hand had to be discovered: sturdier and more productive specimens of animal and plant life had to be achieved, if they could not be found, through cross-breeding.

Out of these new, vast and growing needs, and out of the incipient demand for better and cheaper manufactured goods, rose the imperative need for England and the United States to extend their initial search for a fulfillment of all their fast-growing needs to other parts of the world where the power of the machine had not yet been established and where, consequently, no obstacles in the form of competition could be expected:

To the rest of Europe, then; to Africa, and finally to the new sovereign countries of Latin América, came the British and the United States travellers trained in the science and art of observing. They were the explorers, the surveyors, the collectors of rare specimens, the intellectual offspring of earlier scholars who had opened the way for the birth and rise of industry in their countries.

To different parts of Latin America came entire expeditions of such learned men that were outfitted by the governments as well as by private individuals and new groups of industrial entrepreneurs. One of the most famous of these expeditions was the visit to the Plate, to Patagonia and to other parts of South America made by His Britannic Majesty's good ship, the Beagle, in 1832, bringing men of science and enterprise to study the life and the resources of those parts and to report what they were able to observe. With this expedition came a young naturalist whose chief concern was the animal species in general and its transformation in particular.

Charles Darwin observed animal life in South America and on certain islands lying near that continent, finding the substance that would later aid him in formulating his great theory and work on the origin of the species:

Darwin in the southern Americas, aware of the link between science and industry, growing aware of the links between past and present animal life, gradually growing aware of the evolution of man.

Darwin in Latin America as the scholar, the pure scientist—and Darwin in Latin America no less as the friend of the British wool industry, observing the ways of the wool-bearing guanaco:

The guanaco, or wild llama, is the characteristic quadruped of the plains of Patagonia. It is the South American representative of the camel of the East. It is an elegant animal in a state of nature, with a long slender neck and fine legs. It is very common over the whole of the temperate *From Darwin's Journal of* parts of the continent, as far south as the *Researches* islands near Cape Horn. It generally lives in small herds of from half a dozen to thirty in each; but on the banks of the St. Cruz we saw one herd which must have contained at least five hundred.

They are generally wild and extremely wary. . . . The sportsman frequently receives the first notice of their presence by hearing from a long distance their peculiar shrill neighing note of alarm. If he then looks attentively, he will probably see the herd standing in a line on the side of some distant hill. On his approaching nearer, a few more squeals are given, and off they set at an apparently slow, but really quick canter, along some narrow beaten track to a neighboring hill.

If, however, by chance he abruptly meets a single animal, or several together, they will generally stand motionless and intently gaze at him— then perhaps move on a few yards, turn round, and look again.

What is the cause of this difference in their shyness? Do they mistake a man in the distance for their chief enemy, the puma? Or does curiosity overcome their timidity?

That they are curious is certain, for if a person lies on the ground and plays strange antics—such as throwing his feet in the air—they will almost always approach by degrees to reconnoitre him. It was an artifice that was repeatedly practiced by our sportsmen with success, and it had moreover the advantage of allowing several shots to be fired, which were all taken as parts of the performance.

On the mountains of Tierra del Fuego, I have more than once seen a guanaco, on being approached, not only neigh and squeal, but prance and leap about in the most ridiculous manner, apparently in defiance as a challenge. These animals are very easily domesticated, and I have seen some thus kept in northern Patagonia near a house, though not under any restraint. They are in this state very bold, and readily attack a man by striking him from behind with both knees. It is asserted that the motive for these attacks is jealousy on account of their females.

The wild guanacos, however, have no idea of defence—even a single dog will secure one of these large animals, till the huntsman can come up. In many of their habits they are like sheep in a flock. Thus when they see men approaching in several directions on horseback, they soon become bewildered, and know not which way to run. This greatly facilitates the Indian method of hunting, for they are thus easily driven to a central point, and are encompassed.

The guanacos readily take to the water: several times at Port Valdes they were seen swimming from island to island. Byron in his voyage says he saw them drinking salt water. Some of our officers likewise saw a herd apparently drinking the briny fluid from a salina near Cape Blanco. I imagine in several parts of the country, if they do not drink salt water, they drink none at all.

In the middle of the day they frequently roll in the dust, in saucer-shaped hollows. The males fight together: two one day passed quite close to me, squealing and trying to bite each other; and several were shot with their hides deeply scored.

Herds sometimes appear to set out on exploring parties. At Bahia Blanca, where—within thirty miles of the coast—these animals are extremely unfrequent, I one day saw the tracks of thirty or forty, which had come in a direct line to a muddy salt-water creek. They then must have perceived that they were approaching the sea, for they had wheeled with the regularity of cavalry, and had returned back in as straight a line as they had advanced.

The guanacos have one singular habit, which is to me quite inexplicable—namely, that on successive days they drop their dung in the same defined heap. I saw one of these heaps which was eight feet in diameter and was composed of a large quantity. This habit, according to M. A. d'Orbigny, is common to all the species of the genus; it is very useful to the Peruvian Indians, who use the dung for fuel, and are thus saved the trouble of collecting it.

The guanacos appear to have favorite spots for lying down to die. On the banks of the St. Cruz, in certain circumscribed spaces, which were generally bushy and all near the river, the ground was actually white with bones. On one such spot I counted between ten and twenty heads. I particularly examined the bones. . . . The animals in most cases must have crawled, before dying, beneath and amongst the bushes. . . . I do not at all understand the reason of this—but I may observe that the wounded guanacos at the St. Cruz invariably walked towards the river. . . .

One day the yawl was sent . . . with three days' provisions to survey the upper part of the harbor. In the morning we searched for some watering-places mentioned in an old Spanish chart. We found one creek, at the head of which there was a trickling rill (the first we had seen) of brackish water. Here the tide compelled us to wait several hours; and in the interval I walked some miles into the interior. The plain as usual consisted of gravel, mingled with soil resembling chalk in appearance, but very different from it. . . .

There was not a tree and—excepting the guanaco which stood on the hilltop, a watchful sentinel over its herd—scarcely an animal or a bird. All was stillness and desolation.

THROUGH THE GREEN FOREST

Both before and after Darwin, there were other British and United States expeditions to Latin America. One of the later English explorers who came in a private capacity was Thomas Belt. An engineer by profession, he became a self-made naturalist, and his work on Nicaragua— which he was fortunately able to finish before his untimely death in Colorado—was highly praised by Darwin, who called it "the best of all natural-history journals which have ever been published."

Belt's detailed descriptions of the Nicaraguan forest were a valuable contribution to science and future industry. The forest so richly described by him was later to become the setting for new industrial ventures of far-reaching magnitude. But meanwhile, there was the great primeval wilderness:

As soon as we passed Pital we entered the great forest, the black margin of which we had seen for many miles, that extends from this point to the Atlantic. At first the road lay through small trees and brushwood, a second growth that had sprung up where the original forest had been

cut for maize plantations. But after passing a brook bordered by numerous plants of the *pita*, from which a fine fibre is
obtained—and which gives its name to Pital—
we entered the primeval forest. On each side of
the road great trees towered up, carrying their crowns out of sight
amongst a canopy of foliage; lianas wound round every trunk and hung
from every bough, passing from tree to tree, and entangling the giants
in a great network of coiling cables, as the serpents did Laocoön—the
simile being strengthened by the fact that many of the trees are really
strangled in the winding folds. Sometimes a tree appears covered with
beautiful flowers, which do not belong to it, but to one of the lianas that
twines through its branches and sends down great rope-like stems to the
ground.

Thomas Belt: The Naturalist in Nicaragua

Climbing ferns and vanilla cling to the trunks, and a thousand epiphytes perch themselves on the branches. Amongst these are large arums
that send down aërial roots, tough and strong, and universally used instead of cordage by the natives. Amongst the undergrowth several small
species of palms, varying in height from two to fifteen feet, are common;
and now and then magnificent tree ferns, sending off their feathery
crowns twenty feet from the ground, delight the sight with their graceful
elegance.

Great broad-leaved Heliconiae, leathery Melastomaceae, and suc-
culent-stemmed, lop-sided-leaved begonias are abundant, and typical of
tropical American forests. Not less so are the Cecropia trees, with their
white stems and large palmated leaves standing up like great candelabra.
Sometimes the ground is carpeted with large flowers—yellow, pink, or
white—that have fallen from some invisible treetop above, or the air is
filled with a delicious perfume, for the source of which one seeks around
in vain, as the flowers that cause it are far overhead out of sight, lost in
the great overshadowing crown of verdure.

Numerous babbling brooks intersect the forest, with moss-covered
stones and fern-clad nooks. One's thoughts are led away to the green
dells in English denes, but are soon recalled. For the sparkling pools are
the favorite haunts of the fairy hummingbirds—and like an arrow one
will dart up the brook and, poised on wings moving with almost invisible
velocity, clothed in purple, golden, or emerald glory, hang suspended in
the air: gazing with startled look at the intruder, with a sudden jerk,
turning round first one eye, then the other, and suddenly disappear like a
flash of light.

Unlike the plains and savannahs we crossed yesterday, where the ground is parched up in the dry season, the Atlantic forest, bathed in the rains distilled from the northeast trades, is ever verdant. Perennial moisture reigns in the soil, perennial summer in the air, and vegetation luxuriates in ceaseless activity and verdure, all the year round.

Unknown are the autumn tints, the bright browns and yellows of English woods—much less the crimsons, purples, and yellows of Canada, where the dying foliage rivals, nay, excels the expiring dolphin in splendor. Unknown the cold sleep of winter; unknown the lovely awakening of vegetation at the first gentle touch of spring.

A ceaseless round of ever-active life weaves the forest scenery of the tropics into one monotonous whole, of which the component parts exhibit in detail untold variety and beauty.

To the genial influence of ever-present moisture and heat we must ascribe the infinite variety of the trees of these forests. They do not grow in clusters or masses of single species, like our oaks, beeches, and firs, but every tree is different from its neighbor, and they crowd upon each other in unsocial rivalry, each trying to overtop the other. For this reason we see the great straight trunks rising a hundred feet without a branch, and carrying their domes of foliage directly up to where the balmy breezes blow and the sun's rays quicken. Lianas hurry up to the light and sunshine, and innumerable epiphytes perch themselves high up on the branches.

The road through the forest was very bad, the mud deep and tenacious, the hills steep and slippery, and the mules had to struggle and plunge along through from two to three feet of sticky clay. One part . . . was especially steep and difficult to descend, the road being worn into great ruts. We crossed the ranges and brooks nearly at right angles, and were always ascending or descending.

About two we reached a clearing and hacienda, belonging to an enterprising German, named Melzer, near a brook called Las Lajas, who was cultivating plantains and vegetables, and had also commenced brick and tile making, besides planting some thousands of coffee trees. His large clearings were a pleasant change from the forest through which we had been toiling. . . .

SHAKING-BRIDGES

German and other immigrants, most of them European, were gradually finding a small place in the Latin American wilds. The newcomers, many of them skilled in the ways of farming, were already beginning to cultivate those species of plant and animal life that were most in demand in Europe—especially England—and, to an ever increasing extent, in the United States.

More and more the Latin American countries promised to become a vast and strategic source of agricultural products—grain, coffee, wool, hides—and minerals and other raw materials needed by the expanding industries and commerce of the world, and particularly of the two large English-speaking nations where industrialization was setting off with a giant's stride. More and more, British and United States interest in the climate and the topography of the Latin American countries was concerned with the possibility of establishing effective lines of communication and transportation to and from those areas.

For this purpose, studies had to be made of the already existing natural facilities offered by the land. For this purpose, too, and for the achievement of broader scientific and other aims, a considerable number of astronomical, topographical, and similar expeditions were organized by the United States and British governments and private interests throughout the first half of the nineteenth century and even later. One of the most noteworthy was the astronomical expedition to Chile organized by the United States Navy in 1849.

Out of such pioneering expeditions came valuable accounts of the customs as well as the means of travel and communication employed by the inhabitants of those areas. Out of the United States Navy expedition to Chile came the enlightening description of Araucanian and other south Chilean ways written by one of its members, Edmond Reuel Smith.

Among the more illuminating passages in Mr. Smith's report was his sketch of existing means of transportation in south Chile, which were broadly characteristic of those that prevailed in the other Latin American countries:

Permanent bridges, with the exception of a few near Santiago, are unknown in the country. But when the rivers become impassable, from the rains of winter or the melting of the mountain snows, suspension bridges are generally erected. These puentes de cimbra—shaking-bridges, as they are appropriately called—are extremely rude both in material and

A Report on Transportation in
South Chile. 1855

construction. The narrowest part of the stream is selected. Upon the bank a couple of strong poles are planted in the ground. Two heavy cables, made of rawhide firmly twisted, are attached to these poles near the earth and carried across to the opposite shore, where they are securely fastened to other poles. On these cables a floor of cane and brush is laid. From the tops of the poles are stretched other cables that help to strengthen and support the floor by vertical thongs at short intervals.

So soon as this primitive structure is completed and properly braced, the transit commences, and continues until the bridge is broken down or swept away by some freshet.

Occasionally it happens that, by the breaking of the cane flooring, an animal's foot goes through, and in the struggle to extricate himself, the ropes give way, precipitating him into the raging current.

I shall never forget my first crossing of one of these crazy structures. It was a stormy day when two of us reached the Cachapoal. The bridge swayed and creaked violently in the strong wind, and it was not without some forebodings that we asked the toll-gatherer if we could pass. He answered, dubiously:

"Yes, I think you can pass over—but it won't hold out much longer."

This was not very consoling. But the river was impassable by fording, and we had no alternative.

First a horse was started over. Being an old traveler, he got along very well, and the others were induced to follow, one by one. It was not easy to make them face the bridge—but once started, they went safely over, picking their way carefully, as though fully aware of their danger.

When we came to the last mule he was obstinate. After being bullied and beaten into starting, he went half way over. Then, like the ass that he was, he lay composedly down and began treating himself to a succession of fresh rolls, amidst a tremendous crashing of the baggage entrusted to his care.

As he was heavily laden, it was unsafe to approach him. Shouting, howling, and showers of stones were unavailing, for he would not move. The case seemed a hopeless one, and I began to solace myself by humming the old ditty:

> "If I had a donkey wot wouldn't go,
> D'ye think I'd wallop him? O no, no!"

But the two muleteers seemed to be of another mind. For, losing all patience, they sprang upon the bridge and laid hold of Mr. Donkey in the most summary manner. One caught the brute by the ears, which he jerked incessantly, while the other seized the tail, which he began pulling and twisting as though drawing the cork out of a bottle. To this treatment was added an accompaniment on the offender's ribs by two pair of boots, until at last even mulish endurance was forced to yield.

The hooting and laughter of the bystanders, the curses and kicks of the muleteers, the obstinacy of the mule, the tossing of the bridge, and the wild roar of the foaming river, all conspired to produce a scene of confusion seldom equaled.

Next in order came our turn to go over on foot. As you commence walking upon one of these light structures, a vibratory motion is imparted to it—running from end to end like the movements of a snake— and you have, at each step, a lateral rolling, tossing you from side to side and making you pitch like a ship at sea.

Add to this the sight and sound of the river surging and roaring beneath your feet, and the variety of sensations produced makes the passage of a *puente de cimbra* no easy matter. Many persons are affected by the motion with giddiness to such an extent as to disable them from proceeding, and they have to be carried across.

Some of the larger streams are crossed in launches. But few of the rivers have a sufficient depth to allow of their employment.

We were now upon the central road connecting all the interior southern towns with the distant capital—the great thoroughfare over which passes most of the internal trade of the country. . . . A noise is heard . . . and a long file of mules comes jogging by, loaded with lumber.

Half a dozen boards or joists are tied on to each animal—the ends in front projecting far beyond his head—while behind they drag and clatter along the ground. As they pass, give them a wide berth if you do not wish to be unhorsed. These donkeys are great sticklers for the right of way and make no allowance for the convenience of others.

Again your ears are saluted by a screeching, like that of a hundred wheelbarrows, and turning, you see a yoke or two of oxen coming slowly along. It is only when nearly abreast that you catch sight of the cause of so much creaking. A clumsy pair of solid wheels, hewn from transverse sections of a tree, and without tires, are working ungreased upon a rude axle—to which are fastened a couple of saplings projecting some distance behind and joined in front so as to form a tongue. This tongue is strapped to the yoke, which, resting on the back of the oxen's necks, is tied to their horns with leather thongs.

The body of the cart is simply a hide laid upon the saplings, and rests about a foot from the ground. These dumpy little vehicles are common throughout the country ... laden to their utmost capacity, with a driver on top stirring up the team with a long pole.

DON IGNACIO'S SHADOW

Gradually though still very slowly, the creaking carts and the shaking bridges began to give way to newer and more efficient means of transportation and communication. Little by little the creaking doors of provincialism were being pushed open.

All over Latin America, the rusty-hinged doors of provincialism were beginning to swing open, letting the first light of European and United States science and industry in, letting in the first light of new systems of religion and free education, too.

From England came representatives of the new methods of popular education devised by the British Quaker, Lancaster, after whom the schools as well as the teaching methods were named. From the United States came the influence of educators like Horace Greeley and his wife, directed toward such men as the tyranny-hating schoolteacher and author, traveller and diplomat, and future president of his country, Domingo Fausto Sarmiento, who laid the foundations for free education in his native Argentina, in Chile where he had long taught, in all of Latin America, in fact. And the countries of Latin America forgot their provincial differences at least to the point of honoring the man and adopting his own teaching methods—the methods of Sarmiento, who helped to break down the barriers to thought and education in Latin America; Sarmiento the man of democratic ideas and the energy to carry them out; Sarmiento the advancing pioneer—looking back for an instant only to make certain that the path he had taken was the right one:

Sarmiento recalling the shadow of Don Ignacio, the beloved teacher of his own school days:

Don Ignacio—for thus he was always called—read, wrote, and ciphered perfectly. He dictated and sent to the press in Buenos Aires a grammar, an orthography, and a treatise upon arithmetic. Later, he taught algebra and some geography. One year I saw a book upon his table, which showed that he did not yet know Latin and proposed to learn it. He was religious, which appeared less in cere-monies than in precepts, and explanations of the catechism, and especially in the frequent inculcation of the principles of morality.

From Sarmiento's Recollections of an Argentine Province

His special quality as a master was to inspire respect—and I ought to say that all education is vain in the presence of a deficiency of this quality, as is the case in the generality of masters. . . . In the absence of Don Ignacio, his influence, his shadow I may say, presided over the school. A dull murmur of conversation might be heard; but it did not come to be noisy, and never rose to a shout. As soon as he was seen to pass by the window, that suppressed murmur began to subside and be-came silence, and this silence was never disturbed by anyone in his presence—there was no necessity of calling to order (to which our masters recur in vain).

I preserve still the almost religious impression of this respect which he inspired in us all, without exception, a respect which we saw at home was mixed with love, and which accompanied us to adult years, although many of his pupils have occupied stations more exalted as to social posi-tion than his own.

The sphere of his instruction was not very extensive, but as we only learn by having our intelligence developed, his mode of teaching went straight to the object, and whatever he taught we learned well because he cultivated the thinking powers from the beginning. In San Juan there were fine readers taught by a new and easy method long before they could be found in Chile. . . .

At first he tried the system of emulation: his pupils were Carthagin-ians and Romans. But later he modified this system by giving to each pupil one opponent who always ended by being his best friend. At last he adopted Lancaster's method. But the system which he used to per-fection was that of simultaneous recitation.

He tried every system of punishments during the nine years that I was his pupil, according as his views improved, but he never deprived himself of the resource of corporal chastisement in cases where he deemed it necessary.

A thousand qualities distinguished this man from the generality of teachers, and established his superiority. Most of his teaching was oral, especially in grammar and arithmetic, and was reasoned out and duly exemplified.

Don Ignacio has gone to his grave, but his spirit is enshrined in the hearts of a people who preserve the traditions of popular education. His pupils have diffused it, and San Juan and Buenos Aires, by their improvements in education, testify to the service of the Rodriguez family of blessed memory. . . . San Juan was the first Argentine province . . . which after the revolution of independence elevated primary education to the highest grade of perfection possible at that epoch. From San Juan went forth the impulse which in these later days has stimulated two republics. . . .

San Juan owes it to herself to re-establish the fame of her ancient school. . . . It is the duty of my country and my compatriots to aid me in the full development of a system of common school education which shall put the seal upon the work of thirty years of my life.

BIBLES FOR BABAHOYO

More and more men in Latin America were occupied with the meaning and purpose of living as they concerned not only the growth of the individual, but of the society around him—not only of the society of his village or town or even province, but of the society of his country and of his country's neighbors to the west and south, northward where the pulse of the United States was beating firmer, sure of itself and its future at last, and to the east where England was rewaking in a roar of steel furnaces. Throughout Latin America, and in spite of the stifling, strangling efforts of the recurrent caudillos to impose their will on the people, there was a broader concern and a deeper regard for the growth of man and of all human society.

This was the heritage of the wars of independence, and before them, of the French and American revolutions—and before these, of the Enlightenment and the smaller and narrower periods of gradual human enlightenment back through the ages. This was the growing heritage of men's struggle for freedom in Latin America and in the rest of the world. And this was the brightening heritage that was now deriving greater and greater energy, newer and newer impetus, from the expanding power of steam, from the multiplying array of machines powered by steam, and from the collective enterprise of all the men of science and technical skill and finance and industry and labor that was necessary to start machine-power on its miraculous course over the whole world. The collective enterprise that was being shaped into a brand-new system of life: the system of industrial capital, the system of wealth put into dynamic motion for the creation of cumulative profit out of mass production of goods—on a scale never dreamed of before—for the mass of people everywhere.

These were the simple forces of freedom and fresh-released initiative, the simple forces gradually growing complex, that made the nineteenth century, especially in its first half, a time of new pioneers in Latin America. Their mission was to break through the still stagnant and decaying wildernesses of men's enterprise and men's thoughts, as well as the dark and ancient barriers raised by nature. And sometimes their mission was to break through all these wildernesses at once: through bigotry, through inertia, through devastating plague and earthquake.

Such was the self-appointed mission undertaken by the persevering Englishman who brought the first copies of the St. James version of the Bible into Latin America. Such was the mission carried out by James Thomson, the pioneering peddler of new ideas:

A little after four o'clock on the morning of the fourteenth, I got into the canoe which was to conduct me from Guayaquil to Babahoyo. The river Guayaquil is navigable at all seasons as far as the latter place, a distance of about forty miles; and in the rainy season, when the river is high, boats pass some fifteen miles farther up. The navigation is performed in balsas, or rafts, and in large and small canoes. *From James Thomson's Letters: Selling Bibles in South America* The small canoes are made of a single tree hollowed out, and the large ones are built like our boats, and capable of carrying several tons, but made in the shape of the small canoes.

It was in one of the large ones I took my passage to Babahoyo. It is in general by no means a pleasant voyage that is made between these two places. On the one hand, the heat is very great; and on the other, the mosquitoes are numerous and active. The effects arising from the bite of this troublesome insect are still, at the distance of more than a week, very visible on my hands, and also on my legs, where they were defended by the stocking only.

On the first day, owing to the excessive heat, I felt very unwell, but enjoyed good health on the following day. On this occasion I experienced from some of my fellow-passengers those friendly and soothing attentions which adorn the female character, and which, on several occasions, I have seen exhibited in regard to myself and to others during my residence in this country.

We were nearly three days in our passage. The river abounds with alligators. I might almost say, it is *full* of them. Great numbers lie basking on the banks with their horrible mouths wide open, and upon our coming close up to them, they plunge into the river and swim about like so many logs floating around you. At one time I counted, in a very short distance, all at one view, on one side of the river, to the number of forty. And at another time I saw twenty close together.

Very few are found at or below Guayaquil, as the water is salt for some miles above the town. In the rainy season, however, when the great quantity of fresh water keeps the salt water down below the town, the alligator is found farther down. I made several inquiries as to the feeling of this animal towards man in this quarter, but could not get any well-authenticated information of its seizing upon human kind—and the frequency of bathing in the river speaks the same language. It seems, in this river, still to observe that fear and regard to man which all the animal creation once possessed, but which has now in regard to several animals been effaced—and in most cases, I believe, through the cruelty of man towards the animal creation.

All accounts, however, agreed in affirming that the alligators here often seize upon hogs, and other small animals, when found close to the river. . . .

Many topics of conversation occurred during our passage up the river. The sale of our New Testaments was known to everybody, and thus afforded a subject of conversation in which we could all take a part. Of course I had also something to say upon this subject, as it was well known that I was the seller of them. Two copies were on board, one of which had been purchased by the captain of our canoe, and the other by one of the passengers. . . .

During the many things that were said, arising from what was read (the reading being frequently aloud), a conversation took place, the relation of which will probably interest you—and more especially as it affords a specimen of the progress of *thinking* upon religious subjects in this country.

The subject was a delicate one, but so much the better, as a specimen. The worship of saints was the matter treated of, though I do not remember what gave rise to it. I stated my views upon the subject, appealing to the Scriptures and to common sense in support of my opinion. A very keen and interesting conversation immediately took place, in which four, besides myself, took a part—and you will be surprised when I tell you that three of the four took my side of the question. . . .

You will see in the whole of this conversation a freedom of thinking and of speaking which you probably did not expect, and I confess that I was myself greatly surprised at it, notwithstanding the many opportunities I have had of observing the sentiments of the people of this quarter. In the higher and more enlightened classes of society, I have often met with liberal sentiments, but as the two persons who took the chief part in the above conversation were of the lower class, it was both new to me and interesting.

On our arrival at Babahoyo, I found lodgings difficult to be procured, as the houses seemed all occupied. As soon as this was known to one of my fellow-passengers, he took me to his father's house, where I enjoyed comfortable bed and board, kindly bestowed and free of expense, during the two days I remained in that town.

As I intended to make no stay in this place, but push on, I gave no public intimation regarding the sale of New Testaments. Yet, through means of my fellow-passengers, it came to be known that I had these for sale—and in consequence I disposed of fifty-one copies, for which I received fifty dollars, one copy being a present.

Latin America's horizons were unfolding at last—and what was even more important, they were beginning to reach out to join those of the outside world.

The narrow frontiers between the Latin American countries were being breached by pioneers of the two worlds slowly becoming one. The hinterland wildernesses created by fearful, domineering man as well as by ruthless nature were being pushed back—back toward the nearing horizons that were joining the southern Americas to the rest of the world.

Ships propelled by steam (with sails still held in reserve) were reaching the ports of Argentina and Chile, of Peru and Brazil, of Colombia and the countries of Central America, of still-sprawling Mexico, whose northern border reached to San Francisco in upper California. The power of steam and steam-driven industry was laying a long invisible track for future vehicles of communication and transportation between Latin America and the rest of the world—as it was already beginning to lay the few but clearly visible tracks across sections of the Latin American land itself:

Laying the tracks, rolling the potent little engines of enterprise and industry over those tracks, coupling those engines to new carriers of produce and people, moving into and out of the slowly opening wildernesses beyond which the new horizons of other countries in other continents were drawing nearer and nearer.

The horizons were coming closer, bringing the new pioneers from Europe and the United States and other parts of the world. Bringing men like Darwin and Thomas Belt, bringing other men of science who were the successors to Humboldt and La Condamine and the others who had come before.

Bringing scholars like the United States envoy, Squier, who was pushing the doors of provincialism open in Nicaragua and Honduras, as other savants and explorers were doing in the rest of Central America.

Bringing another United States envoy, Poinsett, whom the world of science would honor by giving his name to the great red flower he found in Mexico. Bringing Poinsett, the pioneer, whose tireless energy kept opening one provincial door after another—not only in Mexico but even in Cuba and Puerto Rico, which were still owned by Spain. Bringing Poinsett and the later pioneers of skill and endeavor like him.

And bringing, at long last, the first big waves of immigrants from Europe and other parts of the opening world to people the new cities and the freshly broken soil where the fragrant stems of new-won freedoms were showing through—in a wheeling, widening arc, clear to the new horizons.

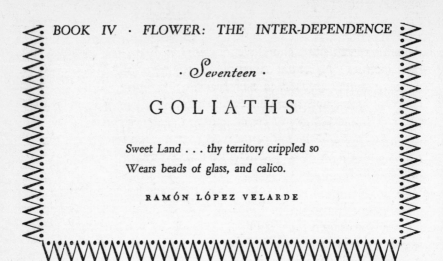

· *Seventeen* ·

GOLIATHS

Sweet Land . . . thy territory crippled so
Wears beads of glass, and calico.

RAMÓN LÓPEZ VELARDE

FROM TORY TO TRAITOR

The first real meeting between the advance guard of industrial power of the two English-speaking nations and the countries of Latin America was about to begin. The two half-worlds that would constitute the modern world—the half-world of industrial and financial power, and the half-world of raw materials and potential markets for goods and capital—were about to come together.

But even before their stretching, vibrant horizons quite began to converge toward each other—like two vast magnetic forces, fresh-born yet already pulled within the mighty orbit of the law of attraction of opposites—the pattern for their nearing encounter was set. And the pattern, too, of the decay as well as the growth that would ensue from that meeting, and would develop through the whole nineteenth century and through at least half of the twentieth century, was outlined in the shadow of new world power advancing to the points and up to the planes where the great meeting would take place.

Even before the countries of Latin America actually launched their wars for independence, in fact, the pattern of the coming meeting and the future relations between them and the new half-world of industrial power being shaped out of the commercial needs of England and of her fast-growing and now independent offspring, the United States, was already there.

The pattern was assembling there in the shadow marching before the substance. The shadow was there to be seen by the few who were able and willing to distinguish its outline moving across the narrowing barrier, moving between the converging separate horizons slowly becoming one. And the approaching shadow was not that of the pioneering savants and the exploring intellects who were few in numbers and whose direct influence was still small—but the shadow of the force that loomed larger and larger behind them: the shadow of new imperial wills to power that were far more potent with energy and skill, and hence potentially greater and more sinister perils to the peace and self-realization of their intended prey, than the Spanish or Portuguese will to empire had ever been.

The shadow that was hurrying to the first great meeting between the two emerging half-worlds was, above all else, England's fears for her empire—shaken and threatened with shipwreck in the wake of the recent American and French revolutions. It was the spectre of a fearful empire bent on controlling—if it could not dominate—the destinies of the remaining weaker territories and the less determined peoples of the earth. It was the force of the British empire-movers—the rising men of industry and finance—moving swiftly to turn the tide of Latin American independence, even before the big fighting had begun, to their own advantage:

It was the force that operated with equal effectiveness through the British volunteers in the Latin American wars of liberation—advocating the establishment of new monarchies, preaching the benefits of trade with England—as through the official emissaries and observers. And it was the same force that kept the opposite side awake and alert as well—encouraging the large landholders and the other men of colonial power throughout Latin America, subverting them against their own people determined to seek and find the freedom they could not live without:

It was the force directed by the British empire-makers coolly but stubbornly striving to turn Latin America's surge for freedom into an almost sterile chaos, into a bloody field of wasted human effort whose only fertility would be for their own imperial purpose.

The ominous pattern of the future was there, as early as 1793, when—to the joy of the native landholding men of power who prepared the way—the British invaded St. Domingue. While the people were readying themselves to declare their Haitian land free and independent from

France, the way for a new though temporary invader was cleared by the tories of St. Domingue—the large landholders and other men of power.

Here was the design for future meetings between the great powers and the emerging nations of Latin America, here in the ubiquitous shadow of British imperialism revived in the gestation-period of the new machine-power and the new form of wealth known as capital. Revived, and already showing its new rending teeth under the admitted guidance and even the goading of the native tory turning to treason: M. de Charmilly, holder of land and slaves, turning traitor in order to preserve his property, in order to retain even a drab remnant of his former power:

After concluding my attendance at the University of Paris, and travelling through a considerable part of Europe, I arrived at St. Domingue in the beginning of the American war. A few months' residence in the colony made me acquainted with its importance. Born with an activity hardly to be surpassed, and favored with a strong constitution, I became desirous to make myself acquainted with the affairs of the island. During a residence at different times of fourteen years, in the full sense of the word I travelled over the whole colony, having been engaged in some important suits, administered to several large estates, and having business of great consequence in every part of the island, which made me acquainted with the principal planters in its various districts.

M. de Charmilly: A Letter to M. Edwards

If you join to that the ambition of becoming one of the richest of its inhabitants, you may judge if I was not, more than any other person, in the possession of opportunities of information respecting the resources of its different provinces, and the advantages of its different manufactures, besides my knowing personally almost all the officers of its administration, both military and civil—with the generous hospitality of the Creoles—and my independence of every tie.

From all these reasons it may be concluded that scarcely any inhabitant of the colony had a greater opportunity of knowing its affairs than myself.

Returning to France at the end of the last war, I was grieved to see the baneful effects of those poisonous principles which the French had imbibed in America. I also saw, with deep concern, the establishment of that philanthropic sect, created first in Philadelphia and afterwards transplanted to Europe. . . .

Since my return to St. Domingue, having re-established several plantations on my own account, I was under the necessity of acquainting myself with everything that related to the commercial resources of the colony. I also had, in conjunction with M. de Marbois, the arrangement of the affairs of one of the most wealthy contractors of St. Domingue. A long residence at Port-au-Prince and the Cape enabled me also to judge of every material occurrence that passed in the two principal cities.

On returning to my plantation at the moment of the revolution, it will not appear surprising that I was nominated a member of the assembly of my parish, afterwards of that of the province where I resided, and finally, deputy of the general colonial assembly.

From the publication of the *Rights of Man*, I foresaw—with the most rational and well-informed inhabitants—the misfortunes that awaited the colony. Residing in the south part of the island, which was in a great measure indebted to the English—and particularly the merchants of Jamaica—for its establishment, and being also, from frequent visits, perfectly acquainted with England, I happily turned my views towards its government, to ensure the safety of St. Domingue.

This sentiment never abandoned me an instant from the first moment of the troubles—I constantly manifested it in my parish, in my province, and in the general assembly at St. Marc, where all my thoughts and actions were continually directed to the means of assuring its success.

The torrent of revolutionary ideas had too much agitated every head not to force the wisest people to conform to circumstances, and I freely own that I was one of those who affected to believe in the possibility of an absurd independence (preferring it, for the interests of the island, to the still more absurd idea of a sugar colony existing with the pretended "rights of man"). Unfortunately, persons of the greatest influence in St. Domingue, dazzled by the remembrance of the great commercial advantages derived during the American war from their increasing trade with neutral nations, hoped and pretended that it might exist.

My opinion was always that such an independence could not take place and that it was necessary for the colony to be under the protection of a mother country, and that it would be well if they were under that of great nation like England.

The diversity of opinions frustrated all my plans and—mine being well known—obliged me to embark, with many of the resident proprietors, on board the *Leopard*. This was with the view of flying from two parties: one of whom saw in us opponents to their ambition, and the other, the enemies of that anarchy which they thought of establishing in this delightful climate.

Arrived in Europe, I soon discovered that France was lost, but still more, surely, was St. Domingue, if a power interested to save her own colonies did not afford her relief. . . . In the year 1790 I had the honor of an interview with the ministers of his Britannic Majesty and proposed to them the means of retaining their colonies by saving St. Domingue. . . .

The revolutionary spirit, which had turned the heads of the French people, furnished the most just and wisest reasons for the British ministry to refuse an offer which had been expressed too late and was become, by the effervescence of the colony and the diminution of its revenues and produce, of too little importance to expose them to the event of a war with the French. I returned to Paris.

But very soon—in 1792—the miseries of France and the king compelled me to seek an asylum in England. From that time I foresaw the certainty of a war. Continually occupied for the welfare of my countrymen and of the first colony in the world, I renewed my solicitations to the British government. In concert with other inhabitants, I never ceased laboring to prove to the ministers of Great Britain that if they saved not St. Domingue, the most considerable colony of the Antilles, they would not save any of their own.

The French declared war against England in February, 1793. Then, the case of those who had exerted themselves to preserve the English and French colonies was heard. Others had evinced as much zeal as myself, and I had no advantage over them but that of a better knowledge of the colony of St. Domingue and being enabled to say, "Behold what must be done: I will accomplish it or perish."

It is for the British ministers to judge if I was so happy as to fulfill my promises—they were pleased to assure me so, and his Majesty himself deigned to testify to me his approbation of the zeal and devotion with which I had placed myself in his service.

HIS BROTHER'S KEEPER

The British empire-makers feared not only the gradual rise of republicanism and democracy in Latin America. They also feared the alliance that had been made between Europe's three most powerful absolute monarchies—the sinister "Holy Alliance" between Prussia, Russia, and Austria—and which was partly aimed at restoring the crumbling power of imperial Spain and Portugal. Any move to restore that power was a threat to England's own imperial needs, emanating from the growth of her industry, for new areas of trade everywhere—including Latin America.

Imperial England's new needs to maintain new power against all rivals and in the face of all obstacles generated greater fears and new anxieties among the British Tories who made and moved the empire. Their fears spread into the world of diplomacy. Their anxieties were leading to new wars.

Rivalry for the world's trade between the two rising industrial powers —England and the still young republic that called itself the United States of America—was growing sharper. Friction between them was almost continuous, until, finally, the first major clash:

The War of 1812.

Out of those two years of fighting on land and sea, little was achieved between the two English-speaking rival powers other than the tacit recognition of each other's imperative needs for broader fields of expansion and for freedom to trade everywhere. The United States' own continental territory now extended to the Pacific, while the borders of Canada as a British possession were clearly defined.

But many questions involving future areas of trade and other influence still remained to be battled over in the continuing war that was all but declared: in the war of diplomacy and intrigue and intervention under many names. The biggest question of the moment still remained to be answered:

Which of the two powers would control, if not dominate—or which would protect and influence, if it could not control—the vast territories in Latin America that were becoming independent though patently weakened nations whose strength and stability would long depend on outside support? Would that support and influence come from Tory England, which was bent on encouraging the establishment of native monarchies throughout Latin America for its own purposes of expediency? Or would the bolstering strength and the guidance come from the young democratic republic of the United States?

For its own national sake as well as the sake of the principles on which it was founded—the young republic feared the rise of the Holy Alliance and *its* avowed aim to restore despotic rule. *But it also feared the reviving power of Tory England, its earlier oppressor and present major rival, which had struck fierce blows at the resources and confidence of the United States in the recent War of 1812.*

The question of United States policy toward the emerging free nations of the Western Hemisphere was the gravest one of the moment. What should that policy be?

In the House of Representatives in Washington, the Speaker himself, a brilliant and warm-hearted man from Kentucky, rose to talk on the subject of the moment:

Henry Clay, letting his powerful voice be heard in the critical year of 1818 when the fate of the Latin American countries as free and sovereign nations still hung in the balance. Clay the statesman, no greater than Clay the ardent lover of human liberties, letting his clear, keen words ring out in behalf of the struggling peoples of the other American latitudes:

Our revolution was mainly directed against the mere theory of tyranny. We had suffered comparatively but little; we had, in some respects, been kindly treated—but our intrepid and intelligent fathers saw, in the usurpation of the power to levy an inconsiderable tax, the long train of oppressive acts that were to follow. They rose; they breasted the storm; they achieved our freedom. Spanish America for centuries has been doomed to the practical effects of an odious tyranny. If we were justified, she is more than justified.

Henry Clay: A Speech Made on March 24, 1818

I am no propagandist. I would not seek to force upon other nations our principles and our liberty, if they do not want them. But, if an abused and oppressed people will want their freedom; if they seek to establish it; if, in truth, they have established it—we have a right, as a sovereign power, to notice the fact, and to act as circumstances and our interest require. I will say, in the language of the venerated father of my country:

"Born in a land of liberty, my anxious recollections, my sympathetic feelings, and my best wishes, are irresistibly excited whensoever—in any country—I see an oppressed nation unfurl the banners of freedom."

Whenever I think of Spanish America, the image irresistibly forces itself upon my mind, of an elder brother—whose education has been neglected, whose person has been abused and maltreated, and who has been disinherited by the unkindness of an unnatural parent. And, when I contemplate the glorious struggle which that country is now making, I think I behold that brother rising, by the power and energy of his fine native genius, to the manly rank which nature, and nature's God, intended for him. . . .

In the establishment of the independence of Spanish America, the United States have the deepest interest. I have no hesitation in asserting my firm belief that there is no question in the foreign policy of this country, which has ever arisen, or which I can conceive as ever occurring, in the decision of which we have had or can have so much at stake. This interest concerns our politics, our commerce, our navigation. There can not be a doubt that Spanish America, once independent—whatever may be the form of the governments established in its several parts—these governments will be animated by an American feeling and guided by an American policy. They will obey the laws of the system of the new world, of which they will compose a part, in contradistinction to that of Europe. . . . The independence of Spanish America, then, is an interest of primary consideration.

Next to that—and highly important in itself—is the consideration of the nature of their governments. That is a question, however, for themselves. They will, no doubt, adopt those kinds of governments which are best suited to their condition, best calculated for their happiness. Anxious as I am that they should be free governments, we have no right to prescribe for them. They are, and ought to be, the sole judges for themselves. I am strongly inclined to believe that they will in most, if not all parts of their country, establish free governments.

We are their great example. Of us they constantly speak as of brothers, having a similar origin. They adopt our principles, copy our institutions, and, in many instances, employ the very language and sentiments of our revolutionary papers.

But it is sometimes said that they are too ignorant and too superstitious to admit of the existence of free government. This charge of ignorance is often urged by persons themselves actually ignorant of the real condition of that people. I deny the alleged fact of ignorance; I deny the inference from that fact, if it were true, that they want capacity for free government. And I refuse assent to the further conclusion—if the fact were true and the inference just—that we are to be indifferent to their fate. . . .

Gentlemen will egregiously err if they form their opinions of the present moral condition of Spanish America from what it was under the debasing system of Spain. The . . . revolution in which it has been engaged has already produced a powerful effect. . . .

It is the doctrine of thrones, that man is too ignorant to govern himself. Their partisans assert his incapacity, in reference to all nations; if they cannot command universal assent to the proposition, it is then demanded as to particular nations—and our pride and our presumption too often make converts of us. I contend that it is to arraign the dispositions of Providence Himself, to suppose that He has created beings incapable of governing themselves, and to be trampled on by kings. Self-government is the natural government of man. . . .

All religions united with government are more or less inimical to liberty. All, separated from government, are compatible with liberty. If the people of Spanish America have not already gone as far in religious toleration as we have, the difference in their condition from ours should not be forgotten. Everything is progressive, and in time I hope to see them imitating, in this respect, our example.

But grant that the people of Spanish America are ignorant and incompetent for free government—to whom is that ignorance to be ascribed? Is it not to the execrable system of Spain, which she seeks again to establish and to perpetuate? So far from chilling our hearts, it ought to increase our solicitude for our unfortunate brethren. It ought to animate us to desire the redemption of the minds and the bodies of unborn millions from the brutifying effects of a system whose tendency is to stifle the faculties of the soul and to degrade man to the level of beasts.

I would invoke the spirits of our departed fathers. Was it for yourselves only that you nobly fought? No, no! It was the chains that were forging for your posterity that made you fly to arms—and scattering the elements of these chains to the winds, you transmitted to us the rich inheritance of liberty.

THE DEVELOPING DESIGN

Mr. Clay's eloquence was applauded in Congress, and his efforts were honored soon afterward with a monument in independent Colombia. But his resolution for full recognition of the independence of the Spanish American countries was voted down.

In view of the pending negotiations in Washington for the purchase of Florida from Spain, Mr. Clay's warm-hearted espousal of republican principles at that critical moment was considered to be untimely and unwise. The question of whose was the timely and the true wisdom—Henry Clay's, or that of the Congress as well as the President, James Monroe, and his Secretary of State, John Quincy Adams—would be debated for years to come. In the meantime, even as Clay spoke, both Florida and Texas were there to be bought from Spain.

There was little interest in Texas as yet, but the negotiations for the purchase of Florida went forward—until, in the following year of 1819, the deal was made and Florida was lost to Spain forever. Florida was lost, and so were all the other American possessions, except Cuba and Puerto Rico, lost to Spain within the next two years. The power of once despotic Spain was vanishing fast—almost as fast as the political power of the republican United States was rising. Almost as fast, in fact, as the economic balance of the United States was changing from agricultural and slave-labor wealth to free enterprise for both labor and the growing giant, capital, that were centered in the expanding, industrializing North of that young and already powerful republic.

By 1822 the United States began to recognize the independence of the new Latin American nations. And one year later came the diplomatic thunderbolt from Washington that struck the deathblow at the shattered power of Iberian empire in the Americas and hurled the mighty challenge at the scheming aspirations of the Holy Alliance—and most important of all, at the soaring New World ambitions of the United States' revived and deadly rival, England:

In 1823, in the President's message of December 2, came the Monroe Doctrine:

". . . the occasion has been judged proper, for asserting as a principle in which the rights and interests of the United States are involved, that the American Continents, by the free and independent condition which they have assumed and maintain, are henceforth not to be considered as subjects for future colonization by any European power. . . ."

And the strict and warning finger was raised for all to see:

". . . with the Governments who have declared their Independence, and maintain it, and whose Independence we have, on great consideration, and on just principles, acknowledged, we could not view any interposition for the purpose of oppressing them, or controlling in any other manner, their destiny, by any European power, in any other light, than as the manifestation of an unfriendly disposition toward the United States. . . ."

The principle of non-interference in the affairs of Europe was coupled with this warning that the affairs of all the Americas were also the affairs of the United States. This was the core of the new doctrine hurled at the Holy Alliance's threat of new despotisms and at the concrete, imperial advances of Tory and Industrial England. This was the hard explosive nucleus of the Monroe Doctrine that was hailed by the new, free peoples and most of their governments throughout the Americas.

But the cold aftermath came soon afterward, when the United States refused to accept offers of alliance from the new Latin American nations. And this was the commencement of Latin American disillusionment over the United States' failure to vivify its basic principles of sovereignty and democracy with specific actions suited to the brave and welcome words. And this was also the commencement of Latin America's turning toward England for the sorely needed security and stability that had found no willing eye or ear in the official acts of their young but mighty brother in the north.

England's race for power in the Americas now began to develop at an unbridled pace—not only in South America, but even in the areas nearer to the United States: in the strategically located islands of the Caribbean, including Cuba and Puerto Rico, both of which still belonged to Spain; in Mexico; in the little republics of Central America where the great patriot, Morazán, was desperately trying to save the Central American Federation he had helped to establish as a strong base for unity and growth as well as a deterrent to ambitious foreign powers. The Federation had been formed in 1823. For nearly twenty years Francisco Morazán labored and fought to save the Federation—against the rising caudillos and their wealthy, conservative supporters. But it was a losing battle, for the selfish and disintegrating aims of the native tories found ready assistance among the British who were always on the lookout for the tories willing to become traitors, eager to become puppets that might be permitted to hold the petty power of paid tyrants over their own people.

The design for British power was spreading fast—to the disgust and dismay of the people of Central America who saw their Federation finally fall in 1842. They saw it fall in the falling body of their hero, Morazán, treacherously shot in the back by the British-backed caudillos and their ignorant mobs, conscripted by force or by the weapons of fear directed at their colonial superstitions, or bribed with strong liquor and a pittance of food.

The full design for English power in the Americas was clear at last. It was clear to a certain keen observer named Ephraim George Squier, the pioneering traveller and diplomat who was the United States Chargé d'Affaires in Guatemala and who lost no time in voicing his feelings as well as his facts concerning the developing power of England in Nicaragua and throughout Central America:

The official agents of Great Britain, in Central America, and particularly at this point, are exceedingly jealous of our operations, and neglect no means to thwart what they conceive to be our objects. . . . To their intrigue, strange as the assertion may seem, we may ascribe the dissolution of the Republic of Central America, and many of the subsequent distractions of the individual States. The confederacy opposed a barrier to their encroachments on the Atlantic coast, and the confederation fell with its last pillar, Morazán, treacherously shot in Costa Rica under British influence—now a virtual province of England.

A Dispatch from Mr. E. G. Squier, U. S. Representative in Guatemala

The seizure of the island of Roatan, and an arrogant claim to half the State of Honduras, followed quick upon these events. The State of San Salvador, more discerning than the other States, endeavored to check further encroachments, and protested firmly against these high-handed measures. It was not long, however, before she was punished by an invasion from Guatemala, incited by British agents, and sustained by British gold, furnished under the disguise of a "loan," secured by a hypothecation of the revenues of the State!

San Salvador successfully resisted her assailants, and turned the tables against them. In less than six months, however, an English fleet blockaded her ports, and all possible means have since been resorted to, to subdue her independent spirit. But however much she has suffered, she has continued to sustain her position, repelling insolence by insolence and yielding nothing to English arrogance. And at this moment, the British Consul General, having succeeded in procuring the return of Carrera (a tool of his own making) to Guatemala, against the wishes of nine tenths of the inhabitants of the State, is inciting that chief against San Salvador, offering a loan of $1,000,000 secured (always!) by the hypothecation of the revenues, and a mortgage on the public domains. So let the collusion result as it may, British interests will be subserved.

My arrival here has been the signal for renewed insolence towards this State, the Government of which is in the weekly receipt of communications, from the above-named official—making all kinds of demands, and loaded with threats in case they are not complied with. The tone of the communications is disgraceful in the extreme, and discreditable to the country of which Mr. Chatfield is the representative. He has demanded amongst other things the immediate payment of certain debts of the State, due to British subjects, the liquidation of which has already been provided for, with Mr. Chatfield's approval, by the appropriation of all the revenues of the State.

To give efficacy to this demand, a steamer of war and a frigate have been ordered before Realejo, the principal port of this State on the Pacific, and their arrival is expected in the course of a few weeks. My information upon the point is positive. . . .

Costa Rica, although there has, as yet, been no public declaration to that effect, and notwithstanding the declaration of her representative in England, has offered to place herself under British protection. And I have no doubt the offer has been accepted. . . . If further evidence was needed upon this point, it is afforded in the recent proposition to this Government, made by the British Vice Consul, Mr. Manning, offering $100,000 for the relinquishment of the claims of Nicaragua over the territories, on the Pacific and the St. Johns, to which Costa Rica has recently set up pretensions. This offer was ostensibly made on the part of Costa Rica, but that State has no $100,000 to give even to preserve her own nationality. . . .

The Department will pardon me for dwelling so much upon the designs of the English and their movements. It is impossible for anyone not on the spot to discover or appreciate their extent and intricacy.

VENDETTA

If the designs of the English in Central America and the rest of the southern Americas were extensive and intricate, those of the ripening power of the United States were no less so. While the jockeying for power in Central America between the two determined rivals was becoming more intense and more feverish over the focal question of who would control the inter-oceanic canal across Nicaragua that was being contemplated, the United States had already taken the lead in Mexico.

Here the pivotal issue was the long-standing question of Texas. The possession of that great border area by the United States was no longer advocated by the far-seeing men like Henry Clay, who had even come to oppose the idea. But the leaders of the slaveholding states of the South were anxious to strengthen their hand in Congress through the addition of another slave state.

For years, with the slaveholding interests in control of the government at Washington, a policy of peaceful but determined encouragement of the settling of Texas by Americans had been carried out—until the Mexicans commenced to realize that they were losing their northern territory by their failure to temper a generous policy with proper control. Instead of control, however, a blundering, cruel policy of repression was initiated by their own hated tories in power. Texas, like the rest of Mexican territory, began to feel the lash of oppression wielded by such tyrants as General Antonio López de Santa Ana. And Texas fought back.

The people of Texas fought to keep the land they had settled and the rights they had won by their labor. They fought the tyranny of Santa Ana as their forefathers had fought the tyranny of George III. Their leaders—Travis and Bowie and Crockett and the others—went down in bloody massacre at a little San Antonio fort named The Alamo. But other men rose up to lead the Texans to final victory at San Jacinto, where they won their independence in the year 1836.

It was one thing for Texas to be free from the despotism of Santa Ana and his clique of tories who were turning Mexico into another monarchy, modelled after Iturbide's brief but flamboyant rule, in everything but name. It was quite another thing, however, for Texas to be made the stepping-stone to United States power sought by the slaveholders and other ardent advocates of the idea that the "manifest destiny" of the United States was expansion and more expansion of its southern borders at any cost. Texas was free, but the conflict over the political issue of its future status was barely beginning. The ramifications of that issue were reaching far and wide beyond the United States' borders, charging the air with distrust and growing friction—until the blast came. The annexation of Texas as part of the United States was all that was needed to provoke Mexico into war against her fast-expanding neighbor to the north. In 1846, the year following Texas' admission into the Union, the first hostilities between the United States and a fellow American nation broke out—and the shots echoed like thunder across the whole aroused hemisphere.

While Ephraim George Squier and other official United States envoys were complaining bitterly over the designs and the intrigues of the English in Central America and the rest of the Latin American countries, the United States had already fired its own cannon of ruthless expansion across its borders—and the meaningful roar went echoing down the hemisphere.

"Manifest destiny" was well underway, and its course would be farther-reaching and more tumultuous than any previously planned course of conquest. Its course would be marked with the heavy smoke of growing, relentless machine-power, as well as the smoke and blood of war. And its course and duration would be so long that even a century later the end would still not be in sight.

Meanwhile, the regular Mexican army fell back before the strong invaders from the north, and some young officer cadets hurled themselves off the ancient heights of Chapultepec in the Mexican capital in a heroic but hopeless gesture of defiance, as the people of Hispaniola had done before the Spanish invaders three centuries earlier. But the Mexican people did not commit suicide or surrender before the advancing Americans from the north. They fought the well-equipped and well-fed invaders as men forced to take to guerrilla warfare must fight. For two years they fought them, without warning and sometimes without mercy:

One night I was sent in command of a scouting party to reconnoitre a guerrilla camp supposed to be some five miles away in the country. It was during the mid-hours of the night, but under one of those brilliant moonlights for which the cloudless sky of southern Mexico is celebrated. Near the edge of an opening—the prairie of Santa Fe—our party was brought suddenly to a halt at the sight of an object that filled every one of us with horror. It was the dead body of a soldier, a member of the corps to which the scouting party belonged. The body lay at full length upon its back; the hair was clotted with blood and standing out

Mayne Reid: A Memoir of His Life

in every direction; the teeth were clenched in agony; the eyes glassy and open, as if glaring upon the moon that shone in mid-heaven above. One arm had been cut off at the elbow, while a large incision in the left breast showed where the heart had been torn out, to satisfy the vengeance of an inhuman enemy. There were shot wounds and sword cuts all over the body, and other mutilations made by the *zopilotes* and wolves.

Notwithstanding all, it was recognized as that of a brave young soldier who was much esteemed by his comrades, and who for two days had been missing from the camp. He had imprudently strayed beyond the line of pickets and fallen into the hands of the enemy's *guerrilleros*.

The men would not pass on without giving to his mutilated remains the last rites of burial. There was neither spade nor shovel to be had; but, fixing bayonets, they dug up the turf, and depositing the body, gave it such sepulture as possible. One who had been his bosom friend, cutting a slip from a bay laurel close by, planted it in the grave. The ceremony was performed in deep silence, for they knew that they were on dangerous ground, and that a single shout or shot at that moment might have been the signal for their destruction.

I afterwards learnt that this fiendish act was partly due to a spirit of retaliation.

One of the American soldiers, a very brutal fellow, had shot a Mexican, a young *jarocho* peasant, who was seen near the roadside chopping some wood with his machete. It was an act of sheer wantonness, or for sport, just as a thoughtless boy might fire at a bird to see whether he could kill it. Fortunately the Mexican was not killed, but his elbow was shattered by the shot so badly that the whole arm required amputation.

It was the wantonness of the act that provoked retaliation; and after this the *lex talionis* became common around Vera Cruz, and was practised in all its deadly severity long after the place was taken. Several other American soldiers, straying thoughtlessly beyond the lines, suffered in the same way, their bodies being found mutilated in a precisely similar manner.

Strange to say, the man who was the cause of this vengeance became himself one of its victims. Not then, at Vera Cruz, but long afterwards, in the Valley of Mexico; and this was the strangest part of it. Shortly after the American army entered the capital, his body was found in the canal of Las Vigas, alongside the *chinampas*, or floating gardens, gashed all over with wounds, made by the knives of assassins, and mutilated just as the others had been.

It might have been a mere coincidence, but it was supposed at the time that the one-armed *jarocho* must have followed him up, with that implacable spirit of vengeance characteristic of his race, until at length, finding him alone, he had completed his vendetta.

ON A BURNING SURFACE

As the United States' war with Mexico dragged on, it became more and more evident that the main purpose of the war was the acquisition of more Mexican territory—the acquisition that would be realized, in fact, of all of New Mexico and Upper California, and eventually, the southern border strip of Arizona. The acquisition of all that, and the establishment of the Texas border with Mexico on the river known as the Rio Grande. These were the aims, these the coming acquisitions that would be paid for with "conscience money."

But as the months of war dragged on, and the scores of American lives lost were turning to hundreds, and the hundreds were threatening to turn to thousands, people in the United States began to clamor for an end to the war. The rising clamor came from the opponents of "manifest destiny," from the strengthening voice of prominent men of the North who opposed the existence of slavery in their own country as they opposed its expansion into any and all bordering lands.

The clamor came from the increasingly strong North, which believed that the future belonged to free labor and the free growth of industrialization of which it was a part, and which demanded peace and the full rights of people everywhere for their sake and for the sake of its own development. The clamor came from the North and from its growing number of representatives in the United States Congress:

From a certain lanky Representative from Illinois:

From the Honorable Abraham Lincoln, raising his hand to speak on President Polk's policy toward Mexico.

Mr. Lincoln, the friend of man as he was the enemy of man's tyranny over others, driving his probing words deep into his country's conscience:

. . . Let the President answer the interrogatories I proposed . . . or some other similar ones. Let him answer fully, fairly, and candidly. Let him answer with facts and not with arguments. Let him remember he sits where Washington sat, and so remembering, let him answer as Washington would answer. As a nation should not, and the Almighty will not,

Abraham Lincoln, in a Speech Made before Congress. 1848 be evaded, so let him attempt no evasion—no equivocation. And if, so answering, he can show that the soil was ours where the first blood of war was shed—that it was not within an inhabited country, or, if within such, that the inhabitants had submitted themselves to the civil authority of Texas or of the United States . . . then I am with him for his justification. . . .

But if he can not or will not do this—if on any pretense or no pretense he shall refuse or omit it—then I shall be fully convinced of what I more than suspect already—that he is deeply conscious of being in the wrong; that he feels the blood of this war, like the blood of Abel, is crying to Heaven against him; that originally having some strong motive —what, I will not stop now to give my opinion concerning—to involve the two countries in a war, and trusting to escape scrutiny by fixing the public gaze upon the exceeding brightness of military glory—that attractive rainbow that rises in showers of blood—that serpent's eye that charms to destroy—he plunged into it, and has swept on and on till, disappointed in his calculation of the ease with which Mexico might be subdued, he now finds himself he knows not where.

How like the half-insane mumbling of a fever dream is the whole war part of his late message! At one time telling us that Mexico has nothing whatever that we can get but territory; at another showing us how we can support the war by levying contributions on Mexico. At one time urging the national honor, the security of the future, the prevention of foreign interference, and even the good of Mexico herself as among the objects of the war; at another telling us that "to reject indemnity, by refusing to accept a cession of territory, would be to abandon all our just demands, and to wage the war, bearing all its expenses, without a purpose or definite object." So then this national honor, security of the future, and everything but territorial indemnity may be considered the no-purposes and indefinite objects of the war!

But, having it now settled that territorial indemnity is the only object, we are urged to seize, by legislation here, all that he was content to take a few months ago, and the whole province of Lower California to boot, and to still carry on the war—to take all we are fighting for, and still fight on. Again, the President is resolved under all circumstances to have full territorial indemnity for the expenses of the war; but he forgets to tell us how we are to get the excess after those expenses shall have surpassed the value of the whole of the Mexican territory.

So again, he insists that the separate national existence of Mexico shall be maintained—but he does not tell us how this can be done, after we shall have taken all her territory. . . .

The President is in no wise satisfied with his own positions. First he takes up one, and in attempting to argue us into it he argues himself out of it, then seizes another and goes through the same process, and then, confused at being able to think of nothing new, he snatches up the old one again, which he has some time before cast off. His mind, taxed beyond its power, is running hither and thither, like some tortured creature on a burning surface, finding no position on which it can settle down and be at ease. . . .

He knows not where he is. He is a bewildered, confounded, and miserably perplexed man. God grant he may be able to show there is not something about his conscience more painful than all his mental perplexity.

SILENT AS THE GRAVE

Mr. Lincoln's words were brave and intelligent words—but like the words of Henry Clay before him, they went unheeded if not unheard in the martial din of the United States' military successes against her weaker neighbor. In the noisy acclaim of the ensuing transfer to the victor of huge chunks of Mexican territory, Abraham Lincoln's bold words were all but forgotten.

The policies proposed by Clay and by Lincoln had been passed over by the short-sighted men of government whose gaze was fixed on the goal of expansion. But Latin America did not pass over the fact that the proposed policies of peace and true friendship and real brotherliness had been rejected by the various governments of the United States, which still bowed to the will and the desires of the slaveholding men of the South.

This fact had not been passed over by the Latin American people at large—who now began to distrust their strong neighbor to the north. This fact had not been passed over, either, by the powerful caudillos and their tory supporters—who now began to plot open alliances with European monarchies as a means of halting or at least slowing up the opening drive from the north.

In all the countries of Latin America, opposition to the United States gained new momentum as the power of that slaveholding and expanding republic grew and its yearning for new aggressions and new territories rang louder over the hemisphere. The filibustering expedition into Nicaragua led by the Southern adventurer, William Walker—who declared himself president of that republic but was taken at last and shot—gave further impetus to the growing fears in Latin America over the ultimate aims of United States policy.

Latin American fears of United States expansionism were leading to sharper antagonism and deeper opposition against the republic of the north, and these were leading to tory intrigues and plots involving the aid of European powers. As soon as the northernmost republic of the hemisphere found itself caught in the most severe trial and the greatest test since its birth, as soon as the United States found itself faced with an all-absorbing civil war of its own—the tories in Latin America appealed to the ambitious powers of the Old World, seeking their support for the many projects aimed at setting up new monarchies on New World soil.

In Santo Domingo, at the request of the caudillo, General Pedro Santana, the sovereignty of his struggling country was sacrificed to the reviving power of the old Spanish dragon. In Peru, the dragon also returned through the connivance of Spanish officials and native tories: the Spanish colors were raised over Peru's Chincha Islands, and the threat of invasion hung over the whole country with the appearance of a Spanish squadron.

Finally, across the United States' own southern continental border, a group of Mexican tories succeeded in obtaining financial, political, and open military backing from the covetous Napoleon III of France. They declared Mexico an empire, with an Austrian prince as its hereditary head. He arrived in Mexico in the sombre year of 1864, with the Civil War full-blown in the United States and the French invasion victorious in Mexico:

Maximilian I and his empress, Carlota, arriving in the Mexican port of Veracruz, in the frigate sent by their imperial French patron, with their whole royal retinue:

On the 28th day of May, at two o'clock in the afternoon, we sailed by
the fort San Juan de Ulloa, which is built upon a small rocky island, and
cast anchor in sight of the town of Vera Cruz. It would appear scarcely
possible to land in the New World at a spot whose appearance is so little
adapted to content the impatient expectation with which one draws near
to a strange quarter of the globe, as is the case
Countess Kollonitz, Attendant to at Vera Cruz. The coast is flat and sandy, with-
Carlota, Arrives in Mexico out vegetation. The roofless white houses of the
town, which are built in straight rows, and form broad, uniform streets,
give to the whole the appearance of a large cemetery—and, alas! not
unjustly.

La Villa Rica de la Vera Cruz, founded by Cortez, is one of the most
unhealthy spots in the world. During eight months every year the yellow
fever rages and diminishes the number of Europeans who have been attracted to it by the interests of trade, and also of those Mexicans who,
having been born in the higher part of the country, are obliged to pass
some time in the dreaded port (the dangerous miasmas of the town are
quite harmless to the real inhabitants). The causes of the peculiarly raging character of the disease are to be attributed in part to the high sand-
downs which hinder the free current of air, and in part to the morasses
which surround the town, and which exhale noisome vapours from the
decaying animal and vegetable stuff, or to the bad drinking-water and
the excessive heat that prevails in Vera Cruz.

The wreck of a stranded French vessel upon a coral reef close by
helped to engrave the melancholy appearance of the place still more
deeply upon our memory.

Westwards, upon the island, Sacrificio, the French fleet had chosen
its anchorage. In front, scattered along the coast of the mainland, are
the graves of many thousands of French soldiers, who had landed here
at the commencement of the expedition, under the command of the
able Admiral Jurien de la Gravière, and who had fallen victims to the
epidemic. Their countrymen have named this place with sad humor,
"Le Jardin d'Acclimatation."

The *Thémis* had gone on in advance, and had announced our arrival.
Yet all was silent as the grave. There was no motion in the harbor and
none upon the coast. The new ruler of Mexico stood in sight of his
kingdom, and was on the point of landing. But his subjects remained in
concealment—no one came to receive him.

An uncomfortable feeling stole over us all, but the Emperor maintained a sarcastic tranquillity. It seemed as if he endeavored to turn his tolerably cutting satire against himself.

The atmosphere was, from every point of view, oppressive. The situation cleared up at length. General Almonte, who had held the reins of government until the arrival of the Emperor, and during the negotiations as to the acceptance of the throne, was awaiting at Orizaba news of the landing—since the dread of yellow fever kept him and his suite as long as possible away from Vera Cruz. From Orizaba to the port is, however, a good day's journey, and therefore he had not yet arrived.

Vera Cruz itself was by no means favorable to the new position of affairs. Of its eight thousand inhabitants most are foreigners, who, connected with the large business houses of the capital, had profited by the disorders to enrich themselves by smuggling and evasion of laws. Every firm and resolute government was odious to them. . . .

After a considerable period, the commander of the French fleet, Rear-Admiral Bosse, appeared on the scene with his aide—both of them apparently in very bad humor because the Emperor had not anchored in the midst of the French fleet, according to their desire. The Rear-Admiral stepped on board with an unparalleled want of consideration and propriety, and gave vent to his anger, whilst he set before us, in sharp colors, all the dangers and disagreeables to which we were exposed by remaining where we were. Above all he maintained that we had anchored in the most contagious spot, that to remain through the night here would be very dangerous—he quoted the cases in which sailors and passengers had in a single night fallen victims to the vomiting-sickness.

And then he spoke of the dangers to which our journey to Mexico City would be exposed, that bands had been formed to take captive the Imperial pair, and that General Bazaine had not time enough at his disposal to look after our safety, etc. He continued to speak for some time in this tone. This was the first—but, alas, not the last—example that we had of French arrogance in Mexico.

At length, towards evening, came Almonte, General Sala, and all the notables of Vera Cruz. . . . With the approach of night, salutes were fired from Fort San Juan de Ulua. The town of Vera Cruz was illuminated with Bengal lights, and the French fleet hung lanterns to every mast, and fired off rockets.

We none of us could sleep—the expectation and excitement were too great. At half-past four Mass was read on the middle deck, and at five we rowed off to the Mole, where we disembarked. The nearer we approached the town, the more distinct became the mephitic odor, the distinguishing feature of Vera Cruz. The yellow fever had broken out but a short time before in consequence of the festival of Corpus Christi, which had been celebrated under a burning sun. For this reason we found no sojourn in the town had been proposed.

As soon as we trod upon Mexican soil the services of the Austrian Court, which had up to this point provided the honors due to the Archducal pair, were at an end. It was here that Mexican ladies were to undertake our duties—but we looked for them in vain. The dread of yellow fever had deterred them even from the reception of their new rulers.

The sinister attempts of European monarchs and statesmen to gain a new foothold in the Americas began to fail even before the final outcome of the fratricidal test on which their future depended: even before the Civil War in the United States came to an end, those attempts began to fail.

One after another they met with doom—because not only the hostile climate but the hostile people of Latin America fought those attempts: with astuteness and stoicism and courage derived from their own determination and from leaders like Benito Juárez in Mexico and General Francisco del Rosario Sánchez in Santo Domingo. One after another the attempts again to establish Old World despotisms in the New World failed, also because of a man named Abraham Lincoln, whose earlier words against tyranny and against aggression for power and territorial aggrandizement had been ignored in Washington. His warnings that nations, like men, must live fully integrated lives of freedom or fall into decay by slavery and disunion, had gone unheeded among the men of influence in his own country.

But during the four years of the shattering War Between the States, Mr. Lincoln used the high and honorable office of President of the United States of America to make it clear to the whole world that his embattled people were not fighting for freedom and progress within their own borders in order to encourage or even tolerate the spread of despotism in the other American countries.

And so Santo Domingo got back its sovereignty, the Spanish flag was lowered in Peru's rich Chincha Islands, and in Mexico the French army was withdrawn—leaving Maximilian to die before a patriot firing-squad, a dupe to Napoleon III's ambition for a stepping-stone to imperial power in the Americas.

The dangerous dreams of European empire-seekers for new realms in the New World were over for the moment. The equally dangerous rivalry between England and the United States, however, was approaching new points of issue in Latin America as in the rest of the world:

The end of the Civil War meant the defeat of the slaveholders and the abolition of slavery in the United States. In the countries of Latin America—except in Brazil, where slavery was gradually dying out, and in Cuba, which still belonged to Spain—slavery had been abolished during the wars for independence nearly half a century before. But in the United States, the belated end of slavery also meant victory for the North's expanding industrialism. The end of the Civil War also meant victory for the North's system of free labor, and the real, secure beginning of an industrial empire for the reunited States.

During the Civil War, England had sought to deal a death-blow to the already weakened United States by openly encouraging and secretly aiding the agricultural South. But England's efforts, like those of the avid European powers that struck at Latin America, had failed—largely because of the far-seeing leadership demonstrated by the President of the American people, Mr. Lincoln.

The Union was saved and—what was most challenging of all to England and the rest of the world as well—United States industry was developing as never before. Industry was reaching out now from Pennsylvania and Massachusetts, from Illinois and West Virginia, reaching out in all directions.

In Latin America, the rivalry between the two English-speaking powers was advancing to new heights of tension. The looming conflict between the two Goliaths was shifting with lightning speed into preliminary, new planes of keener competition, of a more intense struggle over markets, of a furious undeclared war for raw materials—for the new precious sources of energy ushering in a faster and far more powerful age: the age of electricity, the age of gasoline, the age of the formidable Pound Sterling and the almighty Dollar.

· *Eighteen* ·

SMOKESTACKS

*Up that Tower the workman will climb
to heroic redemption.*

JOSÉ SANTOS CHOCANO

STEAMBOAT ON THE AMAZON

By the time the Civil War was over, both the United States and England had launched their large-scale economic penetration into Latin America. As early as 1865, communications were being opened into some of the most remote parts of the southern Americas. People were riding into the Amazon in comfortable steamers, where they sat reading in lounging-chairs or eating luxurious meals served by ships' stewards—while the great savage wilderness moved slowly by:

September 12th, 1865: On Sunday we left Manaos in the steamer for Tabatinga, and are again on our way up the river. . . . Although no longer on board an independent steamer, we are still the guests of the company, having government passages. Nothing can be more comfortable than the travelling on these Amazonian boats. They are clean and well-kept, with good-sized staterooms, which *Professor and Mrs. Agassiz'* most persons use, however, only as dressing-*Journey in Brazil* rooms—since it is always more agreeable to sleep on the open deck in one's hammock.

The table is very well kept, the fare good, though not varied. Bread is the greatest deficiency, but hard biscuit makes a tolerable substitute.

Our life is after this fashion. We turn out of our hammocks at dawn, go downstairs to make our toilets, and have a cup of hot coffee below.

338

By this time the decks are generally washed and dried, the hammocks removed, and we can go above again. Between then and the breakfast hour, at half-past ten o'clock, I generally study Portuguese, though my lessons are somewhat interrupted by watching the shore and the trees— a constant temptation when we are coasting along near the banks.

At half-past ten or eleven o'clock breakfast is served, and after that the glare of the sun becomes trying, and I usually descend to the cabin, where we make up our journals and write during the middle of the day. At three o'clock I consider that the working hours are over, and then I take a book and sit in my lounging-chair on deck, and watch the scenery and the birds and the turtles—and the alligators, if there are any—and am lazy in a general way.

At five o'clock dinner is served—the meals being always on deck—and after that begins the delight of the day. At that hour it grows deliciously cool, the sunsets are always beautiful, and we go to the forward deck and sit there till nine o'clock in the evening. Then comes tea, and then to our hammocks. . . .

September 13th: This morning the steamer dropped anchor at the little town of Coari on the Coari River—one of the rivers of black water. We were detained at this place for some hours, taking in wood: so slow a process here that an American, accustomed to the rapid methods of work at home, looks on in incredulous astonishment.

A crazy old canoe, with its load of wood, creeps out from the shore, the slowness of its advance accounted for by the fact that of its two rowers one has a broken paddle, the other a long stick, to serve as apologies for oars. When the boat reaches the side of the steamer, a line of men is formed, some eight or ten in number, and the wood is passed from hand to hand, log by log, each log counted as it arrives. Mr. Agassiz timed them this morning, and found that they averaged about seven logs a minute. Under these circumstances, one can understand that stopping to wood is a long affair.

Since we left Coari we have been coasting along close to the land— the continental shore, and not that of an island. The islands are so large and numerous in the Amazons that often when we believe ourselves between the northern and southern margins of the river, we are in fact between island shores. . . .

Since we left Manaos the forest has been less luxuriant; it is lower on the Solimões than on the Amazons, more ragged and more open. The palms are also less numerous than hitherto, but there is a tree here which rivals them in dignity. Its flat dome, rounded but not conical, towers above the forest, and when seen from a distance has an almost architectural character. . . .

September 18th: Another pause last evening at the village of San Paolo, standing on a ridge which rises quite steeply from the river and sinks again into a ravine behind. Throughout all this region the banks are eaten away by the river, large portions falling into the water at a time, and carrying the trees with them. . . .

The steamer is often now between the shores of the river itself instead of coasting along by the many lovely islands which make the voyage between Pará and Manaos so diversified—what is thus gained in dimensions is lost in picturesqueness of detail.

Then the element of human life and habitations is utterly wanting. One often travels for a day without meeting even so much as a hut. But if men are not to be seen, animals are certainly plenty. As our steamer puffs along, great flocks of birds rise up from the shore, turtles pop their black noses out of the water, alligators show themselves occasionally, and sometimes a troop of brown capivari scuttles up the bank, taking refuge in the trees at our approach. . . .

September 20th: On Monday evening we arrived at Tabatinga, remaining there till Wednesday morning to discharge the cargo—a lengthy process. . . . Tabatinga is the frontier town between Brazil and Peru. . . .

At this point the Amazonian meets the Peruvian steamer, and they exchange cargoes. Formerly the Brazilian company of Amazonian steamers extended its line of travel to Laguna, at the mouth of the Huallaga. Now this part of the journey has passed into the hands of a Peruvian company whose steamers run up to Urimaguas on the Huallaga. They are, however, by no means so comfortable as the Brazilian steamers, having little or no accommodation for passengers. . . .

There is reason to believe that all the larger affluents of the Amazons will before long have their regular line of steamers like the great river itself. The opening of the Amazons, no doubt, will hasten this result.

THEY DIED BY HUNDREDS

On the coast of Peru and on the islands off the western shores of South America, where millions of birds had made their home from time immemorial, there was a mad scramble for the bird-deposits, known as guano, which farmers in England and the United States were clamoring for. Guano was needed to fertilize their lands. From the precious pearl-gray islands of Lobos de Afuera alone, more than a million tons of the natural fertilizer were removed—until the islands with their giant, erect mounds of guano standing tall and brown over the sea, began to look like decapitated, ghostly figures of death.

Ships owned by private American and British companies were moving up and down the Latin American coasts, into the wildernesses criss-crossed by rivers. Crews of men hired by other private companies with headquarters in London or Boston, New York or Liverpool, Manchester or San Francisco, were pushing into the forests of Central America, felling the king of all trees—the majestic mahogany—and many other varieties of valuable timber.

People from all corners of the globe—from Germany and the United States, from England, from China—were drifting into the opening arms of the Latin American lands. They came as men of enterprise of all kinds—as laborers and farmers, as agents of commerce and representatives of industry, as emissaries of foreign banks. They came to build homes, to build towns, to build cities. They came to build rail and steamship lines, linking the new cities and the old towns and villages, joining the hot coasts to the high sierra lands, ignoring the borders between countries as they ignored the frontier between city and wilderness, crossing and recrossing the borders and the frontiers, spanning Latin America with the great broad hand of industrial venture.

Among them came builders of ships and of harbors, of coal mines and gas works, like William Wheelwright. And builders of railroads, like Wheelwright, like Minor C. Keith, like the fabulous Henry Meiggs, who fled from his creditors in San Francisco, and who planned and carried through the construction of "railways to the moon," through the Andes of Chile and Peru.

The rails were being laid up and down Latin America, through tunnels and over mountains. Across new bridges. And across old and deadly swamps such as the little island of Manzanilla where the Panama Railroad had been started as early as 1850—and where the laborers to do the dangerous job grew as scarce as the hazards were plentiful:

This island is little better than a coral reef, partially covered with a thin layer of muddy soil, which at the highest points of the island is only a few feet thick, and beneath which the salt water of the ocean is every-where reached by digging. The railroad engineers who first landed there describe it as a virgin swamp, covered with a dense growth of the tortuous, water-loving mangrove, interlaced with huge vines and thorny shrubs, denying entrance even to the wild beasts common to the country.

Engineer Kurtze on the Building of the Panama Railroad

In the black, slimy mud of its surface, alligators and other reptiles abounded, while the air was laden with pestilential vapors, and swarmed with sand-flies and mosquitoes.

The laborers were compelled to work with their faces covered with gauze veils, and at night had to seek refuge on board an old brig anchored in the bay. Many of them in a few days succumbed to sickness, others deserted, while those that could be induced to remain could only work a week at a time, and thus made but slow progress.

Further inland, the same and even worse difficulties were encountered. For fifteen miles from the coast the road has to run through a deep, almost bottomless swamp. For months and months the men had to work waist-deep in water, exposed alternately to the broiling sun and to the drenching rains of the tropics, in an atmosphere saturated with malarious poison. The insects left them no peace by day or night. Living on shore was impossible. The men in going to and from their work had to wade their way through two to four feet of mud and water, over mangrove stumps, and through tangled vines and thorny shrubs. They had to sleep crowded together on old hulks anchored in the bay; they lived on sailor's fare, brought down to them from northern ports; they had only rain-water to drink.

And they died by hundreds.

Fresh laborers were brought by thousands from all parts of the world, but the climate seemed equally fatal to all. Natives from the neighboring coasts, Negroes and mulattoes from the West-India islands, North Americans, English, Irish, French, Germans, Coolies, and Chinamen were all tried in turn, and all in turn succumbed. Each mail-steamer that arrived brought its quota of fresh men and carried away a similar number of sick and disabled. The superintending engineers alternated regularly, one in the hospital, the other at work.

Three miles from the coast the first dry mound was discovered in the midst of the swamp, and a hut for the engineers erected upon it. The timber for this hut had to be carried to the spot on the backs of men, and for a long time the men themselves continued to live on board the boats. The country was, of course, totally uninhabited, and produced not a single article of food—everything had to be brought from points thousands of miles distant.

Even when, after two years of incessant and disheartening labor, varied only by a greater or less sickness and corresponding desertion of the men, the first thirteen miles through the morass had been built, and higher ground reached, the difficulties continued nearly the same. The forests were just as dense, the fevers just as deadly, the insects as abundant; only instead of through morass, the road now passed through a rugged country, along steep hillsides, over wild chasms, spanning turbulent rivers and furious mountain torrents, until the summit ridge was reached, whence it descended abruptly over similar wild regions to the same terrible swamps on the shores of the Pacific.

The road in its whole length runs between the eighth and ninth parallel north of the Equator, where the most sultry tropical heat prevails throughout the year, and where for nearly six months the whole country is deluged daily with the tropical rains. The sparse native population, composed of a . . . race of Spaniards, Indians and Negroes, furnished no assistance whatever. . . . They produced scarcely enough for their own support, and could contribute nothing to the maintenance of the foreign laborers.

Every single article of food, every piece of material used, had to be transported thousands of miles. Even the forests in this wretched country, dense as they are, furnish no timber fit for use. Ties or sleepers cut from native timber had to be taken up and replaced by others imported from abroad, even before a train had run over them. The whole country does not provide so much as a telegraph pole, every piece of timber used having to be brought from some of the other Central American republics or from the north.

But in spite of all these seemingly insurmountable difficulties, the road was finally completed, and, after having for some time previously taken passengers and freight partially across . . . the company was at last able to run a locomotive from ocean to ocean, and shortly after to throw the entire road open to regular traffic, which has never since been interrupted.

The enterprising capitalists, who with so much courage and determination persevered in this undertaking in spite of such discouraging experience, were, fortunately, amply rewarded by the pecuniary success of their enterprise. At the end of the third year of their labors—long before the road was finished—they were already in the receipt of handsome dividends.

A SWAPPING SOUTHERNER

At the end of the Civil War in the United States, many men of the
South and their families migrated to Cuba and Brazil, where slavery was
still practiced and where they might recoup their lost fortunes as planters
and employers of Negro labor. Their views on slavery were selfish and
backward, but their comparatively high energies were needed to raise
the poor productiveness of the rich Brazilian soil. And the Emperor
Dom Pedro II encouraged this influx of immigrants from the Southern
States.

They were a strange people in an alien land, and they seemed even
stranger to the Englishmen who were already in Brazil—even to such an
experienced traveller and writer as Richard Burton. He understood their
usefulness to Brazil, but he could only express astonishment at their
ways:

At the door of the pigmy hostelry we caught sight of an elderly citizen
in a hammer-claw, or swallow-tail black coat, and we found a party of
Southerner immigrants wandering about in search of land. The leader
was a Mississippi man, accompanied by two daughters and one son-in-
law, two companions from the same State, and a Georgian who was
hailing back for the River Plate—despite In-

Richard Burton's Observations dians, Gauchos, and other little difficulties.
of a Growing Brazil Mostly these strangers had been accustomed to
the flats of Florida and the plains on the bank of the Yazoo River. None
of them came from the . . . states where men raise cereals and cotton—
at present, perhaps, the most important and certainly the safest industry
in Brazil.

I had already met several parties of these refugees, and they were not
my last experience. The first impression made by our . . . cousins—
speaking only of the farmer and little-educated class—is peculiar and
unpleasant. In them the bristly individuality of the Briton appears to
have grown rank. Their ideas of persons and things are rigid as if cast in
iron; they are untaught, but ready to teach everything. One of them—
and perhaps the best educated—had heard of Hannibal and the vinegar
which split the Alps. I heard him recommend the plan to a Portuguese,

and remember the face of the latter after the trial. In this part of the world vinegar is nearly as dear as wine.

All have eyes steadily fixed upon the main chance—every dodge to "get on" is allowable, provided that it succeeds—and there is no tie, except of blood, to prevent at any moment the party falling to pieces. Amongst themselves there is no geniality. Of strangers they are suspicious in the extreme, and they defraud themselves rather than run the risk of being defrauded. Nothing appears to satisfy them—whatever is done for them might have been done a "heap deal better." As the phrase is, they expect roast pig to run before them, and even then they would grumble because the crittur was not properly fixed for them.

This is not an agreeable account of the pioneers now leading the great Anglo-American movement in Brazil. Yet we presently find out that these are the men wanted by the Empire to teach practical mechanical knowledge, to create communications, and to leaven her population with rugged northern energy. Bred in a sub-tropical country, seasoned to fevers, and accustomed to employ Negroes, they will find the Mediterranean Brazil an improved edition of their old homes. . . .

It was impossible not to admire the pluck and spirit of these pilgrims. Everything was new and strange to them, they saw what they did not understand, they heard what they could not comprehend—it was quite indifferent to them. They mounted their wretched nags; they wandered about at night; they slept in the woods heedless of Maroons—runaway Negroes—and "tigers." And they were brought in by the Negroes to the planters' houses, which they often mistook for hotels.

In fact, they became a standing marvel to the land.

An old man, with a foot and a half in the grave, unaccompanied by a servant, and riding, not as the Rechabim rode, a garran—like the steeds of Agincourt—carrying a carpet-bag and a paper of bread, but without even a blanket, actually set out to descend the São Francisco River, cross to the headwaters of the Tocantins, and float down to the Amazon. He had been wandering upwards of a year in Brazil.

He had not learned a sentence of Portuguese, and probably he never would. Like the British sailor, he instinctively determined that those who cannot understand good English will be better suited with it broken: "Me no sabby, me no carey, me very peculiar, me no drink wine—*vinho*, me no drink coffee—*caffé*, me no drink spirits."

This, aided by the presence of a mighty quid, was intended to enlighten the dullest understanding.

His account of meeting in the backwoods with an English-speaking youth had its comic side. The latter pulled up his galloping nag, stared at the solitary figure dressed in a kind of winter greatcoat, collaring him to the head and skirting him to the heels; at the crumpled-up trousers; at the under-drawers—forming a "lucid interval"; and at the unblacked boots with toes well turned out. Presently he found presence of mind enough to exclaim:

"Who the hell are you?"

"Guess," replied the senior, "that that don't concern yeou."

"Where the devil are you going?"

"Waal," was the rejoinder, "s'pose it don't much matter to yeou."

"What are you doing, then?"

"Calc'late, young man, that you had better move off that way, and I go this way"—suiting the action to the word, and thus they parted.

He offered to accompany me, but I could not bring myself to say yes. . . . This venerable egotist was candid enough to declare that he wanted my company as an interpreter. At every five minutes he would interrupt conversation with, "Tell him so and so," or, "Ask him this and that."

He wanted me to sell his garran, to threaten that it should be turned loose upon the world if it could not fetch its price, to "swap" it for a canoe. . . .

I translated him literally. And the expression of the Brazilian countenance, with a painful tendency to a guffaw—a *gargalhada*—which civility forbade, was a study. . . .

This Southerner emigration will be, to a certain extent, a natural selection from the United States—even as the population of the latter is a selection of species from Europe. What I mean is, that; whereas the old, the sick and the feeble in mind and body remain at home, the young, the brave and the adventurous—even the malcontent, the criminal and the malefactor—go forth in search of fortune, and find it.

THE INSURGENT GOVERNMENT

Whatever their general beliefs and prejudices, the settlers and entrepreneurs from all regions of the United States, the immigrants from England and the rest of Europe, the coolies from China, were bringing potent energies with them that were merging with the new and powerful energies contained in the spread of new industry and commerce through Latin America.

Together, the energies brought by the people and the energies brought by the penetration of American and British industry and trade were releasing still newer energies. And these were shaking the patterns of Latin American life loose from the ways of colonialism that still lingered on, loose from the later but still hesitant and fear-conditioned ways that had come with the caudillos after independence.

In Central America, a bold man named Justo Rufino Barrios now undertook to reunite those countries in the democratic Federation which Morazán had founded and sought to preserve—and like Morazán before him, Barrios, too, paid with his life for his fight for unity and against provincialism and provincial tyrants who, sooner or later, proved to be traitors serving the ambitious schemes of foreign interests. Even as president of Guatemala he fought the caudillos of Central America and the old cliques of landholders and selfish clerics who supported the caudillos with powder as well as prayers. Sadly but willingly he paid for his zeal for progress with his life—sensing that the end of it was near as he took one long look of love at his wife before riding into the battle that was his last.

And finally, insurgent movements aimed at shaking off the dying but brutal hold that Spain still held in the Caribbean sprang up in Cuba and even in tiny Puerto Rico. The new movements had been prepared by men of thought and action, by forward-looking men of Cuba and Puerto Rico and the Dominican Republic, who dreamed of a Federation of Free Antillean States, as Barrios had dreamed and fought for the Central American Federation.

The new dreamers and fighters included men like the brilliant Eugenio María de Hostos, men like the dynamic Céspedes and the determined Aguilera. Men like a certain restless Cuban who was a poet of talent as well as a political pamphleteer: José Martí, organizing the armed fight for Cuban independence from his place of exile in New York and his temporary haven in Haiti. Martí making his way successfully, at long last, to the fields of actual combat, joining the leader of the rebel forces, setting up the insurgent government in the field of action, alongside the fast-moving insurgent forces of Máximo Gómez:

The two eastern provinces, Santiago de Cuba and Puerto Príncipe, are already Cuba Libre—Free Cuba. There the new government is discharging all its functions almost without annoyance. In the other four provinces, the rebels are practically the rulers outside the large cities. For more than two years, with a maximum strength of scarcely thirty thousand indifferently armed guerrilla soldiers, *The Tactics of General Gómez* the insurgents have, on a narrow island, suc- *Against the Spaniards in Cuba* cessfully waged war against two hundred and thirty-five thousand well-armed troops, assisted by militia, supported by a navy, and maintained by constant supplies. . . .

General Gómez never has more than three or four hundred men with him.

His favorite camp is near Arroyo Blanco, on a high plateau, difficult to approach, and covered with dense thicket. He posts his outer pickets at least three miles away, in the directions from which the enemy may come.

The Spaniards, whenever possible, march by road—and, with these highways well guarded, Gómez sleeps secure. He knows that his pickets will be informed by some Cuban long before the Spanish column leaves or passes the nearest village to attack him.

A shot from the farthest sentry causes little or no excitement in Gómez's camp. The report throws the Spanish column into fears of attack or ambush, and it moves forward very slowly and carefully. Two pickets at such a time have been known to hold two thousand men at bay for a whole day. If the column presses on, and General Gómez hears a shot from a sentinel near by, he will rise leisurely from his hammock and give orders to prepare to move camp.

He has had so many experiences of this kind that not until he hears the volley-shooting of the oncoming Spaniards will he call for his horse, give the word to march, and disappear, followed by his entire force, into the tropical underbrush, which closes like a curtain behind them—leaving the Spaniards to discover a deserted camp, without the slightest trace of the path taken by its recent occupants.

Sometimes Gómez will move only a mile or two. The Spaniards do not usually give chase. If they do, Gómez takes a keen delight in leading them in a circle. If he can throw them off by nightfall, he goes to sleep in his camp of the morning happier than if he had won a battle.

The Spaniards learn nothing through such experiences.

Gómez varies the game occasionally by marching directly toward the rear of the foe—and there, reinforced by other insurgent bands of the neighborhood, falling upon the column and punishing it severely. While his immediate force is only a handful, the general can call to his aid, in a short time, nearly six thousand men.

AN ELOQUENT LOSER

Cuba was nearly free. Even the Spanish businessmen in Havana recognized the fact and were already dealing with the insurgent government. But it was not until three years after Martí's death on the battlefield of Cuba Libre, that the final blow came:

It came in 1898 with the mysterious and fatal explosion of a United States battleship in Havana harbor. The ship was the Maine—and the result was a far bigger explosion:

The result was the United States' declaration of war against Spain, the landing of American troops in Cuba and Puerto Rico, the bottling-up of the Spanish fleet in the Philippines. The result was the ultimate smashing of Spanish power in the New World, which had first been sighted by Rodrigo Triana, the sailor, four hundred years earlier, from his look-out on the ship that had sailed out of Palos in Spain.

It came in April, and by December it was over—all but the reading, and subsequent ratification, of the treaty which was being negotiated in Paris. It was over—all but the last-minute plea for magnanimity from the proud and eloquent loser:

I got a private hint on the day after our arrival, from the Foreign Office, about M. Delcassé's purpose to bring the two sets of Commissioners together socially at his breakfast table. . . . At the breakfast, Castillo struck at once what I believe is to be their permanent tone—one of rather proud supplication. He came to me, through the crowd on his side, the moment our presentations to the French Premier were finished, and after a few words about his pleasure at meeting "mon ancien collègue et ami"—"my old colleague and friend"—and messages for Mrs. Reid, began at once:

A Letter from Whitelaw Reid to President McKinley

"You have had a great victory, the first you have really had over a foreign foe—for Mexico didn't count. Now you must prove your greatness by your magnanimity."

After the breakfast he sought me again in the smoking-room and renewed the attack:

"Do not forget," he exclaimed with increasing energy, "that we are poor. Do not forget that we have been defeated. Do not forget that it was Spain that opened the New World. Do not forget that the greatness of your victory will be dimmed by any lack of magnanimity to a fallen foe."

These phrases he kept repeating, with slight variations. Some of them he addressed to Mr. Day, and I translated them promptly. Naturally we both avoided replies that should in any way commit us.

But it seemed plain that their role was to appeal from the outset to our magnanimity.

Subsequent intercourse has convinced me of the justice of our first impressions about them. They are men of high character and position, but not of extraordinary force.

None of them seemed to me the equal of Castillo himself (the Spanish ambassador in Paris). Three or four of them speak a little English, and all speak French—though Montero Ríos (the chairman) seems to know little but Spanish. This is a blessing. He is so long-winded in Spanish that if he had an equal command of one or two other languages he would be intolerable. As it is, the interpreter, from time to time, has to turn the stopcock on the endless flow of his eloquence. . . .

It was really a dramatic spectacle, while these provisions for deeding away the last vestige of their possessions in the world they had discovered and conquered were slowly read and translated. They were all visibly moved, and old Montero looked as a Roman senator might when told that the Goths were at the gates.

PERSUASION IN PANAMA

By the terms of the Treaty of Paris, Puerto Rico—the small but sturdy gate to the Caribbean—passed over to the United States. The Philippines and the island of Guam, Spain's golden doors to the East, became the United States' stepping-stones to penetration of the Orient. Even the new republic of Cuba, whose sovereignty the United States had promised to respect in the treaty which also granted the United States a naval base at Guantanamo Bay, became a virtual American protectorate by 1901 through the blunt provisions of the Platt Amendment.

Cuba, Puerto Rico, the Philippines—all territory now owned or controlled by the United States. Cuba, Puerto Rico, the Philippines—territory where millions of American dollars were invested, and millions more were being poured in. And it was only the beginning:

For Puerto Rico and Cuba and the Philippines were far more than rich spoils of war. They were, above all else, precious gateways to new territories and new trade-channels in Latin America, as well as in China, Manchuria, and other parts of the Far East. They were the new route to the Orient, just as the Hawaiian Islands—which had been annexed by the United States during the Spanish-American War—were the new keys that would unlock the whole Pacific to United States power.

The twentieth century was around the corner, and the United States was already a real world power. There was no turning back now. In fact, other targets for other ultimate goals were already being lined up.

The next was a narrow stretch of land that was part of Colombia, the waist of the Isthmus where the United States had long wanted to build and control a canal between the two great oceans. The next target was Colombia, the goal being the Panama isthmus. And the wielder of the stick was President Theodore Roosevelt himself:

When, in August, 1903, I became convinced that Colombia intended to repudiate the treaty made the preceding January . . . I began carefully to consider what should be done. By my direction, Secretary Hay—personally and through the minister at Bogotá—repeatedly warned Colombia that grave consequences might follow her rejection of the treaty. The possibility of ratification did not wholly

From the Autobiography of Theodore Roosevelt

pass away until the close of the session of the Colombian congress on the last day of October. There would then be two possibilities.

One was that Panama would remain quiet. In that case I was prepared to recommend to Congress that we should at once occupy the Isthmus anyhow, and proceed to dig the canal—and I had drawn out a draft of my message to this effect.

But from the information I received, I deemed it likely that there would be a revolution in Panama as soon as the Colombian congress adjourned without ratifying the treaty. . . . Correspondents of the different newspapers on the Isthmus had sent to their respective papers widely published forecasts indicating that there would be a revolution in such event.

Moreover, on October 16—at the request of Lieutenant-General Young—Captain Humphrey and Lieutenant Murphy, two army officers who had returned from the Isthmus, saw me and told me that there would unquestionably be a revolution on the Isthmus . . . and that the revolution would probably take place immediately after the adjournment of the Colombian congress. They did not believe that it would be before October 20, but they were confident that it would certainly come at the end of October or immediately afterward, when the Colombian congress had adjourned.

Accordingly I directed the Navy Department to station various ships within easy reach of the Isthmus, to be ready to act in the event of need arising.

These ships were barely in time. On November 3 the revolution occurred. Practically everybody on the Isthmus—including all the Colombian troops that were already stationed there—joined in the revolution, and there was no bloodshed.

But on that same day four hundred new Colombian troops were landed at Colon. . . . The gunboat *Nashville*, under Commander Hubbard, reached Colon almost immediately afterward. . . . Commander Hubbard landed a few score sailors and marines. . . .

By a mixture of firmness and tact he . . . persuaded the Colombian commander to re-embark his troops for Cartagena.

PIPELINE TO POWER

A new age of conquest had begun—and war was only one of the means used to attain the ends of expanding influence for security and, if need be, for coercion; of raw materials for the mushrooming home industries; of markets for the threatening plethora of manufactured goods. War was only one of the means—and it was no longer the most effective. There were other, newer means to gain those ends, and they were cheaper, though they were none the less violent, none the less means to further violence and, ultimately, to further war:

Bribing the native men of power—the caudillos, the caciques or provincial political chiefs, and their main supporters among the gentry and the generals—was still a favorite method. But now the caudillos were bought with more than a few arms and a little money. They were purchased with huge loans made by private firms and investment houses to the Latin American governments—whose treasuries, for all practical purposes, belonged to the caudillos.

Not only did these foreign loans draw enormous rates of interest, but they were granted in exchange for fat concessions in given fields of trade, in the building and control of railway and other communications, in the obtaining of old and new vital raw materials. And the heavy, compound interest on these loans had to be paid promptly—or new burdensome loans had to be accepted, and further concessions granted.

The penalty for failure to meet these multiplying obligations was increasing pressure from the governments of the countries whose banking and business and industrial entrepreneurs had advanced the millions in pounds or dollars. Here was the new, grave danger to the security and sovereignty of the Latin American republics. Here was the new danger contained in the very core of the finance capital and the trade and industrial investments that were bringing new life-giving energies to those countries and joining them with indissoluble bonds—cables and rails, canals and breakwaters, and tunnels running horizontally through mountains and even perpendicularly deep into the earth filled with minerals and fuels.

Bands of steel and concrete were joining the republics to each other, joining their cities and jungles, joining Latin America to the whole world with the new bonds of modern finance and industrial and trade concessions that could not be broken without jeopardizing the whole system of economic expansion. Yet here in this very force that was making Latin America inter-dependent with the rest of the world—that was making Latin America an integral and indispensable part of the world's new and growing energies in its mighty strides toward the strengthening and the perfectioning of man's fulfillment of everyday needs—here in the potent, accelerating influx of foreign industry and foreign capital, was the newest and the gravest threat of all:

The loans to the Latin American countries, though made by private firms, were backed by the governments of the firms making them—by the Government of the United States, by His Britannic Majesty's Government. They were backed, at length, by other powers which had begun to loom on the international horizon of growing industry and finance—by France, by Italy. They were backed by the challenging power of a rising Imperial Germany.

As early as 1902—one year before President Theodore Roosevelt's policy of the Big Stick had made Panama an independent and ostensibly sovereign country almost overnight—Great Britain, Italy, and Germany blockaded Venezuela in an effort to enforce the financial claims held against that country by private investors who were subjects of those countries. Germany was the last to remove her fleet and agree to arbitration—and this only after the same President Roosevelt threatened to order American warships to Venezuela.

With the aid of the Government of the United States, meanwhile, powerful, new banking syndicates began to extend their own formidable controls not only over Venezuela but over the entire Caribbean area. The Caribbean was, in fact, fast becoming an American lake.

In 1904 a protectorate similar to the one which had been imposed on Cuba was established over Santo Domingo. Eight years later, another protectorate—granted in exchange for a loan made to Nicaragua, which was ruled by the caudillo Chamorro—brought that country under direct control by the United States. Little Haiti was next—in 1915—but by that time the Great War had broken out in Europe. By that time the intensifying rivalry between the major powers, including the United States, for trade and other concessions throughout Latin America would be one of the factors behind the Great War, the war for world economic supremacy.

In the meantime, United States diplomatic pressures in behalf of American bankers and large business interests were being exerted in Honduras—where a banking combine organized by J. P. Morgan and Company had extended heavy loans—and over the whole Caribbean. In Mexico, however, the rivalry between British and American interests for concessions in trade and concessions of long-term rights to valuable subsoil was growing more acute. The rivalry was becoming a bitter struggle. And the struggle was turning into violence—a new kind of violence emanating from the determination to obtain not only preference but monopoly over the greatest possible number of concessions available to foreigners.

The chief weapon in the drive toward monopoly was the threat of "revolution"—the threat of encouraging or even assisting or perhaps even starting an armed uprising that would end the rule of the caudillo in power. The new weapon had first been used—with quick and resounding success—in the Hawaiian Islands, where a "revolution" during the short-lived Spanish-American War had brought about the early annexation of those islands by the United States. Several years later, the weapon had again proved overwhelmingly successful in separating Panama from Colombia.

With full knowledge of what had happened in Cuba and Panama and Santo Domingo, and in the face of the danger to the political power he had wielded for nearly a generation, the caudillo of Mexico, Don Porfirio Díaz, nevertheless refused to grant exclusive rights to American interests in Mexico. He encouraged the influx of American capital and he gave American entrepreneurs vast concessions of land and of rights to the rich Mexican subsoil. But he also welcomed British capital and British interests:

He welcomed the man who was the very spearhead of British industry's belligerent quest for the newest and the most precious fuel of all—oil.

Dictator Díaz welcomed Weetman Pearson, the entrepreneur from England. Pearson came to Mexico to build harbor improvements, and he stayed to establish a British oil empire which would soon compete with the stronger empire already laid out by Doheny and other men from the United States in the heart of Mexico's richest lands. Pearson, the newest of the pioneers, the industrial captain:

Weetman Pearson, now the first Viscount Cowdray, writing to his son of the hazards that had to be met in the job of laying a pipeline to wealth and to power:

So far I have been occupied to the full. Matters not only of policy but of detail have kept me going at top speed. . . . The refinery is going to be lighted up this week—not of course in full blast for the one-third unit, but still by still. It looks an immense place. Minatitlan market rivals Tehuantepec now. San Cristobal oilfield is in first-class shape. All the tanks are full of oil, and of course the pipeline is in working order. I am afraid the area of the field has been determined, as we have got a complete ring of dry wells round it except for say one-eighth of its circumference. It may be, and we are so hoping—although not very hopefully—that the productive area will extend in that direction. The field

A Letter from Lord Cowdray to His Son, March, 1908

only gives us a two years' life—but surely before that two years has passed we shall have found further deposits of a satisfactory quality, i.e. a refining quality.

The one encouraging feature about the oilfield is the fact that one well has continued to flow about 100 tons of oil a day for ten or twelve weeks. Such vitality shows that we may have a much more lasting field than the depths of oil-bearing sands and rocks have led me to believe.

As you know, we hedged by agreeing to purchase . . . a minimum of 2000 and a maximum of 6000 barrels a day for twelve years. So if we do fail to find more oil—which is an almost impossible assumption—than we have, we avoid a failure.

All this you know already. But it is cheering to put it down on paper when disappointments are all round me.

The oil business is not all beer and skittles. Far-seeing provisions have to be made to ensure success. Wise principles have to be followed. Much detail should hour by hour be gone into to avoid all waste. Everyone, on an oilfield that has been proved, is inclined to be extremely wasteful, as it is considered to lead to untold wealth. And beyond all, it is essential to know the business—otherwise the opinions of one's employees have to prevail. . . .

I entered lightly into the enterprise, not realizing its many problems, but only feeling that oil meant a fortune and that hard work and application would bring satisfactory results. Now I know that it would have been wise to surround myself with proved oil men who could give advice that their past life showed could be relied on, and not, as I did, relied upon commercial knowledge and hard work coupled with a superficial knowledge of the trade.

However, all's well that ends well. And I feel we are out of the wood in any event—and should we have plenty of oil in our lands, we have a great business, one that my sons will be proud of.

The industrial empires of the world were laying out their economic stakes and their financial claims all over Latin America. Beside the chimneys and smokestacks of copper-mines and sugar-mills, beside the towers of textile factories, beside the tall grain elevators and warehouses for hides and bananas, coffee and cinchona bark, there rose the derricks of oil wells. And new derricks were rising besides these. The great machine of modern industry and commerce was going up, slowly but surely

—and with it new groups of men were coming into being throughout the Latin American countries:

Men of business, professional men, and men of skilled labor. In short, new men of enterprise who were not Englishmen or Americans—but Mexicans and Brazilians and Argentines and Bolivians. In every one of the twenty Latin American republics, these new groups of men were coming into being.

Their place was still at the rear of the machine of modern industry and trade that the foreign entrepreneurs and investors and engineers and technicians had brought and installed. But in some of the Latin American countries the new groups of men were already beginning to climb into the front seat—and in a few of the Latin American countries the new groups of men were even preparing to take the driver's wheel themselves in order to guide the machine forward with greater precision and at a steadier and faster speed over their own lands!

· *Nineteen* ·

FORWARD

Over mine and mausoleum
against the abominable appetite of death . . .
forward!

PABLO NERUDA

THE DEAD SHRINK SO

The turn of the century saw the swift extension over Latin America of a diplomacy, based on the power of the pound and the might of the dollar, that was backed by veiled threats of "revolution." But it also saw the rapid surge of the new native groups of business and professional men determined to make their own real revolution in their own countries, where radical social changes were radically needed once more.

The primary objective of these groups was to achieve the decisive liberation of their countries from the last trammels of feudalism which hindered the extension of trade and industrial benefits among them and among the people at large. Their target was the decrepit but clinging power of the feudal order—the old ways maintained by the new caudillos and their cliques—which still held their lands in the grip of a backward agricultural economy, which still held the mass of the population in the grip of peasantry, which still held the people in the grip of poverty, illiteracy, hunger, disease, premature death.

These were the targets of the rising jefes or chiefs of revolution in the making—of the men of professions and businesses whose aspirations and ambitions could find little outlet and less fulfillment in the predominant pattern of agrarian ways and a new, hybrid, semi-colonial life. Most of these jefes came from the conglomerate of Latin America's racial mixtures known as the mestizaje, just as most of the independence leaders

358

one hundred years earlier had come from the angry groups of Creole whites.

And once again the leaders formed the core, and once again around them gathered the long-impoverished, still hopeful peasantry.

But now more and more leaders began to emerge from the peasant perimeters of the new armies of revolution, and to take their place, at least for fitful periods of a few years or maybe even a bare few months, in the very core of the armed revolution as officers and senior officers, as colonels and generals. In Mexico such men even rose to command combined groups of guerrilla forces and to occupy and govern vast areas of the national territory.

Around the little lawyer, Madero—who led the movement in 1910 that toppled the old caudillo, Díaz, from his well-worn seat of power—gathered the peasant host. Around the little idealist with the black goatee, around the future martyr, Francisco Madero, rose a host of peasants and coming leaders—with guns in their hands, with their own ideas of bread and land, of schools, and of sovereignty over the nation's subsoil and the national wealth, in the back of their own long Indian heads.

And even the murder of Madero, and even the American bombardment and landing at Veracruz in 1914—ostensibly because of an insult to the American flag—could not shake those ideas from the back of those Indian heads, or the guns and machetes from those peasant hands. Not even the people's abiding hatred for the foreign invader, not even their own patriot oath of "death to the Gringos!" scribbled on the walls of schools that had been taken over as barracks by the American forces in Veracruz, nor the wad of saliva spat in contempt, out of nowhere and against the invader's face and chest, could make those armed peasants and their leaders deflect the force of their wrath and their avenging blows from Victoriano Huerta, the betrayer and usurper of their revolution.

Mexico's revolution was moving with a momentum that would not be stopped. It was moving in the small and sturdy hooves of the fast Mexican ponies, and in the wheels of the rebels' armored trains intoning new corridos, or ballads, as they turned. It carried forward the revolutionary peasants with their guitars and their women, their strong liquor, their pet dogs and parrots, and sometimes even their poor but handy household effects along with the loot taken from the Huertista foe.

The Mexican Revolution of the growing middle-class and the peasants was marching in the scattered, far-flung, but determined ranks of the Constitutionalist rebel armies. These included the forces of Venustiano Carranza, the bearded landowner who had thrown in his lot with the people; of Emiliano Zapata, the beloved peasant leader from Morelos; of Pancho Villa, the fighting peon and scourge of the north; and of many other new generals leading many new rebel bands.

Their common enemy and their common target of hate was the betrayer, Huerta, who had turned against the revolution and was trying to bring back the false and bloody discipline of the Díaz tyranny. He and his ally, Felix Díaz, a nephew of the ex-dictator, were admirers of Kaiser Wilhelm and the Prussianism that Imperial Germany was seeking to extend. The year was 1914, and the Great War was only a few months away.

But the revolutionary armies of Mexico had their own war to fight at home, and it would be years—years of sporadic civil war, of revolution and counter-revolution—before the issue would be settled. Meanwhile, the common enemy and the immediate target of the Mexican rebel armies was Huerta—"The Jackal"—and his rurales, and all his other armed supporters, known as the Federales:

The first car of the repair train was a steel-encased flat-car, upon which was mounted the famous Constitutionalist cannon, El Niño, with an open caisson full of shells behind it. Behind that was an armored car full of soldiers, then a car of steel rails, and four loaded with railroad ties. The engine came next, the engineer and fireman hung with cartridge belts, their rifles handy. Then followed
Villa's Revolution in Mexico, as two or three box-cars full of soldiers and their
Seen by John Reed. 1914 women. It was a dangerous business. A large force of Federals were known to be in Mapimi, and the country swarmed with their outposts. Our army was already far ahead, except for five hundred men who guarded the trains at Conejos. If the enemy could capture or wreck the repair train, the army would be cut off without water, food or ammunition.

In the darkness we moved out. I sat upon the breech of El Niño, chatting with Captain Diaz, the commander of the gun, as he oiled the breech lock of his beloved cannon and curled his vertical mustachios. In the armored recess behind the gun, where the Captain slept, I heard a curious, subdued rustling noise.

"What's that?"

"Eh?" cried he nervously. "Oh, nothing, nothing!"

Just then there emerged a young Indian girl with a bottle in her hand. She couldn't have been more than seventeen, very lovely. The Captain shot a glance at me, and suddenly whirled around.

"What are you doing here?" he cried furiously to her. "Why are you coming out here?"

"I thought you said you wanted a drink," she began.

I perceived that I was one too many, and excused myself. They hardly noticed me. But as I was climbing over the back of the car, I couldn't help stopping and listening. They had gone back to the recess, and she was weeping.

"Didn't I tell you," stormed the Captain, "not to show yourself when there are strangers here? I will not have every man in Mexico looking at you. . . ."

I stood on the roof of the rocking steel car as we nosed slowly along. Lying on their bellies on the extreme front platform, two men with lanterns examined each foot of the track for wires that might mean mines planted under us. Beneath my feet the soldiers and their women were having dinner around fires built on the floor. Smoke and laughter poured out of the loopholes. . . . There were other fires aft, brown-faced, ragged people squatting at them, on the car-tops. Overhead the sky blazed stars, without a cloud. It was cold. After an hour of riding, we came to a piece of broken track. The train stopped with a jar, the engine whistled, and a score of torches and lanterns jerked past. Men came running. The flares clustered bobbing together as the foremen examined the damage. A fire sprang up in the brush, and then another. Soldiers of the train guard straggled by, dragging their rifles, and formed impenetrable walls around the fires. Iron tools clanged, and the "Wai-hoy!" of men shoving rails off the flat-car. A Chinese dragon of workmen passed with a rail on their shoulders, then others with ties. Four hundred men swarmed upon the broken spot, working with extraordinary energy and good humor, until the shouts of gangs setting rails and ties, and the rattle of sledges on spikes, made a continuous roar. It was an old destruction, probably a year old, made when these same Constitutional-ists were retreating north in the face of Mercado's Federal army, and we had it all fixed in an hour. Then on again. Sometimes it was a bridge burned out, sometimes a hundred yards of track twisted into grape vines by a chain and a backing engine. We advanced slowly. At one big bridge that it would take two hours to prepare, I built by myself a little fire in order to get warm. Calzado came past me, and hailed me. "We've got a hand-car up ahead," he said, "and we're going along down and see the dead men. Want to come?"

"What dead men?"

"Why, this morning an outpost of eighty *rurales* was sent scouting north from Bermejillo. We heard about it over the wire and informed Benavides on the left. He sent a troop to take them in the rear, and drove them north in a running fight for fifteen miles until they smashed up against our main body and not one got out alive. They're scattered along the whole way just where they fell."

In a moment we were speeding south on the hand-car. At our right hand and our left rode two silent, shadowy figures on horseback—cavalry guards, with rifles ready under their arms. Soon the flares and fires of the train were left behind, and we were enveloped and smothered in the vast silence of the desert.

"Yes," said Calzado, "the *rurales* are brave. They are *muy hombres*. *Rurales* are the best fighters Diaz and Huerta ever had. They never desert to the Revolution. They always remain loyal to the established government. Because they are police."

It was bitter cold. None of us talked much.

"We go ahead of the train at night," said the soldier at my left, "so that if there are any dynamite bombs underneath—"

"We could discover them and dig them out and put water in them, *carramba!*" said another sarcastically. The rest laughed. I began to think of that, and it made me shiver. The dead silence of the desert seemed an expectant hush. One couldn't see ten feet from the track.

"*Oiga!*" shouted one of the horsemen. "It was just here that one lay." The brakes ground and we tumbled off and down the steep embankment, our lanterns jerking ahead. Something lay huddled around the foot of a telegraph pole—something infinitely small and shabby, like a pile of old clothes. The *rurale* was upon his back, twisted sideways from his hips. He had been stripped of everything of value by the thrifty rebels—shoes, hat, underclothing. They had left him his ragged jacket with the tarnished silver braid, because there were seven bullet holes in it; and his trousers, soaked with blood. He had evidently been much bigger when alive—the dead shrink so.

RUBBER CARAVAN

Behind the rising revolutionary movements of Latin America, there was more than the need of the middle class and the peasant leaders to unseat the feudal caudillos who were selling their countries to foreign concessionaires, and getting wealth for themselves but ruinous loans for their countries in return. There was more than the need of the growing middle class and the aroused peasantry to smash the puppet power of the old-time caudillos and caciques in new disguises, who were granting the foreign companies and foreign trusts long-term leases and outright ownership to the national soil, juicy with petroleum and rich with minerals.

There was more than the necessity to get rid of the false leaders who were obtaining few or none of the benefits of modern industry and modern techniques and training for the people of their countries. There was more than the will to oust those unscrupulous henchmen of foreign monopoly who were converting their countries into half-colonies dependent on the favors and subservient to the wishes of foreign concessionaires and the governments back of them.

Behind the new revolutions that were springing up in every part of Latin America, there was the gathering force of a new laboring class—the steadily multiplying numbers of semi-skilled and unskilled industrial workers:

The workmen in the mines and the oilfields. The workers in the slowly lengthening chain of factories and industrial plants across the narrowing expanse of the southern Americas. The agricultural laborers—twentieth-century peons beginning to dress in store-bought clothes from the United States:

The dark-skinned rural workers on the coasts and the islands where the cane was being cut and refined to make white sugar. The Negroes and the Indians, the poor mestizos and the poor mulattoes in the jungles where the green and gold banana plantations were being industrialized and transformed into real empires in all but name. The workmen of all colors and all castes of poverty in the forests where the colorless chicle that would become chewing-gum, or the caucho that would be turned into smooth, polished rubber, were being drawn.

Behind the Latin American revolutions that were getting underway, there was the gathering force and the gathering protest of the unskilled workers in every country against the chicanery and the greed of the foreign boss and the native foreman. There was the protest against the continuing poverty in the midst of the mounting wealth they were helping to produce, and against the continuing illiteracy and disease and premature death in the midst of their new and harder conditions of work— conditions which sometimes amounted to brutal slavery, such as those that prevailed in 1912 in the American and British-owned rubber-forests of Peru:

. . . I accompanied a caravan of some two hundred Andokes and Boras Indians—men, women and children—that left Matanzas station on the 19th of October to carry their rubber that had been collected by them during the four or five preceding months down to a place on the banks of the Igaraparana, named Puerto Peruano. . . . The distance . . . is one of some forty miles, or possibly more. The rubber had already been carried into Matanzas *A British Consul-General De-* from different parts of the forest lying often *scribes Slavery in Peru. 1911* ten or twelve hours' march away—so that the total journey forced upon each carrier was not less than sixty miles. . . .

The path to be followed was one of the worst imaginable, a fatiguing route for a good walker quite unburdened.

For two days . . . I marched along with this caravan of very unhappy individuals—men with huge loads of rubber weighing, I believe, sometimes up to 70 kilograms (154 pounds) each, accompanied by their wives, also loaded with rubber, and their sons and daughters, down to quite tiny things that could do no more than carry a little cassava bread (prepared by the mothers before leaving their forest home) to serve as food for parents and children on this trying march.

Armed muchachos, with Winchesters, were scattered through the long column, and at the rear one of the racionales—"men of reason"—of Matanzas . . . beat up the stragglers. Behind all, following a day later, came Señor Normand himself, with more armed racionales, to see that none fell out or slipped home, having shed their burdens of rubber on the way.

On the second day I reached Entre Ríos in the early afternoon, the bulk of the Indians having that morning started at 5:15 A.M. from the place where we had slept together in the forest. At 5:15 that evening they arrived with . . . the armed muchachos at Entre Ríos, where I had determined to stay for some days. Instead of allowing these half-starved and weary people, after twelve hours' march, staggering under heavy loads, to rest in this comparatively comfortable station of the company —where a large resthouse and even food were available—Negrete drove them on into the forest beyond, where they were ordered to spend the night under guard of the muchachos.

This was done in order that a member of the company's commission . . . who was at Entre Ríos at the time along with myself, should not have an opportunity of seeing too closely the condition of these people— particularly, I believe, that we should not be able to weigh the loads of rubber they were carrying. I had, however, seen enough on the road during the two days I accompanied the party alone to convince me of the cruelty they were subjected to, and I had even taken several photographs of those among them who were more deeply scarred with the lash.

Several of the women had fallen out sick on the way, and five of them I had left provided for with food in a deserted Indian house in the forest. . . . An opportunity arose the next day to weigh one of these loads of rubber. A straggler, who had either fallen out or left Matanzas after the main party, came into Entre Ríos, staggering under a load of rubber . . . when Mr. Fox and I were about to sit down to lunch. The man came through the hot sun across the station compound, and fell before our eyes at the foot of the ladder leading up to the veranda, where, with the chief of the section . . . we were sitting. He had collapsed, and we got him carried into the shade and revived with whisky, and later on some soup and food from our own table. He was a young man, of slight build, with very thin arms and legs, and his load of rubber by no means one of the largest I had actually seen being carried.

I had it weighed there and then, and its weight was just 50 kilograms —110 pounds.

This man had not a scrap of food with him. Owing to our intervention, he was not forced to carry on this load, but was permitted the next day to go on to Puerto Peruano empty-handed in company with Señor Normand. I saw many of these people on their way back to their homes some days later, after their loads had been put into the lighters at Puerto Peruano. They were returning footsore and utterly worn out through the station at Entre Ríos on their way back to their scattered houses in the Andokes or Boras country. They had no food with them, and none was given to them at Entre Ríos.

I stopped many of them and inspected the little woven string or skin bags they carry, and neither man nor woman had any food left. All that they had started with a week before had been already eaten, and for the last day or two they had been subsisting on roots and leaves and the berries of wild trees they had pulled down on the way. We found, on our own subsequent journey down to Puerto Peruano a few days later, many traces of where they had pulled down branches and even trees themselves in their search for something to stay the craving of hunger. In some places the path was blocked with the branches and creepers they had torn down in their search for food, and it was only when Señors Tizon and O'Donnell assured me that this was done by "Señor Normand's Indians" in their hungry desperation that I could believe it was not the work of wild animals.

Indians were frequently flogged to death. . . . Deaths due to flogging generally ensued some days afterwards, and not always in the station where the lash had been applied, but on the way home to the unfortunate's dwelling place. In many cases where men or women had been so cruelly flogged that the wounds putrefied, the victims were shot. . . . Salt and water would be sometimes applied to these wounds, but in many cases a fatal flogging was not attended even by this poor effort at healing, and the victim—"with maggots in the flesh"—was turned adrift to die in the forest or was shot and the corpse burned or buried, or often enough thrown into the bush near the station houses.

At one station . . . I was informed by a British subject, who had himself flogged the Indians, that he had seen mothers flogged on account of shortage of rubber by their little sons. These boys were held to be too small to chastise, and so while the little boy stood terrified and crying at the sight, his mother would be beaten "just a few strokes" to make him into a better worker.

FOUR O'CLOCK SIGNAL

The revolutionary movements were spreading over Latin America as inexorably as the independence fires had spread one hundred years earlier. And already, the concrete of the needed new principles that could eventually solidify those movements—within the countries and even beyond the national borders—was being mixed.

Out of the fresh and positive concern for the plight of the increasingly harassed "underdog," out of the growing awareness that only violence could spring from that condition unless the finger of guidance was raised, the new ideologies of the times were rising to the surface in every country of the world. The new social philosophies establishing the right of working men and women and their families to a better life was sweeping over Europe and, like the ideas of the revolutionary Age of Reason before them—which had been concerned mainly with political rather than economic change—were speeding to the rest of the world:

To the Near and the Middle and the Far East. To Czarist Russia, where the rumble of protest from the oppressed would soon turn to thunder. To Spain, the gateway to Africa and the bridge to Latin America. To the United States, the factory for all the Americas, came the raw materials of the new social philosophies, challenging the foundations of the old order.

To every country in Latin America, from the United States and directly from Europe, went the finished products of the ideas that were beginning to change the world: the revolutionary socialism of Marx and the anarchism of Bakunin, the reformism of Pope Leo XIII and the militant trade unionism of larger and larger numbers of working people everywhere, even if the price was death and martyrdom, as the Haymarket victims in Chicago had found.

No aura of peace surrounded the preaching and the efforts to put the new theories of more just government and saner life into practice. In Latin America, the people's widening struggle to achieve control over their national economies—as the only sure guarantee of their political sovereignty—was fought on every hand. It was fought by the foreign interests controlling those economies. It was fought by the caudillos, emboldened with foreign bribes in the form of loans and fees and magic-working favors.

In Venezuela, where United States oil interests held an iron grip on the land, the people's efforts to achieve simple national hegemony were fought by one of the most bloodthirsty caudillos Latin America had ever known—the tyrant called Gómez. Still, the effort toward freedom had to be made. Again and again, the signal to strike had to be given:

And now our last preparations were being made. It had been agreed that Colonel X was to seize the police headquarters and, acting in liaison with the group who were to take possession of the automobiles that were in the public garages, patrol the city and concentrate reserve bodies of troops in the suburbs. These would act in cooperation with General

José Pocaterra: The Memoirs of a Venezuelan Revolutionist

Y . . . who was to surprise La Guaira, where his arrival was already expected and which would give him the control of the harbor. In the meanwhile, General Roberto González, commanding a group of a hundred men, was to arrest Marquez Bustillos, acting President at Dos Caminos. Bustillos, in view of the change in the situation, would be forced to sign the proclamation which would be placed before him, and at the same time announce his resignation.

As for the troops garrisoned at Caracas, they, having been assembled in the courtyards of the respective barracks, and the leaders who sympathized with the Gómez regime having been arrested, the rest were to proclaim the formation of a national civic union. Keeping the same staffs of officers and reinforcing the regular troops with the volunteers from Caracas, a few leaders would be enough to raise the necessary forces to combat Gómez in the valleys of Aragua.

It would be impossible for the latter to attack us for at least three days. By that time we would have been able to reach an understanding with the provinces of Carabobo, Lara, and Falcón. We did not count on the support of Miranda. The other provinces knew what was going on and were too far away to be able to interfere in any way. Moreover, by driving forward along the Tachira, Arauca, and the eastern seacoast, one energetic push would be sufficient. . . .

It had been agreed that a volley fired at four o'clock in the morning in the courtyard of the San Carlos barracks, situated just north of Caracas, should be the signal which would set the vast machine in motion.

One of those present took up the enormous parcel of proclamations which were to be stuck on the walls. Another distributed a few weapons. When I left the meeting-place, only two of my companions remained crouching in the courtyard. Their eyes were fixed on the stars. I went down towards the Grand Hotel in order to change my clothes, take a little rest, and see to certain private papers that I had in my room.

On my way there an automobile filled with policemen passed me. It was going south. I stepped aside, retreating into the shadow cast by a gateway at the corner of Pajaritos. The strange car passed out of sight.

My watch said half-past two. All precautions had been taken. The lines of the web were in telephonic contact with two outlying posts equidistant from the center. No matter what unlooked-for incident might occur, nothing, at this eleventh hour, could interrupt the execution of our plans. The only thing it might do would be to modify them. And in every case, two plans of campaign had been worked out to meet every possible emergency.

I only remained in my room a few moments. Leaving the hotel, I hired a broken-down old carriage, one of those vehicles whose coachman is always asleep. In it I drove by the Mamey barracks and the one situated at the Planta Eléctrica del Pariaso, then on past the long, gloomy, yellow wall of the Rotonde facing the esplanade, in front of which two sentinels walked up and down. Everything was quiet. I left the carriage and strolled up, by way of San Francisco, to the square beside the entrance to the Police Headquarters, smoking as I did so.

There, under a little tree, stood two men—the head of the local police, Pedro García, and the Prefect. I thought they had recognized me. A few moments later I felt I was being followed. Two police spies were walking behind me, quite casually humming a tune as they came along. Considering that it was late for an arrest to take place, I did not worry, but went over to a newsstand and bought a package of cigarettes. After which, without hurrying in the least, I returned to my hotel. The spies went off convinced that I was going to bed.

I went out an hour later and walked towards the Place du Pantheon.

San Carlos barracks, also known as La Trinidad, is a couple of dozen yards away. I sat down in the shelter of a tree, facing the clock which dominates the square. How slowly, how desperately slowly the hand moved. Half-past three, a quarter to four, seven minutes to four. Four o'clock. Slowly the four strokes sounded over the silent park. The Avila loomed like a shadow out of the mist. The lights grew dim. A forewarning of dawn stole over the sky.

The volley which at four o'clock was to wake the city and the nation had not been fired.

Something had gone wrong. The shape of the Pantheon, with its ugly outline like an unsightly church, showed itself in the growing light.

What had happened to Captain Andrade Mora and the officers of Trinidad barracks?

Never—not the time I was shipwrecked, nor a little later on when I lay waiting for death in my prison cell, nor during the long nights of anguish and terror which lay before me—did I feel an agony comparable with that which flooded my being at this instant.

BREAD BARONS

Out of the effort and out of the agony, out of the rending of the old ideas and the old orders, and out of the clinging-together of the forward-moving principles and the men who were shouting and fighting for them, a new social pattern was emerging in Latin America.

In some of the countries, groups of native industrialists and other entrepreneurs were beginning to appear as a strong challenge to the power still wielded by foreign banks and foreign business and the foreign governments behind them. This was true in Mexico. It was even truer in Argentina where the new prosperity, engendered by the Allies' need for food in the war against Imperial Germany and the other Central Powers, was already creating a formidable group of native business monopolists:

The outbreak of the Great War was the cause of considerable disturbance in the commercial relations of the republic. . . . The situation of the country outside the sphere of direct action led the majority to prophesy that of all lands the Argentine Republic was to be exceptionally favored. It was universally accepted that the chief articles in demand would be articles of food—and wheat *A Report on Grain Growers'* and meat being the staple exports of the re-*Grievances in the Argentine. 1919* public, they would be called into greater demand, and this would mean increased prices, enlarged areas under cultivation, eventually heavy profits, with considerable increase in the wealth of the country at large, and in particular for the farmers. In short, an era of great national prosperity seemed certain.

There is no denying that generally speaking these premises have proved correct. We have seen an unparalleled increase of prices accompanied by an increment in the value of the articles from the first stages of production . . . remarkable total value in exports . . . the rise of a considerable national industry. . . .

General prosperity has undoubtedly characterized the country's history throughout the period of the European war. Gold . . . has flowed into the country's coffers as never before. We have established a new era in political finance, selling our produce on easy terms of payment.

We have given credit instead of soliciting it. A new precedent in business has been set. The inhabitants of the Argentine Republic may well be proud. . . .

But . . . the interests of the nation as a whole are that its products shall obtain a fair return. . . . It would be idle to suppose that the solution of this problem will engage the serious attention of the small clique who control the export in cereals. . . . This aggregation of capital has been so skilfully engineered that it constitutes a growing evil and a monopoly of almost unlimited powers, and also of almost unlimited resources. . . .

It is perfectly clear that the introduction of methods likely to foster competition and afford relief to the grower from the present usurious and iniquitous system in vogue will meet with the most strenuous opposition of the daring few and skillful monopolists who now subordinate all other interests to theirs. The producer is absolutely at their mercy, and even the big railroads must bow to their dictum.

This, however, is but a particle—their powers are without limitation. Not only the cereal market, but the freight and exchange markets they manipulate and swing to suit themselves by their gold imports and operations. . . . Woe betide any little trader who crosses their path, or any enterprising cereal or ship broker who has the temerity to arouse their cupidity. . . . "War to the knife" is the motto of this little band of highwaymen. . . .

The wealth of Argentina is in the hands of some three or four firms—and absolutely at their mercy.

BANANA RULE

As the pattern of Latin American life changed, so did the struggle for greater political and economic freedom assume newer and more dynamic forms. The continuing fight against the continuing native tyrannies—against Gómez in Venezuela, against Machado in Cuba, against Leguía in Peru—was also a fight of the peasants for land, of the growing numbers of industrial workers for better wages and better hours, of all the people for education and for health. It was a fight for the security of men and women and children. And it was a fight for national hegemony over their land and over the real and potential wealth in agriculture and industry that might be drawn from that land.

THE SOUTHERN AMERICAS

was inevitably, therefore, also a fight for the freedom to discuss and determine the ways and means that might afford a solution to those problems for the general welfare of the nation and its people.

In this fight, the opposition to the people was no longer confined to the native tiranzuelos, or petty tyrants, or to the military, the landowners, and the high clerics that supported the caudillo tyrants. More and more often, the people's chief opposition was a British or American company operating in a given field of agriculture or industry in which it held a monopoly and which enabled it, for all practical purposes, to control and sometimes even run the national affairs of the country.

The age of the buccaneers was over. But even influential members of government and owners of newspapers in these countries were not safe from the new scourge represented by such large monopolies as the American company known as United Fruit. For the rule in the "banana republics" was as ruthless in its own way as the methods employed by the earlier corsairs of the same Caribbean. And woe to the men who stood in the way of the company's demands for an additional port or for other concessions!

Woe to the men like Dr. Eduardo Aguirre Velásquez of Guatemala, who put his country's interest before the company's demand:

When I discussed with Mr. Wilson my observations on the contract for the Pacific port . . . he remarked that due to our friendship I should not oppose the project. I considered the remark as a mere casual one, thinking that he was sincere in referring to our personal relations—one of his references having been to my acceptance of an invitation to dinner in his house, in company with Mrs. Wilson and Mrs. Aguirre (my wife). I dispassionately replied that I was sorry to have to say that my position as a government official placed obligations on me that were superior to any other considerations.

Dr. Eduardo Aguirre Reveals an Attempt to Intimidate Him

I could not interpret Mr. Wilson's ambiguous expression when a Cabinet member—but it became very clear to me upon the transfer of my note from the bank to an employee of the fruit company, when I was merely the *jefe político* of Sacatepéquez.

I would have liked to settle this account at once. But I found it impossible to obtain the money from any source. The Anglo-South

American Bank—that had recently advanced $2000 when I applied for it—now advised me through its manager that orders had been received from the London office not to extend further credit under any circumstance. Then I called on Mr. Wilson, asking him to accept the press machinery involved in the debt as a security, as I did not care by any means to continue this tie-up with the fruit company, although this tie-up had been secured from me through a—what do you call it?—trick or intrigue. The reader may perhaps find the right name for it.

What steps were then taken by the fruit company, or by Mr. Wilson, to be more exact?

He went to Ubico, then the President—whom the *Excelsior* (my paper) criticized daily—and combined to force settlement of the claim. But it was not the fruit company that did the collecting—that was done by a José María Grajeda, a baker whose house had been sold at auction because of his inability to settle a small debt, and who consequently did not have money to take over my loan, as he appears to have done.

The loan note contained a clause under which the bank—later the fruit company, through its employee—could at any time demand settlement.

One afternoon there appeared the secretary of the Civil Judge, with a retinue of police, a receiver, some secret police, etc. By authority of the new holder of the note they demanded payment from me—and when I said I could not meet it, they began to take an inventory.

In spite of the duress and the coercion, in the face of persecution and imprisonment, and regardless of banishment or death, throughout Latin America the fight for the new social rights moved forward.

At first the fight centered around the need for internal national reforms. As early as 1888, the Brazilians, for instance, had demanded and won an end to slavery and, one year later, an end to the monarchy as well. But little by little, notwithstanding the strengthening of republicanism everywhere in Latin America, the domestic social issues were found to be indissolubly joined to the larger problem of foreign economic domination.

It was becoming more and more difficult for the people of the Latin American republics to obtain their own internal political and economic and even cultural freedoms without breaking or at least radically loosening the hold exerted on their economies and on their very governments

by the powerful American and British banks and industrial monopolies
—by Electric Bond and Share in Cuba, by the Guggenheim copper interests in Chile, by Standard Oil and Royal Dutch Shell in Mexico
and Venezuela, by British railway companies in Argentina and American
fruit and steamship companies in Central America. By the Bank of England and the National City and Chase National Banks of the United
States—and by scores of other American and British industrial and business corporations, banking and insurance and engineering firms, with
hundreds and even thousands of agents and representatives scattered
over the growing cities of Buenos Aires, largest in Latin America, and
Rio de Janeiro and Mexico City and Lima and Santiago and Havana and
all the other multiplying and expanding cities and towns and even
villages of all the other American countries.

To protect the widespread interests of American big business against
the spreading movements for social reform throughout Latin America,
the United States Government was already beginning to intervene in the
internal affairs of those countries to a degree and in a manner scarcely
dreamed of before.

In Haiti, in Santo Domingo, in Nicaragua—the affairs of the nation
and the everyday fate of the people came under the direct control of the
United States Marines. Along the Mexican border and into the interior
of the country, American troops pursued the revolutionary forces of
Francisco Villa who had dared to defy the authority of American oil and
other propertied interests in his awakening country. And soon, in the
great continent of South America itself, which had hitherto been more
or less of a British economic bailiwick, diplomatic pressure from Washington became bolder and more blatant—opening the way to further
waves of armed violence, with British and American interests backing
opposing sides.

As a result, the sporadic and recurrent skirmishing for social rights in
all the countries of Latin America, by the very force of opposition within
and without those countries' borders, was fast merging into a single and
protracted struggle—far more complex and higher in aspiration than the
merging of the independence battles a hundred years earlier.

In Haiti, the cacaeus, or native guerrillas, fought the American invaders with gun and with knife as their ancestors had fought Napoleon's men a century before. In Santo Domingo the people fought back.

In Nicaragua, leaders like Augusto Sandino arose to face the mighty intruder with meager but determined handfuls of men in the thick of the tropical jungle. And by this time—leagues against the "Colossus of the North" were formed among the thickening ranks of organized labor and armed peasants and angry students in the universities and preparatory schools all over Latin America. And even the small but growing groups of native business and professional men—lawyers and doctors and engineers—joined their voices to the deepening roar of "Hands Off Nicaragua!" and "Down With Yankee Imperialism!" that startled the hemisphere all the way from Fuegia up to that city, on the very border facing the aggressor, named Juárez after an earlier man of liberation.

This was the period of prohibition and flappers and Teapot Dome and other graft without precedent in the United States, the period known as the "roaring 'twenties." There was plenty of roaring in the southern Americas, too, at this time—but the noise was of a somewhat different kind. And the message and the meaning of that roar were there for all who cared or dared to hear it:

The meaning and the message were there, not only in the armed resistance of the guerrillas in the green Haitian hills, and of Sandino and his men in the dark jungles of Nicaragua—but also in the new institutions of discussion and learning that were springing up over the length and breadth of Latin America. The meaning was there in the collective bodies of industrial workers and students beginning to merge their strength with the vast numbers of peasants throughout those agrarian lands. The message was there in Mexico's radical new Constitution of 1917, which the new governments of Mexico were finally undertaking to put into effect.

Above all, the message as well as the meaning were there in the initial flowering of a new social philosophy, a new education, a new art and architecture, a new literature, in all the countries, big and small, that formed part of the great family of nations known as Latin America. A new continental unity was being born in the popularity of the earlier philosophical writings of the Uruguayan Enrique Rodó and of the earlier poetry of the Nicaraguan genius, Rubén Darío.

A new and shining unity among the people of Latin America was coming to life—in the essays of the revolutionary critic of Peru, José Mariátegui, and in the social novels by Eustasio Rivera of Colombia and

Rómulo Gallegos of Venezuela and Jorge Icaza of Ecuador. In the music of Heitor Villa-Lobos, the Brazilian. In the paintings of the Mexican titans of contemporary art—Siqueiros, Rivera, Orozco, and a score of others.

The new spirit of unity in Latin America shone like a new star through all these and a thousand other works of culture conceived and carried out by a thousand other new and promising men and women artists, scientists, educators, and even politicians and statesmen, who called themselves workers of the intellect.

The meaning of the fresh trend toward progress as well as unity was also there in the growth of textile, paper and other industries owned by native men of business, in the rise of scientific and medical institutions, such as the Brazilian Institute for the Study of Tropical Diseases, in the emergence of outstanding figures in aviation and other fields of modern science and modern technique. And the message was no less there in the swift rise of the Argentine labor movement, in the slow but steady spread of Protestantism throughout Latin America. It was there in the appearance of organizations everywhere in the hemisphere advocating friendship with the world's first socialistic state—the Union of Soviet Socialist Republics.

Both the message and the meaning were clearly there as the 'twenties turned to 1930 and the students of Havana University—those who had managed to elude the dungeons or the shark-filled waters around them —led the people of Cuba in a general strike that brought the tyrant, Machado, down from his seat of power with a force of unity and decision that shook the whole hemisphere. Both the meaning and the message were already there, too, in the financial crash that all but broke the bank in Wall Street, as the roaring 'twenties vanished into the bleak horizons of the 'thirties.

But the cry of "forward!" had been launched, and the echoes were resounding across all borders and beyond all frontiers. The desire and the will to advance to new life were already planted deep in the soil of the hemisphere. And the first shoots of unity of principles and of interdependence of action were already beginning to flower.

In the face of all the old conflicts over boundaries and borders, in the face of all the new frictions caused by the changing economic circumstances of all nations and all peoples, throughout the southern Americas the first flowering of inter-dependence of thought and word and deed among the twenty Latin American republics was already there.

It was full of the promise of radiance, like the first visible rays of the rainbow, trying to break through the gray and still threatening horizons around the borders of every part of the world. It was trying to break through the world depression, and the decay and the fear that were rising from it and bringing a new storm of hatred and violence to the whole world as well as to the whole Western Hemisphere, which was now an integral part of it.

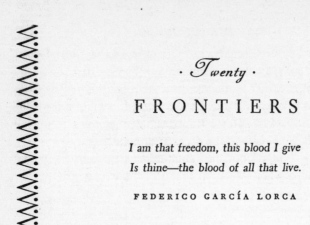

· *Twenty* ·

FRONTIERS

I am that freedom, this blood I give
Is thine—the blood of all that live.

FEDERICO GARCÍA LORCA

THIRST IN THE CHACO

While the fresh spirit of inter-dependence among the twenty republics of the southern Americas sought new strength in the recognition and extension of common social and cultural bonds, foreign monopoly interests continued to view those countries as their colonial or semicolonial domain. While the Latin American people groped their way toward nationhood and toward a new solidarity based on their common traditions of culture and growth and on their common aspirations toward greater economic freedom and wider political sovereignty and fuller social benefits, United States and British big-business interests were heaping the coals of provocation and distrust and rivalry on the old and dying fires of friction among those countries and their peoples.

The foreign monopolists, enjoying the tacit and sometimes open support of their governments, were determined to crush the incipient flower of Latin American unity before it could reach full bloom.

While the governments of the Latin American republics and the United States met in solemn sessions of the Pan-American Union, which had been established several decades before—in the interests of hemisphere unity and peace—down in the rich oil lands of the Chaco, in the very heart of South America, a bloody war of conquest was launched on the dark, foreboding wave of the world depression.

On the surface, the war was being fought between the two countries which laid claim to the precious strip of more or less barren land, hiding a treasure in oil and known as the Gran Chaco, which lay between them. On the surface, the new war without mercy was being waged between two of the weakest and most vulnerable countries of South America: between Bolivia—landlocked and preyed upon since its defeats, decades before, at the hands of the stronger nations of the continent—and Paraguay, which had also been all but exterminated in previous wars against the South American major powers.

But the real antagonists battling over the Chaco were not Bolivia and Paraguay, or the stronger South American nations backing one side or the other. The real antagonists were the two great rivals for the control of the world's oil. The war was really being fought between Standard Oil of the United States, and Royal Dutch Shell of Great Britain—and the real issue was their thirst for oil. But to the men of Bolivia and the men of Paraguay who were doing the fighting and dying, thirst in the Chaco had a different meaning:

We have attacked, the enemy has counter-attacked—and has just been beaten back. There is no firing for the moment. In the tangled brush lie the corpses of Bolivians and Paraguayans piled upon each other. Machine guns, hand grenades, daggers, and rifle butts have all had their say, leaving the fields to the dead: bodies pinned to the ground by steel yataghans, faces smashed by rifle butts. Corpses, tree trunks, leaves, the soil; everything is stained a dark red. Sergeant Candia is lying with a yataghan stuck through his throat. What was once his face is turned skyward: tongue out, eyes mashed to a pulp, nose shattered. On top of his body are the corpses of three Bolivians, their bellies ripped open by the Sergeant's dagger.

The Story of a Combatant, by Arnaldo Valdovinos. 1934

From the fields and brush come the groans of the wounded. The soil clings to torn flesh and bones. Piercing cries, echoing across the belly of the mountainside, seem to thunder at me from every corner of hell.

"Water, lieutenant!"

"Kill me, lieutenant—for the love of God, kill me."

All around me: the shrieking of the badly wounded, begging me to kill them. So many wounded, and so few stretcher bearers.

The sun burns down on us pitilessly, and the water canteens are empty. To breathe the thin mountain air becomes more and more difficult; it is impossible to fill one's lungs with sufficient oxygen. On top of this, the heavy stench of sweat and blood has never been so nauseating. Some of the thirsty men are growing violent, shouting filthy insults at everyone. Others are on their knees, whimpering like beggars:

"Water water water water water water water—"

Suddenly a fellow officer hits upon an idea. Grabbing up a few canteens, he asks the soldiers to urinate in them. He insists, however, that certain scruples of hygiene must be observed—so men suffering from disease are disqualified.

The canteens are soon filled. Opening his knapsack, the officer draws out a small bundle of herbs, then another containing sugar. He drops an equal amount of herbs and sugar into every canteen. Now, one after another, the canteens are shaken—with elaborate flourishes. When ready, serve in a tin can.

Before long the canteens are empty, and many of our wounded haven't had a sip.

Meanwhile, the field is being cleared as quickly as possible. But this is dangerous business: from the brush nearby, the enemy blasts away with deadly fire every time we make the slightest move.

"Son of a bitch!" I cry to no one in particular. On every side of me our wounded are dying, their parched tongues jutting stiffly from wide-open, gasping mouths. In a few moments the messenger whom I have dispatched to our sadistic captain with a request for water comes crawling back.

"Captain Reinoso is dead," he whispers. "Shot in the back, four bullets—by our own."

And he hands me a note from the Comandante. . . . The message is interesting to me only because of the promise that water is being sent. I hasten to inform the men of this. But so many are already dead or dying. Others are raving, delirious.

The rest are busy stripping their comrades' bodies, in a frenzied search for valuable rings and gold teeth. There is no time to ascertain whether a man is dead or wounded. The minute an open mouth reveals a gold tooth or filling, the prize jaw is smashed by a well-aimed rifle butt and the gold extracted in a hurry. These operations are carried out in silence.

Suddenly the grim quiet is broken by a burst of brutal jibes aimed at the wretched men, who only a few moments earlier were living comrades. One badly wounded man clutches at the ankles of a soldier standing over him, and begs:

"A little water, brother—just a sip, brother—"

"Too bad, old boy," is the reply in native Paraguayan, "you won't get to enjoy any more of the warm herb—"

"Nope," adds the soldier beside him, grinning malevolently, "*ne mahína cué chembaerá*—from now on your girl friend is for me."

"Stop firing—you scabs!" shouts a voice from the enemy lines, scarcely thirty-seven yards away. "Can't you see it's supper time?"

"Here goes your supper—!" is the reply from one of my machine-gunners as he directs his fire at the hungry Bolivian's voice.

Then there is quiet.

Silence spreads over the entire front. It is nightfall. And there is the sky offering the aloof beauty of its stars, splaying their light over the cleared, gutted mountainsides and the soil charged with the fury of cannon thunder momentarily hushed. And there are shadows: moist, saturated with the sickening stench of rotting human bodies, a stench from which there is no escape—as though it were part of one's nostrils.

Fighting has been steady all day; but now, thanks to general fatigue, a brief—and unofficial—respite has been declared. From time to time, scattered firing breaks out on both sides. It never lasts long, but it is enough to keep one awake.

After a series of advances, we have won this new position near the enemy's lines. With the aid of a sharp-pointed steel *yataghan* and an ordinary spoon, each of us has fashioned his own shallow, coffin-shaped dugout. There we lie, watchful. Those close enough to each other's dugouts take turns watching and sleeping.

At intervals the heavy sleepers among us open fire in order to stay awake. Then there is a brief exchange of shots, and once more quiet takes over. During the lulls, jibes and insults are tossed back and forth between the enemy lines:

"Hey there, you Bolivian bastards, your ribs show through from here!"

"You Paraguayan pimps—"

"Come on over—we'll feed you raw meat!"

Shrill, whore-like laughter, and fresh epithets and insults are exchanged in mounting crescendo—until rifles and machine guns launch a brisk fire. Five minutes later, silence breaks through again, only to be stabbed the next instant by new cries, more obscene diatribe. Gradually, from every sector of our lines, the name of the Bolivians' military leader,

Kundt—the name we Paraguayans have learned to hate above all others
—begins to resound like the barking of a thousand dogs:

"Kundt! Kundt! Kundt!"

Kundt, Salamanca, Ayala, Casado, Standard Oil, the Paraguay River,
and Titicaca Lake—all the real and imaginary issues of the war, jumbled
into incoherent confusion—are springboards for a fresh abundance of
vile epithets. In the midst of this verbal chaos, officers on both sides
soon introduce a *leit motif* with shouts of *status quo*, Soler-Pinilla,
utiposeditis, parallels, meridians, all of which no one understands.

Finally the debate is reduced to two individuals. The speaker for the
affirmative begins to interpret Paraguay's claims to the Chaco territory.
Suddenly his carefully phrased legal terminology is cut short by the impatient, categorical bark of a machine gun from his opponent's side.
What—no more words left? Well then, back to bullets! And again rifles
and machine guns go into action.

A few moments of savage unburdening—and once more there is calm
and silence and the night.

"The goddamned imbeciles!" I mutter to my friend and former school-
mate beside me. "Arguing about legal claims across a field covered with
corpses—"

He does not answer. I turn to him with some trifling remark. He is
still silent, his position unchanged. "Say, you certainly can sleep," I
whisper—more to myself than to him—as I reach out a hand to wake
him.

Something wet and warm causes me to draw my hand away instinctively. It is blood. I scarcely have time to realize that my friend is dead,
killed during the "debate," when a soldier creeps up to me with a note
in his hand.

"From the *Comandante*," he mumbles. . . .

I unfold it, lay it on the floor of my dugout, and in the faint glow
from my pocket flashlight, read it. . . . I crush the piece of paper in my
fist, and turn over. Lying on my back in my coffin-like dugout, bitter,
questioning, I look up at the clear night sky—and I see no answer there.

A LEGATION IS SACKED

*The answer was not to be seen in the sky—or in any other part of the
giant American landscapes. But the answer was there to be seen and
understood by any and all who were not afraid to look—at the fast-*

spreading growth of foreign monopoly holdings over the land, at the new undeclared war that was being fought between the two great world powers bent on winning complete mastery over the oil and the other wealth and all the other resources in materials and purchasing power of the southern American republics.

The reply was discernible in the intense struggle for markets and raw materials, especially in the South American continent, between the United States and Great Britain. It was perceptible, too, in the recurrent eruptions of new controversies and frictions over frontiers between the Latin American countries—fearful of the spread of the financial power of the "Colossus of the North," or, clinging to the other extreme, declaring their eagerness to serve that power, through one of their own petty tyrants, even to the jeopardy of a neighboring state.

The answer to the rising flood of ill-will among neighbors and neighboring states was also to be found in the birth of the new ultra-nationalist movements everywhere which were being used to oppose and combat the spread of socialist and democratic programs of principles over the hemisphere and over the world. The reply was there in the ominous appearance of a new type of caudillo espousing those ultra-nationalist aims in Salvador and Nicaragua and the Dominican Republic and even in Brazil and Argentina and other countries of the Western Hemisphere.

And the answer was already written in dark and menacing letters in the revival of the old aggressiveness of the Peruvian militarists against their neighbors—against Ecuador later, against Colombia now:

At about eight-thirty o'clock on the night of Saturday, the 18th, a Peruvian citizen and public officer called at the Legation and told the Colombian Minister that he had knowledge of the fact that the Ministry of Government and the Municipality of Lima were organizing, through the secret police and the Sánchez Cerro clubs, an assault upon the Colombian Legation that would be carried out *A Note from the Minister of Foreign Affairs of Colombia* as a result of the reading of a patriotic address that the President of Peru was going to deliver over the radio that evening. The Colombian Minister called His Excellency, the Papal Nuncio, on the telephone, advised him of the possible assault and asked him, if he found it in order, to speak to the Peruvian Government about the matter. The Nuncio talked with the Government and was told that there was not the least danger of an assault, but that, anyway, all measures had been taken to prevent it and to protect the Legation fully. The Nuncio so advised the Minister of Colombia by telephone.

A little before ten o'clock that night (of February 18), when the reading of the President's proclamation was finished, a small rabble appeared in front of the Legation, burst out in shouts, insults and threats, and commenced stoning the building, breaking window panes and frames, without the six or eight armed policemen who were on duty making the least sign of interference to stop it.

The Colombian Legation was situated on the Avenida Chorrillos of the Balneario (Bathing Resort) de Barranco . . . in the principal and highest class residential section of the locality—and only a few blocks away from the office of the Police Commissioner and the Military Academy, where there are more than a thousand armed men.

When the attack became more intense and the mob invaded the building, the Colombian Minister called the office of the Police Commissioner and the Military Academy on the telephone, advised what was going on and asked for protection, and was told that it would be sent immediately.

He called the Nuncio—and as he was told that the latter had gone to a reception at the Italian Club, he called the Venezuelan Minister and asked him to find the Nuncio and tell him what was occurring. The Venezuelan Minister did so. The Nuncio spoke to Foreign Minister Manzanilla and the latter reiterated the assurances of having taken and continuing to take all the precautions to protect the Legation of Colombia.

In the meantime the mob had invaded the building and commenced a vandalic and shameless pillage. The Minister, his wife and daughter who was confined to her bed by illness, took refuge in a room on the lower floor of the house. At the end of about an hour, the fury of the rabble subsided and the Minister was able to take his wife and daughter to a house nearby. He returned to the telephone but the lines were tapped by the police; he was unable to obtain connection with the American Embassy; and with the Chilean Embassy, as soon as he commenced to talk he was cut off.

At this moment, a much larger mob than the first one, which came from Lima and Callao and had been carried in automobiles, trucks and express tramcars, arrived and intensified the pillage and destruction to extremes that seem incredible.

The Minister again took refuge in the lower floor, and from the window witnessed the scenes of destruction that took place until two o'clock in the morning—at which time a detachment of the Guardia Republicana (Republican Guard) arrived and the Legation building was already a despoiled ruin, illuminated by the flames from burning furniture, doors, windows and everything that on account of its nature or size could not be plundered.

The authorities then entered to offer guarantees to the Minister. The prefect . . . insisted on the Minister allowing him to accompany him somewhere, pointing out that the house was destroyed and also flooded, dark and unsafe, since it had neither doors nor windows and that even the iron gratings that separated the garden from the street had been torn off. The Minister repeatedly asked to be excused—for it was his intention to remain in the Legation—but he finally acceded to being accompanied to see his wife and daughter at the Chilean Embassy, where they had been taken by the family that had first given them shelter. . . .

The rabble was in possession of the Legation for nearly five hours without anyone opposing it. The material losses . . . are extremely large. The various furniture, picture, mirrors, *objets d'art*, table service, glassware, antiques and collections; the jewelry of the Minister's wife; the clothing of all the occupants of the house; the Legation library and the Minister's private library; documents of great importance to the history of America, such as the originals of two unpublished manuscripts concerning the liberating work of Colombia, were broken or torn to pieces, burned or plundered by the rabble.

Two of the Legation automobiles were completely destroyed—and one of them was thrown into the ocean.

THE INCIDENT IS CLOSED

As in the days of the early caudillos, the rise of the latest type of military tyrannies, patterned after the new totalitarian dictatorships of Europe but depending for support on the United States, on the high clergy, and the large landowners, as well as a few native industrialists, meant the beginning of further acts of aggression across the Latin American borders. It meant the vengeful settling of age-old scores against neighboring states, and against minority groups within the aggressors' borders: It meant the massacre, in one long night of terror, of thousands of innocent Haitian men, women, and children along the Dominican-Haitian border. And the Dominican dictator, Trujillo—General Rafael Leonidas Trujillo, who placed his name alongside that of God—brazenly sought to quiet the storm of protest over the mass slaughter of Haitian peasants and their families by declaring the matter closed:

In view of the importance given by the press to the incident that took place in the month of October last, on the Dominican-Haitian border, between Dominican landowners and Haitian citizens, I have deemed it necessary to make the following statements: This incident is similar to others which have taken place in the past, in various points along the border, as a consequence of the irregular pene-

A Statement by the Dominican Minister in Washington. 1937

tration of Haitian elements into Dominican territory, and of the justified alarm of agriculturists and cattle ranchers of the Dominican Republic in those sections —who only entertain the legitimate aspiration of working in peace and with due guarantees for security of the fruits of their labor.

The statements of the Secretary of State for Foreign Affairs of the Republic of Haiti, Mr. Leger, which undoubtedly have been misinterpreted, have contributed to attach to the incident in question a character which it does not possess. Likewise, they have facilitated the description of the incident in a manner which is wholly apart from the truth of the facts.

There were bloody clashes between Haitian citizens determined to maintain an illegal residence in Dominican territory, and Dominican landowners interested in defending their properties and the fruit of their labors. The so-called collective slayings, which have been mentioned by the press, are wholly absurd. . . .

The Dominican Government considers the incident as closed.

ITS ALMONDS ARE FAMOUS

While arch-nationalism was spreading over Latin America, and the friction over boundaries and frontiers was growing sharper, throughout the world the lines of a coming global conflict were being drawn tighter and tighter:

In Manchuria and China and the South Seas, the determined Empire of Japan was threatening the old control from the West. In Africa, hordes of Italians sent by the dictator, Mussolini, were sweeping over the ancient land of Ethiopia in preparation for further conquest in more vital and more strategic areas of the world. And in the new German state, the most sinister force of them all, the force of Nazism in the person of Adolf Hitler, was already rising to menace the world with fire and poison unparalleled.

But the new challenge against the domination of England and the United States and their allies over the world, was more than a challenge for economic supremacy this time. It was a challenge of the new, tyrannical credo of fascism against the very foundations of democratic thought, against the very structure of all principle and action aimed at achieving and insuring security along with freedom for all people:

Under the guise of an anti-Communist agreement, the three main challenging powers—Japan and Germany and Italy—and their willing and unwilling allies over the world had created a twentieth-century version of the old Holy Alliance. Under the guise of the Anti-Comintern Pact, the three fascist governments formed an Axis whose policy and propaganda were presumably directed against the Union of Soviet Socialist Republics and against the growth of communism everywhere. But the real function of the Axis was something else:

The real, fanatical aim of the Axis was the overthrow and utter extinction of all forms of democracy and republicanism—now gasping for breath in the tightening ring of the worst economic crisis the world had ever known.

And while the two great English-speaking powers reproved the growing aggressiveness of the Axis with a mild and vacillating finger, in the southern Americas most of the countries were preparing to take a stronger stand against the perilous influence of the Axis and its fascist credo—both of which were already beginning to threaten the internal security of those countries. The fascist threat was more than apparent now in the rising activity of new caudillos supported by the old landowning and clerical groups and by the arch-nationalist admirers of fascism—some of them in the pay of the Axis itself. The threat was more and more apparent—until it burst upon the world from the land that had been the homeland of most of the southern Americas for more than three hundred years, from the country whose culture and traditions were still a live and nourishing force in the roots of Latin American life, from Spain itself.

In July of 1936, the fascist forces of Spain, aided and armed by the Axis, rose up to overthrow the young Spanish Republic. Overnight, from all parts of Latin America, and from the rest of the hemisphere, people rallied in defense of that growing democratic republic. In spite of the opposition of their own fascist groups—some of which already held the reins of government—and in the face of the apathy and the false position of "non-intervention" adopted by the United States and England and even France, the people of Latin America, and most of the people of the United States, took their stand on the side of the beleaguered Republic of Spain.

In defiance of all the propaganda, fomented by the Axis and spread by willing as well as ignorant messengers of public opinion everywhere, charging the Spanish Republic with being communist, atheist, and a tool of Soviet Russia—the people of Latin America took their stand by the side of the people of Spain. They took their steadfast stand against the Axis invaders and the credo of destruction they preached. They sent supplies. They sent fighting volunteers—including a young and promising Cuban poet:

Pablo de la Torriente Brau, a name that would be remembered:

Pablo, the fighting poet from Cuba, writing a letter now to tell of the beauty he found time to observe in the little town of Castile where the great Cervantes was born.

Pablo de la Torriente Brau, writing home from the world's first battle-field against fascism, writing home from Spain:

Here goes another letter. The cannon bark louder than ever. It seems that our batteries have been increased considerably and that they have orders to do a little destructive work. There is plenty of booming from the other side as well. I have just arrived from Pozuelo de Alarcon, a tiny town with twisted and climbing streets and whites houses with blue mosaic bases jutting from their thick brick walls. Until last night the battalion was there, and now when I managed to rejoin it they have transferred us to Alcalá de Henares, the city where Cervantes was born. At this rate I will soon have covered half of Spain.

A Letter from Spain by Pablo de la Torriente Brau. 1936

The other day an insolent squadron of fifteen Italian tri-motors, accompanied by pursuit planes, flew over Madrid early in the day and unloaded in a brutal, pitiless manner. These dogs are murdering more women and children in Madrid than men on the front. In the crowded workers' neighborhood, Cuatro Caminos, the bombs smashed streetcars full of people. It was an especially hard day at several points along the Madrid front. The Frenchman's Bridge, where the enemy started a desperate attack, had to be blown up. Their tactic hasn't changed, and as a matter of fact, it cannot very well be changed. No other road is open to them but to capture Madrid, and they won't be able to do that.

Despite the deficiencies of our infant military apparatus, despite a harmful inactivity on other fronts at a moment when there should be greater pressure from our forces, they won't enter. Moreover, they may soon have to flee. Our aviation is wrecking their bases and their planes on a large scale. But they always restore these; their planes fly directly from Germany and Italy . . .

The indebtedness of the Spanish fascists to Germany and Italy is growing alarmingly. It may become so huge that there will be no solution but an international war.

How the artillery is thundering! It's worth listening to, if only once in a lifetime. It's like a tempest of thunder and lightning in the mountains of Oriente in Cuba.

Their aviation, which has shown itself to be inferior to ours in close fighting, does not tire of acts of vandalism which defy description. Last night, after a thrilling beating which they had received during the afternoon from our machines, their planes appeared and threw incendiary bombs on the city. In the blackness of the night, there arose over the horizon, out towards the Casa de Campo, the glare of the fire they had caused. A hospital was also bombarded. Such are the methods of their desperation.

Every time I feel their cannon closer to Madrid, I fancy ours closer to Seville and Burgos.

I suppose that the international press has mentioned something about their most recent bestiality. They dropped a box by parachute over Madrid containing the horribly cut-up body of one of our aviators who had fallen behind their lines. Not even the cannibal tribes would do this —they are not exhibitionists of barbarism.

On our side, General Miaja, head of the Defense Junta, has just issued an order that the lives of all fascist aviators who fall over Madrid be respected.

At dawn yesterday an intense shelling took place. In the neighborhood of Abascal and Quevedo Streets, the smoke and the crashes of falling buildings filled the air. Families evacuated their homes, weeping, dragging their children along and leaving the dead behind. . . .

We have our headquarters in the convent of Las Claras. Miguel de Cervantes Saavedra was born and lived in Alcalá de Henares. I have not had the time to visit his home. From our auto, I have seen that it is an ancient town with that simple dignity typical of Castile. Large buildings of old brick; elegant church towers and convents; a peaceful silence in the streets. It also has its plaza for band concerts, its original fiestas, and numerous artistic and historical treasures. They say, too, that its almonds are famous. And I can't tell you anything more of Alcalá de Henares. Someday I'll know it better.

Today has begun badly for me. They have told me that Candón, the other Cuban commandant, has died. How happy he was to tell me the other day:

"I'm going to lead the attack."

Let's hope it is not true. He wanted me to go with him. . . .

Well, I leave off here. I will write you from the land of Cervantes.

But the letter from the land of Cervantes was never written:

On the following day, the writer-that-was and the writer-to-be fell to his death before the fascist bullets in Spain. And in his fall, as in the fall of thousands of other fighters for freedom in Spain, as in the fall of the Spanish Republic in 1939, a newer and still stronger bond of unity among all the southern American republics was born.

The last vestiges of bitterness against the old Imperial Spain were gone. Spain had become a symbol of struggle and heroism, watering with its own blood the flower of Latin American freedom and inter-dependence with the rest of the torn and troubled world—the flower that could not be crushed by force or by neglect, the flower of Latin American unity that was growing toward full bloom.

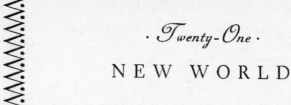

· *Twenty-One* ·

NEW WORLD

Union with the whole world—
not with one part of it,
not with one part against another.

JOSÉ MARTÍ

A FIGURE OF HOPE

The 'thirties were the grimmest years the world had known. On the heels of the Wall Street crash of 1929 came the long-drawn-out, even more cruel depression. And it spread over the earth and among most of the earth's population.

As the depression grew worse, the growing ill-will among people and society in general began to threaten the whole existing order—not only the system of capitalist economy but also the basic, dynamic principles of democratic thought and action that had little or nothing to do either with that economy or with the depression which had sprung from its agony of failure.

The credo of hate and destruction—the credo of fascism—was spreading over the whole world, dressed in a gaudy array of "shirt" movements preaching the rule of the blackjack and the culture of the concentration camp. No country in the world was quite free any longer from this newest and most ominous scourge of them all.

In Mexico there were the Gold Shirts, and in Brazil the Green Shirts or Integralistas as they called themselves—patterned after the fascist movement of Portugal that had managed to seize and hold power in the former motherland. Throughout the southern Americas the forces of fascism were rallying around the new banners of hate and the new violence whose pretended enemy was communism and the Union of

Soviet Socialist Republics, whose immediate victims were the Freemasons, the Jews, the leaders of trade-unions—but whose main target,
whose ultimate target, was the United States of America and the principles of democratic freedom for which it stood.

The 'thirties were grim. But in the midst of their grimness, in the
middle of the rising tautness and the spanning tension among individuals and social groups and entire nations, and in the face of the
world-wide challenge already being hurled by Hitler and Mussolini and
the other directors of the new doctrine of ill-will that could only resolve
itself into another war for conquest and domination—there was a figure
of hope:

There was Franklin Delano Roosevelt, President of the United States,
who knew that, first of all, much of the suffering of his countrymen—
millions of them living "ill-clothed, ill-housed, ill-fed" amid a very real
though not apparent abundance—could and must be alleviated at once,
could and must be eventually ended. And he launched the New Deal to
bring all the sense and the planning and the organization that the ailing
economic system could bear into the government and into American
life.

In the thick of the world's anxiety, in the midst of the Axis' preparations for war, in the very middle of the growing movements of hatred
sweeping over Latin America and directed toward the United States,
there was the hopeful figure of the man who walked with difficulty—
with a cane, and sometimes two, in his hands, and with ten pounds of
iron around his stricken legs—but who could never admit defeat:

Franklin D. Roosevelt, who reached the highest office in his country
a second time—as he would a third and a fourth—to launch a new and
unprecedented international policy, as he had previously launched the
domestic reform program known as the New Deal. President Roosevelt,
reelected to office in 1936 and increasingly aware of the good that had
been achieved by his bold and progressive program—domestically through
the New Deal and its measures of greater employment and security for
the people, and internationally through his recognition of the Union of
Soviet Socialist Republics, and equally through his action in ordering
the withdrawal of United States marines from Nicaragua and Haiti and
Santo Domingo.

Franklin Roosevelt, aware of the many fears that were being allayed among people everywhere because of his words and his actions, because of the persistence of his broad and humanitarian views in a time of apprehension and narrow fears. Aware of the fears that were being allayed, but also aware of the many fears that lingered and were throttling the lives of men. Aware of this danger as he planned his first stern warnings to the fascist, Axis powers, against the snarling opposition of the "economic royalists" of his own country.

F.D.R., as his people liked to call him, aware of the good that had been done, as he was aware of all that remained to be done, waiting now aboard the good ship Indianapolis in the harbor of Buenos Aires. Waiting there to welcome the Argentine president, and to inaugurate another policy that would bring further confidence and rejoicing to the hearts of millions of men and women and children the world over:

The policy that lay ahead, like a new road of new hope, with a Roosevelt who did not believe in wielding the "Big Stick" pointing the way. F.D.R.'s way—

The policy of the Good Neighbor:

At 1:40 P.M. President Agustin P. Justo of Argentina arrived on the quay to meet the President. The Indianapolis rendered passing honors as we arrived. . . . On either side of the gangway a guard of honor in immaculate uniform of blue and white was formed and made a most impressive appearance. The roofs of the nearby buildings were crowded with people. Beyond the quay building on the road *From the Log of Mr. Roose-* leading from the enclosed reservation, two hun- *velt's Trip to South America.* dred Argentine naval cadets flanked the auto- *1936* mobiles assigned to take the staffs of the two presidents to the American Embassy.

At 1:50, the President . . . left the ship. Full Presidential honors were rendered. As the President left the ship, the Argentine Marine Band played *The Star-Spangled Banner* while the guard of honor presented arms.

President Justo greeted the President warmly and after the two presidents had exchanged handclasps they embraced each other and on doing so President Justo exclaimed: "The democracy of the South embraces the democracy of the North"—this in Spanish, our President replying with warm words of thanks in English. President Justo then presented the members of his suite.

President Justo and President Roosevelt embarked in on open car while the staffs of the two presidents embarked in other cars beyond the quay. In the procession the presidential car was flanked by mounted grenadiers of the famous San Martín regiment. Motor and bicycle policemen were also close by, and Argentine secret service men ran alongside the car the entire length of the trip, some four miles, being relieved at frequent intervals.

The procession proceeded through the gate leading from the quay into the city. The order of the cars in the procession was the reverse of that normally followed. The presidents' car was last.

Beyond the quay gate, a regiment of mounted grenadiers was formed and preceded and closed the procession as it motored through the city. From the quay through the Avenues of San Martín, Santa Fe, Callao, to the end of Avenida Alvear where the Embassy of the United States is located, approximately two million Argentines packed in every conceivable point of vantage, greeted the President with wild acclaim and showered him with flowers as he passed.

Apparently no effort had been spared by the Argentine people to pay a sincere tribute to the President. The entire city was in brilliant festive garb. The famous jacaranda trees along the avenues were in full bloom. Their loveliness added greatly to the picture.

As the procession continued, the tumult grew—each square, each section of the city, and each of the regiments of armed forces seemed to vie with each other in welcoming the President. Along the route to the Embassy, twenty thousand Argentine troops with forty-three regimental bands lined the *avenidas*. As the procession passed, each regiment presented arms and the regimental band played *The Star-Spangled Banner*.

The immense throngs uncovered or saluted during these honors. It was an impressive and stirring tribute. From all reports the reception given the President by the citizens of Buenos Aires exceeded in warmth and spontaneity anything that has ever occurred in Argentina.

The day was declared a national holiday and special trains were run from all directions to bring eager visitors to the capital. The streets through which the procession passed were solidly lined with people. Windows, roofs, and balconies—all were filled with enthusiastic onlookers. American flags fluttered everywhere, and flowers were showered every few yards until the hood of the President's car was completely covered.

Upon arrival at the Embassy, President Justo of Argentina and his suite withdrew in a motor car to the Casa Rosada (Government House) where he and the members of his Cabinet and household were to receive President Roosevelt. . . .

At 4:30 the President left the Embassy to pay his respects upon the President of the Argentine Republic. . . . At the Embassy gates the procession was joined by the troop of mounted grenadiers to escort the procession to Government House. . . . Along the Avenidas Alvear, Callao, Rivadavia, and de Mayo, the Horse Guard and other Argentine troops lined the streets.

Behind the armed forces, crowds cheered and applauded as the President passed.

Upon arrival at the Casa Rosada, President Roosevelt and his party were received by President Agustin Justo of Argentina, members of his Cabinet, and his civil and military household. The presidents went to the Salon Blanco—the White Room—immediately, where they chatted quietly for fifteen minutes. . . .

During this time continuous cheering could be heard from the surrounding avenues and the Plaza de Mayo. By the time the two presidents had completed their conversation, the cheering had grown so loud that the presidents proceeded to a balcony overlooking the Plaza de Mayo and acknowledged the cheers of the crowd.

The barriers had been let down. Throngs from the nearby avenues poured into the Plaza below the balcony. Thousands upon thousands crowded in, shouting enthusiastically and waving flags, hats, and handkerchiefs.

It was mob violence—but of a most friendly sort. The strength of the people in their enthusiasm beggars description and left a lasting impression on each one of us.

OUT OF THE MEDDLING HANDS

Encouraged by the bold program of government launched by Franklin D. Roosevelt in his own country and in behalf of friendly nations and colonial and semi-colonial people everywhere, a wave of courage and courageous action was sweeping over the world. Governments were more and more concerned with the collective, key problem of strengthening the economic security, the social welfare, the political self-determination, and even the cultural aspirations of their people.

In the United States, an organization of industrial unions was formed to supplement and revivify the older federation by crafts known as the

A.F. of L., the American Federation of Labor. The new and growing organization of industrial unions was called the CIO—the Congress of Industrial Organizations.

And in Latin America and other parts of the world, similar progressive trade-union federations were bolstering not only the cause of the increasing numbers of industrial and agricultural workers and their families in those countries, but also the larger fight against fascism—along with the renewed struggle for further democratic rights and greater economic security.

Just below the Rio Grande of the North, another president of far-reaching vision and determination concluded that it was high time to take the affairs of the Mexican government and the welfare of his people out of the meddling hands of the powerful American and British oil companies—the Huasteca and the Aguila—which were subsidiaries of the giant world monopolies, Standard Oil and Royal Dutch Shell. There was only one sure way to accomplish this—and so, in 1938, President Lázaro Cárdenas of Mexico, who had long ago decided that the soil of Mexico must be returned to its people, declared the oil resources of Mexico to be the property of the nation:

How many of the villages near the oilfields possess such things as hospitals, schools, social centers, water supply, or purification plants, or athletic fields, or electric plants, even if only fed by the untold millions of cubic feet of natural gas wasted in oil operations? What center of oil activities, on the other hand, is not provided with a company police force, designed to safeguard private interests, *A Message from President* invariably selfish and occasionally unlawful? *Cárdenas on the Oil Question* Many stories are told about these organizations, whether authorized or not by the Government—stories of abuse, outrage and even murder, invariably for the benefit of the companies.

Who does not know, or is not acquainted with the irritating discrimination that governs construction and lay-out of company oil camps? Comforts of all kinds for the foreign staff; poor accommodation, misery and unhealthfulness for our nationals. Refrigeration and insect protection for the former, indifference and neglect, doctors and medicines but grudgingly supplied, for the latter; lower salaries and hard and exhausting work for our people.

All these are the abuses due to a tolerance that grew up under cover of ignorance, dereliction of duty and weakness on the part of the Nation's rulers, we admit. But the machinery was set in motion by investors lacking moral qualities sufficient to induce them to give something in exchange for the wealth they drew from the land. . . .

Another unavoidable consequence of the power in the hands of the oil industry, strongly characterized by its anti-social tendencies, and even more harmful than all those previously mentioned, is persistent and improper interference by these companies in the politics of the Nation.

No one now argues whether or not strong rebel factions were supported by the oil companies in northern Veracruz and on the Isthmus of Tehuantepec, from 1917 to 1920—forces that fought against the constituted government.

No one is ignorant of the fact, either, that at sundry times subsequent to the years mentioned and even in our day, the oil companies have encouraged, almost openly, the ambitions of persons discontented with the administration of the Country, every time their business has in some way been affected either by taxation or the suppression of privileges theretofore enjoyed, or by the withdrawal of a tolerance they had become used to.

They have had money, arms, and munitions to support rebel bands. Money for an unpatriotic press that defends their interests. Money to enrich their unconditional defenders. But for the progress of the country, for establishing true balance by means of fair remuneration for work done, for sanitation of the districts in which they operate, or for saving from loss that enormous wealth consisting in natural gas occurring in company with petroleum in nature—for none of these has money ever been forthcoming, nor economic assistance, nor even the will to draw same from the volume of their earnings.

Nor is there money, either, to acknowledge a responsibility marked out for them by a judgment—for they hold that their economic strength and their pride shield them against the dignity and sovereignty of a nation that has with such liberality handed over to them its enormous natural resources and that cannot, by legal means, obtain satisfaction of even the most rudimentary obligations.

It therefore becomes unavoidable, as a logical consequence of this brief analysis, to take final measures, under our laws, to put an end to this never-ending state of affairs under which the country labors, its industrial progress checked by those who hold in their own hands the power to throw all obstacles in its way . . . and who . . . abuse of that economic strength to such an extent as to jeopardize the very life of the Nation that seeks to uplift its people by means of the enforcement of its own laws, by turning to account its own resources, and by freely managing its own destinies. . . .

I now call upon the Nation for moral and material support sufficient to carry out a decision so justifiable, so transcendent, and so indispensable.

SIDE BY SIDE

The world was awakening at last to the mortal danger confronting it. The advances of the new doctrines of hate in politics and public opinion, the futility and shame of the policy of appeasement of fascism as manifested in the signing and subsequent failure of the Munich Pact, and finally, the military offensives already launched by the Axis in Spain, in Austria and in Czechoslovakia, in China and even along the Siberian borders of the Soviet Union—all these developments had brought the presence and the peril of the Axis closer to the people of every land. And in Latin America as in the rest of the world, the people were waking up.

By now fascism was racing against time. But even time could be set ahead if necessary, as it had been set back for expediency's sake until now—and fortune might still continue to smile, as long as the people of the world were not fully and militantly aware of the fascist peril confronting them. And they were not yet aware and alert to the point where they could compel their governments to act swiftly in their behalf. So that fortune continued to favor the fascists:

This time, in fact, she smiled her widest smile where she had first begun the job for the fascists. She smiled her widest now where the shortsightedness of the governments of England and France and the United States was most acute and most fatal—the shortsightedness that was the hardest of all to bear in the minds and the hearts of the millions of Spanish-speaking people all over Latin America. Fortune smiled for the fascist side in Spain:

By 1939 most of the fight was gone out of the exhausted Spanish people. By April of 1939, when General Francisco Franco, the friend of Hitler and Mussolini—and their military ally in everything but official name—marched into Madrid, fascism had won a firm foothold in Spain.

The Axis could now turn its efforts confidently in another direction—and only five months later, Hitler's powerful mechanized forces rolled into Poland. The Second World War—the most cruel and most destructive war since time began—was underway.

After France and the rest of Europe were overrun, the Axis hurled its mighty armies at the people of the Soviet Union, whose strength was known only to themselves. And within the next six months—on December 7, 1941—the Japanese partner of the Axis struck a shivering blow at America's chief fortress in the Pacific. The Japanese dealt an all but mortal blow at Pearl Harbor in the Hawaiian Islands. The Axis struck at the United States.

The American people were in the war—with England and with China, with the free part of France, and with the whole Union of Soviet Socialist Republics, with all the resistance movements, all the "armies of freedom" in the Axis-occupied lands and even within the Axis countries themselves. The American people were at war against the fascist foe, and almost at once nearly all the other nations of the hemisphere rallied to the side of the nation that had proved itself a good and a friendly neighbor. With only one or two exceptions—chiefly Argentina, where fascism had already struck deep roots among the ruling cliques—the Latin American nations hastened to break relations with the Axis and even to declare war against the central powers of fascism.

One of the first countries to enter the war actively alongside the good neighbor of the north was the United States of Brazil, which sent a contingent of well-trained men to fight beside the American Fifth Army in Italy. Soon Americans and Brazilians were advancing side by side against the fascist enemy. Brazilians and Americans were winning battles together, smashing ahead together toward the Eternal City that was still held by the fascists.

And American and Brazilian boys were also lying side by side in military hospitals for the sick and the wounded:

I met Robert W. Jackson in a hospital. We were operated on on the same table by the same doctor. Jackson was in the vanguard of the American Army and had his left leg nearly crushed under a tank from his own unit. He fought in North Africa, in Sicily, at Anzio, and he would be at the Bologna front today if that accident hadn't occurred which made him unfit for service. I am in the rear echelon of the Brazilian Army and therefore I was sent to the hospital only to treat an illness. One

An Interview with a Brazilian Soldier in Italy

afternoon in December I was seized with a pain in the abdomen, which ultimately resulted in an appendectomy.

Christmas morning I awoke from the deep sleep of the anesthetic and saw before me a big Christmas tree, all decorated, erect and motionless —as motionless as most of the men there.

In the next bed, a husky youth with firm features and brown hair was reading a comics book. I turned toward him slightly and was greeted with a friendly smile and a cheery "hello!"

It was Robert W. Jackson.

We lived together there for fifteen days and fifteen nights. He told me his life story and I told him mine.

It would have been difficult if we hadn't known some Italian—which is the Esperanto of foreign soldiers here. I received visits daily from my friends and chatted with them for half an hour each day.

No one came to see Jackson. But he had many friends among the American patients in the ward. He could talk with them until the nurse turned out the lights after serving the hot chocolate. Nevertheless, he devoted most of his attention to me.

He acted as if he were the very author of the Good Neighbor Policy —as if he considered it his responsibility to maintain the impression that the people of the north have a feeling of good will for those of the south.

When I left the hospital, we parted with an embrace. We were both touched—although we weren't sure then that we would never see one another again.

ANTELOPE CHAIRS AND WATERED MILK

The turning point in the war came toward the end of 1942 when the Soviet armies began their mighty counter-offensive at Stalingrad on the Volga, when American troops landed in North Africa to join the British battling there, and when American naval, air, and land victories over the Japanese in the Pacific and South Pacific began to mount with increasing force and in growing numbers. But it was not until the spring and summer of 1945, not for nearly three more bloody and shattering years, that the Axis was forced to surrender.

The "total" war was over, but millions of men and women and children over the world were dead from the bombings and strafings, the hunger and cold, the slaughters en masse in the towns and villages and fascist concentration-camps. Millions were dead and millions were homeless and starving. Millions were dying.

And in the hemisphere of the west—though its towns and cities were still standing, though the bombs had not fallen there and the population had been spared from the ravage by fire and epidemic—a new plague was spreading over every land:

The plague of shortages of almost every kind of commodity, of rising prices and falling wages, of black markets and profiteers. The post-war plague of inflation brought an unprecedented wave of want in its wake. No country was exempt from the curse of inflation. And one of the worst sufferers of all in the southern Americas was one of the countries that had contributed most in ships and supplies, in loss of markets and loss of men:

One of the worst sufferers was Brazil:

Rio de Janeiro today is not the happy playground of three years ago, when an American dollar provided luxury for the tourist on the Brazilian exchange. Prices have soared so high that the poor smash store windows, middle-class residents wonder how long they can support their families, and tourists gape at an inflation that has leaped ahead of the United States. In three years prices have jumped an *Emily Towe: An Awful Lot of* estimated 300 percent. Milk went up a few *Inflation in Brazil. 1946* weeks ago from 10 to 15 cents a quart. The residents accept a certain amount of watering of milk as inevitable, but a recent demonstration opposed "excessive watering of milk."

Housewives shudder at the bread shortage. When they can get it, they find it has jumped from 10 or 12 cents a loaf to 25 or 35 cents.

A few weeks ago Rio even went through a coffee shortage. The tiny cups served in the open-air cafes rose from 1½ to 2 cents—and they have an awful lot of coffee in Brazil!

Oranges, a balancing item in the Brazilian's diet of beans and rice, are beyond the pocketbooks of the poor. And on the outskirts of the city orange groves stretch for miles.

The tourist pays seven cruzeiros—35 cents—for a pack of good Brazilian cigarettes and 50 cents for United States cigarettes. Gin tonic, favorite drink in Rio bars, costs 75 cents.

At the time of my visit to Rio there was a serious water shortage. During certain hours of the day, water was unobtainable in hydrants, so that hotels warned their guests to fill their bathtubs.

Taxi fares shot up during the war when free-spending American servicemen, unfamiliar with the exchange, paid exorbitant rates. The fares have not been lowered. The cleaning of a man's suit costs $1.25. . . .

In late August angry mobs expressed resentment by smashing windows and in some cases interiors of stores and theaters. The outbreak was touched off by the death of a student who was sold a poisonous sweet at a midtown bakery, but the rock-throwing started simultaneously throughout the city, and an organizing hand was suspected. Some blamed the Communists, who have been gaining influence in Brazil, and others accused the followers of Vargas, the former dictator.

I queried a number of persons about the cause of the inflation. It was generally agreed that the main trouble was inadequate transportation from one section of this huge, undeveloped country to another.

Brazil lost many ships during the war. Railroads that were never adequate could not handle the waterborne freight. Thus the cattle country in the south was cut off from the meat-consuming north. Lack of sufficient transportation was also responsible for the temporary coffee shortage in Rio.

Rio has changed considerably since the casinos were closed last spring. Though hotels are packed to capacity, the businessmen and tourists find even in the Copacabana Palace Hotel a mild play center. Because income from gambling paid for the elaborate floor shows, the caliber of entertainment has fallen to the lowest Rio residents can remember.

I spent a weekend at fabulous Quitandinha in the hills, near Petropolis (the summer capital). This ten-million-dollar hotel is the answer to a little girl's dream of a fairy castle.

Started just before the war and completed during the last year, its lounge chairs are covered with antelope skin and it has its own movie theater seating several thousand persons. A restaurant adjoins the warm-water indoor swimming-pool. Among the many dining rooms is one for children where a Mickey Mouse movie is shown after meals. Among the ingenious decorations is a bird-cage the size of a room where Brazilian birds twitter.

The gambling room in the midst of this luxury is closed. Quitandinha was built for the profit on its gambling games. It is remaining open despite tremendous loss because rumors persist that President Dutra's ban on gambling will soon be removed.

AIRPLANE IN THE JUNGLE

The ban on gambling of all kinds would be removed in more than one country in Latin America—and the solution of more than one knotty problem would be left to chance, in the tradition and spirit of the widespread lotteries, and in the press of the whole world's post-war perplexities and needs. The solution of more than one of the many problems of living and problems of government facing the people of Latin America in the post-war world would be postponed with the hope that a more secure and stable future was not far off.

In the meantime, the people as well as the governments of Latin America rallied around the newly formed international federation for peace and security known as the United Nations, the UN, which the late Franklin Roosevelt, President of the United States, but bereaved the world over, had helped to plan.

Within the UN, delegates from Latin America in the Security Council and in the Assembly took the floor to insist that collective action be initiated against the fascist government of Spain; to condemn British rule in Palestine, and urge a solution there for the good of Arabs and Jews alike; to denounce Dutch aggression against the still unrecognized Republic of Indonesia; and to hail the birth of the independence of the Philippines and of India.

And in the meantime, the closer cooperation achieved between the southern American republics and the United States during the war years pointed the way at least to a partial solution of some of the urgent problems faced by the people and the nations of Latin America—the problem of transportation and communication, for instance, between the cities and the huge hinterlands of South America; the problem of health and hygiene; of such primary needs as safe drinking-water and simple sewage-disposal.

A bare beginning had been made toward the solution of such problems with the aid and assistance of an official United States wartime agency known as the Office of Inter-American Affairs. Under the initiative and partly under the direction of this agency, doctors, engineers and other skilled personnel were sent to the Amazon and other remote parts of the continent—where rubber and other vital war materials were being produced—to study the conditions and the basic needs of the people.

Men like David S. Lozano were sent as part of a group to survey the conditions and report their findings. And one of the best reports was the account prepared by one of the more observant of the official observers—by Mr. Lozano, describing the visit made to a remote village in Bolivia, the Indian village of San Ignacio de Mojos:

We arrived at San Ignacio about 2:00 P.M. From the air the town looked rather small. About three rows of houses (or streets) two blocks long each way formed an exact rectangle surrounding a large green plaza—the village square. On the southern corner of the square was a very large church. The lake—or lagoon, as the people called it—was approximately a kilometer from the town in a southeast direction from the center of town. The town was more accurately situated near the corner of its western segment. It appeared oval from the air, the long axis of the lake parallel to the long axis of town.

David S. Lozano's Account of a Survey Trip in Bolivia

The airfield was three kilometers from the town and due south. On landing the field proved to be a rather bumpy grass-covered strip.

The radio was inside a mud hut in the center of a huge thatched roof structure on bamboo poles, with no walls. The air was pleasant with an exhilarating odor like a clean new forest.

Many people from town were awaiting the plane. The people appeared relatively large, of rather heavy build, dressed lightly in loose clothing of white or light colors and with pleasant expressions on their faces. In front of this group the mayor was awaiting us with horses—the only means of reaching the village at this time, due to the mud.

The other passengers and the baggage were brought along behind in a brown, bullock-drawn, two-wooden-wheeled cart roofed with picturesque tan-and-white, blotched cowhide, in covered-wagon style. The official transportation for the Lloyd Aereo Boliviano airline consisted of two bullock-carts—one uncovered, for baggage; one covered, for passengers.

There had been heavy rains, and as a result the road was a good deep mud. It took us a half-hour to get into town, detouring often from the road through any little pass in the jungle.

Along the way we saw several native Indians dressed in loose white gowns about to their knees—the men always with machetes. The ride was very beautiful: the jungle full of palms, huge vines dangling down, and the chatter of monkeys and birds all about. Upon entering town there were many pools of apparently stagnant and not very deep water on both sides. A few adults and children were seen bathing in these waters; they seemed rather shy, but only at the sight of strangers.

We arrived at our lodgings—in a long white house—on the square. . . . The patio was a large courtyard surrounded by a roofed top and open-sided passage on all sides. All the rooms of the house opened on the plaza, and a door on the opposite side of each room opened on a courtyard—horse-stable style, with swinging doors divided across half-ways up so as to use the upper half as a window. There were no windows. The passages contained—in different places—storerooms, hooks for hanging meat, flour mills, clay urns for clarifying and crystallizing sugar, the kitchen, the dining room, hammocks, a huge bronze pot, some green coffee, some whole dry corn, a hand centrifuge for sugar, and a rice peeler.

The center of the patio—some 30 by 30 feet—was covered with cowhides. Some stretched on pegs, on top of which were coffee beans drying. Some of it was shelled, some just harvested with its outer reddish coats on. Along the edges of the passage were huge Ali-Baba-like clay vases or urns sunk two thirds into the ground and covered with a beautiful bright green moss that contrasted with the red fire-baked clay. These were used for storing rainwater collected from the roofs for drinking purposes. The water had an earthy taste—as if it rained only after long intervals of breeze, accumulating dust from the fields.

We hoped it would be clean dust. . . .

We spent a hectic afternoon trying to clear the room of all types of objectionable insects—chiefly spiders, two to three inches across, on the walls and ceiling, a couple of scorpions in the corners of the room, and various flying insects. That evening we had an invasion by a few bats. Next day we battled huge field roaches, centipedes, beetles and small grasshoppers—every night we saw a new species. . . .

We . . . found the committee waiting to take us to the lagoon. We turned one block down to the right and one over, and entered a built-up path that led straight to the lake. On both sides there was a narrow ditch and the wonderfully fragrant jungle. The deputy said that the road had been built up higher to keep it dry at all times and consequently the ditches formed at the sides. He showed us the jungle on the right-hand side, pointing out that it was somewhat higher ground, and just at the edge of town—two blocks from the center.

As we advanced halfways to the lagoon, we began to notice a great deal of low, sunken, swampy ground. Somehow the whole region gives one the impression of endless water-soaked ground. We saw much beautiful flora and fauna, some deer tracks, beautiful birds and butterflies. The water lilies had many beautiful flowers—purple, red, yellow, etc. We also saw a few large, green, triangular-headed lizards. We were told boas and rattlesnakes (we thought they must mean water moccasins) lived in the swamp—and still some alligators.

When we arrived at the water's edge, we saw a beautiful little grove of trees clumped at the far, left-hand edge of the inlet that must have once been a shallow mud-bottomed swamp, sloping gradually into the water. Next to the trees were three piles of logs on which women were washing clothes—some sitting on the logs, and some standing knee-deep in the water.

Men, boys, horses—and a team of bullocks—were also bathing. Only the women and girls used a light dress for bathing. The bullock team proved to be filling barrels of water to bring into town.

We were told that the town was pitifully in need of a water system. Here they were, so near the water; and yet when a drouth came, even the town wells would dry up and nothing would grow because there were no means of transporting sufficient quantities of water to town. Even when the wells were full, the water was rather brackish. When it rained, the wells would fill very high temporarily, thus giving the impression of superficial (ground-water) wells.

It seems that their drinking water depended mostly on collected rain. However, they said the people who drank and used the lake water for cooking never became ill. This seemed rather strange, and of course was not quite consistent with the fact that in spite of the surprising freedom from disease, especially highly contagious ones, there was quite a bit of intestinal disorders about. . . . The people were very clean, but had a very difficult time bathing because of the two-kilometer round-trip involved; likewise, bathing near horses, cattle, and dogs was not the best hygiene.

The deputy hopes to combine the water-works and the clinic in one construction project, and run the water-system on a small charge basis to insure maintenance regardless of politics. . . .

We had a half day before us previous to the plane's departure for our return trip. We were awakened early by several bullock-carts loaded with rice coming into our back yard. The baskets which held the rice were curiously boat shaped and made of wide palm, like the type given out in churches on Palm Sunday. The carts had improvised divisions or pockets made of cowhide. . . .

It was with real regret that we left this beautiful place to which we had become attached for its peacefulness, beauty, and kindly people. The ride back on horseback was just as lovely as our coming. Almost everyone we had met accompanied us to the airfield. . . .

Apart from what Indians—mainly women—can carry on their heads, there is no means of transportation except horses, bullock-carts, and airplanes. Horses were never seen to be used for anything except the transportation of people. Bullock-carts, of which there are a moderately large quantity—perhaps twenty-five—are very slow. They take about two weeks to reach Trinidad in good weather. Rice, coffee and other exports are taken . . . by these carts. . . .

Airplane service to San Ignacio is only once a week. From Trinidad there is service four times a week—however, the plane is always loaded to capacity, coming and going, with passengers and freight.

DOCTORS VERSUS DOGS

Airplanes were moving into the jungles of Latin America where not even automobiles had penetrated before. A bare beginning was being made toward solving the multiple problems of the people in the cities and towns as well as the vast rural domains. But the solutions to most of the major problems were being ignored or postponed until some later day.

There were some problems, however, too pressing to be ignored or even postponed, problems that had to be faced without delay and with little if any aid from other countries:

The problem, for example, of the curse of the Andes. The problem of hydrophobia—which was being met with courage and resolution in the mountains and highlands of Ecuador:

As the inspectors pushed southward into the back country, they found more and more resistance. The priests, who keep their ears to the ground, reported that the people were threatening to make the inspectors swallow their own poison. By an unfortunate coincidence, it happened that hundreds of Indians near the place where the inspectors were working had risen to defend their land against the claims of a big landowner. The police had intervened, killing several Indians and wounding a good many more. Before the inspectors had time to decide on a plan, the storm broke. Five hundred Indians fell on them with every primitive weapon known to them. In half an hour the inspectors were so thoroughly beaten that they withdrew.

Lilo Linke: Hydrophobia, the Scourge of the Andes

Dr. Garcés came down from Quito. Taking a priest with him, he talked to the excited crowd, explaining that the Health Department was trying to protect their lives and—even more valuable to the Indians—their sheep and cattle. Then he took his beaten men back to Quito.

"The Indians lost so many sheep that they grew alarmed," said Dr. Cárdenas. "I'm sure they want us back now. Our first attempt wasn't altogether useless, though. Dr. Garcés, a few other doctors, and I lectured all over the place to schoolteachers, farmers' representatives, heads of Indian communities, and soldiers stationed near the region. So they're all on the lookout for new outbreaks, and if anything should happen to them, they'll know where to go."

"Are there new cases all the time?" I asked.

"Definitely. And the worst is that north of Quito hydrophobia is spreading among wolves. How are we going to control those? One of them entered a hut at the outskirts of Cayambe and bit three children. The animal was killed and its brain examined, so we know it had rabies. We must prevent a spread toward the coast, where there are vampire bats. In Brazil they've found that these bats carry the disease but don't die of it themselves. Imagine what that means!" he sighed heavily.

Dr. Garcés' position is not enviable. Yet he sticks to his job with a determined enthusiasm undiminished by disappointments. Thanks to him and his staff, hydrophobia is declining slowly.

Occasionally one even hears voices raised in support and applause. As Dr. Garcés hoped, people are definitely getting health-conscious. But the greatest triumph is to hear people ask, "Why doesn't the Department do something about it?"

Three Quito newspapermen had accepted Dr. Garcés' invitation to see the hydrophobia case held in grim old San Juan de Dios Hospital. We went across the inner patio to a door through which we could hear a hair-raising sound that was half groan, half growl.

I was the only woman present. Dr. Cárdenas stopped a few steps from the door. "Perhaps—," he began uncertainly, pointing at me.

"She's no child, is she?" Enrique Garcés cut him short. "Let her see for herself and maybe she'll stop crying over the 'poor little dogs!' "

A male nurse unlocked the door and quickly shut it behind us. Once inside, none of us dared move. The room was completely dark. The only sign of life was that inhuman voice. Dr. Garcés opened the shutters. As the gray light entered, the groans turned into cries.

On a bed in the corner lay an Indian tightly strapped to the wooden planks. Only his head was free, and it rolled wildly. His face was ravaged, with fury or unbearable pain.

He looked straight at us with bloodshot eyes, yet did not see us. His teeth were bared in a mad grin. His twitching lips were covered by white foam exactly like those of the dog I had seen earlier in the day. His big hands twitched open and shut.

The Indian had ceased to be human. Had he been in hell or in a concentration camp, we would have jumped to stay the hand of the torturer. Here we were powerless.

"Can't you make it easier for him?" I asked Dr. Garcés when the Indian grew quiet for a moment.

"We're giving him injections to calm him. That's all we can do. He'll die in a day or two."

"Why don't you kill him now?"

Dr. Garcés looked at me through half-closed eyes, his heavy chin sagging.

"It's against the law," he said curtly.

"Even when everyone knows there is no hope?" I insisted stubbornly.

"That's his wife over there," the nurse said, pointing to an Indian woman crouching on the ground outside the patio. "The resident doctor has cleaned her wound and given her the first vaccine injection. She doesn't want to lie down. Just sits there."

The woman looked up with frightened eyes, her whole body like a bundle wrapped in brightly colored shawls and wide skirts. Dr. Garcés bent over her.

"Will he die?" she asked, still motionless.

"Not yet. We'll let you know."

He spoke more gently than I had ever heard him address anyone.

"Keep those shutters closed," he told the nurse. Then to the journalists, "We had better leave now."

BEFORE THE THIRD GRADE

The great problem throughout Latin America, overshadowing all others, was the problem of economic want. It was the uninvited guest, the poor relation that showed up unexpectedly to cast a sombre shadow over the bold undertaking. Poverty was the chief obstacle even in the enterprising attempts of some of the Latin American countries to do away with illiteracy, which was still widespread over the southern Americas. Poverty was the immense hurdle—even in Costa Rica, where public instruction had reached a higher percentage of people than in any other country of Latin America:

Despondent as teachers and observers are concerning the grinding poverty which prevents the average youngster from reaching the third grade, they are also aware that poverty is the chief problem of those who remain in school. "The children don't have notebooks; a lot of them have lice and are dirty," said one. "Our school has a uniform for the girls," said a director, "but we don't require that they wear it because many cannot afford it." "When we have processions," explained another, "we ask the girls who have an extra uniform to loan it to another girl. We are always covering up the poverty of our school and the students for the sake of appearances. I think it might be better if we just let the public and the government see that children in my school have to stand throughout hour-long assemblies because there are not enough chairs."

John and Mavis Biesanz on Education in Costa Rica

A fifth-grade teacher in Heredia says that of her eighteen students only five can buy books or make any other monetary sacrifice, no matter how small. One girl's school-work suffers because before school begins—at seven—she sweeps and does the marketing for a family to earn her breakfast, and she leaves school at ten to prepare the midday meal.

Ragged clothes and bare feet do not seem to preoccupy the teachers greatly, for they are worried about something more fundamental—the actual hunger and malnutrition of a large number of the youngsters. Not only does the undernourished child have a stunted body as a result of scanty and improper food, but he also advances more slowly in his studies. In talking of physical education, teachers invariably point out that they cannot demand too much of children who, as a result of malnutrition, lack physical stamina. Some children have to be excused from marching in Independence Day parades because of weakness.

Preventive and educational measures are being taken to relieve poverty. Each school has a *Patronato Escolar* (School Guardianship) composed of parents and teachers, which raises funds for milk, uniforms, and school supplies for the poorest pupils. There is some free dental and medical inspection and service. . . .

Few Costa Ricans go to high school. For every twenty now in grade schools, there is only one in high school. The youngster's parents must pay tuition, buy books and uniforms, and—unless they live in one of the few towns where a high school is located—either pay commutation fees or have the child live away from home. As many as one third of the students have scholarships . . . while many also receive a stipend for room and board. . . .

Wealthy men have never subsidized schools or laboratories, and the state rarely devotes money to research.

A MAYAN REFLECTS

Illiteracy and ill health, inflation and black markets, and lack of transportation and sanitation facilities—these were some of the main stumbling-blocks in the way of Latin American efforts to achieve economic and social well-being. But behind many of these problems, and behind the ubiquitous, all-pervasive problem of poverty, lay one of the most ancient lacks of all:

The lack of an equitable distribution of land.

In many of the southern American republics the soil still belonged to a small minority of latifundistas or large landowners. Even in Mexico— which had been carrying out broad and sometimes drastic agrarian reforms since 1910—many peasants were without tillable land.

Theoretically one of the main objectives of the long and violent Mexican Revolution was the revindication of the rights of the Indian peasant. But in practice the program was far from being fulfilled—at least that was how one Indian peasant, the straight-talking mayor of a Mayan village in Yucatan, felt about it:

Many times I reflect that, although our race is very fierce in battle, making our leaders of the Revolution triumph, for just laws and for liberty, nevertheless it seems that we do not enjoy its fruits. We ought to laugh with our leaders, with those who live in the cities, but up to now we have not achieved what we sought, although it has cost the lives of many of our race. If the plan of the revolutionary laws has triumphed, the country ought to know it. The Revolution which was made, and which cost the lives of many in humble villages in all this countryside, ought to bring its benefits especially upon these.

Reflections of a Village Mayor in Yucatan

It is plain to the whole general public that the villages of our sort are without doctors or sanitary aid. Only sometimes they are visited by the priests, or by officials, or by armed police, that come to exact payments.

But the people die with sickness, or are sickly from childhood, without having any doctors. This happens even to those who know how to read—sometimes even to the teachers, while they are fulfilling their mission in the villages. It is true that there arrive notices explaining hygiene, but we are far from being able to buy the materials, the medicine.

The way quickly to improve the humble villages far from the cities—would that it might be possible!—would be to have, even for a week, a doctor or a hygiene officer to explain this in general assemblies. Only in this way can our land be made to prosper and flourish.

In truth, the customs and ambitions of today are something like those of the time of the dictatorship and of *caciquismo*.

In the time of General Don Salvador Alvarado, who brought liberty, law and justice, all were occupied in work, from the humblest to the highest class. Ambition and its vices disappeared or were forgotten. The forces of public safety went from village to village. One heard music and flourishes of the band.

Today these villages lack music—but they have a right to music. Chan Kom, for example, hasn't any, and we have to go long distances to the cities to hear it.

Another thing which happens in the villages, and to which those concerned ought to give strict attention in watching over the villages—even to those out in the bush with their respective properties—is that although there are plenty of lands, there is not enough food: principally such things as fruit trees. In these lands there are just weeds and useless trees. Often it happens that there are people who do not have garden lots—the lands are monopolized by others.

In all these matters those concerned should take measures.

Another thing that happens is that many villages lack playgrounds. In this village there is no playground.

There are other very urgent needs in all the villages that are far from the cities. All those who work with energy—defenders of the proletarian class—ought to give enthusiastic aid in the opening of roads to the villages. When we go to the cities, we see with pleasure the paved streets, and sometimes even airplanes. But it is just that for us too should come a time for improving our streets by which we go out to obey the orders of, or to receive, our superiors.

AUTHORS IN NEON

In spite of the failures that lay behind and the stumbling-blocks that lay ahead, all over Latin America the trails and the paths and the roads and highways to new progress and new learning were being cleared. And the main driving-force was the basic principle on which the war had been fought and won—the principle of anti-fascism and its concomitant: the right of all people to economic and social security as well as political and cultural freedom.

It was only just, that one of the greatest stimuli to the spread of learning and to the rise of new popular movements based on the new-found aspirations of the people of the southern Americas, should come from the still oppressed land where the world's resistance to fascism had really begun. It was only logical that one of the brightest beacons in the new-found unity of the Latin American people with the whole post-war world should be the presence and the inspiring energy of thousands of Spanish Republican exiles—in Mexico, in Cuba, in Argentina, in the Dominican Republic, in Chile, and in all the other southern American republics that had offered them a haven. Many of the exiles from Spanish fascism—which still held that country in its grip and still spread its sinister propaganda over the Americas through its Falangist and other agents—were men and women once famous in their professions:

Teachers, librarians, professors and other educators. Doctors of medicine and doctors of law and philosophy and literature. Engineers and technicians and scientists in every field. Writers and painters, sculptors and architects, composers of music and composers of the dance—artists and craftsmen of every kind:

Able, at long last, to take up their cherished professions again. Able and eager to make their worthy and valuable contributions once more to the people and the society around them:

Men like the former publisher, Rafael Giménez-Silés—exile from fascism and still the man of burning Republican convictions. Giménez-Silés, publisher of books to enlighten the people of Mexico and of all the other American lands:

In the glare of lavender neon—advertising an author, not a movie star—Indians verging on illiteracy wait for buses these mild evenings outside one of the strangest stores in the world: the *Librería de Cristal*, or Glass Bookshop, in the heart of Mexico City. Often the mother nurses a baby under a dark shawl as her husband peers dumbly at row upon row of *Milton Bracker: Mexico City's* vivid bindings in the forty curved and glisten-*"Glass Bookshop"* ing windows. Older children flatten noses against a pane rimmed with thick paper-backs like *El Ratón Mickey*, Mickey Mouse—and *Mandrake el Mago*, Mandrake the Magician.

Meanwhile, the crackling neon etches the best-sellers into the night and classical music pours from spaced loudspeakers. The store is open from 9:00 A.M. to midnight 364 days a year—the exception is May 1.

The *Cristal* is completing its fifth year now, and plans are afoot for an upstairs art gallery and an adjoining outdoor literary café. . . . The *Cristal's* proprietor seems determined to build it into the unique literary haven of the Americas. On the basis of his neon display, his endless concert of Tchaikovsky, Beethoven and Strauss, and his stock—from *Espaguetti (Popeye and Wimpy)*, to *Microparasitology and Serology* by Gutschich and Schumann—he has made an impressive start. At the proposed café, which would extend into Alameda Park, books would be on call—as well as apéritifs.

The idea man is Rafael Giménez-Silés, fiftyish Loyalist Spaniard.

Head of the Madrid Publishers Association, he ran three book fairs for Republican Spain before 1936. He escaped from a concentration camp via France and came here (to Mexico City) in 1939.

With Mexican associates, he founded EDIAPSA—Ibero-American Publishers—with one unit of the present *Cristal* as its retail outlet. The store now has a glass periphery of 470 feet, broken into a chain of narrow islands, by pleasant walks leading to the park.

Señor Giménez decided to put his authors up in lights because he was getting tired of "movie stars and brands of beer." He thought it was about time the writer got a break.

There are now four separate spectaculars above the store. The signs are changed monthly, after the *Cristal* checks on sales and consults other publishers. This month, fluorescent tubing will hail General Fulgencio Batista and his *Sombras de América*. Last month, *Rosenda*—newest novel by J. Rubén Romero—shared the best space with *Poesías Completas*, by Luis Urbina.

Imagine, if you can, an electric sign advertising someone's collected poems in Times Square! And imagine the glow helping illumine a lesser billboard for Balzac's *Comédie Humaine*—a current and constant best-seller at all local shops.

LOST IN BROOKLYN

The influence of Republican Spain in exile was great and glowing in the new flame of enlightenment and will for the new freedoms—the flame rising from the aspirations of millions of people, higher and higher over the Latin American lands:

The flame lifting like a giant incandescent torch—lifting, being transmuted into a glowing brightening sphere, becoming the people's patient scrutiny and clearer understanding of their old ways and their new wants. The sphere of new determination being lifted into its high and proper orbit by the people and their leaders and the many new influences exerted upon them:

Influences like the movements in Bolivia and other countries of the northern Andes and in Guatemala and Mexico and Venezuela, aimed at giving the Indian and the poor mestizo the land that was really theirs and the equal place in the life of the nation that they were beginning to demand.

Strong and sturdy influences like the movements that were studying and publicizing the vast contributions made by the millions of Negro people throughout the southern Americas: trends and currents of lasting significance such as the Afro-Cuban movement initiated by the Cuban savant and foe of fascism, Fernando Ortíz, and spreading to all the countries of the Caribbean and to Brazil where the priceless hand of labor and leisure from Africa had made its deepest impress.

Influences, too, like the slow but continuous diffusion of Protestant ideas over Latin America, challenging the hold of the clergy on the life of the nation and the minds and hearts and hopes of the people. The healthy competition offered by Protestantism in Latin America, encouraging the people in their age-old longing and struggle for the separation of church and state. And other influences, other trends and other currents of far-reaching importance:

Influences like the extensive cooperation that had grown up between the United States and the other American republics during the war against fascism:

Main currents for better Pan-American understanding—such as an American surgeon's discovery that curare, the ancient and deadly Indian poison used by the Caribs' kin on the southern continent, could be transformed into a powerful healing drug, could be turned by modern science into a cure for rare diseases of the bone. Main trends toward a broader and more frequent contact between the people of all the Americas—such as the nearing fulfillment of the old dream of a great highway linking all the countries of the Western Hemisphere. Permanent influences for real appreciation between the people of the United States and the people of Latin America—like the mutual interchange of visitors from every social group, including such men of prominence as the Peruvian writer, Manuel Seoane, travelling in the United States during the war, observing the North American customs, and candidly noting the bad along with the good as he was able to see them:

My speaking-English is almost as bad as the Spanish of a certain professor of Castilian in Cincinnati, who was never able to understand me in either Spanish or English. On several occasions, during my recent trip through the United States, when I asked for an extra slice of bread in a restaurant, they gave me, instead, a small square of butter stamped with an American flag, a charming forget-me-not, or the menacing statement: BUY WAR BONDS! Yet, I managed to get along very well, thanks to the Good Neighbor Policy. The Good Neighbor idea impressed me as being a living thing, an actual state of conscience in the North American people. For example, during my first night in New York, there was a blackout. Since we Latin Americans eat rather late, I left my hotel at nine o'clock to look for a restaurant. Hungry and friendless though I was, the sirens forced me into a dark doorway with several other people. Since they were all women, my sense of chivalry forced me to try to engage them in conversation in order to make them forget the war. They seemed quite interested in what I was saying, and soon two very pretty girls, whom I would personally not bother to look at more than twenty or thirty times in broad daylight, became very friendly after they managed to learn that I was a South American. After the "all-clear" sounded, they helped me find a restaurant, and would not leave until they were sure that I understood their detailed directions for getting me back to the hotel.

Manuel Seoane: Impressions of a Peruvian in the U. S.

After that incident an amazing number of others followed. One afternoon in Macy's, while I was trying to explain my desire to buy five little turtles of various colors and with a picture of Popeye on each of them, the salesgirl startled me by speaking Spanish. It gave me the strangest feeling of fantasy. There I was, thinking of how my children would like the little beasts when I took them back with me, and thinking, too, of how far I was from home and people I could really talk to, when this turtle saleswoman addressed me in my own tongue.

In Denver, also, while visiting Lowry Field, an officer and I were trying to discuss aviation. We were still grounded, misunderstanding each other's excited gestures, when a sergeant happened by and set us on the runway by acting as interpreter.

Almost everywhere I went in the United States, from coast to coast, in this casual manner I found people who could speak Spanish with varying degrees of skill. And this is good; it is what I meant when I said earlier that the Good Neighbor Policy is an active state of conscience in the North American people.

You and we have some important things in common; we both saw the light of day a relatively few decades ago because of a violent desire for freedom. We do not know the old hates, the rivalries of Europe. We do not have her decadent scepticism; we are young and creative.

Still, we have our surface differences, and these were as apparent to me when I visited your country as ours unquestionably would be to you should you visit one of ours.

For instance, there is your concept of time. The people in New York rush along the streets in such haste that many times at first I ran after them, thinking that some exciting event had occurred, which, being a newspaperman, I did not want to miss. After I found out that they were just rushing into some office building, store, or subway station, I relaxed and began to enjoy myself. On four separate occasions, because I had rushed madly behind a crowd, I found myself lost in Brooklyn.

As a result of these episodes I began to take an almost fiendish pleasure in standing on some street corner and watching the crowds shove by. This led to my actually timing myself against the crowds. I discovered, for example, that it takes fifty seconds of brisk walking to make the average city block, from corner to corner. But the most surprising thing was that it takes only one minute to do the same distance walking casually and not attempting to shove all New York City out of your way en route.

Using these figures, I worked out a table showing the time saved by the average New Yorker. On the basis that a person will hardly walk more than fifty blocks a day, at high speed he will save about five hundred seconds, or eight and one-third minutes. In the process he will have perspired copiously and increased his laundry bill; he will have overtaxed his heart and kidneys, and will surely have to have his shoes repaired once a month. . . .

This high-pressure living and its consequent waste holds over in even so simple a thing as eating. I have had any number of embarrassing experiences at North American tables because we, like the Europeans, hold the knife in the right hand and the fork always in the left throughout our entire meal, while you meticulously use the right hand only for eating and change your fork from the left to the right with a frequency and use of energy that at times made me think those eight minutes and twenty seconds saved could be increased easily to ten by simply changing over to our way.

"I HAVE SEEN THE MONSTER"

Other visitors to the United States had reason to be more critical. Other visitors after the war—which the people of Latin America and the world had come to believe was a struggle for the freedom of all human beings regardless of race, religion or color—were quick to point out the fatal gap that still existed in the United States between the preaching and the practice of democracy:

Visitors like one of the most influential leaders in the strong labor movement of Cuba. Men like Jesús Menéndez, head of the Cuban Sugar Workers Union—describing his first visit with his neighbors of the north:

I had never before been in the United States. The airplane that carried us landed in Miami at ten o'clock in the morning after a splendid flight of one hour and forty minutes. On arriving in Miami, we learned that we could not proceed on to Washington, D.C. until 8:00 A.M. next day, by a fast train. Then we spoke by telephone with the America Hotel,

A Cuban Labor Leader Discovers Prejudice in the U. S.

where, as we had been informed in Cuba, Cubans generally stay, its owners being Cuban. They answered yes, they had rooms reserved for three. We immediately took a taxicab and went to the hotel.

As we arrived, a Cuban girl met us, ready to welcome us—but on seeing us, she paled and was hardly able to explain that we could not stay at the hotel. She was ashamed to tell us that there was a state law forbidding her to lodge colored persons in the hotel.

Finally she told us how very sorry she was, that she was a Cuban, and angry about racial intolerance in the United States, especially in the South, and asked us to excuse her. She further explained that José Luís Amigo and Jacinto Torras could stay, but that I should go on to some other place where colored persons could board, and recommended me the Mary Elizabeth Hotel—on the outskirts of the city.

I was full of indignation, and so were my friends. I could not help but compare that humiliating situation with the thoughts that my father took arms and fought in the Cuban Revolution to end slavery and for freedom and democracy in my country. The thought came to my mind of the thousands and thousands of American boys—white and Negro—who offered their blood and died just the other day on the battlefields of the world, fighting bigotry and race intolerance in the form of Nazism and fascism, and to make the world safe for freedom and democracy.

Then I recalled the thought of the Master—Martí—who, when referring to the retrograde forces in the United States, said:

"*Conozco el Monstruo, porque he vivido en sus mismas entrañas*— I know the Monster, for I have lived in its very entrails."

And echoing the words of the Master, I drowned deep in my breast of a Negro and a Cuban the profoundest damnation of those responsible for such humiliation.

I convinced my companions to stay at the America Hotel. There was no other alternative but to part, and I went to the hotel which had been suggested to me. When night came, I spoke by telephone with my friend Torras. It was about nine o'clock, but he warned me not to leave the hotel, as he had learned that after ten o'clock in the night colored persons are not allowed to be in the street in some sections of Miami.

On hearing this I could hardly believe it. I wondered whether I was in the United States of America in peaceful times or in a Nazi concentration camp. I felt as though the room were a straitjacket choking and suffocating me.

Then I thought of Cuba, and a sense of relief and gratification pervaded me as I thought of the liberties, the people's rights and true sense of democracy attained by my country through her struggle. However, I realized I ought to bear in silence and go on. I was not in the United States for pleasure or on my own accord. I was there on a mission in behalf of over four hundred thousand sugar workers who had entrusted to us the interests of the Cuban people in the sugar negotiations.

As I do not speak English, I asked by gestures for soap, a towel and a glass of milk. The hotel owners are Negroes like me, but they did not understand me. Though Negroes, they talked a different language. All they knew was that my companion and my interpreter could not stay along with me because of our different skin color, notwithstanding that we talk and feel alike.

Next morning we boarded *The Champion*, a fast train, which conveyed us to Washington, D.C. We traveled the three of us in a compartment for which we had made reservation from Havana. Apparently because of war conditions, Negroes and whites are allowed to travel together, as many Negro officers and privates travel in the trains—many of them returning maimed from the battlefields.

But Negroes and whites are not allowed to dine together in the dining car. When dinner was ready, I was set apart in a corner, and then they drew a curtain to separate me from the rest of the diners.

From the train one can see the richness and fertility of the soil at some places, and the sugar mills, cattle pastures, pine woods, here and there stretches of barren land, vast extensions of uncultivated land. At times one would believe himself to be traveling through the provinces of Camaguey and Oriente, where almost all of the lands—chiefly large latifundia—are owned by American imperialistic companies.

We arrived in Washington, and immediately went to the Cuban Embassy, where we were very well received. But we could not all lodge at the same hotel. My friends stayed at the Hotel Roosevelt, and I had the good luck that through the Cuban Consul a Negro family of good reputation agreed to lodge me.

This question of race intolerance is one that should preoccupy seriously the peoples of America. . . . We, all of the peoples of America—in the United States and elsewhere—should struggle with all the resources at hand to do away wholly and forever with all tendencies toward bigotry and race intolerance, fully aware that all such tendencies can only lead to destruction of natural human fellowship, democracy, and the very fundamentals of human society.

THE ART OF SWIMMING

There were other American attitudes, too, that were troubling the people and the nations of the southern part of the hemisphere. There was the matter of Puerto Rico—the little Caribbean island that had been taken from Spain in 1898 and whose people had been promised their freedom then by the American forces landing there. Yet Puerto Rico was still a colony of the United States, was still far from enjoying even full autonomy, to say nothing of independence.

There was the knotty problem of Puerto Rico and its Spanish-speaking population—more than two million in all—whose traditions and whose culture were shared by most of the inhabitants of Latin America. There was the steadily worsening problem of Puerto Rico and its people—whom even half a century earlier, the first U.S. Commissioner to the island had judged to be capable of governing themselves:

The question of capacity for self-government lies at the threshold of the whole subject. . . . If the desire to assume the burdens of local self-government may be taken as indicating some degree of capacity for self-government, the people of Puerto Rico certainly have the desire. They may be poor, but they are proud and sensitive, and would be bitterly disappointed if they found that they had been delivered from an oppressive yoke to be put under a tutelage which proclaimed their inferiority. Apart from such qualifications as general education and experience constitute, the commission has no hesitation in affirming that the people have good claims to be considered capable of self-government.

Commissioner Carroll's Report on the Puerto Ricans. 1899

Education and experience, although too high a value can hardly be set upon them, do not necessarily make good citizens. Men may be well educated and yet be bad morally. Moral conduct is the first and most indispensable qualification for good citizenship. The ignorant and the vicious are often spoken of as though always in one class. In some measure they are; but so are the intelligent and the vicious. Education is not the invariable line which separates good citizens from bad, but active moral sense.

The unswerving loyalty of Puerto Rico to the Crown of Spain, as demonstrated by the truth of history, is no small claim to the confidence and trust of the United States. The people were obedient under circumstances which provoked revolt after revolt in other Spanish colonies. The habit of obedience is strong among them.

Their respect for law is another notable characteristic. They are not turbulent or violent. Riots are almost unknown in the island; so is organized resistance to law—brigandage flourished only for a brief period after the war, and its object was revenge rather than rapine.

They are not a criminal people. The more violent crimes are by no means common. Burglary is almost unknown. There are many cases of homicide, but the number in proportion to population is not as large as in the United States. Thievery is the most common crime, and petty cases make up a large part of this list of offenses. The people as a whole are a moral, law-abiding class, mild in disposition, easy to govern, and possess the possibilities of developing a high type of citizenship.

The fact that so many of them enter into marital relations without the sanction of state or church is, of course, a serious reflection upon their social morality. Half or more of their children are illegitimate. From this stigma they cannot escape. But too much to their discredit may be easily inferred from this scandalous state of affairs. Their apparent defiance of social, civil and ecclesiastical law is not due to immoral purpose, but to conditions of long standing, against which they have deemed it useless to struggle. It is the general testimony that persons living together without the obligations of marriage are as a rule faithful to each other, and care for their offspring with true parental love and devotion.

They are industrious and are not disposed to shirk the burdens which fall, often with crushing force, upon the laboring class. Their idleness is usually an enforced idleness. No doubt the ambition of many needs to be stimulated, for their lot has been so hopeless of an improvement that the desire for more conveniences and comforts may have been well-nigh lost. . . .

The question remains whether, in view of the high rate of illiteracy which exists among them, and of their lack of training in the responsibilities of citizenship, it would be safe to entrust them with the power of self-government. The commissioner has no hesitation in answering this question in the affirmative.

Who shall declare what is the requisite measure of capacity for self-government? It may be put so high as to rule out all the Central and South American nations and some of the nations of Europe which have demonstrated practically their capacity for self-government. . . . Tribes living in a very primitive state show capacity to maintain order, to protect their common interests, and defend themselves against enemies, and to hold individuals accountable to a more or less crude and imperfect system of law. Some measure of such capacity is common to the human race, better developed among some peoples than among others, but characteristic of all.

Puerto Ricans are surely better prepared than were the people of Mexico, or of the colonies in Central and South America, which have one after another emancipated themselves from foreign domination and entered upon the duties and privileges of self-government. Revolutions marked their earlier history with violence and bloodshed, because they were a warlike people—but out of it has come increased capacity and steady advance toward settled peace, with prosperity.

The Puerto Ricans will make mistakes, but they will not foment revolutions or insurrections. They will learn the art of governing the only possible way—by having its responsibilities laid upon them—and they will fit themselves for the discharge of their obligations by establishing at once a system of free schools that will give every boy and girl a chance to remove the reproach of illiteracy.

The father who wishes his son to learn to swim does not row him all day upon the lake, but puts him into the water, and the child's fear of drowning will stimulate him to those exercises which lead to the art of swimming.

BULLETS AND BALLOTS

Among the post-war problems facing the people of the southern Americas, none was more vital, few were as grave, as the gradual emergence of the new ultra-nationalist and fascist-minded movement headed by Colonel Juan Perón of Argentina into a position of power in that rich and rising country.

It was becoming clearer and clearer that the tactics used by Perón during his own candidacy for the presidency of his country in 1946 might some day be employed against the democratic-minded people of neighboring countries. And the tactics employed by Perón to win the election, as well as the measures he would soon take to relegate absolute power to the state—with himself as the state—were ominously reminiscent of the methods pursued by the late fascist dictators of Europe, thousands of whose hirelings had found refuge and favor in Perón's Argentina.

The tactics and methods used by Perón and his followers were, indeed, something to be concerned about:

The pro-Democratic mass meeting was orderly enough at first. Long before three-thirty, when the meeting was scheduled to begin, the Plaza del Congreso overflowed with a crowd estimated at a quarter of a million, despite the mass concentration of mounted police and tear-gas squads on Avenida Nueva de Julio, four blocks away. Here and there groups paraded under the hot December sun, singing the anthem of the Democratic Union and yelling "Down with Perón!" When speakers gathered on the steps of the padlocked Congress building called the meeting to order, the huge throng surged forward, breaking the rope barriers and packing the steps of the building with a solid mass of humanity. Every speaker was acclaimed by roars of applause.

Scott Seegers Notes Some Birth-throes of Peronism

About five-thirty I heard the first shots, across the Plaza at the corner of Cevallos Street. By the time I worked my way through the crowd with my camera, an ambulance had removed the body of a man shot down by the police. Democratic Union youths had linked arms, forming three solid human chains across Cevallos Street, and were holding back their enraged fellows who wanted to fight the gangs of peronistas a block away. The *peronistas*, armed to the teeth with clubs and stones, shouted insults at the *democráticos* and challenged them to fight. Occasionally, police rode through the *peronista* crowds to reconnoiter, but made no attempt to disarm or disperse them. Every time the police showed up they were greeted by *peronista* cheers.

A few *democráticos* were stopped by *peronistas* on their way to the meeting. I saw two of them badly beaten with sticks, fists, stones, and feet. The *peronistas* who fell into Democratic hands were merely searched for weapons and slapped around a bit. The shooting started when one Democratic youth who was being beaten broke away and ran toward the Plaza, followed by a shower of stones and by *peronistas*. Half a dozen *democráticos* broke through the chain and rushed to run interference for him. Before they returned to the corner, a few scattered shots came from the *peronistas*, answered by the *democráticos* with light pistol fire.

Suddenly, as if at a signal, the cordon vanished and no less than forty pistols appeared in the hands of the *democráticos*, directly below my balcony. They blazed away with heavy fire at the *peronistas*, who disappeared magically behind building corners a block away. I don't see how such volume of fire could have missed the tightly packed mob, but I saw none fall except a few who threw themselves down on the pavement to make a smaller target and immediately scrambled for safer spots.

The *democráticos* barricaded their end of Cevallos with park benches and with building tile from a construction job across the Plaza. They tore up other park benches for clubs. For the next two hours they fired at any male figure appearing at the other end of the block. The only exception was a peddler of ice cream suckers, who undoubtedly set the world's record for short bicycle sprints when he looked up the street and saw the barricades and the gleam of pistol barrels.

In general, the *democráticos*' fire was heavier than the *peronistas*', although the latter bounced enough bullets off surrounding buildings and steel shutters to keep everybody's head down. The barricades could not have stopped any bullets heavier than thirty-two caliber. Poor marksmanship must have accounted for the fact that there were so few casualties, if the widespread reports that the *peronistas* were armed with police weapons were true.

The police did not show up at Cevallos, but the occasional rattle of rapid-fire weapons and the swirl of running crowds in other points of the vast Plaza indicated they were busy.

The battle finally wore itself out, and the defenders left the barricades

426 THE SOUTHERN AMERICAS

just before dark. The Plaza was almost empty when I unloaded my camera and left it with the janitor of the building for safe-keeping until morning. As I left the building, two armored cars, each followed by a double file of police with eyes watchful and carbines ready, pulled aside enough benches to get through. The battle was over, but the atmosphere remained tense. The score was four killed and thirty-three wounded.

IN THE CITY CALLED "PEACE"

The apprehension of the other southern American republics over the rise of Peronism and its aggressive policy of expansion began to show itself in more than words:

In Bolivia, for example, the people finally rose up against the repressive government of another colonel, Villaroel, who had made himself president by means of a coup engineered with Argentine backing:

The anger of the long-oppressed people of Bolivia—bowed down with cold and hunger and gruelling labor in the tin mines owned by the magnate, Patiño, and others and the foreign monopolies they were associated with—finally turned to fury. And the fury was aimed not only at the tin barons but also at the new political masters in the pay of the Argentine fascists.

The fury finally burst into violence in the summer of 1946. In the capital, La Paz—the city called Peace—the people of Bolivia rose up against their oppressors in a way that could scarcely be forgotten—particularly by the U.S. ambassador who kept a diary and who witnessed the scenes from his own office across the way.

July 21: This morning I arrived at the office about ten-thirty and found several ranking members of my staff also there on this momentous Sunday morning. The strangest thing is the lack of any armed forces in the city. La Paz is obviously unarmed. We learned later that Saturday night the regimental commanders of the troops in La Paz, acting among themselves, decided that they would take no
U. S. Ambassador Flack's further part in the warfare between the gov-
Diary of a Bolivian Revolution ernment and the people. They so informed the President. Therefore, the troops are all quartered in their barracks and have no intention of leaving them.

Suddenly from my office windows we see civilians running down the streets with rifles and ammunition.

We learn immediately that the large MNR (official "National Revolutionary Movement") deposit of arms at the municipal headquarters has been left unguarded and that the people are willy-nilly arming themselves. At first we are not sure whether these are the MNR people or the students, but we soon discover that the mayor—from spite, because the MNR has been thrown out of the government—withdrew the guards from the municipal headquarters with the intention of causing havoc.

This is not long in breaking loose—there is now anarchy in La Paz. Hundreds of students and their supporters, all armed with rifles, are already gathering outside the Embassy windows for an attack on the traffic-police headquarters, and still no representative of the law appears.

The traffic headquarters are soon taken, and part of the mob moves on to the prison and another part to the police school. These points are reduced, and now the whole group joins for an assault on the Presidential Palace.

The only persons in the Palace are the President, one aide-de-camp, one minor secretarial official, and some twenty-five heavily armed soldiers. For the first time the mob encounters resistance and it is strong.

But the mob is too much for the resisters. Although many are killed among the students, the firing is so heavy that the soldiers are overcome. Finally a tank is brought up by an army unit sympathetic to the students and the Palace doors are burst open.

The crowd enters. Not long after, the President and his two assistants are thrown to the pavement. They are all horribly mutilated, and are subsequently hanged to lamp posts.

Horror is added to horror. At the police school, ammunition cases are found with the bodies of students killed previously which had been burned by the government in an effort to destroy their identity. (Subsequently it is learned these are not student bodies, but those of the prominent men murdered in November, 1944.)

Most of the killing is over now, but we have yet to know how many died. The number of wounded is staggering, and it is difficult to imagine the condition of the La Paz hospitals and clinics, which were never sufficient anyway, now that they have been loaded with the wounded from several successive engagements. There are also many wounded hidden in private houses, and there is a temporary shortage of bandages, serums, and medicine. Many will die through lack of attention who would have been saved under happier circumstances.

We don't know what has happened to the leading members of the fallen regime, but undoubtedly some have escaped in six AT-6's and one C-47 military aircraft. Others are hiding, and still others are seeking the asylum of foreign missions.

NO MORE GLASS BEADS!

If the people of the other Latin American countries were watching the mounting strength and aggressiveness of the Perón regime with an anxious eye, they were also disturbed at the growing friendliness and favoritism that were being displayed toward that regime by the United States itself.

They were even more disturbed by other changing aspects in America's foreign policy:

They were concerned over the abandonment of the Roosevelt policy toward the U.S.S.R. They were sorely troubled by the insistence of the United States Government, in spite of its possession of the annihilating atom bomb, on armaments and a military alliance among all the nations of the hemisphere of the west. They were troubled and fearful and anxious—because the urgent need among all the people of the southern Americas was not armaments for war, but a vast exchange of peacetime commodities; because the great need was not armored tanks and planes, but money and materials for schools and hospitals and sewage-disposal plants; because the basic need was not military maneuvers, but industry and more industry.

All over Latin America the chief problem was still poverty. And behind the poverty was the continuation of an agrarian and semi-colonial economy—the kind of backward system that had made it possible for the old conquistadors to obtain a fortune in gold and other goods in exchange for a few beads made of glass.

But now the cry all over Latin America was, "No more glass beads!" The cry was for industrialization and for diversification of crops—for a sovereign economy as well as a sovereign government. The cry was for bold measures urgently needed to end the prevailing low standards of living—among the coffee workers of Colombia, for instance, who, after a twelve-hour day in the wet outdoors, the women and children along with the men, came "home" to sickness and want.

The difference between the standard of living of Colombian coffee workers and U.S. laborers is about the same as that between U.S. laborers and Hollywood stars. . . . Here is the way one of our more prosperous coffee workers lives: He gets up at five o'clock in the morning. He breakfasts on a cup of coffee or *agua de panela* (water with brown sugar) and corn bread. He wears a shirt and trousers and a piece of hemp cord for a belt.

A Colombian Paints an Exotic Picture—of Want

These two pieces of clothing are a solid mass of patches . . . resembling a mosaic, a checkerboard, or a cubist painting . . . for a few yards of cloth cost more than the workers can afford.

After breakfast, he crosses himself—for we are very Catholic down here—takes his basket, and goes to the plantation. These coffee plantations are beautiful and picturesque, but they are also deadly. After working for several weeks, all the men—and the women and children, for they, too, must work from sun to sun—suffer from malaria, anemia, and other illnesses. So people say we export blood, not coffee.

The atmosphere of the *cafetales* is heavy with perfume and moisture. The tree branches, with their red, green and garnet clusters, are covered with the morning dew. Beautiful but murderous! When a worker plunges his arm through the branches to break off the clusters, a light rain falls on his body. Soon he is drenched and stays wet all day. At the foot of the tree there is an accumulation of rotting leaves. These, too, are part of the plantation "perfume." On the ground crawl beautifully colored animals whose names I don't want to remember because among us it is bad luck even to mention them. . . .

Work on the plantation goes on from six in the morning to six in the evening, with a half hour for lunch and a half hour for supper. This meal is abundant and filling, but has little nutritive value. There are never any eggs, milk, fruit, vegetables, fish, cheese or butter. Sometimes a piece of meat wanders into a plantain or bean soup, or a wisp of bacon lands in a kidney-bean broth. The ever-present, basic food is cereal, which, like some of our politicians, looks good, but has little substance.

At six, the workers go home, invariably a straw hut with a dirt floor. In oil or water colors, these huts portray the picturesque for satisfied beings. . . . But only those who for centuries have been heir to misery can possibly live in them.

Usually these huts have only one story and an adjoining lean-to where the cooking is done. This one floor is used by the family and other inhabitants of various species—dogs, chickens, cockroaches, scorpions, etc. Sometimes the coffee workers gather around the fire of an evening and a peon, stopping off on his way somewhere, takes his guitar and strikes up a sad wistful song, or a story-teller recounts century-old tales. These evenings are the motion picture, the night-club, or the opera of U.S. cities.

Some Sundays, the families go to market or to hear Mass and a sermon. Or to suffer the temptations of parish demagogues at election time. For these events the countryman brings out his best trousers, shirt, and straw hat. His wife wears a dress of printed cotton with bright flowers, practically the only luxury in her life.

If they have something to sell in the market—a pig, their own coffee, a few fruits from their small orchard—or if they have been paid, they take a turn through the village shops. . . .

But these are workers who are well-off. Usually they have nothing but the blackest and most obscure misery.

The cry for a sounder economy and a clearer promise of security was growing louder over the hemisphere. And in spite of the new caudillos and the agents of foreign monopolies, in the face of the new coercion by the force of power, against the threat of a worse depression and against economic aggressors wearing the mask of humane concern— against these and for unity with the entire world—the incandescent torch of new resolution, subjecting the old and archaic ways of thought to its persevering, critical glow, was being raised high over the southern Americas. The torch of resistance, against outmoded social patterns and against the bankrupt ways of governments willing to play the puppet for the big foreign interests, was held by 120,000,000 men and women and children.

Here was the aspiration to achieve untrammeled political freedom for themselves and for their countries. Here at last was their resolve to lift their lives to a height of economic sufficiency and social fulfillment and cultural expression never dreamed of before. Here was the torch to light their future—

Illumining all the lands that curved, from head to toe, from the burning Rio Grande down to the verdant Amazon, down to the melting snow of Fuegia:

Illumining, by its fire and by its light, the whole body of the green and waiting land below.

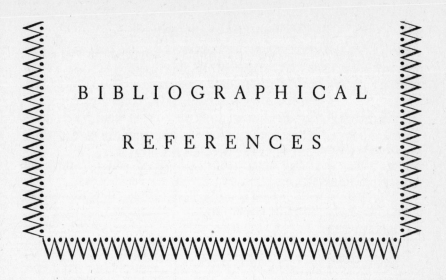

BIBLIOGRAPHICAL
REFERENCES

CHAPTER I

Page 4   Roys, Ralph L. *The Book of Chilam Balam of Chumayel*. Washington: Carnegie Institution, 1933.

Page 6   *Popol Vuh* (*Las Historias del Origen de los Indios de esta Provincia de Guatemala*, traducidas de la lengua Quiché al Castellano por el R.P.F. Francisco Ximénez). Vienna: Dr. Karl von Scherzer and Carlos Gerold e Hijo, 1857. (Excerpt translated by Abel Plenn)

Page 9   Radin, Paul. *The Sources and Authenticity of the History of the Ancient Mexicans*. Berkeley: University of California Press, 1920.

Page 13   Sahagún, Fray Bernardino de. *A History of Ancient Mexico*. Nashville: Fisk University Press, 1932.

Page 16   v. Page 9 above.

Page 18   Garcilasso de la Vega, The Inca. *Royal Commentaries of the Incas*. London: Hakluyt Society, 1871.

Page 21   Avila, Dr. Francisco de. *Narrative of the Rites and Laws of the Incas*. London: Hakluyt Society, 1873.

Page 24   Hernández, Pero. "The Commentaries of Alvar Núñez Cabeza de Vaca." In *The Conquest of the River Plate*. London: Hakluyt Society, 1891.

Page 26   v. Page 13 above

CHAPTER II

Page 32   Markham, Sir Clements R. *The Journal of Christopher Columbus*. London: Hakluyt Society, 1893.

Page 34   Curtis, William Eleroy. *The Authentic Letters of Columbus*. Chicago: Field Columbian Museum, 1895.

Page 37   Azurara, Gomes Eannes de. *The Chronicle of the Discovery and Conquest of New Guinea.* London: Hakluyt Society, 1896.

Page 41   v. Page 32 above.

CHAPTER III

Page 47   Díaz del Castillo, Captain Bernal. *The True History of the Conquest of Mexico.* New York: Robert M. McBride & Co., 1927.

Page 51   *The Despatches of Hernando Cortes, the Conqueror of Mexico, Addressed to the Emperor Charles V.* New York: Wiley and Putnam, 1843.

Page 55   Pizarro, Pedro. *Relation of the Discovery and Conquest of the Kingdoms of Peru.* New York: The Cortes Society, 1921.

Page 60   Graham, R. B. Cunningham. *Pedro de Valdivia.* London: William Heinemann, Ltd., 1926.

Page 63   Schmidt, Ulrich. "Voyage of Ulrich Schmidt to the Rivers La Plata and Paraguai." In *The Conquest of the River Plate.* Trans. and ed. by Luis L. Dominguez. London: Hakluyt Society, 1891.

Page 67   Staden, Hans. *The True History of His Captivity.* New York: Robert M. McBride & Co., 1929.

Page 70   Carvajal, Friar Gaspar de. *The Discovery of the Amazon.* New York: American Geographical Society, 1934.

Page 75   Jiménez de Quesada, Don Gonzalo. "Relación . . . sobre los Conquistadores. . . ." In *Historia del Nuevo Mundo,* by Don Juan Bautista Muñoz. Madrid, 1793. (Excerpt translated by Abel Plenn)

CHAPTER IV

Page 79   Las Casas, Fray Bartolomé de. *The Tears of the Indians.* London: Nath. Brook, 1656.

Page 81   Vespucci, Amerigo. "Account of His Third Voyage." *Old South Leaflets,* IV, 90. Boston: The Old South Association.

Page 84   "Annals of the Cakchiquels." In *Documents and Narratives Concerning the Discovery and Conquest of Latin America,* No. 3. New York: The Cortes Society, 1924.

Page 87   v. Page 18 above.

Page 92   Acuña, Father Cristóbal de. "A New Discovery of the Great River of the Amazons." In *Expeditions into the Valley of the Amazons.* Trans. and ed. by Sir Clements R. Markham. London: Hakluyt Society, 1859.

CHAPTER V

Page 97   Lasso de la Vega, Br. Luis. *Huei Tlamahuicoltica.* Trans. into Spanish and ed. by Lic. Don Primo Feliciano Velásquez. Mexico City: Carreno e Hijo, 1926. (Excerpt translated by Abel Plenn)

Page 99 Hansen, Father Leonhard. *The Life of Saint Rose of Lima*. Philadelphia: Peter F. Cunningham & Son, 1855.

Page 102 v. Page 79 above.

Page 104 Hanke, Lewis. "Pope Paul III and the American Indians." *Harvard Theological Review*, XXX, 2 (April, 1937).

Page 107 Pope Paul III. "Apostolic Letter of . . . A.D. 1537." In *Life of Bartholomew de las Casas* by one of the Dominican Fathers of New York. New York: P. O'Shea, 1871.

Page 108 Vieyra, F. Antonio. "Sermon of the First Sunday in Lent, 1653." In *History of Brazil* by Robert Southey. London: Longman . . . and Brown, 1819.

CHAPTER VI

Page 115 Fleurian, F. Bertrand Gabriel. *The Life of the Venerable Father Claver, S.J.* London: Thomas Richardson & Son, 1849.

Page 117 Ewbank, Thomas. *Life in Brazil*. New York: Harper & Brothers, 1856.

Page 122 Rainsford, Marcus. *An Historical Account of the Black Empire of Hayti*. London: James Cundee, 1805.

Page 124 Knolls, Francis. *The Life and Dangerous Voyages of Sir Francis Drake*. London: H. Dean, 1780.

Page 126 Benzoni, Girolamo. *History of the New World*. London: Hakluyt Society, 1857.

CHAPTER VII

Page 132 v. Page 32 above.

Page 134 Ulloa, Antonio de and Juan y Santacilia, Jorge. "A Voyage to South America." In *A General Collection of the Best and Most Interesting Voyages and Travels* by John Pinkerton. London: Longman . . . and Brown, 1813.

Page 137 Pazos, Don Vicente. *Letters . . . Addressed to the Hon. Henry Clay*. New York: J. Seymour, 1819.

Page 141 Anonymous. *The Spanish Empire in America*. London: M. Cooper, 1747.

CHAPTER VIII

Page 147 Anonymous. "The Art of Stealing." In *History of Brazil* by Robert Southey. London: Longman . . . and Brown, 1819.

Page 149 Zárate, Don Francisco de. "Letter . . . to Don Martín Enríquez, Viceroy of New Spain." In *New Light on Drake*. Trans. and ed. by Zella Nuttall. London: Hakluyt Society, 1929.

Page 151 Vallejo Aldrete, Lázaro de and Costilla, Hernando. "Letter to His Catholic Royal Majesty." In *Spanish Documents Concerning English Voyages to the Caribbean, 1527–1568*. Selected by Irene A. Wright. London: Hakluyt Society, 1929.

Page 154   Lussan, Sieur Raveneau de. "A Journal of a Voyage into the South-Sea." In *The History of the Bucaniers of America*. London: T. Evans . . . and Richardson and Urquhart, 1771.

Page 156   "The Exploits and Adventures of Le Grand, Lolonois, Roche Brasiliano, Bat the Portuguese, Sir H. Morgan, etc." In *The History of the Bucaniers of America*. London: T. Evans . . . and Richardson and Urquhart, 1771.

CHAPTER IX

Page 162   Anonymous. *A Sketch of the Customs and Society of Mexico*. London: Longman and Co., 1828.

Page 163   Graham, Maria (Lady Calcott). *Journal of a Voyage to Brazil*. London: Longman, Hurst, Rees, Orme, Brown, and Green, 1824.

Page 165   Laborie, P. J. *The Coffee Planter of Saint Domingo*. London: T. Cadell and W. Davies, 1798.

Page 168   Wimpffen, Baron de. *A Voyage to Saint Domingo*. London: T. Cadell and W. Davies, 1817.

Page 170   Robertson, J. P. and W. P. *Letters on Paraguay*. London: John Murray, 1839.

CHAPTER X

Page 180   v. Page 134 above.

Page 183   Aguirre, Lopez de. "Letter to Philip II." In *Personal Narrative* by Alexander von Humboldt. London: Longman . . . and Brown, 1819.

Page 185   Vieyra, F. Antonio. "Sermons." In *History of Brazil* by Robert Southey. London: Longman . . . and Brown, 1819.

Page 187   Gage, Thomas. *The English-American . . . or A New Survey of the West Indies*. London: George Routledge & Sons, Ltd., 1928.

CHAPTER XI

Page 194   Baker, Reverend Mr. J. *A Complete History of the Inquisition*. Westminster: O. Payne, 1736.

Page 198   Llorente, Juan Antonio. *History of the Spanish Inquisition*. New York: Morgan . . . and Bunce, 1826.

Page 202   Mackenna, B. Vicuna. *Francisco Moyen: or the Inquisition as it was in South America*. London: Henry Sotheran & Co., 1869.

Page 204   Pons, François Raymond Joseph de. *Travels in South America*. London: Longman . . . and Orme, 1807.

CHAPTER XII

Page 208   Stevenson, W. B. *Historical and Descriptive Narrative . . .* London: Longman . . . and Green, 1829.

Page 209   v. Page 117 above.

Page 213   v. Page 168 above.

Page 215   Humboldt, Baron Alexander von. *Political Essay on the Kingdom of New Spain*. New York: I. Riley, 1811.

Page 218   Leonard, Irving A. *Don Carlos de Sigüenza y Góngora*. Berkeley: University of California Press, 1929.

Page 221   Flinter, Col. George Dawson. *An Account of the Present State of the Island of Puerto Rico*. London: Longman . . . and Green, 1834.

Page 223   Pinkerton, John. *A General Collection of the Best and Most Interesting Voyages and Travels*. London: Longman . . . and Brown, 1813.

CHAPTER XIII

Page 232   Nariño, Antonio. "Escrito presentado . . . al Tribunal de Gobierno de Sante Fé de Bogotá." In *El Precursor* by Eduardo Posada. Bogotá: Imprenta Nacional, 1903.

Page 234   Biggs, J. *The History of Don Francisco de Miranda's Attempt to Effect a Revolution in South America*. Boston: Edward Oliver, 1811.

Page 237   v. Page 137 above.

Page 239   Pennaforte, Frei Raymondo. "Descripção dos Ultimos Momentos de Tiradentes." In *Tiradentes* by Assis Cintra. San Paulo: Irmãos Marrano, 1922. (Excerpt translated by William Hepper and Abel Plenn)

Page 241   Mackenzie, Charles. *Notes on Haiti*. London: Henry Colburn and Richard Bentley, 1830.

CHAPTER XIV

Page 248   Dessalines, Jean Jacques. "Communication of the Intentions of the Black Government . . ." In *An Historical Account* . . . by Marcus Rainsford. London: James Cundee, 1805.

Page 251   v. Page 137 above.

Page 255   v. Page 163 above.

Page 257   Calleja, General F. "Decree . . ." In *Outline of the Revolution in Spanish America* by a South-American. New York: James Eastburn & Co., 1817.

Page 259   Miller, John. *Memoirs of General Miller*. London: Longman . . . and Green, 1829.

Page 263   v. Page 208 above.

Page 266   Flinter, Major George Dawson. *A History of the Revolution of Caracas*. London: T. and J. Allman, 1819.

Page 269   Anonymous. *Recollections of a Service of Three Years in the Colombian Navy*. London: Hunt & Clarke, 1828.

Page 272   *Memorias del General O'Leary*. Caracas: Imprenta de la Gaceta Oficial, 1881. (Excerpt translated by Abel Plenn)

Page 275   v. Page 259 above.

CHAPTER XV

Page 282   Poinsett, J. R. *Notes on Mexico*. London: John Miller, 1825.

Page 284   Baylies, Francis. "Despatch. July 24, 1832." In *Diplomatic Correspondence of the U. S.* Washington: Carnegie Endowment for International Peace, 1932.

Page 287   v. Page 170 above.

Page 290   Sherwell, Guillermo A. *Antonio José de Sucre*. Washington, 1924.

Page 292   Garibaldi, Giuseppe. *Autobiography*. London: Walter Smith and Innes, 1889.

CHAPTER XVI

Page 299   Darwin, Charles. *Journal of Researches*. London: John Murray, 1852.

Page 301   Belt, Thomas. *The Naturalist in Nicaragua*. London: Edward Bumpus, 1888.

Page 304   Smith, Edmond Reuel. *The Araucanians*. New York: Harper & Brothers, 1855.

Page 308   Sarmiento, Domingo F. *Life in the Argentine*. New York: Hurd and Houghton, 1868.

Page 310   Thomson, James. *Letters on the Moral and Religious State of South America*. London: James Nisbet, 1827.

CHAPTER XVII

Page 316   v. Page 122 above.

Page 320   Clay, Henry. *The Works of Henry Clay*. New York: Barnes & Burr, 1857.

Page 325   v. Page 284 above.

Page 328   Reid, Elizabeth Hyde. *Mayne Reid: A Memoir of His Life*. London: Ward and Downey, 1890.

Page 330   Lincoln, Abraham. "Speech . . . (January 12, 1848)." In *Abraham Lincoln: Complete Works*. New York: The Century Co., 1894.

Page 334   Kollonitz, Countess Paula. *The Court of Mexico*. London: M. A. Saunders, Otley, and Co., 1868.

CHAPTER XVIII

Page 338   Agassiz, Prof. and Mrs. Louis. *A Journey in Brazil*. Boston: Ticknor and Fields, 1868.

Page 341   Kurtze, F. *The Interoceanic Railroad Route*. New York: John A. Gray & Green, 1868.

Page 344   Burton, Richard F. *Explorations of the Highlands of Brazil*. London: Tinsley Brothers, 1869.

Page 347   Alvord, Thomas Gold. "The Tactics of General Gomez . . ." Forum, July, 1896.

Page 349   Reid, Whitelaw. "Letter to President McKinley, October 4, 1898." In The Life of William McKinley by Charles S. Olcott. Boston: Houghton Mifflin Company, 1916.

Page 351   Roosevelt, Theodore. The Works of Theodore Roosevelt, vol. 22. New York: Charles Scribner's Sons, 1925.

Page 355   Pearson, Weetman (Lord Cowdray). "Letter to his son, Clive. March, 1908." In Weetman Pearson, First Count Cowdray by J. A. Spender. London: Cassell and Company, 1930.

CHAPTER XIX

Page 360   Reed, John. Insurgent Mexico. New York: D. Appleton and Company, 1914.

Page 364   Casement, Sir Roger. "Report . . . to Sir Edward Grey, March 17, 1911." In Slavery in Peru. Washington: U. S. House of Representatives, Feb. 7, 1913.

Page 367   Pocaterra, José Rafael. Gómez, the Shame of America: Fragments from the Memoirs of a Citizen of the Republic of Venezuela. Paris: Andre Delpeuch, 1929.

Page 370   Holm, Gert. The Argentine: Grain Grower's Grievances. Buenos Aires: Imp. Rugeroni Hnos, 1919.

Page 372   Aguirre Velásquez, Dr. Eduardo. Article in La Prensa Libre, San José, Costa Rica, July 3, 1933. In The Banana Empire by Charles David Kepner, Jr. and Jay Henry Soothill. New York: The Vanguard Press, 1935.

CHAPTER XX

Page 379   Valdovinos, Arnaldo. Cruces de Quebracho . . . Relatos de Un Combatiente. Buenos Aires: Editorial Claridad, 1934. (Excerpt translated by Abel Plenn)

Page 383   Memorandum sent to the Colombian Legation at Washington by the Minister of Foreign Affairs of Colombia (March, 1933). Washington, D. C., 1933.

Page 386   Pastoriza, Andrés. Statement. Washington, D. C.: Legation of the Dominican Republic, November 8, 1937.

Page 388   Torriente Brau, Pablo de la. "Letter, November 30, 1936." The New Masses, January 26, 1937.

CHAPTER XXI

Page 393—The Cruise of President Franklin D. Roosevelt to South America (Log of the U.S.S. Indianapolis, November 18 to December 15, 1936). Washington, D. C.: United States Government Printing Office, 1937.

Page 396   Cárdenas, Lázaro. "Message to the Mexican Nation, March 18, 1938." In Messages to the Mexican Nation on the Oil Question. Mexico City: DAPP, 1938.

Page 399 Homen de Montes, J. M. "Adeus, Robert W. Jackson." In *O Cruzeiro do Sul*, newspaper published by the Brazilian Expeditionary Force in Italy, February, 1945. Translated into English from the original Portuguese, by Frank V. Norall.

Page 401 Towe, Emily. "An Awful Lot of Inflation in Brazil." *The Washington Post*, October 20, 1946.

Page 404 Lozano, David S. *Official Account of a Survey Trip to San Ignacio de Mojos (Bolivia), May 18th to 25th, 1946.* Washington, D. C.: Institute of Inter-American Affairs.

Page 408 Linke, Lilo. "Scourge of the Andes." *The Inter-American.* Washington, D. C., March, 1946.

Page 410 Biesanz, John and Mavis. *Costa Rican Life.* New York: Columbia University Press, 1944.

Page 412 Ceme, Eustaqui. Autobiography. Chan Kom, Yucatan, January 20, 1929. In *Chan Kom, a Maya Village*, by Robert Redfield and Alfonso Villa. Carnegie Institution of Washington, 1934.

Page 414 Bracker, Milton. "Mexico City's Glass Bookshop." *New York Times Book Review*, July 7, 1946.

Page 416 Seoane, Manuel. "Impressions of a Roving Peruvian." *Tomorrow*, March, 1943.

Page 419 Menéndez, Jesus. "Letter." *New Masses*, January 22, 1946.

Page 421 Carroll, Henry K. *Report on the Island of Porto Rico . . . to Hon. William McKinley, President of the United States, October 6, 1899.* Washington: Government Printing Office, 1899.

Page 424 Seegars, Scott. "Editor's Eye-Witness Account." *The Inter-American*, January, 1946.

Page 426 Flack, Joseph. "Diary of a Successful Revolution, Official Despatch." *The American Foreign Service Journal*, Washington, D. C., September, 1946.

Page 429 Vallejo, Alejandro. "Open Letter to North Americans." *The Inter-American*, April, 1946.

INDEX